T0358197

ECONOMIC
SEMANTICS

ECONOMIC SEMANTICS

Second Edition

Fritz Machlup

With a New Introduction by

Mark Perlman

Routledge
Taylor & Francis Group

LONDON AND NEW YORK

Originally published in 1963 by Prentice-Hall, Inc. as *Essays in Economic Semantics.*
Published 1991 by Transaction Publishers

Published 2019 by Routledge
2 Park Square, Milton Park, Abingdon, Oxon, OX14 4RN
52 Vanderbilt Avenue, New York, NY 10017

Routledge is an imprint of the Taylor & Francis Group, an informa business

New material this edition copyright © 1991 by Taylor & Francis.

Library of Congress Catalog Number: 90-10965

Library of Congress Cataloging-in-Publication Data

Machlup, Fritz, 1902–
    Economic semantics / Fritz Machlup; with a new introduction by
Mark Perlman. — 2nd ed.
        p.   cm.
    Rev. ed. of: Essays on economic semantics. 1963.
    Includes bibliographical references.
    ISBN 0-88738-836-1
    1. Economics.   I. Machlup, Fritz, 1902–   Essays on economic
semantics. II. Title.
HB34.M2   1990
330'.0142—dc20   90-10965
                                                                 CIP

ISBN 13: 978-0-88738-836-1 (pbk)
ISBN 13: 978-1-138-52260-2 (hbk)

CONTENTS

CONTENTS

INTRODUCTION
TO THE
SECOND EDITION

Mark Perlman

My remarks in this prefatory note cluster about two poles. The first involves some discussion of the first edition of the book, its reception, and Machlup's views. The second concentrates on some additional materials we have added in this edition to round out certain aspects of Machlup's views. I conclude by offering some of my own observations.

1. The Book's History

Presented to Machlup on his 60th birthday in 1962, the first edition was a collection of his own essays. It was an effort on the part of several of his students to honor Fritz in an unusual way. By collecting and reprinting a few of his straight-forward principally pedagogical (as distinct from his mainly research) efforts they wanted to mark particularly that aspect of his many-sided influence. Their choice, perforce, had to be extremely limited, and what resulted was a selection clearly designed for an audience of

American graduate students. That their gift became something of a derivative classic speaks volumes of their prescience as well as an indication of Machlup's historical significance.

Machlup lived and worked at full pace into his 83rd year. He was only a mere 60 in 1962, when Professor Merton Miller, leading the aforementioned students, presented this gift. Selection of material to be included was made from what had been written earlier, what Machlup was interested in then, and in one case something that had not previously been published in English. What were possibly the richest of his pedagogical-research products, his final work on the economics of knowledge and the knowledge industry, *Knowledge and Knowledge Production, The Branches of Learning,* and *The Economics of Information and Human Capital,* were still well in his future. In a very real sense, these final, very lengthy studies, supplement as well as complement what his students had chosen because, if his audience for those last volumes were scholars at large (rather than graduate students), he was writing from a lofty paternal lectern—as an elderly seer teaching the adults of his old age the body of learning he had been taught as well as what he had discovered as an autodidact, throughout a long life.

From early on Machlup had wanted to be a professor of economics, but initially fate did not seem likely to afford him that opportunity. By the time he did secure a true professorial appointment (in the United States, at Buffalo), he had already absorbed a feeling for the importance of the kind of empirical details usually required of market-place outsiders—what many academic self—styled intellectuals consider the crassest type, namely profit-hungry entrepreneurial businessmen. Thus, if his professional career was built in good part on the traditional foundations of an academic training at an Austrian *Gymnasium* and then at the University of Vienna under Professor *(ordinarius)* von Wieser, generally, and afterwards under Professor *(honorarius)* von Mises and the von Mises circle (including Hayek, Haberler, Morgenstern), particularly, it also included the battering of a non-academic experience, as well. As a Jew (indeed, one with a slightly confused lineage[1]), Machlup was not in any real sense during the 1920s and 1930s, specifically, eligible for a regular academic appointment—if they were rare in the United States, they did not exist in Austria. For this reason (if not for others, as well), Machlup, while still a graduate student, created a firm in the paperboard business. Perhaps like Ricardo, he was led by his mind in one direction, and by his observations in another, to delineate between what it was rational for a business man (qua businessman) to do, and what from time to time he (fun-loving and aesthetic, fiercely logical and diligent Fritz) actually did. In any event, he was a product of those two cultures (academia and the market place).

These aspects of his academic and non-academic experiences show up in this volume. The essays reflect mostly the early evolution of the history of his economic thought between his training under von Mises and his final massive efforts concerning the knowledge industry.

The book, originally published by Prentice-Hall in 1963, was reprinted in 1967 and again in 1975. A desire, decades later, for a new edition shows a rare continuity of interest.

2. The Contents of this Book

The first edition.   At first sight, the book has 11 essays. Closer examination suggests that it really has only "ten," with two being quite short and accordingly less substantive. The first (really one of the two "halves"), written especially for the first edition, simply contains Machlup's effort at trying to provide a rubric. His choice, obviously, was economic semantics. It is mainly in this very brief essay where he makes his case for *general* philological rigor, and even there Machlup's ability to see several sides to every question can be observed. It is not a profound writing; it leans heavily on

---

[1]Machlup was a natural child, something which he took even greater pains to explain in his last year than he had ever taken pains previously to conceal. When John Chipman wrote his splendid biographical entry for the 1979 Biographical Supplement of the *New Encyclopedia of the Social Sciences,* according to a recollection of my last visit with Fritz (in Vienna in 1982), he suggested that Chipman explicitly mention this point. What ever—Chipman's text carries the message implicitly. As I had always been impressed, but puzzled, with Machlup's combination of a passionate respect for social traditions and his extreme willingness to tolerate eccentric behavior, this element in our last long conversations explained something significant to me.

patristic quotations from Malthus and Senior rather than on insights, any explicit reasoning, or even the assembling of episodic data. Had Machlup, instead, leaned on John Stuart Mill's views on the advantages of ambiguity (the less preferable alternative to an ambiguous statement might be no statement), he could have had a patristic (surely that describes J. S. Mill's role) view giving the alternative conclusion. Also, this essay eschews any consideration of institutional considerations which might explain why a phrase, created for one time and/or place, was insufficiently descriptive, directly or by analogy, of a second, similar phenomenon found in another time and/or place.

We were thus left with the "ten and a half" reprinted articles—articles originally printed between 1934 and 1960. One was translated and appeared in English for the first time in this volume.

The next four essays deal with imprecision as found in the usage of such word combinations such as *statics and dynamics; equilibrium and disequilibrium, structure and structural,* and *micro-and macro-economics.* Machlup thought the unifying tie was in his treatment of these four was economic methodology, particularly insofar as methodology offered the most obvious key to the differences between the deductive and the empirical methods. Besides showing each author's methodological preferences, he also thought that the choice and usage of words revealed the quality of a writer's deductive abilities.

Letting these asides pass, the essays show several things. The 1959 "Statics and Dynamics: Kaleidoscopic Words" opens with reference to five previous such essays.[2] Within such a framework he proceeds to show, often with quotations, how no less than 38 different more-or-less modern economic theorists have used the two words. These ranges from Comte and Veblen, both Keyneses, both Clarks, to Samuelson, Patinkin, Baumol, and himself (interestingly, Allais, Arrow, Hurwicz, and Debreu are not included); Schumpeter the younger is quoted against Schumpeter the older, however. From these examples he constructs his own generalizations regarding the way that the terms were bent for creative as well as rhetorical

---

[2]Four of these are contained in this collection. The omitted one is the 1950 "Three Concepts of the Balance of Payments and the So-called Dollar Shortage."

purposes. In all, it is a fine exercise in comparative *explication de texte.*

The next is a 1958 essay, "Equilibrium and Disequilibrium," in which the rhetoric, that is the order of presentation, is reversed. It starts with his generalizations regarding the usages of the terms, and then in the final segment shows how a variety of writers in the international trade subfield have employed the concepts. If the older Schumpeter differed from his younger self (as noted immediately above), in this case J. E. Meade flipped and then flopped back again. Here what Machlup seems intent upon showing is not the inconsistency of usage, but the problems of specifying adequately as against the problems of inadequate specification.

A second 1958 essay, "Structure and Structural Change: Weasel-words and Jargon," comes next. It sets out a 10-point check list to help would-be users of the two terms identify the "clearer meanings." It then moves to a 9-point list of vulgar usages of the terms. The essay concludes with six illustrations of the use of the term to postpone (perhaps to occlude) just what the author was saying scientifically and what he was implying normatively.

The fourth of these essays, "Micro and Macro-economics: Contested Boundaries and Claims of Superiority," appeared first in 1960. As I reread it, it is an exercise in intellectual orientation, rather than an exercise in definition. I was his colleague during the period, and I can recall the debate which went on at Johns Hopkins. Machlup had taught three theory courses; (1) the theory of relative prices, (2) the theory of relative incomes, and (3) methodology. While he was expressly impressed with Don Patinkin's fusion of the traditional Walrasian general equilibrium analysis with the Keynesian disequilibrium system, *Money, Interest, and Prices,*[3] he was less enthusiastic about the compression of applied topics including fiscal policy, monetary policy, and employment policy into the Ann

---

[3]Patinkin's book, a reworking of a brilliant dissertation, managed to explain much of the Keynesian model in terms of Walrasian general equilibrium. Two things are particularly worth historical note about the book: Patinkin explained the Keynesian disequilibrium model in general equilibrium terms, and what Patinkin thought was required for that explanation shortly became the discipline of modern macroeconomics. The book is not so much the first modern treatment of macroeconomics as it was a definition of what modern macroeconomics encompassed.

Arbor *macroeconomic* theoretical, mold, as designed sequentially by Richard Musgrave (1959) and Gardner Ackley (1961). However, when Evsey Domar left the Hopkins to go to M.I.T., the faculty voted to offer the vacated position to Musgrave, and Machlup, ever ready to admit those with whom he differed, enthusiastically accepted the choice. I see this essay as part of Machlup's effort to express, if not to clarify, his thinking about micro- and macroeconomics.[4] In it he reveals his antipathy for "persuasive definitions," a kind of elusive rhetoric which seemingly permeated Musgrave's work. Machlup thought such definitions were the kind of thing honorable and intelligent men had to take extraordinary care to avoid. Not so much for reasons of their sneaking in implicit value judgments consciously or unconsciously, but because their doing so made most systematic economic analysis impossible. At Hopkins the relationship between him and Musgrave was brief; Musgrave came in September 1960 and twelve months later Machlup had left for Princeton, where his responsibilities were not in the micro-macro theory fields but in international trade and finance.

The ensuing "two and a half" essays relate to a "debate in the journals" with Richard A Lester. It started with the second of the essays (as presented), one which was published in 1937 shortly after Machlup had accepted his appointment at the University of Buffalo. He was then perceived (both by himself and others) as a prototype Austrian economist. "On the Meaning of the Marginal Product" is an expository treatment, really a textbook statement. Nonetheless, it served as a classificatory personal label for the

---

[4]Machlup's political positions were a mixture of (1) his conviction that in the end the market's truths, unvarnished supply vs. demand were bound to prevail, and (2) his warm humanity which suggested that weak parties entering the market were well-advised to try to ameliorate their condition politically. We had, as might have been expected, many extended conversations about the "good and bad" of trade unions; I recall Machlup asserting that in the long haul unionism, if it was successful, "distorted" the natural outcome (a *bad thing*) but that he, himself, would join a union (a *good thing*) if he could, and particularly if he felt that he faced a monopsonist. I think that the record shows that Machlup used his role as a union leader in the American Association of University Professors effectively to speed the upward movement of the salaries of well-known professors (the skilled workers, if you please). Characteristic of his warmth and sense of social equity, he set up the AAUP Committee T (the one on salaries) to benefit all of the professoriat.

immigrant, Machlup, and when given the opportunity Machlup, "the theorist," decided to do battle with Richard A. Lester, "the empiricist," albeit one trained at Yale under Fisher. In March 1947 Lester's article, "Shortcomings of Marginal Analysis for Wage-Employment Problems," purported to show that few if any of the firms that he had studied appeared consciously to model their policies along the lines of conventional marginal analysis; therefore, such analysis was, at best, irrelevant, and certainly in that sense wrong. Machlup's reply in September 1946 (Machlup had been editing the *Review* for part of the period of the War and he was in the position to undertake the reply to Lester if he wanted to, and he wanted to) attempted to show that Lester's empirical methods were too crude to justify any conclusions, he thought that what underlay the problem is not what business men said that they did but what they logically had to do if they wanted to remain in business. Self-description, Machlup averred, was not usually a reliable source of scientific description. Except for a brief (4-page) 1955 half-essay, printed here as "Reply to Professor Takata," there is no mention of several sequels to the Lester-Machlup *Methodenstreit*. Such there was, however; one case was its choice as the topic selected by Machlup for his 1967 Presidential Address to the American Economic Association. By that time Lester and he were colleagues at Princeton; the verve of Machlup's language suggests that he felt that there remained need for continued battle.

The remaining three essays in the original edition were grouped under the rubric, "Semantic Issues in Macro-economics and Economic Policy." They deal with several of the hot topics of the post-war decades. His 1943 essay, "Forced or Induced Saving: An Exploration Into Its Synonyms and Homonyms," however, is as illustrative of the era as it is of the topic. It was a time when journals carried clarifying, what Bacon called light-casting (as distinct from fruit-bearing) articles, and here Machlup was trying to eliminate what one TV series more recently called "mushy-headedness." It is a measure of the advance in the method of argument to note the more limited time-applicability if greater sophistication, but also the greater caginess, in the second essay in this section, the 1960 "Another View of Cost-Push and Demand-Pull Inflation." The last essay, "Disputes, Paradoxes, and Dilemmas Concerning Economic

Development" is far more an essay on the futility of planning economic development than it is on semantics, albeit on the semantics side it has merit. What seems trenchant about these last essays is Machlup's desire to combine the precision of academic scholarly discipline with the kind of messiness of the political world and the active material market place. If economic semantics, as seen in academe had a strong transcendental side, Machlup seems intent on showing that economic semantics could be considered in the forum, as well.

The second edition. Machlup was a many sided person. For this and other reasons we are including in this second edition two major additions. One is a reprint of the session on methodology at the 1951 annual meeting of the American Economic Association. It contains several essays, one each by Frank H. Knight, Kenneth E. Boulding, and Paul A. Samuelson, as well as Machlup's response. Machlup had organized the session, his choice of these three prominent theorists was made in pursuit of his pedagogical plan.

Three additional volumes of collected Machlup essays appeared in 1964, 1974, and 1978. The first dealt with his work on international trade and finance; the second and third[5] included much material on his views relating to methodology. Nothing contained in them, however, put forth so starkly his underlying concern about the limits to the role of Cartesian thinking in economics. For this reason, we have chosen to put his 1951 response, particularly to Samuelson, within the contextual setting of the session in which it was delivered.[6] The other addition is an article, "Are the Social Sciences Really Inferior," he wrote for publication in 1961 in the *Southern Economic Journal.*

---

[5]Indeed, the title of this collection was *Methodology of Economics and Other Social Sciences.* It contained 26 essays of which only the first appears for the first time. I draw particular attention to this first essay; Machlup, the advocate of semantic discipline, almost "gives up" and nearly admits that *"Mrs. Malaprop Takes Over:"* "Methodology," as such, has come to mean in practice not only what it ought to mean (criteria for the selection of methods), but a description of the "cookbook- approach" to particular methods.

[6]See Machlup 1978 for many of his articles on methodology; of these, one was published in 1936 and another in 1951, the remaining two dozen were published after the 1951 meetings.

His choice of the reporting of his session on methodology for the 1951 American Economic Association meetings in New York is revealing. It starts with a short Machlupian statement distinguishing methodology from comparative methods. First, Kenneth Boulding (in some sense then only approaching the zenith of his career at Michigan) was invited to give his views under the rubric, "Implications for General Economics of More Realistic Theories of the Firm;" they involved a defense of theorizing, generally, and the use of some maximization methods, specifically. Boulding's approach reveals his developing interest in orgainzation, communication, and control theory. His comments are divided between static and dynamic theorizing; he gives marginal analysis all its points on the former, and he urges the theory of organization for the latter.

Frank H. Knight (then nearing the close of his brilliant career at Chicago), using as his title, "Institutionalism and Empiricism in Economics," gave what he, himself, termed, "A Few Brief and Hasty Observations on the Topic Printed in the Program." It dealt in good measure with the roles of uncertainty or the unknowable and of human intent in economic thinking. His remarks on institutionalism explicitly abstracted from the quantitative approach associated with Wesley Clair Mitchell, clearly damned Veblenian "diatribes against any 'meliorative trend' and insistence upon colorless mechanism," and strongly disassociated any personal approval for the kind of thing that John Rogers Commons had been doing.

It was Paul A. Samuelson's essay, "Economic Theory and Mathematics—An Appraisal," which served to focus the session on Machlup's concept of methodology. It served as the real target of Machlup's rebuttal. Quoting Willard Gibbs' "only speech" before the Yale faculty, albeit a statement of four words: "Mathematics is a language," Samuelson went on to improve it in three words: "Mathematics is language." Samuelson continued with wit and imagination to drive home his point—mathematical knowledge may not be necessary or even sufficient for a contribution in economic theory, but it is overwhelmingly desirable.

I eschew summarizing Allan G. Gruchy's comment, but Machlup's is what we are here for. It is a frontal consideration of Samuelson's underlying view that without mathematics most (really, virtually all) work in future economic theory is impossible. It is a statement about epistemology; it should be seen as such. Machlup thought mathematics, at best was *a* language; and there were some things which all languages could not express equally well. Mathematics was clearly unsuited to express certain emotions, etc. His views, as given in a brief form, explain why in his last years Machlup despaired of the direction most academic economics was taking and tried to recapture ground by trying to integrate economics with other branches of learning.

His 1961 essay on the social sciences is a broad, sophisticated, and many-faceted comparison of that body of knowledge,[7] generally (and implicitly of economics, specifically), to knowledge in the physical sciences, particularly physics and chemistry. Machlup's comparisons include, (1) invariability of recurring situations, (2) objectivity of observations, (3) the capacity to use controlled experiments to verify (sic) hypotheses, (4) exactness of measure, (5) numerical quantification, (6) existence of mathematical constants, (7) use of predictability of future events as a test, (8) rigorousness and acceptability of specialized scientific language, and (9) average competence of professionals. The result of this multi-faceted comparison is a mixed verdict—two comparisons are irrelevant, four suggest "no real difference," and three suggest inferiority to the natural sciences. True to his nature, he ends the essay with a discussion of the "Crucial Question: 'So What'?"

3. The Book's Initial Reception

When the first printing of the first edition of the book initially appeared, an unsigned review in the *Economist* gave it generous space but devoted most of the space to summarizing his argument with Lester. It concluded by noting that Machlup, for all of his "political views (extreme liberalism)" was still offering "a trenchant

---

[7]Machlup suggests that the list could include more than Sociology, Cultural Anthropology, Social Psychology, Human Geography, Demography and Population Theory, Ethnography and Ethnology, Political Science, Economics, History, and International Studies, but that there is also so much overlapping, that it could also be said to include less.

criticism of loose usages, even if it annoys some of his readers. Some very respectable economists are found guilty of semantic impropriety; now they have been warned to behave better in future and so have we all" (*Economist* 1964, p. 1007).

More scholarly reviews appeared in three other journals. Kurt Klappholz, writing in *Economica,* gave the LSE-Karl Popper School's judgment; it was not favorable. Although his review contained several detailed criticisms, the main point was that "a preoccupation with the 'meaning of terms' tends to encourage futile methodological approaches . . . verbalism and [Popperian] essentialism." Popper, Klappholz points out, noted "that . . . physics which worries hardly at all about terms and their meaning, but about facts instead has achieved great precision." Moreover, Machlup (whom Klappholz writes, "is not an *apriorist* after the manner of Mises . . .") gets thrown because in one of his essays he asserts on the one hand that equilibrium is not an operational concept, yet, on the other hand, he concludes that one can "verify" the appropriate theoretical predictions. *Verification,* from the standpoint of the LSE-Popperian crowd, was not "the name of the game in town;" it was *falsification.* Machlup's efforts were not successful, and "the deficiencies of the subject could be better remedied by a greater concentration on its explicanda rather than on the meaning of terms" (Economica N.S. 1965).

In the *Journal of Political Economy,* Don Gordon gave more of a summary of the contents of the book. While Gordon commented on Machlup's reputed prowess as a teacher and even as a theorist, he disagreed with Machlup's rationale for the book and concluded that viewed *ex post* semantic confusion was really in and of itself not much of a problem. The problem was theoretical confusion. There is an apocryphal story about a conversation between Hans Bethe and Nils Bohr. In inviting Bohr to give a 'name lecture' at Cornell, Bethe implored him to speak clearly. Bohr's reply was that the problem was not his speech, it was his thinking.

Professor Terence W. Hutchison, who had recently been engaged in fierce journal debate with Machlup, was asked to review the book in the *American Economic Review.* His assessment, featured as the opening review in that issue, was presented in three long paragraphs. The first dealt swiftly with the pedagogical virtues of the book—the initial set of essays was not only the best., "but all graduate students of economics would do well to read them."

In the second paragraph Hutchison raised the ghost of his own differences with Machlup. The issue involve the relevance of empirical testing of theories, particularly since Machlup seemed unclear ('ambiguous' was the word) about whether he felt that empirical testing could prove a theory erroneous or merely irrelevant.

The third paragraph states that the third part of the book, although "[containing] models of how economic policies should be discussed by academic economist . . . [they] are not especially concerned with semantic issues . . .". Alas, unlike Machlup, Hutchison was never a businessman, and does not relize that advertising is built on the premise of roses smelling differently when sold under other names. Words do matter.

4. Some Concluding Remarks

This collection offers even now, almost a third of a century later, things of value and of interest.

The *organization* of the essays, using the materials of the history of thought as intellectual evidence combined with assertive definitions and chains of syllogisms, remain among the finest examples in the economic graduate student curricular literature. As such, Machlup remains a "living" teacher.

As essays in the history of economic thought, these also offer splendid starting places for further analysis.

Machlup's policy views, particularly seen in the last essays of the first edition, are, as phrased, more time- and place-bound than his subjects warrant, but even they are pedagogically relevant in this time (1989–90).

Machlup's defense of abstract theorizing, as seen in his debate with Lester, is probably of more historical interest than of current value. J. A. Schumpeter is said to have remarked that Lester had the argument, but that Machlup won the debate. There are many, including specifically Terence Hutchison, who have held that Machlup's 'victory' reflected more Lester's incompetence than

Machlup's competence. Perhaps, it was Machlup's desire to go over that ground again which led him to take up the topic anew in his 1967 American Economic Association presidential address.

During his last years Machlup, the abstract theorist, came to despair of the ultra-abstraction of formal, mostly advanced algebra, formulations of economic relationships. For most of his career, however, he stood for the Carl Menger Austrian tradition (Carl, but not Karl [the son], was also antimathematical), which favored use of the syllogism and verbalized abstraction, but not the headiness of easy mathematical transformations. As we have already seen his concern with this topic had led him to organize a blue-ribbon panel for the 1951 American Economic Association meetings. As I have already noted, some of his considerable writings on the topic were collected and published (he records, at my suggestion) in 1978 under the title, *Methodology of Economics and Other Social Sciences.*

But, let us consider the basic topic—economics and semantic discipline. Machlup, unlike Humpty-Dumpty, preferred to believe that words should not be allowed to mean anything that the writer wanted them to; nor did he assign higher values to arcane words that should be "paid extra." Words, in his view, should be tools, and it was a sloppy workman who neglected his tools by not keeping them as sharp as was expedient. Yet, Machlup argued as though he believed that philological imprecision resulted from ignorance of etymology, inadequate care given to literary style, and individual arrogance. And, while much can be said for understanding etymology, does the point that in one era a word had a particular association bind it to mean the same thing later on?[8] Perhaps because he lived in early 19th century Britain long before the Reform Act, Ricardo may have appropriately posited that only land was in fixed supply, but should the classical economists' hijacking of that word *rent* preclude Pareto's choice of the same word *rent* to apply to any force of the factors in short supply later on? Should there be a verbal analog to Fisher's Ideal Index Number which handles the weighting both forwards and backwards?

---

[8]The origins of the word *fornicate,* for example, suggest only that prostitutes plied their trade in the basements of public buildings—fornix refers to the *vaulted* areas.

One can, of course, assert that the "mis-usage" of words may not only be the result of carelessness and ignorance, but it can also be a reflection on organic changes in thinking. Indeed, Machlup knew this, and one of his wonderful teaching skills was to misunderstand purposefully a student's language to lead the student to things the student had not realized were there—like Moliere's M. Jourdain, many of Machlup's students found after he had finished with them that their thinking was deeper than they had ever imagined.

Earlier I indicated that the crowning achievement of Machlup's career was probably the scope of his final 8-volume project on learning and knowledge, and particularly the execution of the first 3 (the ones he completed). Now I suggest that these essays represented the initial phase of Machlup's thinking about the nature of learning and economic knowledge, but that that initial phase was incomplete. What seemed pedagogically straight-forward and effective during most of his career was on reflection more a set of questions than it was a set of answers. The final major project was his effort to present *both* a better set of questions as well as of answers. It is a pity that they are not available, particularly in an inexpensive edition.

References

Ackley, Gardner (1961). *Macroeconomic Theory.* New York: Macmillan.

Gordon, Don (1964). Review of F. Machlup. *Essays on Economics Semantics. Jour.Pol.Econ.* 72, 103-04.

Hutchison, Terence W. (1956). "Professor Machlup on Verification in Economics." *South.Econ.Jour.* 22 (April) 476-83.

———— (1964). Review of F. Machlup. *Essays on Economic Semantics. Amer.Econ.Rev.* 53, 1104.

Klappholz, Kurt (1965). Review of F. Machlup. *Essays on Economic Semantics.Economica N.S.* 32, 101-02.

Machlup, Fritz (1952). "Issues in Methodology: Introductory Remarks." *Amer.Econ.Rev.Supp.* 42 (May), 35 ff. "Discussion," *ibid.* 69-73.

———— (1955). "The Problem of Verification in Economics." *South.Econ.Jour.* 22 (July) 1-21.

———— (1956). "Rejoinder to A Reluctant Ultra-empiricist." *South.Econ.Jour.* 22 (April), 483-93.

————— (1964). *International Payments, Debt, and Gold.* New York: Scribner's.

————— (1967). "Theories of the Firm: Marginalist, Behavioral, Managerial." *Amer.Econ.Rev.* 57 (March) 1-33.

————— (1976). *Selected Economic Writings of Fritz Machlup.* Edited by George Bitros. New York: New York University Press.

————— (1978). *Methodology of Economics and Other Social Sciences.* New York: Academic Press.

Musgrave, Richard A. (1959). *The Theory of Public Finance—A Study in Public Economy.* New York: McGraw-Hill.

Patinkin, Don (1956). *Money, Interest, and Prices: An Integration of Monetary and Value Theory.* Evanston: Row, Peterson.

PREFACE TO THE
PAPERBOUND EDITION

The original edition of this collection of essays was published in January 1963. The essays were assembled and edited by Professor Merton H. Miller of the University of Chicago on behalf of a group of my former students. The first copy of the volume was presented to me in December 1962 on the occasion of my 60th birthday. I hope that the availability of this collection in a paperbound edition will further help my essays to realize the purpose for which they were written: to dispel semantic and conceptual fog and allow greater visibility in areas in which both the fog and the traffic have been dense.

The essays differ in design and exposition. The four essays in the section entitled "Semantic Issues in Economic Methodology" have a common objective, namely to clarify widely used terms and concepts, but the approach is different. The essay on "Statics and Dynamics" includes references to about 90 writers and to many more works, and it produces more than 120 quotations from them. Thus, a bit of doctrinal history is presented here, partly as evidence for the variety in the use of the two terms. In contradistinction, no quotations and no references are included in the essay on "Structure and Structural Change." I felt that reviewing the intellectual history of these terms would serve no good purpose and I wanted to avoid naming the perpetrators of the semantic misdemeanors exposed in this essay. It distinguishes ten "clearer meanings," nine "vaguer meanings," and six "crypto-apologetic meanings" of the terms in question.

The other two essays in this section fall between these extremes in exposition. The essay on "Equilibrium and Disequilibrium" starts out as a methodological analysis without references to particular writers, but after the deck is cleared proceeds to apply the lesson to selected examples from the literature. The essay on "Micro- and Macro-Economics" contains enough references to show the varied use of these terms, but no attempt is made to comb the literature for quotable statements. I considered it more important to present the methodological issues involved than to provide a survey of opinions on this pair of labels.

The three essays in the next session deal mainly with the methodological problems of marginal analysis in general and the concept of marginal productivity in particular. In the article on "Marginal Analysis and Empirical Research," semantics remains in the background once it is clear what marginalism means and what it does not mean. This article has become well known among students of economics as one of the basic statements of the neoclassical position in the "marginalism controversy." The essay "On the Meaning of the Marginal Product" is more nearly in the nature of a semantic study, unless one wishes to see a difference between semantic and conceptual analysis, the former explaining the meaning of words, the latter clarifying the concepts designated by these words. The brief note "Reply to Professor Takata" is intended to shed light on some of the many misunderstandings regarding the contents of marginal-productivity theory.

The last section combines three essays of disparate character. The study of the concepts of "Forced or Induced Saving" serves semantic differentiation as well as conceptual clarification as it exhibits 34 concepts involving the idea of involuntary or induced saving. The essay on "Another View of Cost-Push and Demand-Pull Inflation" was intended to provide an analytical demarcation of some significance for practical-political judgments. Its contribution toward this task was recognized by the late Sir Dennis Robertson in his Marshall Lectures.[2]

The last essay in the volume, "Disputes, Paradoxes, and Dilemmas concerning Economic Development," discusses the many conflicts in the definitions, the objectives, the recommendations, and the theories of economic development. This piece, though once called "required reading" for all students of development economics, has not been widely noted, perhaps because it was first published in a foreign journal and republished in this collection of essays in semantics, where specialists on developing countries

---

[2] Sir Dennis Robertson, *Growth, Wages, Money* (Cambridge: Cambridge University Press, 1960). Robertson spoke of my article as "much the clearest analysis of the matter" he had seen (p. 29).

would hardly look for any contribution to their subject.

I am grateful to Prentice-Hall for assigning the copyright to me and thus enabling me to authorize the reissue of this volume in a paperbound edition. I am especially obliged to its publishers, W. W. Norton & Company, for issuing this edition purged of a large number of misprints. In several instances the corrections called for much typographical effort and ingenuity.

Two items in the preliminary material of the first edition—a list of my students and a bibliography of my writings from 1925 to 1962—are not included in the present edition. They were part of the commemorative design of the original volume and have nothing to do with the essays collected.

Perhaps it should be noted that a preposition was changed in the title of the volume. The first edition was called *Essays on Economic Semantics;* but since only one essay was explicitly *on* semantics as a specialized scholarly activity, while the rest were essays *in* semantics, the title has been appropriately revised.

Nothing else has been changed and nothing else omitted. All eleven essays are reproduced here in full.

FRITZ MACHLUP

PREFACE TO THE
ORIGINAL EDITION

This collection of *Essays In Economic Semantics* has been assembled in honor of Fritz Machlup on the occasion of his 60th birthday. The precedents for this form of appreciation have been well established in economics; the commemorative volumes for Jacob Viner, Professor Machlup's predecessor as Walker Professor of Economics and International Finance at Princeton, and for Professor Frank H. Knight at Chicago being two noteworthy examples.

The particular essays reprinted here are not a representative cross-section of Professor Machlup's work, which ranges widely over economics and the social sciences generally. Rather, they are intended as a tribute to his virtuosity as a teacher since their precision and lucidity so epitomize the man and his methods. By forcing ambiguities, sloppy reasoning, and implicit theorizing out into the open, Professor Machlup has alerted his own students and the profession at large to the tyranny of words. He has been a life-long foe of Mephistopheles, who advised the student in Goethe's *Faust* to use words to conceal ignorance, to substitute words for what he did not understand: "Denn eben wo Begriffe fehlen, Da stellt ein Wort zur rechten Zeit sich ein."

For advice and suggestions in the preparation of this volume we wish to express our thanks to a number of Professor Machlup's present and former students and colleagues, especially to Professor T. C. Liu of Cornell University. We are indebted to Dr. Edith Tilton Penrose of the London School of Economics for the translation from the German of "Micro- and Macro-Economics." And, of course, the usual acknowledgments and thanks are due to the following publishers for permission to reprint the articles presented here: *The Southern Economic Journal, The Economic Journal, Der Zeitschrift für Nationalökonomie*, the McGraw-Hill Book Co., *The American Economic Review, The Osaka Economic Papers, The Review of Economics and Statistics*, and *La Rivista Internazionale di Scienze Economiche e Commerciali*.

Finally, we wish to thank Professor Machlup himself for allowing us to pry loose from his notes his reflections on the cultivation of economic semantics to serve as the introductory essay for this volume.

MERTON H. MILLER

WALTER D. FACKLER

TOM E. DAVIS

Introduction

On the Cultivation of Economic Semantics

ON THE
CULTIVATION OF
ECONOMIC SEMANTICS

Some people regard exercises in semantics as a waste of time. I consider them useful, if not indispensable, if we care to understand one another. A good many earlier economists have felt this way and devoted considerable effort to the terminological cleaning-up job that becomes necessary from time to time. A few reminders of past essays in economic semantics may be of interest.

Malthus published in 1827 a volume on *Definitions in Political Economy*.[1] In his preface he stated that "one of the principle causes" of the notorious differences of opinion among political economists "may be traced to the different meanings in which the same terms have been used by different writers." In the first chapter he laid down four rules: "First. When we employ terms which are of daily occurrence in the common conversation of educated persons, we should define and apply them so as to agree with the sense in which they are understood in this ordinary use of them." Second. Where this does not apply, "the next best authority is that of some of the most celebrated writers in the science, particularly if any one of them has . . . been considered the principal founder of it." Third. Changes of terms or definitions should be made only when necessary and useful. "A change which is always itself an evil, can alone be warranted by superior utility taken in the most enlarged sense." Fourth. "That any new definitions adopted should be consistent with those which are

---

[1] Rev. T. R. Malthus, *Definitions in Political Economy, preceded by An Inquiry into the Rules Which Ought to Guide Political Economists in the Definition and Use of their Terms; with Remarks on the Deviations from these Rules in their Writings* (London, 1827).

allowed to remain, and that the same terms should always be applied in the same sense, except where inveterate custom has established different meanings of the same word; in which case the sense in which the word is used, if not marked by the context, . . . should be particularly specified."[2]

Malthus then proceeded to discuss the terminological deeds and misdeeds of a number of economists, including Smith, Say, Ricardo, James Mill, and McCulloch. He sternly rebuked writers—e.g., Ricardo and Mill—for having altered definitions or meanings of words "without improving them" (p. 37). In one chapter Malthus undertook to present definitions for 60 economic terms, beginning with "Wealth" and ending with "Unproductive Consumption."

In 1826, a year before the appearance of Malthus' *Definitions*, Archbishop Richard Whately published a revised edition of his *Elements of Logic* with an Appendix "On certain terms which are peculiarly liable to be used ambiguously in Political Economy." This appendix—or the basic information for it—had been "furnished by the kindness of the Professor of Political Economy" [in the University of Oxford], Nassau W. Senior, whose *Political Economy* appeared in its first edition in 1836.[3] In this appendix, Senior (or Whately) stated that "there would be as little difference of opinion among Political-Economists as among Mathematicians" if only "they had possessed a vocabulary of general terms as precisely defined as the mathematical." Instead, hardly any one of the terms used by the writers "has any settled and invariable meaning, and their ambiguities are perpetually overlooked." Senior then proceeded to show the inconsistent uses of seven different terms by Smith, Say, Ricardo, James Mill, Malthus, Lord Lauderdale, McCulloch, Storch, Sismondi, and Torrens. In a concluding sentence—obviously by Whately—renewed reference is made to "both the frequency of an ambiguous use of language, and the importance of clearing up such ambiguity."

Senior's insistence on terminological discipline was partly founded on his rationalist position. Thus he wrote: "If Economists had been aware that the Science depends more on reasoning than on observation, and that

---

[2] *Ibid.*, pp. 4-7.

[3] Nassau W. Senior, *An Outline of the Science of Political Economy* (London, 1836; 6th ed. 1872). The appendix to Whately's *Logic* is reproduced in the Allen & Unwin reprint of Senior's book published in 1938.

4

its principal difficulty consists not in the ascertainment of its facts, but in the use of its terms, we cannot doubt that their principal efforts would have been directed to the selection and consistent use of an accurate nomenclature."[4] One does not, however, have to share Senior's extreme anti-empiricism in order to agree with him on the importance of clear language. Senior may have been right in attributing "the slow progress which has as yet been made by Political Economy" to most writers' "inattention to established usage," and in believing that with greater care in such matters "its advancement may be accelerated."[5]

One of the pioneers of quantitative economics in the modern sense, Henry Moore, who was convinced of the "imperative necessity" of better "statistical knowledge" of economic conditions, was no less concerned about the need of greater care in the use of terms. In an article in which he spoke out against the linguistic muddle prevailing around the word "competition" with all its inconsistently used qualifying adjectives—such as "perfect, unlimited, indefinite, free, pure"—he begins with the following fine statement:

> Economic terms seem to pass in their historical development through a series of stages which, without pretension to rigidness, may be described as follows: first, no definition is given, but it is assumed that every one has a sufficiently clear idea of the subject to make a formal definition unnecessary; second, a definition is attempted and a number of exceptional forms are noted; third, with the further increase of data, the relative importance of the various forms changes, confusion in discussion is introduced, logomachy takes the place of constructive investigation; fourth, a complete classification of the forms embraced under the original term is made, and problems are investigated with reference to these classes. The bewildering vagueness of economic theory is largely due to the fact that the terms used are in all of these stages of development.[6]

This may sound like the description of an unavoidable development through which technical terms have to pass, irrespective of the scholars' terminological sloppiness. Moore does not, however, propose to drop the charges against writers who confuse their readers, as well as themselves,

---

[4] Senior, *op. cit.*, p. 5.

[5] *Ibid.*, p. 5. The "inattention to established usage which so diminishes the usefulness of his writings" was a rebuke to Ricardo, on p. 62.

[6] Henry L. Moore, "Paradoxes of Competition," *Quarterly Journal of Economics*, Vol. XX (Feb. 1906), p. 211.

by the use of ambiguous terms. He shows how much can be done, and must be done, by way of semantic analysis.

I hope that no one will misinterpret my propensity to engage in semantic exercises as an approval of the use and defense of "the hunt for the meaning of words as a method of research."[7] We know the difference between necessary and sufficient. Semantic clarification is necessary but, as should hardly be necessary to state, it cannot be sufficient in the search for improved knowledge.

---

[7] Joseph A. Schumpeter, *History of Economic Analysis* (New York, 1954), p. 485.

Semantic Issues
in Economic
Methodology

STATICS
AND
DYNAMICS:

Kaleidoscopic Words

Reprinted by permission from *The Southern Economic Journal*, Vol. XXVI, No. 2, October, 1959.

This essay is one in a series of studies in economic semantics: inquiries into the meanings of some of the most widely used terms in economics. Serious terminological ambiguities and conceptual obscurities have been found to exist, some of them curable, others beyond hope of clarification. Previous essays have dealt with the "marginal product,"[1] with "forced saving,"[2] with the "balance of payments,"[3] with "equilibrium and disequilibrium,"[4] with "structure and structural change;"[5]

---

[1] Fritz Machlup, "On the Meaning of the Marginal Product," *Explorations in Economics* in Honor of F. W. Taussig (New York: McGraw Hill, 1937), pp. 250-63. Reprinted in *Readings in the Theory of Income Distribution* (Philadelphia: Blakiston, 1946), pp. 158-174. Reproduced in the present volume, pp. 191-206.

[2] Fritz Machlup, "Forced or Induced Saving: An Exploration into its Synonyms and Homonyms," *Review of Economic Statistics*, Vol. XXV (1943), pp. 26-39. Reproduced in the present volume, pp. 213-40.

[3] Fritz Machlup, "Three Concepts of the Balance of Payments and the So-called Dollar Shortage," *Economic Journal*, Vol. LX (1950), pp. 46-68.

[4] Fritz Machlup, "Equilibrium and Disequilibrium: Misplaced Concreteness and Disguised Politics," *Economic Journal*, Vol. LXVII (1958), pp. 1-24. Reproduced in the present volume, pp. 43-72.

[5] Fritz Machlup, "Structure and Structural Change: Weaselwords and Jargon," *Zeitschrift für Nationalökonomie*, Vol. XVIII (1958), pp. 280-298. Reproduced in the present volume, pp. 73-96.

the present essay will deal with "statics and dynamics" and the truly kaleidoscopic variety of meanings that have been given to these learned terms.

Statics is derived from the Greek στατικός, which means "causing to stand," and Dynamics from δυναμικός, which means "causing to move." Thus, an extremist may say, since all economics is designed to explain *change,* there can be no such thing as "Economic Statics"—and all economics must needs be dynamic. On the other extreme, since all economics must use a method of isolating some factors from others, which involves assuming some variables to be *unchanged,* there can be no such thing as "Economic Dynamics"—and all economics must needs be static. The fact is that economists in their reasoning must always cause some variables to "stand" and some variables to "move"—which leaves us nowhere in deciding this argument.

I. Statements on the Distinction
Between Statics and Dynamics

Not all writers who have used the terms have bothered with defining them. But often, even where there are no definitions, some statements can be found in which a writer reveals what he means. I have examined a representative sample of the literature for statements defining or distinguishing Statics and Dynamics, and shall present a collection of them. But first I should explain some conspicuous omissions in the collection.

1. Some of the great system builders whose works have been widely discussed as significant contributions to Economic Dynamics have not themselves used this term. For this reason, Ricardo, Malthus, Sismondi, List, Marx, the writers of the German Historical School, and finally Robertson are not represented on the list. But we shall return to them—and also to Keynes—in Section II in order to find what in the eyes of their critics or admirers characterizes their methods as Statics or Dynamics.

2. Some of the great names in the history of economic thought are absent from the list because these authors said nothing at all or nothing worth quoting on the distinction between Statics and Dynamics; this is true, for example, for Jevons, Menger, Böhm-Bawerk, Wieser, Cassel. Jevons made one, quite casual remark in the preface of his *Theory,* which

was interpreted in contradictory ways.[6] Menger said nothing about Statics and Dynamics, which is noteworthy in the case of an author of two books on the methodology of economics. Böhm-Bawerk used the terms only in review articles when he referred to the uses J. B. Clark and Schumpeter had made of them, but he did not propose alternative definitions or suggest alternative meanings.[7] In Wieser's work only a short and misleading statement about Statics, and nothing about Dynamics, can be detected.[8] Cassel used "static" as a synonym for "stationary," and contrasted his model of a stationary economy with one of the "steadily progressing economy," without using the term "dynamic."[9] Perhaps Mitchell should be mentioned in this company; although sometimes named among the pioneers of "quan-

---

[6] Jevons referred to "a close analogy" of the theory of wealth and value "to the science of Statical Mechanics" because the former is "explained by the consideration of indefinitely small amounts of pleasure and pain, just as the Theory of Statics is made to rest upon the equality of indefinitely small amounts of energy." He added that the "dynamical branches of the Science of Economy may remain to be developed"—but he failed to say just what they should deal with. W. Stanley Jevons, The Theory of Political Economy (London: Macmillan, 1871), pp. viii-ix. Streller had no doubts that Jevons meant Dynamics to be "Practical Economics" while Statics was "Theoretical Economics." Rudolf Streller, Statik und Dynamik in der theoretischen Nationalökonomie (Leipzig: Streller, 1926), pp. 45-46. Kuznets, on the other hand, inferred from "the analogy . . . with static and dynamic mechanics" that "statics would deal with the relation of forces at the equilibrium level, dynamics with the same relations in the changes that lead toward equilibrium." Simon Kuznets, "Static and Dynamic Economics," American Economic Review, Vol. XX (1930), p. 426; reprinted in Essays in Economic Change (New York: Norton, 1953), p. 32.

[7] Böhm-Bawerk did not reject the terms; he spoke of "this certainly important and fruitful distinction, which in the most recent theoretical literature, chiefly thanks to Clark's influence, has received great honors." Eugen von Böhm-Bawerk, "Eine 'dynamische' Theorie des Kapitalizinses," Zeitschrift für Volkswirtschaft, Sozialpolitik und Verwaltung, Vol. XXII (1913), p. 3. It is not understandable why Schumpeter—whose theory was criticized in that article—should later remark that "Many, among them Böhm-Bawerk, would not hear of statics and dynamics at all." Joseph A. Schumpeter, History of Economic Analysis (New York: Oxford University Press, 1954), pp. 966-67.

[8] Wieser, in this statement, rejected all Statics—which he confused with a mathematical system, "like mathematical physics," that disregarded some of the essentials of human action and economic choice. Friedrich von Wieser, Theorie der gesellschaftlichen Wirtschaft. Grundriss der Sozialökonomik, 1. Abteilung, 2. Teil (Tübingen: Mohr-Siebeck, 2nd ed., 1924), p. 40.

[9] Gustav Cassel, The Theory of Social Economy (New York: Harcourt Brace, 1924), pp. 29, 34.

11

titative dynamics," he can be quoted only as the author of somewhat emotional pronouncements on the two concepts.[10]

3. Several well known names in contemporary economics are not included, simply because the list is designed to be merely a "sample." There would have been no point in multiplying restatements of points of view already clearly stated by others. Needless to say, some more original definitions or characterizations may have been overlooked. Their authors are requested to pardon the oversight, and to take comfort in the thought that this essay is, in a sense, a pillory of terminological originality. Writers are implicitly castigated for their originality in the meanings given to accepted terms!

The statements included in the list are, whenever possible within the brief space, quoted literally, though some of the statements are synthetic in the sense that they have been put together from different pages or different chapters of a book, or even from different books of an author. In a few instances, for the sake of brevity, a concise paraphrase was substituted for a long statement; the absence of quotation marks indicates where the authors' own language was replaced by the compiler's paraphrase.

The order of the entries is roughly chronological; only very roughly though, because the statements quoted have often been made in similar form in earlier works by the same author, or because several statements are put together from passages of different publications that have appeared many years apart. Thus, if a statement is quoted from a book first published in 1955, it is quite possible that virtually the same ideas were expressed in a book the same author had published in 1939. As a result, the order of the entries should not be taken to reflect "priority." (Let me repeat that priority in the use of a novel meaning of a term is no cause for pride; in fact it betrays a lack of "terminological discipline" and a want of linguistic inventiveness—for when a writer creates or modifies a concept he ought also to coin a new word to denote it, rather than corrupt the language and spread confusion.)

---

[10] Mitchell wrote that static theory was providing an "escape from stern reality into a romantic world," whereas Dynamics furnished "scientific" theories of "the cumulative change of institutions." Wesley Clair Mitchell, "The Prospects of Economics," in Rexford Guy Tugwell, ed., *The Trend of Economics* (New York: Alfred A. Knopf, 1924), p. 27.

A COLLECTION OF STATEMENTS
ON THE DISTINCTION BETWEEN STATICS
AND DYNAMICS IN ECONOMICS

Author	*Statics*	*Dynamics*
A. Comte[11]*	Abstract theory of social order	Theory of social progress
J. S. Mill[12]	Study of "the economical laws of a stationary and unchanging society," especially "of the economical phenomena considered as existing simultaneously" and of "the principles of their interdependence"	Study of "the tendencies" of "the economical conditions undergoing progressive changes"; "thereby adding a theory of motion to our theory of equilibrium"
L. Walras[13]	Analysis of interdependence in which we "imagine an economy establishing . . . equilibrium *ab ovo* over a given period of time during which no changes take place in the data of the problem"	Analysis of interdependence in which we "suppose the data of the problem . . . to vary as a function of time," with "the fixed equilibrium . . . transformed into a variable or moving equilibrium," "constantly being disturbed by changes in the data and . . . constantly being reestablished"
J. N. Keynes[14]	Study of "phenomena . . . as they present themselves under given conditions"	Study of "manner in which (economic and social) conditions change over . . . time," especially "study of economic progress," chiefly by "historical method"
A. Marshall[15]	Study "of some group of tendencies . . . isolated by the assumption other things being equal": "we fix our minds on some central point" and "treat variables provisionally as constants"	Study of economic "change and progress," taking account of "complex mutual interactions" and gradually approximating the world in which "all these mutual influences take time to work themselves out, and, as a rule, no two influences move at equal pace"
J. B. Clark[16]	Methodological device of "isolating" by holding conditions constant, yielding	"Laws" accounting for "variations of actual incomes from . . . natural standards" and "for the

* Footnote references for this section appear on pp. 22-24.

Author	Statics	Dynamics
	"real laws . . . working" both in a "stationary state" and in a society in "movement and disturbance"	slow and steady change" in these standards, especially under the influence of "five generic changes" in conditions—population, capital, technology, business organization, and tastes
T. Veblen[17]	(a) "Taxonomic" Statics —where "the activity ("not to disturb the equilibrium . . . between variables") goes on in perfection, without lag, leak, or friction" (b) Clarkian "Dynamics" —a conception "of an imperfectly static state," involving "changes in the absolute or relative magnitude of the several factors comprised in the equation," but still an "equilibrium between variables"	"Evolutionary Economics"—"a close-knit body of theory . . . of an unfolding sequence," giving "a genetic account of the life process" and of "the growth and mutations of the institutional fabric"; a "theory of genesis, growth, sequence, change, process, or the like, in economic life," "of a process of cultural growth as determined by the economic interest, a theory of a cumulative sequence of economic institutions stated in terms of the process itself" —not of the "determination . . . of the outcome of the process" —where "each new situation is a variation of what has gone before it and embodies as causal factors all that has been effected by what went before"
K. Wicksell[18]	(a) "Aspect of the problem of equilibrium" which concerns itself with "the conditions necessary for the maintenance, or the periodic renewal, of a stationary state of economic relations" (b) Analysis based on the assumption of "a society which retains unchanged from year to year the same ᵕopulation, the same area	(a) "Complete analysis of economic phenomena" taking account of changes in "the total supply of labor," capital, and land, and "in the efficiency of the available supply of labor," etc. (b) "Can only be successfully presented in combination with the practical part of our subject" (c) "Transition to dynamic point of view": treatment

Author	Statics	Dynamics
	of territory and the same amount of capital, and remains on the same level of technical achievement."	of "the problem of saving or accumulation of capital—which is equivalent to production without corresponding consumption—as well as its negative counterpart, capital consumption"
		(d) (Imputed by Myrdal) Theory of the "cumulative process" by which a deviation from monetary equilibrium evolves and progresses
V. Pareto[19]	First part of "pure economics," studying "equilibrium" under the assumption of given and unchanged conditions	(a) Second part of "pure economics," studying "successive equilibria" under changing conditions;
		(b) Third part of "pure economics," studying "the movements of economic phenomena"
M. Pantaleoni[20]	"Study of equilibrium positions"	"Studying of movements taking place in positions of disequilibrium and leading to a return to equilibrium positions"
F. Y. Edgeworth[21]	Study of "properties" of "positions of equilibrium" of the economic system	Study of "the path of the economic system from any . . . random [position] to a position of equilibrium
J.A.Schumpeter[22] (early writings)	Theory or "logic of the economy's circular flow," explaining "changes in the equilibrium position of the economy as originating in changes of the data," that is, as adjustments to "exogenous disturbances"	Theory of "economic development . . . changing the data of the static system" through "innovations" by "dynamic entrepreneurs
F. Oppenheimer[23]	"A part of dynamics," studying, "not a state of rest, but a state of movement . . . that is not exposed to disturbances through changes in the data during the interval	The entire "social process," the subject matter of sociology, "containing Statics and Kinetics as its two parts"; "Kinetics . . . comprises all studies of movements which change in magnitude or direction or both" be-

Author	Statics	Dynamics
	of observation"; includes "comparative statics"	cause of "changes in data"
F. H. Knight[24]	"Reasoning" about "economic change" in the only possible method: varying one thing while holding others constant	Cannot exist as "economic science"—though perhaps as "evolutionary or historical economics"
N. D. Kondratieff[25]	"Conception [which] considers economic phenomena, essentially and as a matter of principle, without taking into account their variations in time. It deals with reality as if its elements were in a state of fixed equilibrium"	"Conception [which] considers economic phenomena in the process of changes in their elements and in the interrelations of the latter in the course of time, and seeks to discover regularities in the progress of these variations," with special attention to "quantitative variations" and to "reversible and non-reversible processes"
R. Streller[26]	"A conception which abstracts from all time intervals that may arise between individual economic acts"; "derived from dynamics by way of abstractions made on methodological grounds"	"A conception of which time intervals are an integral part"; "coextensive with the subject matter of economic theory"
J. M. Clark[27]	Theory of "equilibrium," based upon "the relative stability of economic values" and upon the assumption of an "unchanging pattern of action"	Study "which focuses attention on processes of change," "restores realism by putting in everything that statics leaves out": (a) dealing with "quantitative departures from static norms," (b) "Second level of dynamics" —"perhaps to be called evolutionary"—dealing with "qualitative evolution of the basic legal institutions . . . , of forms of business organization and of competition, or dynamic changes or long run evolution in human nature itself"

Author	*Statics*	*Dynamics*
H. L. Moore[28]	Theory of "static equilibrium" showing "the interdependence of all economic quantities" and through "simultaneous mathematical equations the conditions of their common determination"	Theory of "moving equilibria, oscillations, and secular change" which "presents all of the interrelated economic quantities in a synthesis of simultaneous . . . equations" where all the variables in the constituent problems are treated as functions of time"
S. Kuznets[29]	Study of economic "relations and processes on the assumption of a uniformity and persistence of either the absolute or relative economic quantities involved," based on "a single principle of individual activity"	"Study of changes in the social phenomena over historical time" —"without descending to the level of individual activity"— with "emphasis on statistical research"
E. Lindahl[30]	Study of "economic developments taking place in time," though "the variables studied do not change their values with the lapse of time"; thus, "a ·special application of general dynamic theory for stationary conditions"	(a) "General dynamic theory" —"to determine certain variables as functions of time . . . with the help of equations based on . . . initial values of these variables and the conditions which determine their fluctuations," with emphasis on plan making and plan changing; (b) "Special dynamic theory" —an "application of general dynamic theory to . . . changing and evolutionary" conditions
R. Frisch[31]	Theory of economic interdependence in which "all the variables belong to the same point of time"	Theory "that explains how one situation grows out of the foregoing," by considering "the magnitudes of certain variables in different points of time," and introducing "certain equations which embrace at the same time several of these magnitudes belonging to different instances";

Author	Statics	Dynamics (a) "micro-dynamics," (b) "macro-dynamics"
G. Myrdal[32]	Study of "the changes of certain interdependent factors," such as "relative prices," by an "instantaneous analysis," assuming "that a deviation from the equilibrium position brings about reactive forces which restore equilibrium again"	Study of "the changes of certain interdependent factors" and "the time sequences" by a "period analysis" of "the development from one point of time to a second and a third and so on," assuming that equilibrium may be "labile," that "the mutual adjustments . . . take time" and that "the time order in which they occur is decisive for the outcome"
E. Lundberg[33]	Study of "how certain variables . . . adapt themselves to given data until a state of equilibrium has been reached," whereby "the adaptation process itself does not influence the fundamental conditions of equilibrium" and "all variable factors . . . are simultaneously variable" and "simultaneously interdependent"	"Sequence analysis" "explaining how each state is derived from a preceding one and, in turn, induces the next," and thus explaining "how the conditions of equilibrium themselves are changed," taking account of different "reaction times" and "reaction patterns"
L. Mises[34]	"Method of all scientific work, designed to analyze the effect of the change of any one factor *ceteris paribus* . . . The assumption of perfect changelessness of all other conditions . . . is a fiction indispensable for science and for thinking in general." ". . . its aim is the explanation of change"	"Everything that can be said about the theory of action of change, and in this sense would have a claim on being called Dynamics." Beyond this, the search for "dynamic theory . . . is devoid of any sense"
J. A. Schumpeter[35] (later writings)	Analysis "expressed in terms of the values which our variables assume at any single point of time," i.e.,	"Theorems" which "include in our functions values of variables which belong to different points of time"—this terminol-

18

Author	Statics	Dynamics
	connecting "economic quantities that refer to the same point in time"	ogy adopted "in deference to Professor Frisch"—"practically coextensive with sequence analysis" and "includes period analysis," but "not coextensive with the theory of economic growth, or development, or progress"
J. R. Hicks[36]	Theory in which "we do not trouble about dating" the economic quantities involved	Theory in which "every quantity must be dated"
G. Haberler[37]	"Theory where all the variables relating to a certain . . . time are explained by data relating to the same point or period of time," —hence without time lags "in the causal nexus"	Theory where "a magnitude is explained by another relating to an earlier . . . time,"—hence the "lags in the causal nexus"
R. F. Harrod[38]	Theory which, taking "certain fundamental conditions to be given and known," will "determine the values of certain unknowns," such as annual rates of inputs and outputs and products	Theory where "the fundamental conditions will themselves be changing, and the unknowns... to be solved will not be rate of output per annum, but increases or decreases in the rates of output per annum"
A. G. Hart[39]	"Timeless equilibrium theory"	Theory which concentrates "on the time element" and, especially, "allows for anticipations of change and for uncertainty"
F. A. Hayek[40]	(a) "Timeless" equilibrium theory"	(a) "Intertemporal equilibrium" theory, analyzing the "fictitious state" of "complete compatibility of ex ante plans" at "successive moments of time"
	(b) Theory of "stationary state"	(b) "Explanation of the economic process . . . in time," not through interdependences, but "as chain of historical sequences"
F. S. C. Northrop[41]	A deductive system based on "empirically verified postulates" but without	Impossible—would be "an empirically verified deductive system" enabling us "through its

19

Author	Statics	Dynamics
	verification of its "deduced consequences"	postulates and theorems . . . to deduce a future state" once the "quantitative values" "defining the present state" are empirically determined
J. Tinbergen[42]	"Theory . . . based on the assumption of a stationary position," confined to "exogenous movements," i.e., those "that may be considered as the immediate, or the almost immediate, adaptation to changes in data"	Theory "to explain . . . endogenous processes," "which will follow step by step the process of adaptation and the succeeding movements," with time " as one of the variables"
P. Samuelson[43]	"Simultaneous and instantaneous or timeless determination of economic variables by mutually interdependent relations"	Study of "functional relationships" among "economic variables at different points of time" or, that is, "between economic variables and their rates of change, their 'velocities,' 'accelerations,' or higher 'derivatives of derivatives' " (a) "discrete processes, treated in 'period analysis'" [with "difference equations"], (b) "continuous processes involving flows, treated in 'rate analysis'" [with "differential equations"]
G. J. Stigler[44]	Theory "which explains the equilibrium position in the particular problem on the assumption that the data of that problem do not change"	Study "of the path by which a set of economic quantities . . reach equilibrium within a static framework"
F. Machlup[45]	Theory of "economic change," explaining change as "adjustment to change," where "time is eliminated as a variable and time sequences do not affect the results of a process"	Theory of "step-by-step adjustments . . . as sequences in time," showing "these movements from period to period" and the effects of different "time sequences" depending on "in what order [certain] steps are

20

Author	Statics	Dynamics
		taken" and on the "time intervals between the steps"
W. J. Baumol[46]	Analysis of "a time-slice, a cross section . . . , thereby eliminating the passage of time from the problem, though . . . not necessarily eliminating the influence of time altogether"	"Study of economic phenomena in relation to preceding or succeeding events," (a) "Magnificent dynamics" — "broad generalizations, often in the nature of alleged . . . laws," concerning secular changes and "the development of the whole economy over long periods"; (b) "Statics involving time"— "concerned with features of the system other than the process of change itself"; (c) "Process (or sequence) analysis"—"step- by-step analysis of economic changes" over relatively short "spans of time"
G. L. S. Shackle[47]	"Economics of perfect adjustment," an analysis in which "time has no significant place, and uncertainty no place"	(a) "Calculable dynamics"— introducing "dynamic time"" "in the form of lagged reactions or of steady growth" (b) Expectational dynamics— introducing "expectational time and uncertainty," i.e., uncertain expectations of the future
F. Zeuthen[48]	"Approach" which "does not include anything about the connection between conditions at various points of time (about movements in time, increases, lags, uncertain expectations, etc.)"	"Approach" where "differences in time are taken into consideration. . . , for instance, . . . the velocities with which changes take place," or "growth, the process of adjustment, subsequent effects or time-consuming processes on the whole," also "uncertain or mistaken expectations"; divided into (a) "momentary dynamic analysis," analyzing "the conditions of a single moment where movement is going on"; (b) "the

Author	Statics	Dynamics
		course of economic phenomena through a period of time" (sequence analysis); (c) "comparative dynamics" analyzing "alternative movements . . . under alternative conditions"
D. Patinkin[49]	(a) "Analysis of . . . the nature of the equilibrium position" (b) Comparative Statics: "Comparison of equilibrium positions before and after a specified change in one or more of the independent variables"	Analysis of . . . the nature of the market forces which bring the economy to equilibrium from an initial position of disequilibrium"

[11] Auguste Comte, *Cours de philosophie positive* (Paris, 1839-42).

[12] John Stuart Mill, *Principles of Political Economy* (London, 1848), Book IV, ch. 1.

[13] Leon Walras, *Elements of Pure Economics,* Translated by William Jaffé (Homewood, Ill.: Irwin, 1954), pp. 318, 319. [Published in French in 1873.]

[14] John Neville Keynes, *Scope and Method of Political Economy* (London: Macmillan, 1890, 2nd ed., 1897), pp. 144, 145.

[15] Alfred Marshall, *Principles of Economics* (London: Macmillan, 8th ed , 1920). pp. xv, 366, 368, 369, 380, [First edition 1890.]

[16] John Bates Clark, *The Distribution of Wealth* (New York: Macmillan, 1899), pp. 30, 36, 56, 60.

[17] Thorstein Veblen, *The Place of Science in Modern Civilisation and Other Essays* (New York: Viking Press, 1932), pp. 70, 72, 77, 165, 190, 232, 242, 243. [First published in 1898, 1900, 1908, and 1909.]

[18] Knut Wicksell, *Lectures on Political Economy* (London: Routledge and Kegan Paul, 1934), pp. 7, 105. [Published in Swedish in 1901.]

[19] Vilfredo Pareto, *Manuel d'Economie Politique* (Paris: Girard, 2nd ed. 1927), p. 147. [First Italian edition 1906.]

[20] Maffeo Pantaleoni, "Some Phenomena of Economic Dynamics." *International Economic Papers,* Vol. V (London: Macmillan, 1956), p. 28. [Italian version in *Giornale degli Economisti,* 1909]

[21] Francis Y. Edgeworth, *Papers Relating to Political Economy* (London: Macmillan, 1925), Vol. II, p. 311. [Written in 1889.]

[22] Joseph A. Schumpeter, *Theorie der wirtschaftlichen Entwicklung* (Leipzig: Duncker & Humblot, 1912), pp. 96, 464, 489, 522.

[23] Franz Oppenheimer, *System der Soziologie,* 1. Halbband des I. Bandes. 2. Halbband des III. Bandes. (Jena: Fischer, 1922), pp. 68, 71, 74, 76; *Theorie der reinen oder politischen Oekonomie: Die Gesellschaftswissenschaft,* (Jena: Fisher, 1924), p. 618.

[24] Frank Hyneman Knight, *Risk, Uncertainty and Profit* (Boston: Houghton Mifflin, 1921), pp. 16-17; "Statik und Dynamik," *Zeitschrift für Nationalökonomie,*

Vol. II (1930), English translation in *Ethics of Competition and Other Essays* (New York: Harper, 1935), pp. 167, 169.

25 N. D. Kondratieff, "The Static and the Dynamic View of Economics," *Quarterly Journal of Economics,* Vol. XXXIX (1925), pp. 567, 577, 579, 580.

26 Rudolf Streller, *Statik und Dynamik in der theoretischen Nationalökonomie* (Leipzig: Streller, 1926), p. 135.

27 John Maurice Clark, "The Relation between Statics and Dynamics," *Economic Essays in Honor of John Bates Clark,* Jacob Hollander, ed. (New York: Macmillan, 1927), p. 46. Reprinted in *Preface to Social Economics* (New York: Farrar, Straus & Cudahy, Inc., 1936), pp. 196, 203; "Statics and Dynamics," *Encyclopedia of the Social Sciences,* Vol. 14 (New York: Macmillan, 1934), p. 354.

28 Henry Ludwell Moore, *Synthetic Economics* (New York: Macmillan, 1929), pp. 2, 4, 6.

29 Simon Kuznets, "Static and Dynamic Economics," *American Economic Review,* Vol. XX (1930), reprinted in *Essays in Economic Change* (New York: Norton, 1953), pp. 32, 35, 38, 44.

30 Erik Lindahl, *Studies in the Theory of Money and Capital* (New York: Farrar, Straus, & Cudahy, Inc., 1939), pp. 31, 32. [Swedish version 1930.]

31 Ragnar Frisch, "Propagation Problems and Impulse Problems in Dynamic Economics," *Economic Essays in Honor of Gustav Cassel* (London: Allen & Unwin, 1933), pp. 1-2.

32 Gunnar Myrdal, *Monetary Equilibrium* (London: Hodge, 1939), pp. 35, 36, 43, 44. [German version 1933.]

33 Erik Lundberg, *Studies in the Theory of Economic Expansion* (London: King, 1937), pp. 2, 3, 9, 11, 17, 243.

34 Ludwig von Mises, *Grundprobleme der Nationalökonomie* (Jena: Fischer, 1933), pp. 104, 105. *Nationalökonomie: Theorie des Handelns und Wirtschaftens* (Geneva: Union, 1940), p. 244; *Human Action* (New Haven: Yale University Press, 1949), p. 353.

35 Joseph A. Schumpeter, *Business Cycles* (New York: McGraw-Hill, 1939), p. 48; *History of Economic Analysis* (New York: Oxford University Press, 1954), pp. 1142, 1160.

36 John R. Hicks, *Value and Capital* (London: Oxford University Press, 1939), p. 115.

37 Gottfried Haberler, *Prosperity and Depression* (Geneva: League of Nations, Revised edition, 1939), pp. 249, 250.

38 Roy F. Harrod, "An Essay in Dynamic Theory," *Economic Journal,* Vol. XLIX (March 1939); *Towards a Dynamic Economics* (London: Macmillan, 1948), p. 4.

39 Albert Gailord Hart, *Anticipations, Uncertainty, and Dynamic Planning.* Studies in Business Administration, Vol. XI, No. 1 (Chicago: University of Chicago Press, 1940), pp. vii, 1.

40 Friedrich A. Hayek, *The Pure Theory of Capital* (London: Macmillan, 1941), pp. 17, 18, 22, 23.

41 F. S. C. Northrop, "The Impossibility of a Theoretical Science of Economic Dynamics," *Quarterly Journal of Economics,* Vol. LVI (1941), pp. 1, 12.

42 Jan Tinbergen and Jacques J. Polak, *The Dynamics of Business Cycles* (Chicago: University of Chicago Press, 1950), pp. 102, 103. [Dutch version 1942.]

43 Paul A. Samuelson, "Dynamic Process Analysis," *Survey of Contemporary Economics,* Vol. I, Howard S. Ellis, ed. (Philadelphia: Blakiston, 1948), p. 354.

II. Putative Statics and Dynamics

For more than twenty years I have been telling my students that one of the wide spread uses of "Statics" and Dynamics" was to distinguish a writer's own work from that of his opponents against whom he tried to argue. Typically, "Statics" was what those benighted opponents have been writing; "Dynamics" was one's own, vastly superior theory.[50]

Beside this attribution of a "static" character to the writings of others, who might not have so regarded their work, we also find "dynamic" theorizing attributed to writers who had not themselves used this term, either because it had not yet been introduced into economic literature or because they avoided it. It may be instructive to ascertain just what features of their studies have earned for them the label "Dynamics," and whether these putative contributors to dynamics were conscious of their doing something that was "different" from whatever may be regarded as "non-dynamic."

See also *Foundations of Economic Analysis* (Cambridge: Harvard University Press, 1947), pp. 311-317.

[44] George J. Stigler, *The Theory of Price* (New York: Macmillan, 1947), pp. 25, 26.

[45] Fritz Machlup, *International Trade and the National Income Multiplier* (Philadelphia: Blakiston, 1943), p. vii; *The Economics of Sellers' Competition* (Baltimore: Johns Hopkins, 1952), pp. 34, 187, 188, 189.

[46] William J. Baumol, *Economic Dynamics* (New York: Macmillan, 1951), pp. 218.

[47] George L. S. Shackle, *Uncertainty in Economics and other Reflections* (Cambridge: University Press, 1955), p. 218.

[48] Frederik Zeuthen, *Economic Theory and Method* (Cambridge, Mass.: Harvard University Press, 1955), pp. 27, 78, 79, 139, 140.

[49] Don Patinkin, *Money, Interest, and Prices: An Integration of Monetary and Value Theory* (New York: Harper & Row, 1956), p. 32.

[50] My quip was quoted in a recent book review: "In this reviewer's opinion. the best definition—and the one that will command the widest agreement among economists—is still an unpublished one due to Professor Machlup: 'Dynamics is my theory; statics is the other fellow's theory.'" John S. Chipman, review of "La période dans l'analyse économique, une approche à l'étude due temps," by Raymond Barre, *Econometrica*, Vol. 22 (Jan. 1954), p. 126. Virtually the same remark was made by Samuelson: "We damn another man's theory by terming it static, and advertise our own by calling it dynamic." Paul A. Samuelson, *Foundations of Economic Analysis*, p. 311.

What is now widely called "Classical Dynamics" are the theories—associated chiefly with Malthus, Ricardo, James Mill, McCulloch, Senior—

ambitiously attempting to analyze the growth and development of entire economies over relatively long periods of time—decades or even centuries ... The basic theme ... was the development of the economy from a progressive state into a stationary state ... with no net investment, subsistence wages, and low or even zero profits . . .[51]

Baumol calls this theory "Magnificent Dynamics" because of the "sweeping generalizations," "inspired oversimplifications," and the "daring and imaginative" thought on which these theories were based. The chief building stones of "Classical Dynamics" were (a) the Malthusian law of population, (b) the law of (historically) diminishing returns, (c) the propensity to accumulate (invest profits), and (d) the law of wages (which are raised through increased investment demand and depressed through increased labor supply).[52]

Because of the eventual disappearance of profits and the resulting end of accumulation and growth which these theories predict, historians of thought referred to their authors as "The Pessimists."[53] If they are now regarded as builders of a "dynamic" model it is chiefly because theirs is a theory of historical development and economic growth. But also others, who do not see growth and development as the essence of dynamics but prefer to use this term to denote certain methods and techniques of analysis, have been able to attribute a "dynamic" approach to classical economists. For example, Pantaleoni states that the "famous essay by D. Ricardo on the depreciation of English paper money . . . is also a study of economic dynamics."[54] And Schumpeter regards Ricardo as a

---

[51] William J. Baumol, op. cit., pp. 11-12. Although John Stuart Mill is customarily not counted among the "classical" economists, he shared the views characterized as their "Dynamics." He was convinced of the "impossibility of ultimately avoiding the stationary state—this irresistible necessity that the stream of human industry should finally spread itself out into an apparently stagnant sea." John Stuart Mill, op. cit., (London: Longmans Green, 1926), p. 746.

[52] Baumol, op. cit., p. 19. Most other writers emphasize only the first two of the four fundamental laws. Cf. Paul Sweezy, The Theory of Capitalist Development: Principles of Marxian Political Economy (New York: Oxford University Press, 1942), pp. 92-93.

[53] Charles Gide and Charles Rist, Histoire des doctrines économiques (Paris: Recueil Sirey, 5th ed., 1926), p. 137. For the same reason Carlyle called economics the "dismal science."

[54] Maffeo Pantaleoni, loc. cit., p. 31.

contributor to dynamics because of his conscious use of "period analysis."[55]

If thus the label "Dynamics" was so conspicuously bestowed on the classical economists, we must not overlook the label "Statics" which hangs there too. Indeed, for a long time it was highly fashionable to identify "classical" economics with "static" economics; members of the German and English historical schools never tired of criticizing and rejecting classical economics for its "statical" approach. (What many of these critics meant by "statical" approach, however, was the method of abstraction and isolation which they rejected in favor of a "totalistic" or "holistic" approach, comprehending the *"innerlich zusammenhängende, einheitliche Lebenstotalität des Volkes."*[56])

Of course there is no reason why classical economics should not have been both "static" and "dynamic"—whatever this may mean—, static in some parts and dynamic in others. But the classical writers themselves did not indicate that they were conscious of employing two different approaches (as to subject matter or techniques of analysis)—except perhaps when they were speculating about future developments. This is altogether different with regard to one of their most famous critics, who was quite emphatic in differentiating his own approach from that of the classics on grounds of what has been called a thoroughly "dynamic" program. The "dissenter"[57] was Simonde de Sismondi.[58] His program is best described in Schumpeter's words:

The distinctive feature of Sismondi's analysis is that it is geared to an *explicit dynamic model in the modern sense of this phrase.*

He realized that the most important of the reasons why transitional phenomena are of the essence of the economic process—and hence not only relevant to its practical problems but also to its fundamental theory—is that the economic process is chained to certain sequences that will exclude certain forms of adaptation and enforce others.

Sismondi's great merit is that he used, systematically and explicitly, a schema of periods, that is, that he was the first to practice the particular method of dynamics that is called period analysis. Moreover, he saw clearly the

---

[55] Joseph A. Schumpeter, *History of Economic Analysis,* pp. 563-64.

[56] Julius J. Kautz, *Die Nationalökonomie als Wissenschaft* (Wien: Gerold, 1858), p. 320.

[57] Sismondi is treated as the first of the "adversaires" of the classical school. See Gide and Rist, *op. cit.,* pp. 199, 201.

[58] Jean Charles Leonard Simonde de Sismondi, *Nouveaux principes d'économie politique* (Paris: Delaunay, 1819).

difference this makes and in particular the disturbances, discrepancies, and hitches that result from the fact that economic life is bound to sequences of which every unit is determined by the past and in turn determines the future.[59]

The features of Sismondi's work that prompted Schumpeter to call it "dynamic" are, of course, the methodological principles stressed on Schumpeter's definition of dynamics adopted "in deference to Professor Frisch." But also if dynamics is understood in some of the alternative senses can one find reasons for characterizing Sismondi's work as "dynamic." For example, it may be regarded as a study of historical economic development and of the evolution of economic institutions.

Friedrich List's work earned the label of "Dynamics" on similar grounds. It was essentially an analysis of the development of the "productive forces of the nation," a severe critique of the static foundation of classical free-trade theory, and an elaborate infant-industry argument for protective tariffs.[60] The putative dynamics of his work is pointed up in the following statement by Gide and Rist:

List has enlarged the political horizon of the classical writers by substituting for their purely *static* conception a *dynamic* conception of the welfare of the nations. He introduced into the theory of international trade what Sismondi had introduced into domestic economics: the preoccupation with the conditions of economic progress. Only that while Sismondi wanted progress to be slowed down List wanted it promoted.[61]

The system that qualifies for the attribution of "dynamics" on more scores than any other, or under the greatest variety of meanings given to the term, is "Marxian Dynamics." It does so as a theory of development, as a theory of a cumulative sequence, as a theory of historical evolution, as a general sociology interpreting the whole of social life, as a study of the evolution of institutions, as a model where all variables are functions of time, as period analysis, and probably on several other counts. One may wonder how Marx and Engels were able to do all this without using the word "dynamics." They used a substitute, though: "dialectics." To this term they gave just about all the meanings that other writers ascribed to "dynamics." In Engel's words, the "dialectical" method "grasps things

---

[59] Joseph A. Schumpeter, *History of Economic Analysis,* pp. 494, 495, 496. (Italics in the original.)

[60] Friedrich List, *Das nationale System der politischen Oekonomie* (Stuttgart: Cotta, 1841).

[61] Gide and Rist, *op. cit.,* p. 339. (Italics in the original.)

and their images, ideas, essential in their interconnection, in their sequence, their movement, their birth and death."[62] Much has been written about the extraordinary comprehensiveness—defeating all attempts at defining it—of the Marxian concept of dialectics. There can be little doubt that it embraces "dynamics" as one of its essential components—if not as its very essence.

Among the "dynamic" elements in the Marxian system are the theories of accumulation, reproduction on an enlarged scale, mechanization, constant re-creation of the industrial reserve army, progressively increasing misery of the masses, concentration of industry, falling rate of profit, recurring crises, and the inevitable downfall of capitalism. Because of this terminal state in the evolutionary sequence, it has been characterized as an "eschatological dynamic."[63] Schumpeter stresses in Marxian Dynamics the analysis of the sequence of evolutionary (endogenous) change, the

fundamental idea . . . of a theory, not merely of an indefinite number of disjointed individual patterns or of the logic of economic quantities in general but of the actual sequence of those patterns or of the economic process as it goes on, under its own steam, in historic time, producing at every instant that state which will of itself determine the next one.[64]

And Paul Sweezy affirms that Marx, chiefly through his theories of the industrial reserve army and of the progressive mechanization of the process of production,

laid the foundation for a new and amazingly powerful attack on the problems of economic evolution . . . [and] . . . discovered one of the most im-

---

[62] Friedrich Engels, *Herrn Eugen Dühring's Umwälzung der Wissenschaft* (Leipzig: Genossenschaftsbuchdruckerei, 1878); English translation *Herr Eugen Dühring's Revolution in Science: Anti-Dühring* (New York: International Publishers, 1935), p. 29.

[63] Cf. Kenneth E. Boulding, "A New Look at Institutionalism," *American Economic Review, Proceedings,* Vol. XLVII (May 1957), p. 9. Mises had called it a "chiliastic" theory, predicting the arrival of a millenium. Ludwig von Mises, *Die Gemeinwirtschaft: Untersuchungen über den Sozialismus* (Jena: Fischer, 2nd ed. 1932), pp. 250 ff.

[64] Joseph A. Schumpeter, *Capitalism, Socialism and Democracy* (New York: Harper & Row, 1942), p. 43.

portant of the 'laws of motion' of capitalism which it was the announced intention of *Capital* to explore.[65]

The German Historical School has occasionally been characterized as dynamic economics, partly because of its objective to discover "the laws of the development of the economy of a nation,"[66] partly because of its attempts to formulate "stage theories" of economic development,[67] partly because of its "emphasis . . . on the concept of social evolution,"[68] but chiefly because of its opposition to the "static" theory of classical economists.

In our survey John Maynard Keynes deserves a special place because of the intentional "dynamics" but putative "statics" which he produced. This divergence between intention and realization happened twice: first with his *Treatise* and again with his *General Theory*. In the Treatise he had declared that greater concern with "dynamical problems . . . will enormously increase the applicability of theory to practice," and that "This Treatise, in contrast to most older work on monetary theory, is

---

[65] Paul M. Sweezy, *op. cit.*, pp. 93-94. Sweezy explained that the dynamics of the classics had been based primarily on the Malthusian law of population; that, when "facts" forced economists to "abandon" this law, they gave up exploring economic evolution and"proceeded to exclude questions of evolutionary processes from the field of systematic theorizing"; that Marx, who had rejected "all truck with Malthusianism," was an exception and by discovering "the principle of the [industrial] reserve army in place of the law of population" established a firm base for his dynamics.

[66] Wilhelm Roscher, *System der Volkswirtschaft* (Stuttgart: Cotta, 2nd ed. 1857), p. 25

[67] Karl Bücher, *Die Entstehung der Volkswirtschaft* (Tübingen: H. Laupp, 1893).

[68] Edmund Whittaker, *A History of Economic Ideas* (New York: Longmans, Green & Co., Inc., 1940), p. 737. In a most informative description of Gustav Schmoller's work, J. F. Bell writes: "Economic life, he believed, was a part of an active culture pattern which was both dynamic in an evolutionary sense and self-revealing. He believed that it was the task of economic science to determine the means or laws of this cultural exfoliation in its economic aspects, thus providing a sequence of cultural changes of growth and decline. Since history shows a repetitive sequence of events, a comprehensive record of past cultural developments would therefore provide a historical cultural prospective for the future. Short-run, environmental elements would not do more than briefly interrupt the cultural trend; they would not alter the final outcome of the dynamic march of cultural progress or of the cultural process. This reasoning provided Schmoller with a logical method of making historical inquiry the most important means of determining the laws of economic and other cultural development." John Fred Bell, *A History of Economic Thought* (New Ronald Press, 1923), pp. 341-342.

intended to be a contribution to this new phase of economic science."[69] However, the critics of the *Treatise* were unanimous in the conclusion that Keynes' argument, especially his supposedly "dynamical equations" were "purely statical in type."[70] Keynes himself, prefacing his next work, pleaded guilty for his earlier "lack of emancipation from preconceived ideas" and for the fact that "the dynamic development, as distinct from the instantaneous picture, was left incomplete and extremely confused."[71] But the renewed effort, though unequalled in all economic literature for its revolutionary impact upon contemporary thought, did not succeed in building a "dynamic" system. Indeed, "Mr. Keynes' system is still completely static," as Haberler summed up the results of several years of debate.[72]. Many features of the system presented in the General Theory have been pronounced "essentially static"[73] in nature, but none more so than the interpretation of "the multiplier as an instantaneous relationship." Keynes apparently had an aversion to period analysis: "forget about periods!" he once told a student, according to a very credible report.[74]

In contrast to Keynes, Dennis H. Robertson is most widely acclaimed as an architect of economic dynamics, though he has never claimed to be one. "Robertsonian Dynamics" has become the accepted designation for period analysis based on the income-expenditure lag. Robertson himself, it seems, went out of his way to avoid using the word "dynamics." He can, however, be found to speak of "a more explicitly temporal method of analysis" and of an "analysis of processes of change, . . . following a step-by-step method, and starting again at each point in the light of all

---

69 John Maynard Keynes, *A Treatise on Money* (London: Macmillan, 1930), Vol. II, pp. 406-407.

70 Evan F. M. Durbin, *The Problem of Credit Policy* (New York: Wiley, 1935), p. 248. With this verdict Durbin confirmed earlier opinions by F. A. Hayek, "Reflections on the Pure Theory of Money of Mr. J. M. Keynes," *Economica*, August 1931 and February 1932, Vol. XI; James E. Meade, *The Rate of Interest in a Progressive State* (London: Macmillan, 1933), and several others. For a good discussion see Arthur W. Marget, *The Theory of Prices, Vol. I* (Englewood Cliffs, N. J.: Prentice-Hall, 1938), pp. 101-140.

71 John Maynard Keynes, *The General Theory of Employment, Interest and Money* (London: Macmillan, 1936), pp. vi-vii.

72 Gottfried von Haberler, *Prosperity and Depression: A Theoretical Analysis of Cyclical Movements* (Geneva: League of Nations, 3rd enlarged ed., 1941), p. 473.

73 Joseph A. Schumpeter, *op. cit.*, p. 1174.

74 *Ibid.*

that has gone before"[75]—which describes perfectly what many mean by "dynamics."

III. Typology and Classification

After listing the statements in which 39 authors attempted to say what they meant by Statics and Dynamics, and after discussing another group of economists whose work was characterized by other writers as either Statics or Dynamics, one should think that we now have a pretty good idea of these concepts. Unfortunately, we have gained only two strong impressions: one, that many of the authors in the first list were quite clumsy in expressing themselves, and some of them unsuccessful in saying clearly what they had in mind (assuming they had a clear conception); and secondly, that there is a great variety of meanings attached to the terms in question.

It might be an interesting undertaking to attempt interpretations of some of the obscure statements. When Mill spoke of a "stationary society," J. B. Clark of a "stationary state," Wicksell of a "stationary state of economic relations," Lindahl of "stationary conditions," Hayek of the "stationary state," Tinbergen of a "stationary position"—did they mean the same thing? Or were, as it seems more likely, five or six different ideas involved here? When J. B. Clark stressed for his Dynamics "the influence of five generic changes"—population, capital, technology, business organization, and tastes—did he mean merely a one-way direction of "influence" or did he mean a two-way street, a shuttle connection between variables in mutual interdependence? When Veblen formulated his incredibly ambitious program of searching for a body of theory that would account for practically everything—where "each new situation . . . embodies as causal factors all that has been effected by what went before"—did he mean what he said or was he merely exuberantly eloquent? Did J. M. Clark really want to put into Dynamics "everything that statics leaves out"?

---

[75] Dennis H. Robertson, "Some Notes on Mr. Keynes' General Theory of Employment," *Quarterly Journal of Economics*, Vol. LI (1936), pp. 172, 186. In an earlier article, Robertson speaks of a "treatment" that stresses "the successive existence of a short number of slices of time during each of which the money which appears as income for A cannot also appear as outlay by A (and therefore income for B)." D. H. Robertson, "Saving and Hoarding," *Economic Journal*, Vol. XLIII (1933), p. 413.

This is only a small sample of the many questions raised by some of the statements collected in our list. We shall not take the time which such an interpretation would require. A different task seems more fruitful: an attempt to develop a typology and a classification of the distinctions made between Statics and Dynamics. If successful, a modicum of order may be brought into the semantic chaos. An earlier attempt, made over thirty years ago, was not successful. Rudolph Streller, in a monograph on the subject, proposed to sort the distinctions into the following five classes:[76]

I. The two concepts are equivalent to the two fields of "Theoretical Economics" and "Practical [Applied] Economics"—the customary division of economics in German universities.

II. The two concepts signify two branches of theoretical economics.

III. All economics is Dynamics; Statics does not exist.

IV. The two concepts refer to different subject matters, namely, the study of "static countries" and the study of "dynamic countries."

V. Statics is the study of equilibrium conditions, Dynamics the study of the forces leading toward equilibrium positions.

It is perfectly correct that all of these meanings of Statics and Dynamics have been expressed in the literature and that authors can be cited for each of the five classes. But a good many authors could not be classed as representatives of any of these views. Moreover, some of the classes are so broad that very different types of distinctions between Statics and Dynamics would have to be left undifferentiated. For a better grasp, not only the obvious and conspicuous differences but also the finer nuances in the conceptions developed by different authors should be taken into account. Hence, we shall attempt to build a typology that accommodates most or all of the variants found in the literature.

It seemed expedient at first blush to separate the views according to which Statics and Dynamics meant two different *methods of analysis* from the views according to which they referred to two different *subject matters*. This has proved unworkable. One may say, for example, that a stationary economy and a growing economy, or the phenomenon of stationariness and the phenomenon of growth, are different subject matters. Yet, in order to understand why an economy is stationary, or fails to grow,

---

[76] Rudolph Streller, *op. cit.*, pp. 38, 58. 77, 82, 89.

one will need a theory of growth; and likewise, many aspects of growth will be better comprehended if recourse can be had to the theory of the stationary state. It just is not so that a certain model is useful only to the interpretation of situations which it depicts or schematizes. As a rule we need "contrasting models" in order to study the significance of whatever factors seem to be relevant in a given situation. For this reason, subject matter cannot be made a major independent criterion in the classification. Where authors insist on designating subject matter as the all-important difference between Statics and Dynamics, we shall have to regard this as an "extreme position." In other instances we shall have to lump "subject matter" and "basic approach" into one class.

The typology offered here will be arranged in the following six classes, the first containing absolute contradictories, the other five describing spectra or differences of degree:

A. Extreme positions
B. Regarding basic approach and subject matter
C. Regarding assumptions of invariance, independence, dependence and interdependence of particular variables
D. Regarding the use of the equilibrium concept
E. Regarding individual behavior and social facts
F. Regarding formal properties of variables.

A CLASSIFIED TYPOLOGY OF DISTINCTIONS BETWEEN STATICS AND DYNAMICS IN ECONOMICS

A. *Extreme Positions*

Statics	*Dynamics*
1. The theory of my opponent	My own theory
2. Description of state of rest; hence, worthless as explanation of change	Explanation of change; hence, the only useful theory ("There is no meaningful statics")
3. Method of holding other things constant; hence the only possible technique of reasoning ("There is no meaningful dynamics")	Method of looking at the complex totality of phenomena, with everything changing at once; hence, worthless for explaining anything
4. Naive speculation about imaginary world, based on unrealistic assumptions	Realistic study of the real world, based on observed facts

33

Statics	*Dynamics*
5. Method of explaining certain things by taking other things as data	Method of taking nothing as datum, attempting to explain everything
6. Theory applicable only to "static" (stagnant) economies.	Theory applicable only to "dynamic" (developing) economies

B. *Regarding Basic Approach and Subject Matter*

Statics	*Dynamics*
1. Pure theory: model building, using abstractions, constructions, isolation, idealization	Applied economics: dealing with empirical "reality" in all its complexity
2. Theoretical construction abstracting from historical time	Historical description of observed sequences in historical time
3. Theory of exogenous changes: adjustments to assumed (given) events of changes	Theory of endogenous changes: explanation of changes evolving without "disturbances" from outside
4. Theory of the stationary state	Theory of growth and fluctuations
5. Theory of relative prices and output: analyzing decision making adjustments of costs, prices, outputs, allocation of resources, and distribution of income	Theory of accumulation and progress: analyzing saving, investment, and technical change, and effects on productivity, employment, and income
6. Theory of value and distribution: the same as Statics B 5	Theory of evolution of institutions, including stage theories of economic systems
7. Theory of variation yielding conditional predictions of effects of particular changes *ceteris paribus*	Theory of development yielding unconditional predictions of tendencies in a distant future
8. Taxonomic and tautological economics	Empirical economics
9. Abstract economic theory isolating idealized patterns of actions under given social institutions	Holistic social theory dealing with the "whole" social process and the change of institutions
10. Analytic method (in Marxian sense)	Dialectic method (in Marxian sense)

C. *Regarding Assumptions of Invariance, Independence, Dependence and Interdependence of Particular Variables*

Statics	*Dynamics*
1. Assuming population, capital stock, technology, business or-	Assuming population, capital stock, technology, business organization,

34

Statics

ganization, and tastes—and social institutions—to change only one at a time, and analyzing the effects (adjustments)

2. Assuming the same as Statics C-1 or as Dynamics C-1

3. Assuming capital stock, technology, and business organization to be unchanged, allowing population and tastes (and some institutions?) to change, and analyzing the effects (adjustments)

4. Assuming the fundamental social institutions to be unchanged, allowing everything else to change, and analyzing the effects (adjustments)

Dynamics

and tastes to change simultaneously—as independent variables or as functions of time—and analyzing the process and the effects

Assuming population, capital stock, technology, business organization, and tastes to change in the course of any sort of process—as dependent variables—and analyzing the causes and interactions as well as the process and the effects

Assuming capital stock, technology, and business organization to change in consequence of entrepreneurial innovation (and of bank credit creation) and analyzing the causes and interactions as well as the process and the effects

Assuming all conditions including fundamental social institutions to change in the course of any sort of process, and analyzing the causes and interactions as well as the process and effects

D. *Regarding the Use of the Equilibrium Concept*

1. Analyzing the formal properties of equilibrium, disregarding transitions or the process of equilibration

2. Analyzing the conditions of equilibrium, but not the forces at work to attain, maintain, or restore equilibrium

3. Assuming all data, after the initial disturbing change, to remain unchanged during the process of equilibration

4. Assuming all responses to lead toward positions of equilibrium

Analyzing the forces effecting the changes in economic quantities that are required for equilibrium to be approached, attained, maintained, restored

Analyzing the paths toward equilibrium and the effects on the outcome of different sequences in the equilibrating process

Assuming data to change further before equilibration is completed; hence, hypothesizing a moving equilibrium that can never be attained ("Moving equilibrium")

Assuming some responses to engender cumulative process leading to

35

Statics

5. Assuming equal reaction speeds of dependent variables in the process of equilibration

6. Comparing consecutive or alternative equilibria ("Comparative statics")

7. Assuming indifference of outcome to the order of steps in the process of equilibration if shown as a sequence

8. Analyzing the simultaneous consistency of interrelated variables, disregarding the possible realizations of the expectations of decision makers in the future

9. Assuming absence of anticipations of changes in prices or other conditions, and absence of allowances for subjective uncertainty

Dynamics

progressive deviations from equilibrium ("Cumulative process")

Assuming unequal reaction speeds of dependent variables, resulting in sequences that may or may not tend to eventual equilibrium ("Sequence analysis")

Tracing consecutive disequilibria as a sequence in time ("Sequence analysis")

Assuming dependence of outcome on the order of steps in a sequence which may or may not approach equilibrium ("Period analysis")

Analyzing the compatibility of plans, decisions, and expectations with regard to their possible realizations over time ("Intertemporal equilibrium")

Analyzing the effects of uncertain expectations and anticipations of changes in prices or other conditions

E. *Regarding Individual Behavior and Social Facts*

1. Explanation of certain changes as adjustments to exogenous causes by individuals and firms responding to altered opportunities and given preferences

2. Focus on the ideal type of economic man, constructed with unchanging postulates about individual motivation and action

3. Deductions from assumption of universal pattern of individual action

4. Qualitative reasoning starting from the individual

Explanation of certain changes as emanations from within the economic system (endogenous changes) in the form of innovating actions of entrepreneurs financed by new money)

Focus on the "whole man" and on the totality of changing social facts, especially "social wholes"

Empirical observation of social facts and aggregative quantitative information

Quantitative research starting from statistical data, especially time series over long periods

F. *Regarding Formal Properties of Variables*

Statics	Dynamics
1. Using only undated variables	Using only dated variables
2. Connecting quantities referring to the same point or period of time	Connecting quantities referring to different points or periods of time
3. Assuming no time lags	Assuming time lags, using lagged variables
4. Omitting time as an independent variable	Making some or all quantities functions of time
5. Emphasizing as variables prices and quantities	Emphasizing as variables differences, rates of change, derivatives with respect to time

It must be admitted that, in an attempt to keep the number of classes down, their characteristics have been formulated somewhat loosely and broadly but, nevertheless, some of the types of distinction will be fitted only with considerable strain into one of the boxes so provided. It must further be admitted that some of the differences between separate types of distinction are so small, or merely verbal, that two or three of the types could just as well have been telescoped into one; on the other hand, further subdivisions could have been made if minor nuances of details were considered sufficiently important. All this is natural in the description of spectra. It is a matter of taste how far one wants to go in dividing a spectrum of ideas.

Duplication, or even multiple entry, has been unavoidable because certain meanings of dynamics combine several criteria and thus represent at the same time several different types. Take, for example, Schumpeter's theory of economic development, which he once regarded as the prototype of "dynamics" (before he generously accepted Frisch's definition). This Schumpeterian Dynamics would fit types B-3 (endogenous change), B-4 (growth and cycle theories), B-5 (accumulation theory), C-3 (giving to technology, business organization, and capital stock the status of dependent variables), D-3 (moving equilibrium), D-4 (cumulative processes), D-5 (sequence analysis), E-1 (innovating activity of "dynamic" entrepreneurs), as well as F-1, F-2, and F-3 (dated, inter-period, lagged variables). Many of the theories that are widely recognized as dynamic will qualify as more than one type of dynamic.

Some of the separate and apparently different criteria are in fact closely linked with one another, if they are not logical correlatives. A theory of growth will be closely associated with a theory of capital accumulation; this, in turn, will be a theory of endogenous change, and the resulting processes and sequences will be analyzed under any of the assumptions concerning reactions, responses, etc. The "endogenous" changes themselves, on the other hand, can readily be interpreted in terms of the "equilibrations" on the part of the consumers-savers and entrepreneurs-investors responding to alternative opportunities and given preferences. Thus, a good many "categorical" distinctions are merely different ways of looking at the same things.

Several of the distinctions proposed in the literature and included in our list suggest contrasts and contradictions which disappear on closer inspection. Many writers, for example, have believed that "equilibrium economics" and "evolutionary economics" were diametrical opposites; in fact, however, the equilibrium concept can often be used in explaining an evolutionary sequence and, indeed, it may be impossible to explain certain processes that are part of an evolutionary sequence without the use of the equilibrium concept. Thus, an evolutionary sequence may (a) employ "temporary" equilibria as explanatory devices, and (b) assume the eventual attainment of (or close approach to) an "ultimate" equilibrium. Cases in point, to name only a few, are Classical Dynamics, Marxian Dynamics, and the converging-cobweb theorem. To illustrate by Marxian Dynamics: the very essence of the "dialectic" scheme is a sequence of "syntheses," which are equilibria in the short run as well as disequilibria from a longer-term point of view; and the eventual emergence of socialism is the ultimate equilibrium, the terminal synthesis in the chain of contradictions. Undoubtedly, if "dynamics" were defined by the non-use of the equilibrium concept it would become a rather empty category; at least, many types of economic analysis, now safely regarded as "dynamic," would no longer so qualify.

IV. Complaints About Confusion

Over the years, there has been a long procession of economists lamenting the semantic confusion about the pair of terms under review. Some of the complaints tried to repair the situation by prescribing what economists *ought* to mean when they speak of Statics and Dynamics; each prescription added one more to the many conflicting and confusing distinctions already in stock. Other complaints confined themselves to surveying and analyzing the conceptual and terminological muddle.

The number of articles and books devoted exclusively to discussions of Statics and Dynamics is remarkable. Some of them we have cited above —Pantaleoni, Kondratieff, Streller, J. M. Clark, F. H. Knight, Kuznets, Frisch, Harrod, Hart, Samuelson, Baumol. But this is by no means an exhaustive list. Most probably it omits more than it includes. To name some omissions of which I am fully aware, there is an essay by Simon Patten,[77] a second book by Steller,[78] articles by Barone,[79], Amonn,[80] Honegger,[81] Roos,[82] Moretti,[83] Demaria,[84] Goetz-Girey,[85] Samuelson,[86] and a frequently cited book by Roos.[87] But in addition there are many articles on the subject that have appeared over the last fifty years in Italian, German, French, Dutch, Scandinavian journals, which I have not consulted, plus a number of books in these languages. Finally there are now innumerable publications on the "dynamics" of particular subject matters,

---

[77] Simon N. Patten, *The Theory of Dynamic Economics,* Publications of the University of Pennsylvania, Political Economy and Law Series, Vol. III, No. 2. (Philadelphia: Univ. of Pennsylvania, 1892).

[78] Rudolph Streller, *Die Dynamik der theoretischen Nationalökonomie* (Tübingen: Mohr-Siebeck, 1928).

[79] Enrico Barone, "Sul trattamento di quistioni dinamiche," *Giornale degli Economisti,* Serie II, Vol. IX (1894), pp. 407-435.

[80] Alfred Amonn, "Die Probleme der wirtschaftlichen Dynamik," *Archiv fur Sozialwissenschaften und Sozialpolitik,* 38. Bd. (1914).

[81] Hans Honegger, "Zur Krisis der statischen Nationalökonomie," *Schmollers Jahrbuch für Gesetzgebung, Verwaltung und Volkswirtschaft im Deutschen Reiche,* 48. Jahrg. (1924), pp. 473-490.

[82] Charles F. Roos, "A Dynamical Theory of Economics," *Journal of Political Economy,* Vol. XXXV (1927), pp. 632-656.

[83] Vincenzo Moretti, "Sopra alcuni problemi di dinamica economica," *Giornale degli Economisti,* Serie IV, Vol. LXIX (1929), pp. 449-488.

[84] Giovanni Demaria, "Saggio sugli studi di dinamica economica," *Rivista Internazionale di Scienze Sociali,* Anno XXXVIII, Serie III, Vol. I (1930), pp. 107-130, 222-257.

[85] Robert Goetz-Girey, "Statique et dynamique économiques dans la science allemande contemporaine," *Revue d'Economie Politique,* Vol. L (1936), pp. 1308-1330.

[86] Paul A. Samuelson, "Dynamics, Statics, and the Stationary State," *Review of Economic Statistics,* Vol. XXV (1943), pp. 58-61.

[87] Charles F. Roos, *Dynamic Economics: Theoretical and Statistical Studies of Demand, Production and Prices* (Bloomington: Principia Press, 1934).

such as "dynamics of competition," "dynamic distribution theory," "dynamic programming theory." Does this mean that agreement has been reached about the meaning of the terms in question?

Agreement with a particular set of formal definitions of Statics and Dynamics would not be enough to remove the confusion, as Kuznets has rightly observed, for "there is confusion as to the actual scope and relation of these two bodies."[88] But we are far from an agreement on definitions either. Knight alludes to "the lack of effort at clear definition" and "the paucity of discussion of their [the terms'] meaning."[89] Rosenstein-Rodan calls them "terms of such ambiguity that their use is often positively misleading."[90] Sombart calls the distinction *"zweifellos das dürftigste Schema"* for dividing economic analysis; he remonstrates against the continuous "confusions of the working constructs of static and dynamic states with the empirical concepts of changeless and change"; and he denounces "the authors who speak of statics but mean traditionalism, and speak of dynamics but mean progressivism."[91]

Schumpeter likewise decries the incessant confusions between static and stationary, and between dynamic and evolutionary.[92] Most writers, he says, confuse "static theory" with the "theory of the stationary state,"

witness the growing popularity of the phrase 'static state' which is the hallmark of this confusion. Nevertheless, though more clearly visualized than rigorously defined, the system of economic statics did emerge during the period and in fact constitutes its great achievement. But the nature of economic dynamics was not even clearly visualized—some identified it with a historical theory of change or else with a theory that allows for trends; others with a theory of general interdependence as against partial analysis of sectional phenomena; still others with a theory of a modern as against the tradition-bound economy of the Middle Ages; and a few simply with the theory of small variations of economic quantities . . . And there were those in whose hands the whole discussion degenerated into a quarrel about words. All this goes to

---

[88] Simon Kuznets, *loc. cit.,* p. 32.

[89] Frank H. Knight, "Statik und Dynamik," *loc. cit.,* p. 1; *Ethics of Competition,* p. 161.

[90] Paul N. Rosenstein-Rodan, "The Role of Time in Economic Theory," *Economica,* New Series, Vol. I (1934), p. 77.

[91] Werner Sombart, *Die drei Nationalökonomien* (München: Duncker & Humblot, 1930), p. 187.

[92] Joseph A. Schumpeter, *History of Economic Analysis,* p. 964.

show the importance, even for purely practical purposes, of logically rigorous definitions. . . .[93]

The sternest strictures came from Ewald Schams, who scoffed at the use of "this pretty pair of names" with unknown or unclear meanings. The "peculiarity of a perfect agreement about the terminology" combined with a "perfect disagreement" about its meaning is attributed to the fact that the terms were rashly taken over from a different field. And "now one struggles manfully to find for the two names some sensible contents that would tolerably well fit the subject"; and under the strange influence of the pair of names one feels under a compulsion to divide the subject into two parts, no matter whether it makes sense or not. Schams believes it makes no sense.[94]

This conclusion is too severe. The trouble, as I see it, is not that the division of economic analysis into Statics and Dynamics makes *no* sense, but that it makes *too many* senses. Perhaps this is even worse; non-sense can be shrugged off with a laugh, but multiple sense may be a real nuisance. It involves, in this instance, less the danger of snags and snares in economic theorizing than the waste of time in trying to understand one another.

The danger of a failure to understand one's partner in discussion is serious. Remember that for Schumpeter "Dynamics" once was the theory of development, but later he warned against confusing growth and development theories with "Dynamics." And just when he and others had declared that by Dynamics they would mean period analysis and lagged variables, Harrod announced that Dynamics was growth theory after all. Price theory, based on assumptions of given cost and demand, was definitely Statics for Harrod and many others; yet, when analyzed with different reaction speeds and sequences, with time lags and alternative paths towards equilibrium, price theory became Dynamics for many economists. The notion of equilibrium, as we have seen, is widely held to be a characteristic of Statics, and Dynamics to be completely divorced from equilibrium theory; but to many, perhaps most, writers Dynamics is equilibrium analysis of a particular kind, namely, with emphasis upon the time aspects of the process of equilibration.

---

[93] *Ibid.*, pp. 966-67.

[94] Ewald Schams, "Komparative Statik," *Zeitschrift für Nationalökonomie*, Vol. II (1930), pp. 33, 61.

Although all this recalls to our attention only a small part of the wide choice of meanings, it is enough to establish the point that the words Statics and Dynamics do not convey a definite meaning unless the speaker or writer has given prior notice of his semantic intentions. There are some who do so in a rather authoritarian fashion by declaring, not what they propose to mean, but what Statics *"is,"* and what Dynamics *"is."* This, considering the existence of dozens of conflicting views stated by economists in good standing, betrays a lack of humility on the part of the defining author, who evidently thinks of himself as *the* authority on the subject.

One may discover a convergence in recent years, especially among writers using mathematical forms of expression, toward the "lagged variables" view of Dynamics. This convergence may be enough to permit the reader's presumption that the inclusion of lagged variables in a model is what these writers mean when they refer to Dynamics. But, of course, there are hundreds of writers whose models have no curves and no figures, nor any alphabetic symbols; and there are even writers who do not know that their models are models, but whose prose teems and buzzes with "Dynamics" and "dynamic."

The need for a declaration of semantic intentions reduces the usefulness of the words in question in oral discussions among people with unknown commitment to word meanings. They can be useful in an economic monologue, in a course of lectures, or a treatise, for there it is possible to announce in the beginning what will be understood by the terms. For general use in discussion, however, words the meaning of which cannot be understood without explanation even in the context in which they are used cannot be recommended.

Thus, whenever another, more readily understood word or phrase is available in lieu of either Statics or Dynamics, it should be preferred. For example, when Dynamics is to mean Growth Theory, we are certainly better off saying Growth Theory in the first place. When Statics is to mean Theory of the Stationary State, we can use this (admittedly longer) phrase and avoid the ambiguous "Statics." When Dynamics is to refer to the history or to the theory of the evolution of economic institutions, we should use these longer but self-explanatory phrases. When it refers to Time-Series Analysis, to Trend Analysis, to Sequence Analysis, to Period Analysis,—all these are more or less descriptive terms, far superior to "Dynamics." Probably more often than not we should be able to do without the terms Statics and Dynamics.

EQUILIBRIUM
AND
DISEQUILIBRIUM

Misplaced Concreteness
and Disguised Politics

Reprinted by permission from *The Economic Journal*. Vol. LXVIII, March, 1958.

A term which has so many meanings that we never know what its users are talking about should be either dropped from the vocabulary of the scholar or "purified" of confusing connotations. Since I believe it is impossible to exclude the terms "equilibrium" and "disequilibrium" from the economist's discourse, I propose that they be subjected to a thorough cleaning job.[1] In attempting this task I shall not be concerned with the meanings of these terms in other disciplines.

---

[1] The ruthless criticism to which my colleague Dr. Edith Penrose subjected an earlier version of this paper is gratefully acknowledged. Thanks to her warnings, I was able to eliminate several flaws of exposition and several offences of over-aggressiveness.

I. A Brief Review of the Use of Equilibrium Concepts in Economics

Economists have used the notion of equilibrium in a variety of contexts and for a variety of purposes; in proceeding from one topic to another some have failed to note transformations in the use made of it and in the meanings read into the term. Not a few who have sensed incongruities, fallacies or outright misuse turned against all "equilibrium economics," heaping abuse on any type of analysis that employed the notion.

The Major Uses of Equilibrium Concepts in Economics

The most literal use of equilibrium or disequilibrium in the sense of equal or unequal weights on the two arms of a scale, without any analytical, explicatory, predictive or evaluative connotation, occurs only in connection with practically measurable quantities, such as income and expenditure in a budget, exports and imports in a trade balance, trade items and long-term capital transfers in a balance of payments. Yet even in these contexts economists have rarely been content with merely weighing the items on the two sides; they have usually wanted to connect them with other economic variables which they considered relevant for a more "inclusive" equilibrium or disequilibrium of the balance in question.

The most prevalent use of the equilibrium concept in economics is probably as a methodological device in abstract theory. Here "equilibrium" is employed in connection with "models" containing several interrelated variables; as a "useful fiction," it serves as a part of a mental experiment designed to analyze causal connections between "events" or "changes of variables."

It is a different use of the equilibrium idea when it is employed to refer to concrete economic situations: here it is supposed to characterize a historical situation as one that has lasted or will last for a relatively long time without significant change. The direct application of the concept to observed situations makes it "operational," as it were. The jump from equilibrium as a methodological device (useful fiction, purely mental construct) to equilibrium as a characterization of a concrete historical situation (operational concept) is a big one; that many take it without noticing any strain and without noting the difference, is attributable, I shall argue, to their failure to recognise the function of the analytical concept, and is conducive to considerable confusion.

A jump in a different direction has been taken from an analytical equilibrium concept to an evaluative one. It is easy to see how it happens: the notion of equilibrium as a balance of forces acquires a connotation of "appropriateness" when the balance is thought of as one of "natural forces"; or even a connotation of "goodness" when that balance is thought of as "harmony." Once the use of equilibrium as a value judgment is condoned, the replacement of the mystical "natural" forces by "progressive" political forces appears indicated, and a variety of social goals is incorporated in the concept of equilibrium. Eventually, equilibrium comes to mean conformance with certain objectives which organised society is asked to pursue. I shall argue that such equilibrium with built-in politics often impairs the usefulness of equilibrium as a value-free analytical device.

Another evaluative equilibrium concept is used in welfare economics. In the theoretical models of the household and the firm "equilibrium" is assumed to be sought between the various items of the plans and dispositions of the individual decision maker so that he would find no reason to make further changes. The older welfare economists promoted this equilibrium from a methodological device (for the explanation of change) to a standard of evaluation (marking the best positions attainable); and all these equilibria became "optima" and integral parts of the maximum welfare position for the whole community. Modern welfare economists deal with the value judgments that were implicit in such a procedure, and try to bring them out into the open. Propositions about conditions under which certain "allocative and distributive equilibria" in the economy as a whole would coincide with whatever is regarded as the "highest social welfare function" are then formulated and qualified with care.

The present paper will not be concerned with welfare economics. But it will be concerned, to some extent, with the use of a value-laden equilibrium concept in positive (explicatory) economics. The chief purpose of the paper is to show the dangers to clear analysis that may arise from the failure to notice the differences between analytical, descriptive, and evalua-

45

tive equilibrium concepts. As a prerequisite, we shall have to pay closer attention than has usually been given to the function of the purely analytical equilibrium concept in economic theorising.

The Basic Idea: Disturbance and Adjustment

In economic analysis some events (or changes of economic variables) are interpreted as the "adjustment" of the system to a "disturbance" consisting in some antecedent events (or changes of economic variables). Several alternative expressions are used to express this idea of adjustment to disturbance; for example, responses to an impulse; reactions or repercussions to a substantive change; effects or consequences of a cause; induced changes following an autonomous or spontaneous change; equilibration following a disequilibrating event. A conceptual scheme is constructed to establish a causal connection between two changes, or two sets of changes; this cause-and-effect relationship is understood, for purposes to be shown presently, as disequilibration-plus-equilibration, or a departure from one position of equilibrium followed by a movement toward another position of equilibrium.

The idea of equilibrium is employed in this scheme as a mental tool, a methodological device; it aids in establishing to our satisfaction a causal nexus between different events or changes. Events or changes can be imagined as well as observed; a causal connection between them can only be imagined, and the idea of equilibrium has the function, as we shall presently see, of making this connection plausible.

II. The Role of Equilibrium
in Economic Analysis

After a brief discussion of the contents and working of "models" in economic analysis we shall present a four-step scheme of causal reasoning, exhibiting the strategic use of equilibria. We shall then proceed to a discussion of the relativity of equilibrium with respect to the variables selected, to the interrelations assumed and to the adjustment time allowed. And we shall attempt a definition of equilibrium.

46

The Contents and the Working of a Model

An analytic model in economics need not be "made out of algebraic functions or geometric curves or some other fancy building material."[2] It can be described entirely in plain words, unless this gets too clumsy. But no matter how it is done, the model inspector should be provided with a full specification of its contents.

The model usually contains a number of variables (*e.g.,* prices, outputs, incomes, exports, etc.,) and a number of stipulated relations between variables (*e.g.,* quantity demanded will vary in a certain way with the price charged; aggregate imports will be some function of disposable income, etc.). Besides the relationship of identity (*e.g.,* income is the sum of consumption and investment), there may be technological relationships (*e.g.,* between input and output), institutional relationships (*e.g.,* between tax payments and income), and economic behaviour relationships (*e.g.,* between cash balances and expenditures). The model is put to work when the mental experimenter manipulates a change of an "independent" variable and "watches" how this will affect the dependent variables acting upon one another according to the assumed relationships.

The Four Steps

The following scheme illustrates the step-by-step working of a model; each step is described both in customary technical terms and in terms of catch-phrases in everyday language:

Step 1. *Initial Position:* "equilibrium," *i.e.,* "Everything could go on as it is."

Step 2. *Disequilibrating Change:* "new datum," *i.e.,* "Something happens."

Step 3. *Adjusting Changes:* "reactions," *i.e.,* "Things must adjust themselves."

Step 4. *Final Position:* "new equilibrium," *i.e.,* "The situation calls for no further adjustments."

---

[2] Fritz Machlup, *The Economics of Sellers' Competition* (Baltimore: Johns Hopkins Press, 1952), p. 5. Some of the ideas presented in the present paper were alluded to in the book.

Steps 2 and 3 may correspond to observable changes; sometimes only one of these is actually "observed" and the other merely expected to occur as consequent or to have occurred as antecedent, respectively. If both are observed in conjunction or succession the theorist will take this as a "verification" of the theory which links them in the described fashion, and he will have increased confidence in it.[3] But when the change which corresponds to Step 2 is called "disequilibrating" and a "new datum," and the changes corresponding to Step 3 are called "adjusting" and "reactions" (to the change considered "disequilibrating"), this is not based on observation; it is only an interpretation. To be plausible this interpretation requires two other steps.

In order to ascertain that the changes under Step 3 are the effects of those under Step 2 and of *nothing else,* we must make sure that there is nothing else in the picture that might be responsible for bringing about the changes under Step 3. There is only one way of doing this: we must isolate Step 2 as a possible cause of the changes under Step 3 by excluding from the model any other possible causes. This exclusion of alternative causes is accomplished by Step 1, the initial position of equilibrium, the position in which "Everything could go on as it is," without any inherent tendency to change. If we were not sure of initial "equilibrium" we could not be sure that Step 3 could not occur without Step 2, simply as the result of something already present in the initial situation. The assumption of an initial equilibrium serves to guarantee the "new datum" of Step 2 the status of being the *sole* disturbing change, the *sole* cause of anything that follows in the model (that is, of the changes interpreted as "adjustment" to, or effect of, the "disequilibrating change").

In order to ascertain that the changes under Step 3 are *all* the effects which the change under Step 2 can have in the model and that we therefore have as complete a list of adjusting changes as we care to have, we must make sure that "no further adjustments" are required by the situation. There is only one way of doing this: we must proceed with the sequence of adjusting changes until we reach a situation in which, barring another disturbance from the outside, everything could go on as it is. In other words we must proceed until we reach a "new equilibrium," a position

---

[3] Fritz Machlup, "The Problem of Verification in Economics," *Southern Economic Journal,* Vol. XXII (July 1955), pp. 1-21.

regarded as final because no further changes appear to be required under the circumstances. The postulate of the final equilibrium serves to guarantee that the list of "adjusting changes" under Step 3 is *complete.*

In a nutshell, we have here a mental experiment in which the first and last steps, the assumption of initial and final equilibria, are methodological devices to ensure that Step 2 is the sole cause and Step 3 contains the complete sequence of effects. The function of the initial equilibrium is to assure us that "nothing but 2" causes the changes under Step 3; the function of the final equilibrium is to assure us that "nothing but 3" is to be expected as an effect of the change under Step 2 (although the "completeness" of the list of effects will always be merely relative to the set of variables included in the equilibrium).

Some simple analogies exist between the pattern of mental experiments and that of laboratory experiments. Step 1, the assumption of an initial equilibrium, corresponds to the requirement of a *controlled* experiment that conditions be kept constant and the manipulated change of the selected variable thus be isolated from changes of other independent variables. Step 4, the assumption of a final equilibrium, corresponds to the requirement of the *complete* experiment that all changes be observed and noted until no further changes in dependent variables occur.

Wide Choice for the Set of Variables in Equilibrium

The economic theorist enjoys great freedom of choice in the construction of his models and in the selection of the variables included. The restraints are few and not very confining: logical consistency of the entire model, relevance of the chosen variables to the problem analysed, "understanding" of the assumed relationships between them as plausible, and applicability of the model in the sense that the events or changes assumed and deduced (as Steps 2 and 3, respectively) more or less "fit" events or changes observed or known to occur in reality. This leaves the choice of what to put into the "equilibrium" wide open. The system may contain few variables or many; it may postulate inter-relationships of many different kinds; it may deliberately exclude interactions of variables which take a long time to work themselves out or, on the other hand, it may disregard regular oscillations of some variables within short intervals of time. (It is chiefly this freedom of choice which makes it often almost meaningless to declare a concrete economic situation in the real world, identified by historical time and geographic space but not specified with regard to the variables selected, as a position of equilibrium or disequilibrium.)

To realize the extent of freedom in the selection of variables that are supposed to be in equilibrium, one has only to think of the simple models of "aggregative equilibrium" and of their successive extension through the inclusion of additional variables or relations. One may first recall the standard equilibrium between the three strategic aggregates, national income, consumption and investment, linked by a simple consumption function, with investment assumed to be given. One may then recall the more complicated aggregative equilibria comprising one or more of the following relations or variables: an investment function making investment depend on income or consumption, or on absolute or relative changes in income or consumption; varying proceeds from exports and payments for imports, with the former affecting income, and with the latter dependent on income; varying government expenditures and tax revenues, dependent on income and affecting consumption (and possibly also investment); a consumption function linking consumption to various past values of income, to values of real assets, to values of cash assets; and so forth. The possible combinations of even this small number of aggregate variables and relations permit an enormous variety of equilibrium positions. Yet, all these equilibria still disregard such variables as prices, wage-rates, interest rates, foreign-exchange rates, all of which are possible candidates for inclusion in the system.

The "relativity" of an "equilibrium in international trade" with regard to the relations and variables included or disregarded merits separate comment. For some problems one will choose to start from a position of balanced trade; for other problems one will choose to start from a position of a given volume of foreign investment, and hence from an "equilibrium export surplus," a surplus consistent with an equilibrium in the foreign-exchange market; and again for other problems one will choose to start from an equilibrium of income, consumption, saving and investment, with a surplus or deficit in the foreign-exchange market as part of the volume of investment consistent with the magnitudes of the other aggregates. If the system includes only these aggregates, but disregards the foreign-reserve position and bank liquidity, final equilibrium may be said to be reached with a trade deficit, the latter being equal to the excess of home investment over total saving. This final equilibrium—where no further adjustment is required of the selected variables—may involve continuing changes of neglected variables: for example, the foreign reserves may continue to dwindle towards zero and the loan portfolios of banks may go on expanding without limit.[4]

Frequently equilibrium will refer to a set of variables that fails to include some which are both relevant and significant for practical problems; such an equilibrium is sometimes denounced as a worthless or dangerous tool of analysis. To be sure, if an economist were to base policy recommendations on an analysis confined to such oversimplified equilibrium models he would be guilty of a gross lack of judgment. Yet such models may have considerable heuristic value. This value is not impaired if an important factor is left out, provided the omission is not inadvertent. Indeed, the importance of any factor can be demonstrated only by leaving it out of account and then showing the difference it makes when it is reinstated as one of the variables in the equilibrium system.

Time and Equilibrium

More often than not, time is left out in the construction and operation of equilibrium models. If time is taken into account this is done in various ways, implicitly or explicitly.

In so-called period analysis, time is given two roles: it appears as an independent variable and as a subscript to other variables. In the latter role it "dates" the quantities which are linked by the lagged interrelations stipulated—where the value of a variable at one period is related to the values of the same and/or other variables at other periods. And as a separate independent variable, time will determine the magnitudes which the other variables will have reached at certain points on their way to their equilibrium values and, moreover, will serve to identify final equilibrium as the position where a further increase of t will leave all other magnitudes unchanged.

In period analysis as well as in some other kinds of sequence analysis,

---

[4] Fritz Machlup, *International Trade and the National Income Multiplier* (Philadelphia: Blakiston, 1943), pp. 85-7, 172-3, 208.

successive positions are sometimes "temporary equilibria," regardless of whether or not the model can ever reach a final equilibrium; in other instances, however, the successive positions, although determinate, are not accurately characterized as temporary equilibria. As an example of the former type we may think of the sequence of prices and quantities sold in a model depicting the cobweb theorem. If the (timeless) demand curve is steeper than the (time-lagged) supply curve the model will not yield a final equilibrium, while the intersections of the "instantaneous supply curves" with the demand curve will each mark a point of temporary equilibrium. Every one of these equilibria is stable (in the sense that random deviations are self-correcting); it is also "final" with respect to the particular instantaneous supply curve—although it is "temporary" if the time-lagged supply curve is taken into account. Thus, one and the same position, defined by a definite set of variables of given magnitudes, will be both an equilibrium or a disequilibrium, depending on the length of time that is taken into account.[5]

In dealing with this question, the theorist has a choice between two equivalent procedures: he may either vary the maximum time interval allowed for the process of adjustment (with given time coefficients of the relations involved) or change the combination of variables making up the model. The latter is Alfred Marshall's procedure for showing the adjustments in the supply of a particular product. He distinguishes between an instantaneous market equilibrium, a short-run market equilibrium and a long-run market equilibrium, not in terms of the time needed for the adjustments to take place, but by extending the list of dependent variables: for the first equilibrium, production is fixed; for the second, production is variable, but productive capacity is fixed; for the third, productive capacity is variable, and only the productive resources potentially available to the industry are fixed. Time itself is not a variable in the model; instead,

---

[5] Certain equilibria in physics and chemistry are of the same type. Take the example of a simple scale (*libra*, in Latin) with two pans of different shapes but equal weight and volume, containing equal quantities of water. The equilibrium will be only temporary, since evaporation of the water will be faster from the pan with the larger open surface; there will be instantaneous equilibrium (before any water has evaporated) and long-run equilibrium (after all the water has evaporated from both pans). Similarly, there may be chemical equilibrium after a very small time interval but not for longer periods, depending on whether only the fast reactions or also the slow reactions are taken into account.

there are three models (or sub-models) with separate equilibria; each equilibrium is "final" on its own terms, though "temporary" in terms of a model with more variables.[6]

It would be mistaken to think that an extension of the list of variables is always equivalent to a "longer-run" adjustment. The opposite may be true: the addition of variables to the set may shorten the adjustment period. Take, for example, the simple saving-investment equilibrium in a period model demonstrating the multiplier principle. If consumption is related to income received in the preceding period, and the marginal propensity to consume is high, the number of periods required to bring income close to its final equilibrium value would be enormous. This model implicitly assumes unlimited supplies of unemployed resources and of idle or newly created cash. If the model is expanded to include such variables as (limited) unemployment, wage-rates, (limited) money supply and interest rates the equilibration of this larger set of variables will take place in a much smaller number of time periods (and, of course, the equilibrium value of income will be smaller).[7]

Just as equilibrium may by design take no account of adjustments that go beyond a certain set of variables or beyond a certain time, equilibrium

---

[6] Incidentally, no student who understands these conceptions will fall into the error of identifying a concrete situation, involving the prices paid and quantities produced in a certain country at a certain time, as a position of long-run equilibrium. All these equilibria are purely hypothetical. Never could anybody "know" that all adjustments to past events have been completed—or will ever be completed. If calendar time were substituted for the Marshallian "long run," the long-run adjustment to a decline in the demand for a product might take some thirty years or more, involving the gradual wear and tear and successive scrapping of productive capacity. Could anybody assume for the real world—what *has* to be assumed for the purpose of thinking things through—that demand and technology and all other things will remain unchanged over a period of such length? Surely, the conceptual apparatus with its final equilibrium was not intended to yield a description of an actual *situation,* but rather to ensure that full attention is given to *all the processes of change* which could be interpreted as the effects of the event or change regarded as the disequilibrating datum.

[7] There have been economists grumbling about "how anybody can speak of an *equilibrium* leaving out so many crucial variables." Such grumbles would be justified if they were directed against the choice of variables and relations, against the usefulness of the model and, especially, against policy recommendations that are based on them. But if the grumbles are about "speaking of an equilibrium" in such a case they are methodologically unsound. Equilibrium and disequilibrium refer to whatever model you may have in mind.

may also by design overlook certain short-term oscillations or fluctuations. For example, changes in demand or production that can be interpreted as regular fluctuations—relating to different hours of the day, days of the week, seasons of the year—may be accepted as part of a stationary equilibrium (or simply disregarded if the fluctuations are irrelevant to the problem at hand), provided the "underlying conditions" remain unchanged throughout the process.[8] But oscillations and fluctuations must not be admitted as part of an "equilibrium position" unless one may assume that they can, under the rules of the model, continue in perfect periodicity, without any change in amplitude or rhythm.

Definition of Equilibrium

We have not thus far attempted to formulate a definition of equilibrium, though the meaning of the term has probably become quite clear. In the light of the preceding discussion we may define *equilibrium*, in economic analysis, as *a constellation of selected interrelated variables so adjusted to one another that no inherent tendency to change prevails in the model which they constitute.* The model as well as its equilibria are, of course, mental constructions (based on abstraction and invention).

It has been suggested to me that the phrase "balance of forces" should be a part of any definition of equilibrium. I cannot accept this suggestion; "balance of forces" is simply another metaphor, perhaps a synonym but not an explanation of "equilibrium," and sadly encumbered by the reference to "forces," which is a rather mystical concept in need of a separate time-consuming cleaning job. But if it is believed that additional metaphors can be helpful in defining or explaining equilibrium, then I should propose the phrase "peaceful co-existence" between selected variables of given magnitudes. Where such "peaceful co-existence" is not possible, where the selected variables are *not compatible* with one another in their given magnitudes, one or more of them will have to change, and will continue to change until they reach magnitudes that make it possible for them to live with each other as they are.

---

[8] The technique of "disregarding" oscillations of quantities (demanded, supplied, produced) is either to reduce them to an average or to express them as rates per unit of time where the time unit embraces the whole "cycle."

Thus, as an alternative definition of equilibrium we may propose *mutual compatibility of a selected set of interrelated variables of particular magnitudes.* Assume the set consists of variables *A, B, C* and *D,* and that certain inter-relationships between them are assumed (in the form of behaviour equations, technological, psychological or institutional relations, as well as mere definitions). If these variables are compatible in their "present" magnitudes "everything could go on as it is." Then "something happens" which increases variable *C.* In its new magnitude *C* is no longer compatible with *A, B* and *D,* and "things must adjust themselves." Which of the variables will "give" and by how much will depend on the rules of the game, expressed in the relationships assumed between variables. At last, the new values of the four variables may be such that they are again compatible with one another, and "the situation calls for no further adjustments."

The crux of the matter is that the addition of another variable, somehow related to one or more of the others, would change the picture. The magnitudes in which *A, B, C* and *D* are mutually compatible when they are the only players in the game may constitute serious incompatibility when they are joined by another player, say *E,* of a certain size. But another addition, say *F,* may neutralize the "disturbing" effect of *E,* and *A, B, C, D* in their "present" magnitudes may again be compatible and "everything could go on as it is." One cannot overemphasize this *relativity* of compatibility and incompatibility regarding extra variables included in, or excluded from, the selected set. Only a complete enumeration of the variables selected and interrelations assumed makes it meaningful to assert their mutual compatibility or incompatibility, that is, the equilibrium or disequilibrium of the chosen set. And, while a *specification* of the selected variables and assumed interrelations is required for every model and every problem, the *definition* of equilibrium and disequilibrium must not narrow the freedom of choice.

III. Misplaced Concreteness and Disguised Politics

Although I recognised the existence of other equilibrium concepts in economics, I have discussed only the one designed for theoretical analysis. I strongly suspect that those who use equilibrium concepts for other purposes, such as the description of historical situations or their evaluation, believe that one and the same concept can do double or triple duty. This I challenge. My task in this section cannot be used for other purposes without losing much of its usefulness in analysis.

Not an Operational Concept

Equilibrium as a tool for theoretical analysis is not an operational concept; and attempts to develop operational counterparts to the construct have not been successful.[9] Some of the variables in a model usually have statistically operational counterparts; in rare instances all have. But even in this event the *compatibility* between the variables is always a question of the assumed interrelations and of the limitation of the model to the variables selected. The "real world" surely has infinitely more variables than any abstract economic model, and their "actual" interrelations are neither known nor, I fear, knowable (partly because they probably change unpredictably over time). It follows that the equilibrium between selected variables could not be observed even if each of the variables had an observable counterpart in the real world.

Some of the variables in a model which have observable and measurable counterparts can sometimes be arranged in sub-sets in the form of balance sheets, T-accounts or financial statements, permitting us to strike a balance between the two sides and to speak (confusingly) of an "equilibrium" or "disequilibrium" in that sub-set. For example, exports and imports can be arranged as a trade balance, or foreign-trade items and certain capital and other transfers can be arranged as an accounting-balance of payments.[10] A so-called equilibrium for these items means merely equality of the sums on each side of the account, and a so-called disequilibrium means inequality

---

[9] Schumpeter once proposed a statistically discernible "neighborhood of equilibrium," with reference to cyclical fluctuations of business activity. But he always insisted on the purely fictitious and instrumental character of the equilibrium concept itself. Joseph A. Schumpeter, *Business Cycles* (New York: McGraw-Hill, 1939), pp. 68-71.

[10] For an exposition of the differences between the "accounting balance," the "market balance" and the "program balance" of payments see Fritz Machlup, "Three Concepts of the Balance of Payments and the So-called Dollar Shortage," *Economic Journal,* Vol. LX (1950), pp. 46-68.

of the sums. But only when this sub-set is linked with other variables—income, consumption, investment, prices, employment, wage-rates, exchange rates, interest rates, foreign reserves, bank reserves, bank loans, etc.—does it become a factor in economic analysis And only after the variables are selected and their interrelations assumed can we speak of equilibrium and disequilibrium in the sense in which these terms are used in economic analysis. Despite the operational sub-set, the model as a whole and its equilibrium are not observable, not operational; they remain mental constructions.

Perhaps similar, perhaps very different considerations once led Per Jacobsson to make this observation on the subject: "You can no more define equilibrium in international trade than you can define a pretty girl, but you can recognize one if you meet one."[11] I like this remark for its charm and wit, but I wonder whether it hits the mark. I think I am quite competent to recognize a pretty girl, though my taste may not be the same as that of other expert observers. But I cannot recognize an equilibrium in international trade no matter how hard I look. I can define it, at least to my own satisfaction; but I cannot recognize anything in reality—in the statistical figures representing the "facts" of a "real situation"—as an equilibrium in international trade in the sense discussed, that is, as a position where "everything could go on as it is" and "the situation calls for no further adjustments" to anything that has happened.

To characterize a concrete situation "observed" in reality as one of "equilibrium" is to commit the fallacy of misplaced concreteness. At best, the observer may mean to assert that in his opinion the observed and duly identified situation corresponds to a model in his mind in which a set of selected variables determine a certain outcome, and that he finds no inherent cause of change—that is, that he believes only an outside disturbance, not in evidence at the moment, would produce a change in these variables. This, of course, is a personal judgment, meaningful only if the variables are fully enumerated and the assumptions about their interrelations are clearly stated. As matters stand, any concrete economic situation may correspond at the same time to an equilibrium of one model and a disequilibrium of another.

The use of the analytical equilibrium concept as a designation of a

---

[11] Per Jacobsson, in a speech in 1949.

concrete historical situation is regarded as "misplaced concreteness," first because of the general fallacy involved in jumping the distance between a useful fiction and particular data of observation and, second, because of the fallacy involved in forgetting the relativity of equilibrium with respect to variables and relations selected. An indefinite number of models may be found to "fit" a concrete situation in one way or another, and the choice is not dictated either by any so-called realities of life or by any conventions of the analysts.[12]

The phrase "relativity of equilibrium" gives expression to the facts that any number and combination of variables may be chosen for a model, depending on the analytical or didactic habits, skills and purposes of the economist; that the same values of variables may account both for equilibrium or disequilibrium, depending on the other variables with which they are made to keep company and on the relations assumed to prevail between them; and that different problems (perhaps concerning the same concrete situation) may call for very different models for use in analysis.

Not the Same as Stability

Stability in the sense of invariance over time has some connections with the notion of equilibrium which may easily lead to confusion. Since equilibrium is the position where everything is so well adjusted to everything else—in the model—that things can go on without change, this surely implies stability over time (at least until the next disturbance). And since a disturbing change must be isolated—in the model—from anything else that might require adjusting changes, this implies that "all other things remain unchanged"—particularly the interrelations assumed for the model;

---

[12] To be sure, there are "observed" situations which invite characterization as "disequilibria" without serious danger of confusion. For example, there will be little doubt about just what model and what variables are referred to when some gross instances of price fixing, either with unsold supplies not disposable at the official minimum price or with queues of would-be buyers lined up to get some of their demand satisfied at the ceiling price, are characterized as "market disequilibria." The implication, apparently, is that the situation could not endure were it not for the "interference." On the other hand, a model that includes government price fixing, penalties for violations, unsold stocks, unsatisfied demand, etc., among its variables would show the surplus stocks or the unsatisfied demand as the "final equilibrium"—though only as "temporary equilibrium" if some lagged black-market behaviour functions are added to the list of assumptions.

all in all, we presuppose the stability of a lot of things for the duration of the process that is pictured as "equilibration" in the model. With everything stable at the beginning and at the end of the imagined process, and many things stable while it goes on, the logical tie between stability and equilibrium is certainly a close one.

In addition, there is the very special meaning of "stability of equilibrium" according to which a "stable equilibrium" is distinguished from an "unstable" one depending on the presence or absence of a mechanism for the "self-correction" of random deviations from the equilibrium values of the variables involved.

However, none of these notions of stability has much to do with the stability of a price or quantity observed in actual fact. An actual price may be stable over a long time without forcing us to have it represented by an equilibrium price in the model that we may choose for explaining it. An actual price may be most unstable, jumping up and down like mad, and yet we may find it most expedient to explain these changes by means of models showing a quick succession of perfectly stable equilibria with different equilibrium prices due to a quick succession of exogenous disequilibrating changes.

We may conclude that "observed stability" and "observed instability" should not be confused with, or attributed to, equilibrium and disequilibrium, respectively, in analytic models.

Not a Value Judgment

Equilibrium as used in positive economic analysis—as distinguished from welfare economics—should not be taken as a value judgment, nor as a reference to a "desired state of affairs." Equilibrium is not a Good Thing, and disequilibrium is not a Bad Thing. Nor is the reverse association justified: equilibrium stands neither for the *status quo* nor for *laissez faire,* as some dissident economists have been inclined to think.

If equilibrium analysis is employed to explain a sad situation as the equilibrium outcome of certain conditions and events, it would be silly to transfer our dislike of the situation to the equilibrium concept used in the explanation. And if a sad situation is disliked and deemed intolerable, to call it disequilibrium on that account helps neither in analysing it nor in developing the best policy for improving it.

Of course, it is perfectly legitimate to allow our value judgments to suggest to us the problems for analysis. If we find it desirable to secure full employment at high wage-rates we may construct models to show us what conditions (interrelations between variables) would make full employment and high wage-rates compatible with given values of the other variables in the set; or what values these other variables would have to attain in order to be compatible with full employment and high wage-rates with given interrelations. If we or others advocate a certain full-employment policy we may construct models to show us what effects could be expected, in a variety of circumstances, if various institutional relationships were established to make interest rates, bank loans, government expenditures (or other employment-inducing variables) depend upon changes in (absolute or relative) unemployment. But none of these exercises, valuable and important though they are, would be aided by incorporating our moral values or political goals into the *definition* of equilibrium, as several economists have proposed. Some of these proposals, as we shall see in Section IV, require that full employment at given wage-rates and other desirable objectives be made part of the definition of equilibrium, so that any position in which these objectives are not attained would always have to be called "disequilibrium."

By infusing a value judgment, a political philosophy or programme, or a rejection of a programme or policy, into the concept of equilibrium designed for economic analysis, the analyst commits the fallacy of implicit evaluation or disguised politics. To choose the variables and interrelations suitable for an equilibrium analysis of problems that are dictated by value judgments and political objectives is one thing. It is quite another thing to insist on packaging these valuations with the definition of equilibrium. Indeed, the analysis of the possibilities of their realization may be impeded by such a restrictive definition.

IV. Equilibrium in International Trade Theory

The literature on International Trade probably makes more extensive use of equilibrium concepts than any other field of economics. The pages are generously sprinkled with equilibria and disequilibria, and more often than not the writers indulge in concrete applications and also in policy advice based on some implicit hierarchy of social goals. Even some of the clearer expositors seem to have a hard time reminding themselves of their own definitions, and many a writer does not mind changing *equos* in midstream and equilibrium concepts in the middle of his *libri* (if a Latin pun may be admitted).

Consistent Awareness of Relativity: Joan Robinson

There are a few exceptionally consistent and methodical writers. One of them, fully aware and mindful of the relativity of equilibrium, is Joan Robinson:

It is now obvious that there is no one rate of exchange which is the equilibrium rate corresponding to a given state of world demands and techniques. In any given situation there is an equilibrium rate corresponding to each rate of interest and level of effective demand, and any rate of exchange, within very wide limits, can be turned into the equilibrium rate by altering the rate of interest appropriately. Moreover, any rate of exchange can be made compatible with any rate of interest provided that money wages can be sufficiently altered. The notion of *the* equilibrium exchange rate is a chimera. The rate of exchange, the rate of interest, the level of effective demand and the level of money wages react upon each other like the balls in Marshall's bowl, and no one is determined unless all the rest are given.[13]

Built-in Politics and Simulated Stability: Nurkse

Ragnar Nurkse undoubtedly knew all this, but in his now classic essay on international equilibrium he chose to disregard it.[14] Perhaps he felt strongly that he was less concerned with the niceties of abstract analysis than with the formulation of practical monetary policies (p. 4) instru-

---

[13] Joan Robinson, "The Foreign Exchanges," *Essays in the Theory of Employment* (Oxford: Blackwell, 2nd ed., 1947). Reprinted in *Readings in the Theory of International Trade* (Philadelphia: Blakiston, 1949), p. 103.

[14] Ragnar Nurkse, "Conditions of International Monetary Equilibrium," *Essays in International Finance* (Princeton: International Finance Section, Princeton University, 1945). Reprinted in *Readings in the Theory of International Trade* (Philadelphia: Blakiston, 1949), pp. 3-34.

mental in attaining several social objectives: "full employment" or "good employment at the given wage structure" (p. 16), avoidance of inflation (p. 12), "reasonable stability of exchange rates" (p. 21), "freedom from severe exchange restrictions" (p. 21). He apparently believed that a programme of preventing "protracted departures" from "this happy state" (p. 34) could be more easily developed with the aid of a concept of equilibrium with built-in value judgments.

Thus, far from regarding the notion of *the* equilibrium exchange rate as a "chimera," Nurkse held that "there should be some more or less generally accepted notion as to what constitutes 'equilibrium' and 'disequilibrium' in regard to international exchange rates."[15] Since he found frequent changes in exchange rates undesirable, he made us "turn away from the imaginary system of freely fluctuating exchanges, in which the balance [of payments] is kept in equilibrium every hour or every day." He proposed that "the period which we contemplate in the definition of the equilibrium rate of exchange . . . should certainly not be less than a year" and preferably "long enough to eliminate 'cyclical' fluctuations," that is, "between five and ten years." The balance over such a period should be the "indication of equilibrium and disequilibrium. In brief, the "equilibrium rate" is the rate at which "there would be no net change in a country's reserve of international means of payments" over a period of five to ten years (pp. 6-7). But this is a *true* equilibrium rate of exchange" only if the balance of payments (excluding all short-term capital movements) is "kept in equilibrium" without "additional restrictions on trade" and without "depression and unemployment at home" (pp. 9-11).

Since Nurkse did not conceal his value judgments, he is not open to the charge of disguised politics; but I doubt the analytical usefulness of his evaluative equilibrium concept, and I submit that he might have avoided confusion by choosing a different term. For example, he could have spoken of the "optimum rate of exchange," the "most desirable rate of exchange" or the "full-employment rate of exchange," instead of invoking Truth and Equilibrium by speaking of the "true equilibrium rate of exchange."

Moreover, to speak of an equilibrium over a period "long enough to permit any cyclical changes to cancel out" (p. 15) is analytically highly questionable. It virtually amounts to a confusion between equilibrium and

---

[15] *Ibid.*, p. 4.

price-stability. If it is agreed—and Nurkse does agree—that "at different levels of national income" (p. 11) or "with a different flow of foreign investment" (p. 8) the equilibrium rate of exchange would be different, is it then permissible to assume that national income (or even full-employment national income) and the flow of foreign investment will remain unchanged over the period of a cycle, over five to ten years? To be sure, one can always "average" the changing rates of income and investment over the years, but what right do we have to transfigure statistical *ex post* averages into *ex ante* norms or data to which the exchange rate should be equilibrated? If we stay on the *ex ante* level, as we should for theoretical models as well as for practical policy advice, we have no legitimate reason for assuming national incomes in the countries concerned and investment flows among them to remain even approximately unchanged over several years and, still less, for assuming that all other conditions are frozen on which "equilibrium exchange rates" would depend. Changes in technology, capital stock, labour force, industrial organisation, consumer taste, factor prices, product prices, interest rates, bank loans, government expenditures, money stocks and so forth would surely alter equilibrium exchange rates frequently and significantly.[16] To assume things to remain unchanged for the duration of a particular process in an abstract model is one thing; it is quite another thing to simulate such stability for practical purposes or to make it an integral part of a concept designed for applied analysis.

Political Criteria Supported: Ellsworth and Kindleberger

Nurkse's notion of equilibrium in international transactions and in foreign-exchange rates has been widely accepted and elaborated upon. P. T. Ellsworth and Charles P. Kindleberger, in their excellent text-books, adopt both the "several-years balance" as the standard for a concrete equilibrium and the social goals of satisfactory employment at satisfactory

---

[16] Under the gold standard one may picture the theoretical equilibrium rates as fluctuating, sometimes with considerable amplitude, around the gold par of exchange because expansions and contractions of bank reserves and deposits, enforced by the gold-flow mechanism and by the rules of the game, would raise and lower the equilibrium rates to the level of the gold par whenever they depart from it. *I know of no good reason why equilibrium exchange rates should remain stable unless monetary institutions and policies make them so.*

wages with moderate trade restrictions and reasonably stable prices as built-in criteria of a true (politically acceptable) equilibrium. They offer additional justifications. For example, Ellsworth writes:

> But our concept of what is desirable has modified our concept of what is normal; it is now generally agreed that we must take a broader view of equilibrium. Full employment, or at least the absence of mass unemployment, is now regarded as itself a condition of equilibrium. So likewise is the absence of an inflationary rise of prices. Hence a balance of payments which can only be balanced by means of a sharp decline in income and employment, or by a rise in income to inflationary levels, cannot be considered to be in equilibrium.[17]

The Keynesian notion of an "underemployment equilibrium" appears to be rejected here, not because of any economic repercussions compelling (in an analytic model) full-employment equilibrium to be restored, but simply because unemployment is undesirable. Kindleberger, on the other hand, looks for a less normative explanation. He agrees that "large-scale unemployment . . . is compatible with a market equilibrium," but, on a wider view, "unemployment means disequilibrium, since government action to remove it is likely and will disturb the balance-of-payments position." [18] Here political repercussions are introduced into economic analysis, not through the assumption of given institutional relations (such as tax rates), but as a prediction that governments, either under political pressure or out of political conviction, will decide to do *something* to raise effective demand for products and labour. "It is suggested that, on a wider view of the social sciences, equilibrium in the balance of payments should be combined with political stability into a more generalized equilibrium" (p. 412).

Equilibrium, to Kindleberger, becomes a political concept, partly because of the political repercussions which he predicts (without specifying them), and partly (and this is a very different matter) because to him it is a state of affairs that is "desired" and sometimes "achieved." Yet "the achievement of economic equilibrium" is contrasted with that of "other social goals, such as national political and social equilibrium or international

---

[17] P. T. Ellsworth, *The International Economy* (New York: Macmillan, 1950), p. 607.

[18] Charles P. Kindleberger, *International Economics* (Homewood, Ill.: Richard D. Irwin, Inc., 1953), p. 412; similarly, p. 464.

peace." Economic equilibrium "is at best a limited objective" (p. 519). Will economists now have to agree on political philosophy and on ethical values before they can talk about equilibrium?

Relativity and Value-Neutrality: Meade I

J. E. Meade, in his treatise on *The Balance of Payments,* the most thorough analysis in this field, shows himself as the master of a house divided against itself. He is a strong believer in, and skilled user of, the equilibrium concept as a value-free, abstract methodological device; but he is also a persuasive advocate of the equilibrium concept as a standard of performance and a symbol for a comprehensive programme of economic policy striving for Good Things and avoiding the Bad; yet in the course of the analysis he finds it necessary to reduce the political comprehensiveness of this equilibrium concept, and to break it down into separate equilibria of much smaller scope. A confrontation of these three Meades with one another will be facilitated by referring to them as Meade I, Meade II and Meade III, joint authors of Volume One of *The Theory of International Economic Policy.*[19]

Meade I opens the book with a resolute declaration in the Preface:

The method employed in this volume is first to consider a number of countries in at least partial or temporary equilibrium, domestically and internationally ; next to introduce some disturbing factor (which is often an act of government policy) into this equilibrium; then to consider the new partial or temporary equilibrium which the economies will attain when the direct and indirect effects of the disturbing factor have fully worked themselves out; and finally to compare the new position of equilibrium with the old. [p. viii]

Meade's scheme of the equilibrium model, presented in Chapters IV and V, corresponds in almost every respect to the one proposed in this article. There is the division of the argument into the same four steps—"old position of equilibrium"; "spontaneous disturbance"; "repercussions" with

---

[19] J. E. Meade, *The Theory of International Economic Policy, Volume One: The Balance of Payments* (London: Oxford University Press, 1951).

"ultimate effects"; "new position of equilibrium."[20] There is also the recognition of the relativity of equilibrium regarding selected variables, disregarding variables not included in the model. For example, Meade I allows unemployment to exist in a position of equilibrium[21] initial or final; he allows "a new equilibrium" to be reached which "involves a deficit in [a country's] balance of payments" (p. 60) and which thus would be a disequilibrium if foreign reserves, etc., were included among the selected variables. And all these equilibria and disequilibria are "value-neutral," that is, free from political value judgments, free from connotations of good or bad, desirable or undesirable, politically acceptable or unacceptable.

Alliance with Political Value Judgments: Meade II

Not so for Meade II, who wrote Chapter I of the book. He begins with a country "suffering" from a disequilibrium (p. 3) and he clearly identifies "balance-of-payments difficulties" with "balance-of-payments disequilibrium" (p. 14). After showing that a country's deficit on trade items and unrequited transfers "does not necessarily represent a disequilibrium in its international position" (p. 8), he finds that its true balance-of-payments deficit" is the "balance of autonomous trade and transfers," which "must be matched by what we have called accommodating finance."[22] But even such a "true" deficit "would be much too narrow a criterion

---

[20] "We shall confine ourselves to a comparison of the new position of equilibrium which results when some spontaneous disturbance has occurred and has had time to work out all its repercussions, with the old position of equilibrium which existed before the disturbance occurred" (*ibid.*, p. 58). The scheme is deemed necessary in order to ascertain the "ultimate effects" of the disturbance (p. 52). The only difference between Meade's scheme and mine is his inclusion of "policy changes," besides "induced changes," among the adjusting changes (pp. 42 ff.). I would treat reactions of the Government to the disequilibrating change either as part of the induced changes (though only if they follow from the assumed institutional behaviour equations) or as an additional datum (if they are not sufficiently "regular" to be subsumed among the given relations between the selected variables of the system).

[21] Meade assumes "that there is an appreciable volume of unemployment . . . to start with" (*ibid.*, p. 53). This assumption is necessary for an analysis of the "income effects" in a multiplier model.

[22] *Ibid.*, p. 13. For an earlier formulation of the balance-of-payments problem in terms of accommodating capital movements see Fritz Machlup, *International Trade and the National Income Multiplier*, pp. 134-5.

of a disequilibrium in the balance of payments" (p. 13); to Meade a merely "potential" deficit is a sufficient criterion. For it is not the actual balance or imbalance but rather a "potential" deficit or surplus "which is the proper measure of a balance-of-payments disequilibrium" (p. 15). Such a disequilibrium without actual deficit exists if the deficit is *avoided* by resort to trade restrictions, to domestic-income deflation and unemployment, or to an adjustment in the exchange rate.

Meade II has thus adopted the political equilibrium concept proposed by Nurkse.[23] But Meade II goes on to make another distinction to the effect "that a disequilibrium of this kind may be temporary or may be more or less permanent" (p. 15). Since "it is the latter, of course, which presents the really serious problem" (p. 15), he decides that "perhaps the most basic measure of balance-of-payments disequilibrium is the country's surplus or deficit of potential and continuing payments for autonomous trade and transfers." He resolves that this is what he will mean in the rest of the book (p. 16).

Meade I might now rise and tell Meade II that a theorist is very familiar with temporary *equilibrium* but cannot understand what may be meant by permanent or enduring *dis*equilibrium—except perhaps a case of direct controls interfering with "market equilibrium." Indeed, a disequilibrium, in the theorist's model, is a constellation of variables that cannot endure if left alone, that must give rise to further change, and thus is temporary *ex hypothesi*. Meade II would have to reply that he did not mean disequilibrium in the economic theorist's sense, but instead was referring to a situation that was quite unpleasant and unfortunately could last a long time: a situation where a desired level of employment at desired wage-rates could be maintained, at given foreign-exchange rates and without special trade restrictions, only with the help of accommodating capital imports (loans from abroad, forced liquidation of foreign assets and depletion of gold and exchange reserves). If the accommodating finance cannot be secured actual balance will *inevitably* be attained, through less employment, through lower wage-rates, through depreciation of the currency or through stricter trade controls. But since any and all of these

---

[23] Note, however, that what Nurkse called the "true" balance Meade calls the *potential* balance, to be regarded as the "proper" measure; "true" balance to Meade means *actual* balance, though rearranged for autonomous and accommodating items.

equilibrations are "undesirable," Meade II would prefer to deny the attained balance the name and title of "equilibrium."

Return to Value-Neutrality: Meade III

The sentiment and resolution of Meade II were of little avail, inasmuch as Meade III wrote most of the rest of the book. He soon found it expedient to distinguish "internal balance" and "external balance" (pp. 104 ff.), the former dealing with domestic employment (and related matters, such as price inflation and wage-rates), the latter with the balance of payments (and related matters, such as trade controls and foreign-exchange rates). The full-employment standard is no longer an integral part of balance-of-payments equilibrium. For example, cases are discussed where "an inflation of domestic expenditure is needed" both to increase employment "and also to restore equilibrium to the balance of payments" (p. 115). Or, in the discussion of "conflicts between internal and external balance," the distinction of a "disequilibrium" in the balance of payments and, on the other hand, "in each national income" of the countries concerned, is consistently carried through (Chapter X). Indeed, the distinctions are quite fine, especially when Meade III separates hypothetical situations in which "the smallest element of disequilibrium," or "the least-marked element of disequilibrium," can be found either in the internal or in the external balance (p. 122).

Meade III discards also the criteria of immutable exchange rates and absence of trade restrictions from the meaning of external equilibrium. Thus, at one point he considers the possibility that the authorities of the countries "let the exchange rate between their currencies change as a means of regaining external balance without sacrificing internal balance," and the alternative possibility that they impose "direct controls over their international transactions so as to restore equilibrium to their balances of payments without disturbing their internal balance" (p. 24). And he discusses a case in which "a balance-of-payments disequilibrium is removed by means of the depreciation of the currency of the deficit country," and another case in which "the balance of payments is put into equilibrium" by price adjustments under a system of flexible wage-rates (pp. 328-9). There is little doubt that Meade III had found out that the definitions developed by Meade II, reflecting a commonly shared regret over lapses from socially ideal circumstances, are not efficient tools of economic analysis. Anxious to get on with his work, he left the political equilibrium concept behind (on pp. 13-16) and used an unpolitical one for his economic analysis.

There is still a difference to settle between Meade I and Meade III, but this is not serious. As a matter of fact, it is merely a matter of terminology. Meade I wanted "equilibrium" to be the thinking device, described in this article, while Meade III often wanted it to refer to a balance of payments in which accommodating transactions were zero. If Meade III had spoken of deficit, surplus and zero balances of payments, without using the word "equilibrium," he would have avoided even the appearance of a conceptual difference. But this is perhaps too much to ask. After all, one can get used to words with multiple meanings, and should be able to remember that a so-called "disequilibrium in the balance of payments" means simply a surplus or deficit, which in economic analysis may figure as an initial equilibrium, an adjusting change, or a final equilibrium, depending on the problem at hand.[24]

Attack on Persuasive Definitions: Streeten

Philosophers of science have recently shown that some definitions, supposedly stating what something is or means, are in fact devised to

---

[24] A reader who has successfully learnt from Meade I that disequilibrium was just a step in an explanation of change might be puzzled when Meade III tells him about a type of "disequilibrium which is the most intractable" (p. 122). However, this is quickly cleared up when he is reminded that the chapter is supposed to examine alternative financial policies and their effectiveness in restoring balance-of-payments equilibrium without resort to depreciation or trade restrictions. Translated into the terms used by Meade I, the question is whether, starting from an "initial position of equilibrium" with a payments deficit financed by accommodating transfers, any measures of fiscal and monetary policy can be found which will act as a "disturbance" leading to such "repercussions" that a "new equilibrium" with a zero balance of payments will be reached, while foreign-exchange rates are unchanged and trade is not directly controlled. If the final equilibrium in any such model continues to show deficits no matter what "disturbing change" is devised by the financial authorities, then Meade III, with many practitioners in the field, calls the situation an "intractable" balance-of-payments disequilibrium, that is, one not yielding to treatment by financial policy.

persuade people to do certain things or to do things in a certain way. "Persuasive definitions" is the name characterising such definitions.[25]

Paul Streeten, in an interesting article, showed that certain definitions of balance-of-payments equilibrium fall in the category of persuasive definitions. We have seen how stable exchange rates, full employment at given wage-rates, stable price levels and unrestricted trade have been included as additional criteria in some definitions of balance-of-payments equilibrium. This expansion of criteria, according to Streeten, amounts to "begging the question"; "conceals behind a persuasive definition value judgments not generally shared."[26]

Streeten proceeds to exemplify the dangers of persuasive definitions:

> To include, say, the presence of import restrictions in the definition of "disequilibrium" produces the convenient result that the removal of these restrictions, and devaluation or deflation, become a *necessity,* although it is hoped, presumably, that the difference between logical necessity (what follows from the definition) and political or moral necessity (what ought to be done) will remain undetected [p. 87].

It is implicitly assumed, I take it, that those who make use of a persuasive definition of equilibrium rely on the popular association of equilibrium with a Good Thing, and of disequilibrium with a Bad Thing. Thus, they hope to sell to the public the removal of import restrictions (or the adoption of full-employment policies, etc.) in the same package labelled "equilibrium."

This does not mean that the absence of import restrictions and the pursuit of fiscal and monetary policies to create a full-employment demand for goods and services are not important assumptions, perhaps indispensable ones, for the analysis of certain problems.[27] The methodological standing of these two assumptions, however, is not the same if by import restrictions

---

25 *Cf.* C. L. Stevenson, "Persuasive Definitions," *Mind,* Vol. 47 (1938), p. 331; Max Black, "The Definition of Scientific Method," *Science and Civilization* (Madison: University of Wisconsin Press, 1949), p. 69.

26 Paul Streeten, "Elasticity Optimism and Pessimism in International Trade," *Economia Internazionale,* Vol. VII (1954), p. 87.

27 Streeten himself assumes some sort of full-employment policy, not only explicitly, but also when he defines disequilibrium to "mean a permanent tendency to generate a deficit in the balance of payments" (p. 87). It should be clear that such a "tendency" could not persist without a continuing *policy* of offsetting by means of loan expansions the automatic deflationary effects of sales from exchange reserves.

we mean the use of discretionary allocation controls rather than the use of tariffs and other general rules with "predictable" impact. Discretionary controls must be excluded from many analytical models, not because we do not like them, but because we cannot predict the outcome; we would need to know the "behaviour equations" of the control authorities in order to know how they react to certain changes in the variables of the model. As soon as these behaviour functions are "given," linking certain variables to others in a definite way, the controls are no longer "discretionary," and we can work with them in our equilibrium theory.

The assumption of "freedom from discretionary (theoretically unpredictable) controls" is, therefore, a necessary part of a model that includes the concept of a market equilibrium. In such a model we regularly assume certain relationships between prices, incomes and quantities offered and demanded in the market. If some of the reactions deduced from the assumed relationship become effective only when licensed, and cannot materialise without special permission by an unpredictable authority, the model becomes unworkable. It is only for this reason that "market equilibrium" must postulate effectiveness of "free-market prices," and therefore absence of direct controls. Trade barriers with predictable influence on all adjusting changes are fully consistent with market equilibrium, and with any other equilibrium as well. And, incidentally, the inconsistency of the assumption of discretionary trade restrictions with an analytically workable equilibrium is no good argument against the use of such restrictions in the real world. A policy cannot be rejected merely on the ground that it does not fit into a conceptual scheme which has proved useful in analysis.

The Trouble with Built-in Politics

The objections against persuasive definitions of equilibrium are not based on the fear that gullible people may actually be persuaded to stand up for the measures or policies "deduced" from arguments in which such an equilibrium concept is employed; the real ground for objection is that an equilibrium concept so drastically restricted by built-in political criteria becomes less useful, if not useless, in the analysis of most problems. Most problems that require analysis are such that not all the ideal conditions which are made "honorary criteria" of equilibrium can be "attained"; their analysis calls for a variety of policy variables and institutional (political) behaviour functions combined with a less circumscribed concept of equilibrium that can be used for *any* set of variables and *any* relationships between them. This statement refers chiefly to the kind of analysis in which equilibrium is thought of as the initial and final positions in an imagined process of change involving a chosen set of interrelated variables. But it holds also for an analysis in which equilibrium is thought of merely as the equality of certain (actual or potential) sums on the two sides of the account called "the balance of payments."

Take any change that would create an increase in the demand for foreign exchange, or a decrease in its supply. Whether it is a change in tastes at home or abroad, a change in the technical production possibilities anywhere, a change in fiscal or monetary policy (say, to accelerate economic development), a change in the wage structure (for example, giving higher wage-rates to industrial workers), a change in the flow of investment (perhaps a greater demand for foreign investment), a reduction in the desire to hold cash, or any one of a score of similar "disequilibrating changes"—the adjusting changes will involve first an accommodating outflow of foreign reserve and eventually some of the "prohibited" movements, that is, some deviations from the built-in political requirements of "equilibrium" in the persuasive sense. For example, real wages may be reduced through higher prices of wage goods; interest rates may rise, or bank loans be curtailed, with consequent reductions in employment; foreign-exchange rates may get adjusted, etc., and the final position—the new equilibrium in the analytical sense—will be a "disequilibrium" of the balance of payments in the persuasive (or rather dissuasive) sense. Since none of the results of any of the possible adjustments would qualify for the honorific title "equilibrium," the "disequilibrium" (in the dissuasive sense) could be remedied only by a *deus ex machina:* by another disequilibrating change that happened to neutralise the first disturbance and render the unpleasant adjustments unnecessary. A virtual sabotage of economic analysis!

STRUCTURE
AND
STRUCTURAL CHANGE:

Weaselwords and Jargon

Reprinted by permission from *Zeitschrift Für Nationalökonomie*, Band XVIII, Heft, 3, 1958.

The existence of homonyms in scientific as well as in everyday language raises no problem when the separate meanings of the same word are *sufficiently* different to make confusion impossible in the context in which the word is used. If we economists, for example, use the word "labor," no reader or listener will ever think of the painful muscle contractions preceding childbirth, and if we say "capital" he may not know precisely what we mean, but he will rarely confuse it with the seat of government in a state or country.

If the separate meanings of the same word are *closely related,* overlapping, or otherwise ambiguous so that the context be relied upon to indicate which meaning is intended, the writer or speaker has a moral duty, I would say, to state what he means. Often he can do so quite easily and briefly, perhaps upon the first use of the word or phrase in question, provided he uses it consistently. To use it sometimes in one meaning and sometimes in a different meaning without due warning and clarification, is inconsiderate and mischievous. A thoughtful scholar will either look for less ambiguous terms as substitutes or will use adequate modifiers to remove the possibility of misunderstanding or doubt on the part of his audience.

If most of the various meanings of a word are *undefined and vague,* not merely lacking precision,[1] but so obscure that the writer or speaker could not succeed in conveying a definite meaning, then the use of the word should not be condoned. Of course, a word may have some clean and definable and some undefinable, obscure meanings; in this case its use is permissible where the meaning is clear, but not where clear understanding cannot be expected.

If a word is used not to convey any clear meaning at all, but rather as a screen to hide muddled thinking, or perhaps to becloud issues and help put across a scheme or policy that might not otherwise be accepted, one may suspect not only the scholarship but also the integrity of the user of the word.

When I decided to embark on a semantic study of the terms "structure" and "structural," I did not know in which of the mentioned categories these terms lay. I had the suspicion that most of their meanings were completely undefinable and hopelessly vague. This suspicion was not justified. I compiled and examined scores of statements about "structure" and "structural" by all sorts of economists, and found that several of the meanings were clear and definable. In many instances there was considerable vagueness, but the statements made sense. In some instances, however, the meanings remained so obscure that I am inclined to characterize the terms (to paraphrase a famous line by Goethe) as words concealing voids of thought. I shall attempt to present samples of all three kinds.

In a recent study on *Structural Change* by Shozaburo Sakai, a Japanese scholar and follower of the German Historical School, the words "Structure" and "Structural" are used constantly, but the author nowhere succeeds in making clear what is meant.[2] In addition to the "structure of the econ-

---

[1] We may not know how quickly the air moves and how high the sand is piled up if we are told about a "wind" and about "sand-dunes"—to borrow from K. R. Popper examples of words lacking quantitative precision—yet we know what is being talked about. The vagueness or obscurity to which I refer in the text is of a different nature: there we do not know what is being talked about.

[2] Shozaburo Sakai: *The Theory of Structural Change of the National Economy* (Tokyo: Science Council of Japan, 1956).

omy," there is the "structure of historical cognition" (p. 1) and the "structure of the human community" (p. 23); there are "structural elements," "structural data," and "structural changes;" and there is even an attempt of a definition, apparently inspired half by Sombart and half by Spiethoff, according to which "structure . . . is the style or proportionality within which every part of the national economy finds its integrity in the whole" (p. 57). I believe that Professor Sakai, despite linguistic obstacles, has admirably succeeded in characterizing for us the typical language of "structure theory." Structure, I am afraid, is often a weaselword used to avoid commitment to a definite and clear thought.[3]

Let us first see how a dictionary definition reads. The *Oxford Dictionary* defines "structure" as "the mutual relations of the constituent parts or elements of a whole as determining its peculiar nature or character;" and "structural" as "of, or pertaining to, the arrangement and mutual relations of the parts of any complex whole." Some dictionaries proceed to give the meanings of "structure" in different disciplines, such as biology, chemistry, psychology; wisely, they stay away from economics.

Dictionaries stay away also from sociology, the discipline with the largest weasel-vocabulary, as it seems at least to the layman.[4] Sociologists have a field day with "structure;" and they have not been satisfied with the noun, the adjective, and the adverb—they have made also a verb, "to structure." Sociologists are always busy "structuring" one thing or another and I understand, they are grieved if anything remains "unstructured." Economists have not yet gone that far.

I. Some of the Clearer Meanings of "Structure" in Economics

I do not know in what connection the word "structure" was first used in economics. I do not recall any significant use of the term by the classical economists, though my memory

---

[3] The *Oxford Dictionary* defines weaselword as "a word which destroys the force of a statement, as a weasel ruins an egg by sucking out its contents."

[4] It has been said of the writings of a famous sociologist that he uses "a terminology devised so that practically no word in it shall enjoy its common meaning in the English language." K. E. Boulding, "The Parsonian Approach to Economics," *Kyklos,* Vol. X (1957), p. 317.

should not be relied upon. I have not attempted to establish priorities in the use of the term in the literature. My hunch is that in one of the relatively earlier uses it was supposed to refer to different arrangements of productive activity in the economy, especially to different *distributions* of productive factors among various sectors of the economy, various occupations, geographic regions, types of product, etc. Thus, economists have spoken of the "structure" of production to mean a cross-sectional distribution of inputs or outputs. Indeed, what we now call an input-output matrix of an economy is often referred to as a "structure."[5]

The term structure of production has also been used to denote the distribution of inputs and outputs over time.[6] Apparently a brief term was wanted to replace earlier phrases about the use of round-about methods of production and about different arrangements of productive factors in more capital using (or more time taking) and in less capital using (or less time taking) production processes. "Time structure" of production is the phrase conveniently used to distinguish the vertical or time distribution from the cross-sectional or horizontal distribution of inputs and outputs in an economy. There may be several obscurities in the theories of the capital structure or time structure of production, but the meaning of the term is relatively clear.

The term "structure," especially in its adjectival form, became popular in business-cycle theory when some German writers insisted that one must distinguish "structural changes" (Strukturwandlungen) from "cyclical fluctuations" (Konjunkturschwankungen). The main idea here was to separate, "merely temporary influences" from changes involving *permanent* alterations of the fundamental relationships in the economy.[7] While the distinction may be neither conceptually watertight nor operationally feasible, the basic idea is clear enough and unobjectionable.

Another contrast was sometimes referred to by pairing "structural" with "monetary," especially in connection with disturbing (disequilibrating) changes. According to this view, a change may occur either "on the side of money"—in the supply of money or in the demand for cash bal-

---

[5] W. Leontief, *The Structure of the American Economy 1919-1939* (New York: Oxford University Press, 1941).

[6] F. A. Hayek, *Prices and Production* (London: Routledge, 1931), p. 35.

[7] B. Harms, "Strukturwandlungen der deutschen Volkswirtschaft (Deutsche Wirtschafts-Enquete)," *Weltwirtschaftliches Archiv*, Vol. XXIV (1926), p. 263.

ances, resulting in a change in the total effective demand for goods and services—or "on the side of goods"—in the stock of productive resources, in the technological opportunities, or in tastes and preferences. This type of change, of *"real"* factors rather than the "money veil," was regarded as "structural" in contradiction to a "monetary change."

Some conceptions may be found to be different if they are defined by what they deny or negate, though not different if defined by what they affirm. There is a meaning of "structural change" that contrasts it with "policy change," that is, with some measure or course of action on the part of government. "Structural" meaning *"non-monetary,"* and "structural" meaning *"non-policy"* are different enough; yet in their positive aspects the two meanings are much the same: "structural changes" would be those occurring (autonomously) in real resources, in technology, and in preferences.

A very different meaning made its appearance in empirical studies of applied economics. A price *structure* was contrasted with a price level. This distinction was significant in many instances, and indispensable in regulatory practice, although in the regulation of freight rates the authorities, looking for formulas determining a rate level that would yield a fair return on investment, had curiously little to say about the "rate structure," about the *relations and differences* between freight rates charged for different products. To be interested in the rate structure meant to be concerned with these differences, with relative rates, rather than with some average rate per ton/mile.

Another meaning of "structure" became customary in applied economics after writers began to use this more high-brow word for the unambiguous word "composition." Needless to say, we are interested not only in the total value of exports and imports, for example, but also in their composition. The reason for saying "structure" in lieu of the simple word "composition" was perhaps the hope that the word "structure" would indicate that there is some *constancy in the composition.* Whereas the composition of any aggregate quantity might change drastically, perhaps even erratically, "structure" may convey the idea that the composition has been about the same for a long time and is expected to remain approximately the same in the future; and that a drastic change of that composition should be looked upon as a rare or highly significant occurrence. For example, an economist speaking of the "structure" of Ecuador's export trade means to convey that he would be greatly surprised if the list of exports next year were not made up largely of cacao, coffee, rice, bananas, balsa wood, and some straw hats.

If then the meaning of "structure" in this case is "a composition that is not expected to change easily," one might object that the expanded connotation mixes an observable fact—the composition of an aggregate quantity—with an unverified theory—namely, about the determinateness and constancy of the composition. But once the connotation is made explicit and the blending of observation and speculation is admitted, the use of the word should do no harm.

Another meaning of economic structure, but likewise with the implication of constancy and giveness, is found in the methodology of model building in business-cycle theory. It refers to the explanation of fairly *regular swings* as effects of quite irregular shocks or disturbances exogenous to the system. The transformation of irregular impulses into regular swings is accounted for by the "structure" of the economy, most appropriately defined as a *"set of constant reaction coefficients."*[8] This meaning of "structure" is often exemplified or illustrated by the rocking-chair analogy: all sorts of pushes, pulls, shocks, etc., lead to the same kind of rocking movement, thanks to the structure of the chair, that is, the way it is built.[9] A different kind of chair, say, a straight kitchen chair or a soft parlor-room chair, would react very differently to the same impulses, and probably rarely respond with the regular swings typical of the rocker.

The role that "structure" plays in the translations of an external impulse into a cyclical movement of economic activities is re-enacted, so to speak, in all sorts of economic equilibrium models constructed to link assumed "causes" to deduced "effects,"—to connect so-called disturbances and so-called adjustments. Changes of some independent variables produce certain changes in dependent variables, but only through operations "under given conditions." This *set of given conditions*, if it is assumed to be *invariant for a variety of problems*, may be regarded as the economic "structure" which influences or determines the consequences of changes of all sorts. In this "apparatus of pure economic theory" it is not postu-

---

[8] J. Tinbergen, „De quelques problemes posés par le concept de structure économique," *Revue d'Economie Politique*, Vol. 62 (1952), pp. 27 ff.

[9] G. von Haberler, *Prosperity and Depression* (Geneva: League of Nations, Revised edition, 1939), p. 11.

lated that the structure is known with all its numerical parameters and coefficients, but merely that it is given and unchanged.[10] The invariant background against which certain processes of change are seen on the stage provided by the analytical model is regarded as its structure. It comprises the totality of the relevant technological, psychological, institutional facts of life in the idealized type of economic system in which small changes of some variables are explained by small changes in other variables, that is, in which certain causes are shown to have certain effects—while they would have had different effects if the system, the "economic structure," were different. Perhaps I should add that most economic theorists have had the good sense to do without the word "structure" in that context, for it contributes nothing to the understanding of the whole business. The phrase, "set of given conditions" is much less mystifying.

If the "underlying conditions" are given but not fully known, theory can merely indicate the kind of effects which certain causes are likely to have, often the direction of change—but numerically accurate predictions are excluded. Numerical information about underlying conditions and about changes in independent variables can yield numerically accurate predictions, provided the information is reliable and the conditions are actually invariant for the time in which the changes are supposed to work themselves out. Econometrics has set itself the task of estimating the reaction coefficients which in a chosen model are exhibited as the relevant ones for certain kinds of problems, and of using these coefficients and all the rest for numerical predictions of economic magnitudes in the real world—a rather formidable task, in my opinion, because few of the "conditions" actually remain constant to the extent necessary for such predictions to prove correct.

Now, the econometrician wants to distinguish a merely formal set of conditions—expressed in x's and y's, and a's and b's—from a fully known set of conditions—expressed in real numbers and fractions—and he needed a word for this purpose. The poor, overworked word "structure" appealed to the econometricians, and they adopted it to denote the "minimum information about constant knowns needed to solve certain

---

10 F. Machlup, "The Problem of Verification in Economics," *Southern Economic Journal*, Vol. XXII (1955), p. 14.

classes of economic problems arising for a given economy."[11] In other words, "structure" to an econometrician is a *set of numerically known constants* which, as parameters and coefficients, determine the numerically expressed effects of definite changes in independent variables. Why "structure?" To express the internal relations within the system and the hope that the constants stay constant? Perhaps. In any case, structure in this sense means not merely conditions assumed to be *given,* though not exactly known, but only "*known* conditions"—conditions known with numerical accuracy.

Implied in the concept of "given and invariant conditions," whether they are merely assumed or actually known with numerical precision, is the idea that these conditions are not themselves affected by the movements of the variables in the system, at least not for the duration of the adjustment process in question. Thus, for certain economic problems we take as given and unchanged for the duration (a) the stock of productive resources (the so-called initial endowment), (b) the production functions, (c) the preference functions, and (d) the legal, moral, political and social institutions relevant to the problem. Changes of prices, absolute and relative, or incomes, money or real, of resource allocation, production, and product distribution are all supposed to leave the mentioned ("fundamental") conditions unchanged. The latter are parts of the whole which help determine the outcome of all sorts of events but are themselves unaffected by them (or affected only to a negligible, and therefore neglected, extent). To apply the term "structure" to the *outcome-determining but not outcome-determined conditions* may make good sense. The assumed invariance does not imply that the conditions will never change.[12] The conditions are merely frozen for the duration of the analyzed process, chiefly because this freezing is helpful and convenient for the explanation. Indeed, one of the clearest meanings of "structural change" refers to a

---

[11] J. Tinbergen, *loc cit.,* pp. 34-35. Similarly, Frisch spoke of "structural equations" as those which contain "influencing coefficients, that is to say parameters that determine the numerical character of the equation" and are data in the problem. R. Frisch, "On the Notion of Equilibrium and Disequilibrium," *Review of Economic Studies,* Vol. III (1935-36), p. 100.

[12] Cf. the definition of structure "as a set of conditions which do not change while observations were made but which might change in the future." W. C. Hood and T. C. Koopmans, *Studies in Econometric Method* (New York: John Wiley & Sons, 1953), p. 26.

change in these fundamental conditions which are assumed for many purposes of analysis.

It may be helpful if this discussion of the "clearer meanings of structure in economics" is summarized in the form of a brief check list:

1.1 The structure of production: a distribution of inputs or outputs among areas, industries, or products; or a distribution of inputs or outputs over time.

1.2 Structural changes: permanent alterations,—not merely temporary changes or cyclical fluctuations.

1.3 Structural changes: alterations in real resources, technology, or preferences,—(a) not monetary changes; (b) not policy changes.

1.4 The price structure: relative prices,—not a price level or some sort of average.

1.5 The structure of an aggregate quantity: its composition, determinate and constant—not easily changed.

1.6 The structure transforming irregular shocks into regular, cyclical swings.

1.7 The structure of the economy: the set of given and invariant conditions assumed for theoretical analysis.

1.8 the structure of the model: the set of numerically known constants and coefficients in econometric analysis.

1.9 The structure of the system: the set of outcome-determining but not outcome-determined conditions.

1.10 Structural changes: alterations in the fundamental conditions which are ordinarily assumed unchanged for purposes of analysis.

In order to avoid a possible misunderstanding I ought to state that the words "economy," "model," and "system" in the items 1.7, 1.8, and 1.9 may be used interchangeably; no difference is intended by this variety of expression. The last of these three items, incidentally, may be rejected as a separate entry and regarded, instead, as an elaboration of the two preceding ones.

II. Some of the Vaguer Meanings of "Structure" in Economics

There are at least five other meanings of the so-called "structure of the economy" to be found in the literature but I was not able to rank them among the clear concepts. When concepts are not well defined and their meanings are only vaguely conveyed by the general tenor of the discussions in which they are employed, an interpreter may still be able to do what the authors failed to do: he may supply definitions and clarify the meanings. But the interpretations, charitable or critical, may not reproduce what the authors had intended to say. The choice between a clear but wrong interpretation and an accurate reproduction of vague statements presents a dilemma.

Standards of clarity, however, are not uniform. Many consumers of literary products, in economics as in other fields, are well satisfied where others complain; they affirm that they understand what others call unintelligible. Whether they really can penetrate the ideological fog that troubles others or are content with dim outlines of things, is difficult to say. Conversely, I cannot be sure whether, when I complain about vagueness, my perception is too poor, my sense of discrimination too fine, my insistence on unambiguous expression too pedantic—or whether the writings in question were just too woolly. In order to avoid charging particular writers with woolly writing I shall keep them nameless and confine my discussion to the "type" of statement made.

In one such type of statement economists have used the phrase "structure of the economy" to contrast something *"real," "observable," "describable"* with something merely imaginary, abstract, unrealistic. These economists were suspicious of the speculations of the theorists and wanted them to pay more attention to "facts;" to be less concerned with model building and more with the "actual structure of the economy." There is a superficial similarity between this emphasis on "structure" and the econometricians' search for "structural data;" both are looking for "real" data of observation. But there is this important difference: the econometrician wants measured quantities, statistical data, substituted as constants and coefficients in equations which are parts of theoretical models, admittedly abstract, idealized, unrealistic; the antitheoretical economist wants all abstract models abandoned in favor of the "real structure," whatever that is.[13] His idea, incurably vague, is that you can do in economics with

---

[13] The econometrician wants structural data substituted *in* theoretical equations; the anti-theoretical economist wants them substituted *for* theoretical equations.

"facts" without theory and that the "structure of the economy" is made up of nothing but "facts."

Another type of statement using the phrase "structure of the economy" shares with the one just discussed the antagonism toward pure and general theory. But it is not the idealization and abstraction which it condemns, but the universalism and cosmopolitism of economic theory, that is, the claim or notion that some fundamental postulates or assumptions, or some basic constructs and models, can be valid for all times and places. By emphasizing the "structure of the economy" these critics of classical and neo-classical economics want to point to the limited historical relevance of any economic system: only what exists at a given time and place, not any eternal truths and universal conceptions, can be significant in economics.

There can be no serious argument about the contention that the "underlying conditions" are different in different countries and at different times, and that the economist must not overlook them, but should examine them more carefully than has sometimes been done. Confusion arises, however, when it comes to the question what are the relevant and significant "facts" that would form the "underlying conditions," or the "structure" of a given economy. One group of writers stress the *ideological climate* of the time: it is the "style of the period," the "spirit of the economy." Again, there should be no doubt that mental attitudes religious, ethical, legal, political and other social norms, prejudices, customs, etc., are highly important in many economic problems; that it is methodologically sound to include such matters among the underlying conditions; and that there is no harm in regarding them as part of the "structure of the economy"—as long as one avoids an air of mysticism by specifying precisely what one is talking about, and just when and why it is supposed to be relevant.

A contrast between the first and the second type of "structure of the economy" deserves some attention: the first stresses numerical data, measurable quantities and relations, whereas the second stresses attitudes of mind and patterns of culture.

A third meaning of the "structure of the economy" is related to the previous two through the implied rejection of equilibrium analysis with its imaginary models based on assumed conditions; and, in addition, is related to the second through emphasis upon the limited historical relevance of all economic generalization. But the stress, in the third meaning, is less on the description of the underlying economic conditions of the particular time than on their evolution through time. The interest is less in an explanation of the economic process under given conditions, and of the differences which these conditions make regarding the effects of certain types of events, than in an explanation of the changes of the underlying conditions: of the *evolution of economic institutions.* This type of study of the "structure of the economy" does not primarily ask what institutions are at the time and how they affect economic activity, but rather how institutions have become what they are and how they may change in the future or give way to different ones. In brief, the study of the "structure" means here the study of the evolution of economic institutions in historical time. The word "structure," it seems to me, adds little to this program of study, though those who used the word in the formulation of the program apparently thought otherwise.

The "structure" of the economy or model or system referred to in items 1.7, 1.8, and 1.9 of the preceding section was characterized by invariance; the "structure of the economy referred to in the first three items of the present section is characterized by change. This, however, is only an apparent, not a real contrast: the *invariance* of the structure was only relative to certain events and their effects, the analysis of which required assumed conditions to be held constant; the *change* of the structure over historical time is usually gradual and slow, perhaps even imperceptible to contemporaries (though not to those looking backward). In accordance with this idea, it may be expedient to designate by the word "structure" the totality of *slowly changing* economic variables and relations which are of significance (in their relative invariance) in the explanation of more quickly moving economic processes.[14]

An analogy used by Keynes in a very different context may be helpful

---

[14] This is an interpretation, not a reproduction, of the ideas which some "structure-minded" economists may have intended to convey. I am probably influenced by Knight's writings, such as the following: "In economics we are chiefly concerned with equilibrium, not as a state of rest but as a process in equilibrium, with a slower process forming the 'given conditions' within which a more rapid one takes place and tends toward a moving equilibrium," F. H. Knight, "Statik und Dynamik," *Zeitschrift für Nationalökonomie,* Vol. II (1930); reprinted in Knight, *On the History and Method of Economics* (Chicago: Univ. of Chicago Press, 1956), p. 170.

in illuminating the difference in question. Keynes contrasted a "sticky mass" with a "liquid" when he once wished to refer to certain variables and relations as less amenable to rapid change than others. Structural relations are perhaps the "sticky mass," in contradistinction to other things in the economy which are more "fluid" and respond readily to external impulses. However, this sticky-mass character of the "structure of the economy" does not clarify the doubtful meaning, but may add to the confusion and controversy about what it includes and how sticky it "really" is. The very application which Keynes made of the analogy is a questionable one. It was a country's import surplus—its export potential and its import needs—which he referred to as a "sticky mass."[15] Upon closer examination one can find that in actual fact import surpluses have disappeared in the course of a few months, and imports have been reduced drastically almost overnight. What Keynes must have meant was not that a quick change was not possible, but rather that it would hurt—and that one ought not to hurt people (or will be thrown out of office if one does). Here was a confusion between possibility, probability, and volition—between what cannot be, what probably will not be, and what ought not to be (or will be politically dangerous). If the "structure of the economy is the totality of these economic variables and relations that *cannot* change quickly, a country's imports and import surplus will be no part of it. But they will be part of the "structure" if this concept is meant to include variables and relations which we *do not want* to change quickly, because we fear the consequences might be too painful. In this meaning "structure" has taken on moral and political connotations.

---

[15] "My own view is that at a given time the economic structure of a country, in relation to the economic structures of its neighbours, permits of a certain 'natural' level of exports, and that arbitrarily to effect a material alteration of this level by deliberate devices is extremely difficult. Historically, the volume of foreign investment has tended, I think, to adjust itself—at least to a certain extent—to the balance of trade, rather than the other way round, the former being the sensitive and the latter the insensitive factor. In the case of German Reparations, on the other hand, we are trying to fix the volume of foreign remittance and compel the balance of trade to adjust itself thereto. Those who see no difficulty in this—like those who saw no difficulty in Great Britain's return to the gold standard—are applying the theory of liquids to what is, if not a solid, at least a sticky mass with strong internal resistance," J. M. Keynes, "The German Transfer Problem." *Economic Journal*, Vol. XXXIX (March 1929); reprinted in *Readings in The Theory of International Trade* (Philadelphia: Blakiston, 1949), p. 167.

Another meaning of "structure" with an evaluational connotation refers to the "price structure"—for products and productive services—relative to the "structure" of supply and demand; and an attempt is made to judge whether the *relative prices* are actually what they would be in an ideal competitive equilibrium system. If they are judged to deviate from these ideal levels, the situation is called—at least by one writer—one of "structural disequilibrium." This, it should be noted, is not a disequilibrium in the analytical sense (that is, a stage in the explanation of a process as one of "equilibration" following a "disequilibrating" change). Instead, the term connotes a failure of the price mechanism to do what it "ought" to do in an ideal system; thus "structural disequilibrium" is used as a designation for the *deviation from a standard of performance.*[16]

One of the widely accepted meanings of "structural change" is that of a *drastic* and fundamental change of the economic environment—in contradistinction to those small variations with which customary equilibrium analysis is usually concerned (such as a reduction of tax rates, an increase in import tariffs, a raise in wage rates). Strangely enough, this meaning clashes with two of the ideas often denoted by "economic structure:" the association of "structure" with *slow* change and its association with *permanent* change. An example of a change which many economists have characterized as "structural" is the destruction through war of a large portion of a country's industrial plant and equipment. This was a drastic, catastrophic change in the economic environment, which it took years to repair. It was neither the slow and gradual transformation that others had in mind when they talked about "structural change," nor the irreversible movement, the permanent alteration, which was called "structural" to be distinguished from a temporary change. Perhaps no serious confusion can arise from these conflicting meanings; on the other hand, there is no good reason, at least as I see it, for using the technical jargon term "structural" when ordinary language offers a wide choice of simpler and less ambiguous adjectives, such as sudden, drastic, sharp, severe, violent, catastrophic, and fundamental.

---

[16] "Structural disequilibrium is a maladjustment of the price system," either "a misallocation of resources relative to prices" or "factor prices inappropriate to factor endowments." C. P. Kindleberger, *International Economics* (Homewood, Ill.: Richard D. Irwin, Inc., 1953), p. 469. In earlier statements Kindleberger distinguished "structural disequilibrium at the goods level" (p. 453) and "structural disequilibrium at the factor level" (p. 461).

Two more concepts may be mentioned in this group, having little in common with the preceding seven—except the vagueness of their meaning. I refer to the "structure of the market" and the "structure of the industry," where "structure" probably means nothing in particular and is merely the best sounding of a number of weaselwords—such as "situation," "circumstances," "set-up"—standing for a *body of pertinent facts*, or relevant description.

What do we expect when we are promised an account of the "structure" of a particular market? We expect to be told about the number of separate firms supplying the product and their relative shares in total sales, about the location and size of the establishments producing it, about the different uses of the product and the industries or consumer groups which buy larger portions of the total output, about prices, especially about any differences in prices charged for different qualities, in different locations, and to different customer groups, about the frequency of changes in price and the relative amplitude of fluctuations, etc. The *collection of facts* presented as part of the "structure" of the market varies with the development of the theory of competition, since market analysts usually intend to throw light on the question of the "degree of competition" prevailing in the market. The word "structure" in this use is vague, but the vagueness is of no consequence and, indeed, partly intentional in order to afford the account presented under that title the latitude of scope that is needed to accommodate changing theories about what facts are pertinent.

The same or even greater latitude of scope is allowed to the descriptive accounts presented as the "structure" of an industry. Such accounts will ordinarily include some of the essential technological information, the raw materials used and their sources of supply, the labor requirements, the value of fixed capital, the locations and sizes of the manufacturing establishments, the number and relative sizes of the firms, their shares in total sales, the major outlets for the product, the extent of vertical integration backward and forward, the existence and functions of trade associations, the history of combinations condemned or condoned by the courts, conventional or habitual trade practices concerning price setting, deliveries, terms of sales, advertising, the entry of new firms and the disappearance of old ones through merger or liquidation, the rates of return on investment, etc., etc. That the facts described are selected on the basis of the relevance they have been found to have, by theoretical model analysis, for certain kinds of economic problems becomes apparent when one thinks of the information ordinarily not included in accounts of the "structure" of the industry: the number of acres occupied by the establishments, the number and height of smoke stacks, the number and widths of windows and doors, the number and ages of the members of the boards of directors, and so forth. In brief, the "structure of the industry" is the *information* about the industry that is *regarded as significant* for economic questions.

As in the previous section, a summary may be found useful. The following "vaguer meanings of structure in economics" have been discussed:

2.1 The structure of the economy: real, observable, measurable facts, —not an abstract model.

2.2 The structure of the economy: the style or spirit of the time,— not a universal theory.

2.3 The structure of the economy: the evolution of institutions over time,—not some imaginary equilibrium.

2.4 The structure of the system: the slowly moving parts of the system,—not those subject to quick change.

2.5 The structure of the system: the parts of the system that are not wanted to change quickly,—not the easily adjustable ones.

2.6 Structural disequilibrium: price structure for factors and products deviating from that of an ideal competitive system.

2.7 Structural changes: drastic changes of the economic environment, —not small variations of economic data.

2.8 The structure of a market: a descriptive account of facts pertinent to judge competitiveness, etc.

2.9 The structure of an industry: all sorts of factual information deemed significant.

III. Some of the Crypto-Apologetic Meanings of "Structure" in Economics

I hope I shall be forgiven for proposing a fancy name for the third group of meanings of "structure" in economics. Since I suspect that in many contexts this word is used—not in order to clarify, and as an aid in analysis—but rather to justify, and as a means of apology, I speak of the crypto-apologetic meanings of "structure." The "crypto" part of this designation is not intended as a serious accusation; I do not mean to say that any economist would try under the guise of objectivity to justify a practice or a policy by the sly use of words with doubtful meanings. But I believe it quite possible that many economists remain unaware of hidden implications which make them virtual advocates and apologists.

The first exhibit in this group is another concept of the "structure of an industry." This phrase has been used, not just as a body of pertinent information about an industry; but as a *non-incriminating explanation* of certain practices that had come under the attack of the law. Members of particular industries had been charged with unlawful cartelization or *conspiracy in restraint of trade;* some economists then tried to prove that the most suspicious facts, such as widespread identity of price quotations, were actually not the result of concerted action but rather the *unavoidable consequence* of the "structure" of the industry. It is true that people in general are often too prone to suspect design and conspiracy even where events can easily be explained otherwise. But in the cases in question no adequate explanation was offered; the mystic word "structure" was supposed both to refute the explanation based on collusion and to obviate the need for any other full explanation of events without collusion. Not all economists that were retained as expert witnesses on the "structure" of the industries concerned have taken this line; some held that the "structure" did not really provide counter-evidence for the charge of conspiracy but, from the point of view of economic policy, justified the resort to concerted action as the only way of surviving.

Other instances of the use of "structure," "structural change," or "structural imbalance" with crypto-apologetic meanings can be found in the advocacy of the maintenance of *governmental price controls* and in the justification of *cartels and international commodity agreements.* I am not contending that price controls, export controls, support prices, and other measures of this sort, can never be shown to be the most efficient methods under certain circumstances of attaining certain socially accepted objectives. The point is that the reference to an alleged "structural imbalance" has so often been offered in lieu of any supporting argument for the mentioned measures. The word "structure" works in some "educated" circles just as the phrase "you know what I mean" works among less literate people. To persuade you that a certain measure is needed you are told that the "structure" makes it absolutely indispensable, and that the "structural imbalance" cannot be coped with in any other way,—surely, you understand, don't you?

I shall not confine myself to such sarcastic remarks, but go more deeply into the "structure" argument for *foreign-exchange restrictions*. Here the idea is that none of the orthodox policies would do any good—and, indeed, would do serious harm if they were tried—when after a "structural change" a "structural imbalance" has occurred. The country concerned must not allow the money flow and income level to get adjusted to the foreign-exchange rate, nor the foreign-exchange rate to get adjusted to the money flow and income level; if there is a "structural disequilibrium," the only safe method of dealing with it is to impose or continue exchange restrictions and quantitative import controls. The fact that dozens of countries have disregarded the warnings of the "structure"-Casandras and have successfully applied classical remedies to deal with their dollar shortage, or even to turn it into a dollar abundance, has discredited the myth of the word "structure" in some quarters, but not yet in all. Does it, after all, have a meaning clear enough and sound enough to give it standing in scholarly discourse?

In our review of meanings of "structure" we have encountered one where "structural" was directly linked with "disequilibrium" and where the phrase was supposed to be particularly pertinent to the issue in point. It was the "structural disequilibrium" in the sense of a maladjustment of relative prices (2.6). It must be admitted that a good many generalizations of economic theory will not hold when prices of productive services and products do not respond to excess demand or excess supply. But it does not follow that in such a case matters will be "improved" if additional parts of the price mechanism are shut off and discretionary allocations are introduced for imported materials or products. That the "price structure" at the "factor level" or at the "goods level" deviates from the ideal one is *per se* no reason for exchange restrictions, no reason for resisting exchange-rate adjustments, etc. Incidentally, this is a very special meaning of "structural disequilibrium" and probably not what most of the economists had in mind who used the phrase in their arguments for exchange restrictions.

Let us go over several other meanings that can be given to the phrase "structural disequilibrium," and let us eliminate those that do not make good sense in the present context.

I have argued elsewhere[17] that "equilibrium" as a tool of economic analysis means the mutual compatibility of a set of selected variables which are supposed to be interrelated in specified ways. "Disequilibrium," then, denotes the mutual incompatibility of these interrelated variables in their given magnitudes, and implies a prediction that one or more of them must and will change. The statement that a given historical situation *is* an equilibrium (or a disequilibrium) can be given sense (1) by translating it to say that the situation *corresponds* to an abstract model in equilibrium (or disequilibrium), and (2) by enumerating all the variables, and specifying all the interrelations among them, which are taken into account. (This is necessary because variables A, B, C, D may be compatible with one another, yet incompatible when joined with variable E, and compatible again when joined also with variable F. The real world has an indefinite number of variables and interrelationships, but for analytic models only a few of them are selected. Their specification is indispensable.)

Assume, for example, that an economist contends that the present situation in his country corresponds to a model in disequilibrium in which real resources, production opportunities, consumers' tastes, wage rates, product prices, interest rates, exchange rates, real income, money income, money supply, bank reserves, and exchange reserves are taken into account and certain relations between them are assumed to prevail. This contention means that the present magnitudes of the enumerated variables are incompatible with one another and that some of them will inevitably change. If the theory is complete, it will indicate which of the variables are going to change and how.

Now, what may be meant if the noun "disequilibrium" in this sense is modified by the adjective "structural?" Of the many possible meanings of "structural" let us try one that was associated with several meanings of "structure," namely, the quality of constancy or invariance; in other words, let us translate "structural" as lasting, enduring, persistent. We readily see that this combination of words would yield a contradiction in terms: "disequilibrium," a conjecture of variables that cannot last and

---

17 F. Machlup, "Equilibrium and Disequilibrium: Misplaced Concreteness and Disguised Politics," *Economic Journal*, Vol. LXVIII (1958).

implies an inherent tendency or necessity to change, is now stated to be an enduring one. "Structural disequilibrium" would then be a situation of which it is said that it both endures and cannot endure. This surely will not do, and one of the interpretations must be rejected. Perhaps "disequilibrium" did not mean here what it means in economic theory; perhaps the users of the phrase meant something like an "undesirable," "troublesome" or "distressing" situation; such situations, unfortunately, may be persistent! If this were meant by "structural disequilibrium," one had better drop the learned but misused jargon and say simply "persistent adversity" or "continuing trouble." Needless to say, every pretension of an explanation or diagnosis—entertained under the protection of the jargon of "structural disequilibrium"—would then be ended.

Other interpretations must be tried, this time leaving "disequilibrium" its analytical meaning, but attaching other meanings to "structural." The adjective may qualify "disequilibrium" to indicate that it was "caused" by a "structural change;" and this may mean a permanent, not temporary, change (1.2), or a real, not monetary, change (1.3 a), or a fundamental, not policy, change (1.3 b), or a change of conditions ordinarily assumed unchanged (1.10), or a drastic, not small, change (2.6). If "structural" means to negate all its contradictories at the same time, it must refer to a change or changes not originating from merely temporary conditions or phenomena, not originating "on the side of money" (that is, not attributable to alterations in the supply of, or in the demand for, money and not evidenced by a change in the total effective demand for goods and services), not originating from acts of public policy, not originating from small variations, not from variations of a sort known to occur in the ordinary course of economic activity (but from changes of variables or conditions assumed to be unchanged in customary analysis). In order to be "structural" a change, therefore, has to be a drastic, lasting, irreversible alteration in the stock of productive resources, in the state of the arts, in the tastes and preferences of the people, or in the legal, political or social framework in which they act.

But what would be the logical connection between a "disequilibrium" caused by a "structural change" of the sort described and the policy conclusion that foreign exchange should be rationed at a price which evokes a continuing excess demand? Why, for example, should a drastic change in resources or in technology (foreign or domestic) call for foreign-exchange restrictions and a policy of forestalling the adjustments, either of money incomes or of prices and exchange rates, which would otherwise follow? If there is a reason, it is not an obvious one, nor one that could be demonstrated with reference to the nature of the *cause* of the disequilibrium; it would require a comparative analysis of the probable *effects*. If a certain course of events, expected as adjustment to a disequilibrating change, is dreaded (by the government or by the voters) and hence "must" be forestalled, the issue cannot be whether the disequilibration is structural or not structural, but only whether the uncontrolled, unrestricted equilibration would involve avoidable hardships.

What then may "structural disequilibrium" mean if "structural" is to refer, not to the nature of its causes, but to the nature of the effects to be expected in the absence of restrictions? One sensible answer seems to be that disequilibrium may be regarded as structural if the equilibrating changes—the adjustments—are likely to include such things as geographic or occupational transfers of labor, the construction of new machinery (and perhaps the scrapping of old machinery), or other adaptations that cannot be done quickly or at small cost or without hardship to many. Perhaps these transfers, investments, hardships are regarded as unwanted and unnecessary. Another possible view might be this: Adjustments that cannot be had except over a long time and with substantial investment outlays are obviously long-run effects and must be preceded by short-run effects, by some changes occurring "in the meantime," without much delay and before any new investments are made; perhaps these short-run effects are held to be undesirable as well as unnecessary in the sense that an ultimate adaptation can be achieved at smaller sacrifice.

Thus, two interpretations suggest themselves of the position that foreign-exchange restrictions are indicated in the case of a "structural disequilibrium": (a) the long-run adjustments to be expected in the absence of restrictions involve costly adaptations of the structure of the economy which ought to be avoided; or, (b) although these long-run adjustments cannot be avoided, the short-run effects to be expected in the absence of restrictions are intolerable and can be avoided by means of government measures which by slowing down the long-run adjustments make them (allegedly) less painful, or measures which are hoped to accomplish the adjustments less painfully and yet not any more slowly or perhaps even faster. No matter whether one accepts these positions as tenable and sound, one can hardly say that the use of the term "structural" is well warranted,—especially in the second interpretation, where a disequilibrium is called "structural" because the "structural changes" which are required for equilibration are held to be accomplished more advantageously through direct controls by the government than through the pressures of changing money incomes and market prices.

I am unable to see any explanatory value in the concept of "structural disequilibrium" for the problem at hand. A long and arduous interpretative analysis has been necessary for us to find any sense at all in the use of these words; and the outcome has been that the concept stands for a number of unsupported assertions, in the support of which it cannot assist. Hence, to diagnose any concrete situation as a "structural disequilibrium" that ought not to be allowed to work itself out, but should be treated by exchange controls, is to substitute terminology for analysis. Perhaps others can provide better interpretations of the vague concept—but until they do the verdict that it has at best a crypto-apologetic meaning seems to be inescapable.[18]

The reference to "structural imbalance" has been used also in the advocacy of *import barriers* other than foreign-exchange controls. It would be needless repetition to show that the invocation of the "structure" concept in this connection plays the same role that it had in the previous context: as an apparently learned term conveying the impression that analysis diagnosis, and appropriate therapy are all proved beyond doubt where in fact not even the analysis has been completed.

As one more instance of crypto-apologetic meanings of "structural imbalance" we mention its use in the plea for the suspension of the operation of the price mechanism and for the introduction and maintenance of *allocation controls*. The interpretation is analogous to the one applied to the plea for exchange restrictions: for one reason or another it is held that in certain situations, called "structural disequilibria," adjustments

---

[18] I have not included the pursuit of a certain fiscal and monetary policy among the possible interpretations of "structural disequilibrium," because this has been rejected by almost all writers who claim the existence of "structural" disequilibrium. One might hold, of course, that the "political structure" of certain countries force their governments to pursue politices—say, "full-employment policies"—which are more inflationary than the policies elsewhere. In such a case a chronic excess demand for foreign exchange at the fixed exchange rate must develop in the relatively more inflation-bound countries. But the writers who speak of "structural" disequilibrium have insisted that they were not referring to monetary phenomena or to policy matters. The use of the term "structural" as a euphemism for "addicted to a policy of credit expansion" would really be a trick worthy of a public relations adviser.

through market prices are inefficient, unnecessarily painful, uneconomic, and that allocation controls are indicated. This may be so; but the words "structural imbalance" neither prove it nor explain why it may be so.

"Structural imbalance" as an "argument" in pleas for particular measures of economic policy and control alludes to a possible chronic malaise; it is meant to support a certain policy prescription on the ground that "there is something *wrong*" with the economy, which necessitates the use of the recommended treatment. In a similar vein the "structure of the economy" is often invoked as an "argument" in contentions that "there is something *different*" in the economy, which makes certain explanations, predictions, or prescriptions which hold almost everywhere else, inapplicable to a particular country. Needless to say, conditions in some countries may significantly differ from conditions in other countries and may call for different diagnoses, prognoses, and therapies. But these so-called "structural differences" and their implications should be spelled out. To say that the "structure of the economy" is different does not convey any information whatsoever. Yet rather well-proven generalizations are often rejected merely on the ground of unspecified "structural differences."

Several other instances might be included in this review of "crypto-apologetic meanings of structure in economics," but the idea would probably be quite similar to those discussed. Here is our check list serving as a summary of this section:

3.1 The structure of an industry: an excuse for restricted competition.

3.2 Structural imbalance: a plea for price controls, cartels, commodity agreements.

3.3 Structural imbalance: a plea for foreign-exchange restrictions.

3.4 Structural imbalance: a plea for import barriers.

3.5 Structural imbalance: a plea for allocation controls.

3.6 Structural differences: an excuse for rejecting diagnoses, prognoses, or therapies which apply everywhere else.

IV. Postscript

How often do we discover bias and prejudice in the writings of others and how seldom in our own! But since bias and prejudice are probably quite widely distributed, it would be rather peculiar if somebody should be completely free from it. Let us ask then whether the "findings" of this semantic essay are not unduly influenced by the author's political philosophy.

My suspicion is aroused by the strange "coincidence" that I have found crypto-apologetic meanings of structure only in pleas for policies which I do not like: restrictions of competition, price and allocation controls, import barriers, exchange regulations. Have I perhaps failed to notice similar aberrations in pleas for policies which I happen to like? I will admit this possibility and gladly state that the substitution of words for voids of thought, and of unsupported assertions for findings of analysis, ought to be condemned wherever it occurs, even in pleas for my most-favored notions and causes. But there is also another possibility: that I have been unfair in criticizing the arguments used by the advocates of policies which I oppose.

I have sometimes observed that to grasp an argument that leads to conclusions hitherto rejected is much more difficult than to grasp an argument supporting a preconceived conclusion. Where I do not like the results, I am more eager than otherwise to question the validity of the premises, the consistency of the argument, the clarity of the concepts. Concepts perfectly "clear" to those who accept the conclusions often seem vague, empty, or self-contradictory to the opponents. Aware of these influences of one's political philosophy upon one's understanding of concepts, I must concede the possibility that my judgment has not attained the degree of fairness to which I aspire. But my criticism has been in good faith: I have not shouted "Unclear" unless I sensed a lack of clarity. My vision may have been dimmed by prejudice, but I did not pretend dimness where I saw clearly.

What semantic prescriptions follow from my lengthy review of meanings? I see no harm in using the word "structure" in its "clearer" meanings, discussed in Section I, although even there I should prefer to see it replaced by a less promiscuously used word whenever possible. I would not use the word "structure" in any of the "vaguer" meanings, discussed in Section II. And I would definitely reject the use of the word "structure" or "structural" in the suspect meanings, discussed in Section III. In general, the term is more often used as an unnecessary jargon and as a plain weaselword than it is as a technical term with a clearly defined meaning. This should be reason enough for avoiding it.

I cannot force these prescriptions upon other writers. I can only hope that many economists prefer to be clear and will shun confusing language.

MICRO-
AND
MACRO-ECONOMICS:

Contested Boundaries and
Claims of Superiority *

I. The Concepts, Their History
and Their Interrelations

The terms micro-theory and macro-theory are now so widely used among economists that one should think it is clear what they mean. Unfortunately, it is not.

Since the Greek words *micro* and *macro* mean in English "small" and "large," one would expect macro-theory to refer to a large model, and one would assume that a macro-model would be composed of micro-models and have micro-models as elements of its structure. If this were the case, a macro-theory would be a means of *coordinating* a number of micro-models, perhaps of *integrating* models of individual organisms or individual decision-units into a grand model of the whole economy.

Alternatively, it is possible to construct macro-models that are not made up of micro-models but display by implication some of the rela-

* Published originally as *Der Wettstreit zwischen Mikro-und Makro-theorien in der National Oekonomie,* Walter Euken Institut, Tübingen, 1960. Translated for inclusion in this volume by Edith Penrose, London School of Economics. Reprinted by permission.

tionships that are expressed in micro-models. In this case a macro-theory becomes a means of *cumulating* micro-variables and micro-relations, of *aggregating* them into macro-quantities and relations between such quantities, in a model of the whole economy.

The first of these two ways of constructing a macro-model is exemplified in the theory of general equilibrium; the second in a theory of *aggregative* equilibrium. To most writers a macro-theory means only the second, and the term becomes virtually a synonym for "aggregative" theory.[1] This has terminological disadvantages in my opinion. For, if macro-theory signifies a theory employing only aggregative models, general-equilibrium theory, explicitly embracing all micro-models, belongs to micro-theory. Yet the theory of general equilibrium necessarily implies all aggregative equilibria since the conditions of general equilibrium cannot be satisfied unless all micro-variables are so adjusted to one another that all aggregative quantities likewise satisfy the conditions of aggregative equilibrium.[2] Thus, macro-equilibria are "contained" in the general micro-equilibrium—which contradicts the plain meaning of the words.

For this reason I find the terminology inept, and I would prefer other terms to identify the pair of concepts—for example, "relativistic" and "aggregative" theory. Nevertheless, I shall follow the majority of economists in the rest of this paper and use the terms "micro-theory" and "macro-theory," resigning myself to accepting the singularly odd presumption that the equilibria of all macro-models are logically contained in the allegedly micro-theoretical general equilibrium.

Alternative Distinctions

I find it a bit presumptuous to begin with an authoritarian definition which disregards the interpretations offered by other authors. Let us examine

---

[1] Ragnar Frisch is one of the minority in regarding the theory of general equilibrium as a part of macro-economics, because it is concerned with "the whole economic system taken in its entirety" and includes within it "all individual commodities, all individual entrepreneurs, all individual consumers." See his essay "Propagation Problems and Impulse Problems in Dynamic Economics" in *Economic Essays in Honour of Gustav Cassel* (London, 1933), p. 172. Most later writers have treated general equilibrium as micro-economics.

[2] See Joseph A. Schumpeter, *Business Cycles* (New York: McGraw-Hill, 1939), Vol. I, p. 43.

briefly some of the criteria proposed by various authors for distinguishing micro- and macro-theories.

(1) *Distinctions according to how one looks at the economy*

In order to distinguish different ways of looking at the economy, teachers have sometimes resorted to analogies, and have compared micro-economics to a view through a microscope and macro-economics to a view through a telescope. These analogies are poor for several reasons. One can use a telescope, just as a microscope, to look at details and at small segments of a whole. To the question how general-equilibrium models should be characterized, the analogy is of no help at all, especially since these models are designed to clarify both the details—like "cell movements," as it were—and the broad relationships. One may remember that microscopes and telescopes can be combined in a tele-microscope, but this instrument cannot catch the broad relationships that are so essential for the analysis of the general equilibrium.

(2) *Distinctions according to whose actions are analyzed*

It is certainly important to be clear about whose actions are visualized by an economic theory, and a fundamental distinction in this connection is that between individuals and groups. Micro-theory deals chiefly with the choices and decisions of the individuals who manage households or firms (although it should be understood that not real but only imaginary, fictitious households and firms, as makers of "typical" decisions, are meant here). Macro-theory, on the other hand, is chiefly concerned with the mode of behavior of groups of economic units with respect to cer- (assumed or estimated) aggregate economic quantities.

This distinction, however, is unsatisfactory in that it is not specific about the ways individuals are combined in groups. In "partial-equilibrium analysis" economists deal with multitudes of individuals whom they combine into groups—say, supply and demand in a market—and whose composite decisions or actions with reference to a particular commodity they analyze. For example, all actual or potential producers of sausages are grouped together as an industry—the sausage industry —and their idealized reactions to price changes are pictured as a supply function. Likewise, all actual and potential consumers of sausages are taken together as a group, and their idealized reactions to price changes are pictured in a demand function. Should one now say that, by casting these particular groups in the model of a market, one has built a macro-model? Or should this term be confined to other uses, for example to characterize less homogenous groups of economic units and their behavior with respect to altogether heterogenous aggregate quantities?

In principle it would be possible to take micro-theory to mean exclusively the theory of individual decision-makers, such as individual households and individual firms. If, however, by macro-theory is meant only a theory concerned with such completely heterogenous aggregate quantities as total income and total consumption, then the "realm of the middle" remains without a name.[3] The dichotomy of economic theory would then become impossible, since everything between the single individual and the whole nation—between the atom and the universe—would be left out of the picture. To escape from this dilemma one must expand the concept of micro-theory and relegate to it the behavior models of groups and subgroups with respect to particular commodities or classes of goods and services. If this is done, however, the distinction between individual and group no longer serves as the criterion for distinguishing between micro- and macro-economics.

(3) *Distinctions according to what is being aggregated*

Some have tried to remedy the defects of the previous distinction by drawing the line differently and distinguishing between the *summation of quasi-homogeneous quantities in micro-theory* and the *aggregation of totally heterogeneous quantities* in macro-theory. To be sure, the supply and demand functions of micro-theory do not refer to truly homogeneous quantities. Everybody knows that a Cadillac and a Volkswagen cannot for all purposes properly be lumped together as "two automobiles"; or that ten tons of writing paper and ten tons of newsprint cannot always be totaled as twenty tons of paper. For the purposes, however, for which micro-theory is ordinarily employed, it is as a rule legitimate and useful

---

[3] Schumpeter sometimes found this disturbing. He once remarked with reference to the cobweb theorem—a model of a market with lagged adjustments of supply—that it is "not indeed micro-economics, because it does not reach the individual deciding agents, but is not macro-economics either, because its models do not embrace the whole of the economy." Joseph A. Schumpeter, *A History of Economic Analysis* (New York: Oxford University Press, 1954), p. 1168.

to "homogenize" different products and services that form a distinct class, that is, to disregard the heterogeneity that exists in reality but is not relevant for the problem under investigation, and to assume homogeneity as a useful fiction.

In other words, in micro-theory one works with quantities that consist of fictitiously homogeneous units; the simplifying assumption of an "as-if-homogeneity" of the quantities in the abstract model has great heuristic advantages as long as neither the accuracy nor the applicability of the results is prejudiced by this assumption. Of course there are problems for which the differentiation between certain goods or services is essential. In such cases the summation of the different units would of course be inappropriate.

In the aggregate computations of macro-analysis, such as in the estimates of social accounting, the most different kinds of things are being aggregated (usually with their money values): thus there is total consumption, total investment, total export, total import, and of course total income, all magnitudes in which horses and apples are "added together" without any inhibitions. The problems of aggregation and disaggregation often cause considerable headaches, but the general idea is accepted that quite heterogeneous things are added together without involving us in any pretense at all of a fictitious homogeneity. It should be admitted, nevertheless, that the dividing line between a summation of as-if-homogeneous quantities and the aggregation of hopelessly heterogeneous quantities is sometimes hard to find and is usually quite arbitrary.

(4) *Distinctions according to what role is given to price relationships*

As an alternative to the subtle dividing line between degrees of heterogeneity, it is proposed to take as the criterion for the distinction the role that the model builders assign to relative prices. In micro-theory relative prices play an important role, in macro-theory they are usually left on one side.

But even in this respect there are exceptions: for example the rate of interest appears often quite prominently on the macro-stage, and sometimes the wage level or the price level (or rather indices of wage-rate or price changes) are admitted as actors on the stage. Usually, however, price relationships between different products, or between services and products, are banished from macro-theory, whereas they are essential for micro-theory. Closely associated with relative prices are, of course, relative quantities, for example, the relative inputs of different factors of production and the relative outputs of different products—variables normally neglected in macro-theory. If some time in the future someone should come up with a technique of building variables of this character into otherwise aggregative models, then these models would no longer be in the nature of pure macro-theory but of a combination of micro- and macro-economic elements.

Of the four distinguishing characteristics set out here I am most inclined to the last, for it is the simplest. Some renowned theorists have, however, preferred the third.[4] To this I have no serious objection. There many be circumstances under which the misgivings which I have expressed may become serious, but this, after all, is true for almost all distinctions. It is seldom possible to draw clear and sharp lines that make sense for all purposes.

What is really disturbing, however, with this business of distinguishing micro- and macro-theories is when adversaries in a controversy over the comparative advantages of micro- or macro-analysis draw the boundaries so differently that certain models, the heuristic superiority of which is recognized by both sides, are thought by each to belong to his camp. In such a case the quarrel is about nothing at all since both parties agree on everything except a definition.

There are many examples for such arguments without point. To illustrate, in a discussion between two writers on the theory of international trade the one regarded himself as a champion of micro-theory the other as a champion of macro-theory within their field of specialization. Eventually, however, it became evident that both were thinking of the theory of comparative cost, and how useful and important it was,—only that one of them regarded it as a micro-economic and the other as a macro-economic theory. On the basis of the second of the four grounds of distinction described above, the theory of comparative costs could with some justification be recognized as macro-theory, for it envisages not directly the actions of individual decision-makers but rather the resulting exchange activities of the economies as entities. On the other hand, on

---

[4] For example Kenneth E. Boulding, *Economic Analysis* (New York: Harper & Row, Publishers, Revised edition, 1948), p. 259 ff.

the basis of the third and fourth grounds of distinction, the theory would surely be regarded as micro-economic, since no aggregation of heterogeneous quantities is involved and the price relations between different goods are not only not neglected but in fact are the very essence of the theory.[5]

In any case we must take it as a fact to be reckoned with that there is no agreement on the meaning and scope of the concepts of micro- and macro-theory. We should be content if the different interpretations of the concepts overlap to the extent of perhaps three-fourths of the ideas encompassed.

Micro- and Macro-Theory in the History of Economic Thought

Although all the talk and quibbling over the comparative advantages of micro- and macro-theory began only some 25 years ago, after the publication of Keynes' *General Theory* (1936), we should not, for this reason, be induced to attribute the pair of concepts to Keynes. Even the terms are older: Ragnar Frisch used them as far back as 1933 and it was probably he who introduced them into economics.[6] The ideas can be traced back very far, although they remained nameless most of the time. Even the most superficial glance at the history of economic thought shows that both kinds of theory have been used for centuries and that macro-theories are perhaps older than micro-theories.

Among the best constructed of the early macro-theories were those of the physiocrats. Quesnay's *Tableau Economique* (1758) is one of the most remarkable macro-models that has ever been produced.[7] Wassily Leontief, as a builder of input-output matrices, and Schumpeter, as a historian of thought, both pay full tribute to the pioneer achievement of the physiocratic macro-model builder.[8]

---

[5] Another example of this type of conflict in interpretation is supplied in footnote 17 below.

[6] Ragnar Frisch, *op. cit.*

[7] François Quesnay, *Tableau économique* (Paris, 1758).

[8] Wassily W. Leontief, *The Structure of American Economy, 1919-39* (Cambridge: Harvard University Press, 1941), p. 9.—Joseph A. Schumpeter, *History of Economic Analysis* (New York: Oxford University Press, 1954). He calls Quesnay's work the "outstanding example for the alliance between Monetary and Aggregative Analysis." p. 278.

Theories of money in nearly all schools and doctrines are essentially macro-economic. This is particularly true, of course, of the circular-flow theories and of the quantity theory. In the formulations of the quantity theory from Davanzati (1588) through Irving Fisher (1911) there are virtually no traces of micro-theory,[9] the only exceptions being those of the theorists who discuss the demand for money to hold, that is the demand for liquid balances, on the part of individual households and firms, as a function of prices and incomes.

In classical economics, beginning with Adam Smith's great work (1776), micro- and macro-economic theory are found side by side or following each other, according to the problem in hand.[10] Smith gave no indication that he was aware of any methodological distinction. Apparently it seemed entirely natural in the explanation of relative values to start with individual trading partners, and not at all unnatural to leave out individual decisions when it came to the discussion of economic development.[11] Ricardo (1817) was perhaps more conscious of the difference. The micro-economic nature of rent theory, for example, was clearly brought out, while in his more dynamically oriented distribution theory macro-economic elements predominate, although, to be sure, the underlying methodological considerations were not discussed in either case.[12]

Cournot's work is entirely micro-theoretical.[13] There we find no doubt that each seller strives to maximize his profit and makes his calculations with references to his cost situation and his estimates of demand. Again,

---

[9] Bernardo Davanzati, *Lezioni delle monete* (Firenze, 1588). Irving Fisher, *The Purchasing Power of Money* (New York: Macmillan & Co., 1911).

[10] A great deal of classical theory is macro-theory, and does not depend for its justification or empirical relevance on micro analogies." M. H. Peston, "A view of the Aggregation Problem," *Review of Economic Studies*, Vol. XVII (Oct. 1959), p. 62. Peston's examples are "Smith and Ricardo on accumulation and the stock of capital."

[11] Adam Smith, *An Inquiry into the Nature and Causes of the Wealth of Nations* (London, 1776).

[12] David Ricardo, *Principles of Political Economy and Taxation* (London, 1817). A number of modern authors have commented on the macro-economic elements in Ricardo's distribution theory. See, for example, Robert Solow, "A Skeptical Note on the Constancy of Relative Shares," *American Economic Review*, Vol. XLVIII (1958), p. 618: "Beginning with Ricardo there have been sporadic revivals of interest in macro-economic theories of distribution."

[13] Antoine Augustin Cournot, *Recherches sur les principes mathématiques de la théorie des richesses* (Paris, 1838). Only in Chapters 11 and 12 are found vague hints about the possibility of developing a macro-theory.

the method is determined by the problem chosen—the determination of monopoly price, duopoly prices, etc.—but with Cournot it is deliberately executed and explicitly emphasized.

The vigorous controversies over monetary policy in the nineteenth century were based on current monetary theory, which was essentially macroeconomic. They ranged over questions of gold shortage and the price level, of the needs of trade, the liquidity of bills of exchange, and of the adequacy of the credit supply for the economy as a whole. (Only much later did it become clear that these questions would have been better resolved had one been clear about micro-theoretical presuppositions.)

Marx's Capital (1867) was essentially and consciously macro-economic.[14] This is true particularly for his theories of reproduction and accumulation, falling profit rates, increasing misery of the proletariat, industrial reserve army, concentration, etc.

The introduction of the theory of subjective value by Jevons (1871), Menger (1871), and Walras (1874) brought micro-theory decisively to the fore.[15] To the micro-model of the producer there was now added a micro-model of the consumer, and the choices of the individual household were given special emphasis. We have already noted at the outset that Walras built the many micro-models of the individual decisionmakers into his model of the general-equilibrium system of the economy as a whole. But it was Menger who most clearly formulated the foundations of "methodological individualism" and "methodological subjectivism," and who insisted on the validity of these principles for all theoretical economics.[16] Menger did not deny that the "empiric-realistic" theory of economics could, on the basis of observed "real types," provide useful generalizations without reference to the "ideal-type" models of the individual economic unit; but he considered that "exact theory," as he called it, with its ideal-type micro-models, was indispensable if one ex-

---

[14] Karl Marx, *Das Kapital* (Vol. I, Hamburg, 1867, Vol. II, 1885, Vol III, 1894).

[15] William Stanley Jevons, *The Theory of Political Economy* (London, 1871). Carl Menger, *Grundsätze der Volkswirtschaftslehre* (Wien, 1871). Leon Walras, *Elements d'Economie politique pure* (Lausanne and Paris, 1874).

[16] Carl Menger, *Untersuchungen über die Methode der Sozialwissenschaften und der Politischen Oekonomie insbesondere* (Leipzig, 1883). For a discussion of "methodological individualism" see Ludwig von Mises, *Human Action* (New Haven: Yale University Press, 1949), pp. 41ff.

pected to obtain general explanations from economic theory.[17] Thus the primacy of micro-theory in economics was emphatically proclaimed.

In spite of the widespread acceptance of Menger's methodology, the notion of an independent, autonomous macro-theory in economics was not undermined. Even the writers of the Austrian school did not eschew macro-theoretical constructions. For example, Böhm-Bawerk's capital theory (1889) was partly macro-economic.[18] Also the way in which Wicksell treated money in his general economic model, which had first rested on barter- and micro-models, must be recognized as macro-theoretical.[19]

On the other hand, Marshall, founder of the Cambridge School, was a micro-theorist *par excellence*.[20] His most important models were designed for partial-equilibrium analysis, especially for problems involving a single market or an individual firm, and recourse to the concept of the "representative firm" is characteristic of his style of model building. I mention this particularly because Keynes was a product of the Cambridge School.

---

[17] Menger's methodological individualism is not incompatible with the conviction that the needs, tastes, and behavior of the individual are strongly influenced, or even largely determined, by social norms—customs and manners, moral views, the legal order, or fashion. The economist, however, leaves these questions usually to the sociologist and social psychologist.

[18] Eugen von Böhm-Bawerk, *Positive Theorie des Kapitals* (Wien. 1888). Schumpeter writes that Böhm-Bawerk "started with a theory of individual behavior and with a theory of exchange. That is based upon it; but on the highest floor of his building there is almost nothing left but aggregates, such as (value of) the sum of total wage goods, (value of) total output, and an aggregative 'period of production' to boot." *Op. cit.*, p. 998.

[19] Knut Wicksell, *Lectures on Political Economy*, Vol. I, *General Theory*, Vol. II, *Money* (Swedish edition 1901 and 1906, German edition 1922, English edition London, 1935). Schumpeter considers Wicksell's use of the social production function as macro-theory and adds that "Wicksell reasoned on a social production function without displaying any symptoms of critical discomfort." *Op. cit.*, p. 998. If one stretches the concept of macro-theory to include production possibility curves (the production surface) with their elasticities of substitution, then the whole theory of relative costs and prices is virtually annexed. This does not correspond to the customary meaning of the words.

[20] Alfred Marshall, *Principles of Economics* (1st ed. London: Macmillan, 1890; 8th ed. 1920). In Schumpeter's *History* the micro theoretical attitude of Marshall is strongly emphasized: "it cannot be too often repeated that Marshall himself gave no lead toward macro-analysis." *Op cit.* p. 997.

If one wants to describe the situation in the economic thought of the first four decades of the twentieth century, one may say that in general the theories of money, credit, and business cycles were predominantly macro-economic, while price and distribution theories were micro-economic. But there were exceptions; the monetary theory of Mises (1913) was founded on micro-theoretical principles,[21] and there were attempts to explain the size and stability of relative income shares with the use of macro-theory, for example, by Douglas (1928, 1934) and Kalecki (1938).[22]

Following Keynes' *magnum opus*[23] (1936) the construction of macro-models came to dominate the work of economic theorists for the next twenty years. We shall consider the reasons for this later on. Our brief sketch of the role of the two methods in the history of economic thought was only designed to dispel the misconception that macro-theory began with Keynes, and to show that it is as old as economics itself.[24]

The Hidden Micro-Relations

One of the chief contributions of the Keynesian system is the simplicity with which it presents the macro-relations, that is, the relations between the aggregate quantities. This is especially evident in the case of the consumption function, $C = c(Y)$, which states that aggregate consumption is a function of aggregate income. But is this all there is to say about it? Ought one to stop here?

There are at least three possibilities for pushing beyond this point. The

---

[21] Ludwig von Mises, *Die Theorie des Geldes und der Umlaufsmittel* (München, 1914).

[22] Charles W. Cobb and Paul H. Douglas, "A Theory of Production," *American Economic Review*. Vol. XVIII, *Supplement* (1928), pp. 139-65. Paul H. Douglas, *The Theory of Wages* (New York: The Macmillan Co., 1934). Michael Kalecki, "The Determinants of Distribution of the National Income," *Econometrica*, Vol. 6 (1938), pp. 97-112.

[23] John Maynard Keynes, *General Theory of Employment, Interest and Money* (London: Macmillan, 1936).

[24] In his *History* Schumpeter tried to make this clear and to emphasize it by stating that Keynes had taken over "this Quesnay-Ricardo-Böhm-Wicksell method." *Op. cit.*, p. 998.

simplest is merely to inquire into the magnitude of the marginal propensity to consume, $\dfrac{\triangle C}{\triangle Y}$, or even about its probable limits within the system. This sufficed for Keynes' immediate purposes. The second possibility is to try to ascertain the form of the function from the statistics of aggregate income and aggregate consumption. This has been a popular sport for econometricians. The third possibility is to ask how the aggregate consumption function is made up from the individual consumption functions of all households. This is the problem of aggregating micro-relations in order to produce the macro-relations used in the macro-model.

In view of the imposing and fascinating progress in economic statistics and statistical method, it was to be feared that interest would remain focused on the "how?" of the aggregate functions and would not extend to the "how come?" Thus it is particularly encouraging that most econometricians have now recognized the problem of aggregation to be one of the fundamental problems of macro-theory itself. R. G. D. Allen, one of the leading mathematical and statistical economists, has expressed this in the following way:

Macro-economic models can be set up in their own right . . . on the assumption that, at least approximately, aggregate variables are directly and simply related. However, this cannot be satisfactory to an economist, conscious that relations between aggregates are the resultant of many decisions by consumers and firms. It is natural to wish to go behind the macro-relations, to see how individual decisions lead to stable relations in the aggregate—if indeed they do so at all.

The picture is then completely changed. The economic theory of any model runs on micro-terms, based on decisions taken, *e.g.* by individual consumers or firms; the macro-relations are derived constructions. There must be an explicit translation, through aggregation, from micro-relations to appropriate macro-relations. The translation may be and often is, of the crudest kind . . . Or the translation may involve more subtle (economic and statistical) considerations. The model is then based on *economic* theory in the form of many micro-relations between micro-variables, but expressed in terms of an *economic-statistical* construction of macro-relations between aggregate variables. The method of aggregation is vital, both in its economic aspect and in its statistical connotation in relation to available data.[25]

In this statement the fundamental nature, the primacy, of micro-theory

---

[25] R. G. D. Allen, *Mathematical Economics* (London: Macmillan, 1957), p. 694.

is recognized.[26] Micro-relations may remain empirically unascertainable and their aggregation may be a purely conceptual, theoretical problem. Nevertheless, theory ought not to stop where measurability ends. In the social sciences *"understanding"* (in Max Weber's sense)[27] stands above *measuring* in the hierarchy of methodological precepts.

Needless to say, it is not a duty for every macro-theorist to search for the hidden micro-relations that lie at the root of the macro-relations. No one is obliged to adapt his scientific curiosity to any methodological norm. To specialize in the construction of macro-models without worrying about the underlying micro-theories is neither unsound nor dishonourable. But to deny that all macro-theory requires a micro-theoretical underpinning, or to deride the efforts of those who do investigate it, would be unreasonable and obtuse. Fortunately such narrow-mindedness is becoming less frequent than it used to be.

---

[26] Similarly, Klein refers to "the behavior of individual households or firms which must form the basis of all theory of economic behavior." Lawrence R. Klein, "Macro-economics and the Theory of Rational Behaviour," *Econometrica,* Vol. 14 (April 1946), p. 93. Tinbergen regards macro-relationships as averages of micro-relationships. Jan Tinbergen, *Statistical Testing of Business Cycle Theories,* Vol. I: *A Method and Its Application to Investment Activity* (Geneva: League of Nations, 1938).—Both these views are criticized by Peston: "If macro-theory is first of all treated as subsidiary to micro-theory, and is then expected to produce conclusions which depend on the structural interrelations of micro-variables, either contradictions will result because the demand is impossible, or the macro-theory will be successful and leave no place for micro-theory." M. H. Peston, *op. cit.,* p. 59—The apparent contradiction between these views can be resolved when we reflect on what is meant by a "successful" theory. If the success of a theory—a macro-theory, in this instance—consists in its yielding correct predictions and surviving several statistical tests, then nothing more is needed. If, however, success of a theory means also that it fits in with a grand deductive system and can be derived from the fundamental postulates which have proved valid for a whole body of knowledge representative of the particular science, then the position rejected by Peston, that is, "the doctrine that micro-theory is fundamental theory and all other theory must be built up from it," (*op. cit.,* p. 60), must be sustained.

[27] The role of "understanding" in the social sciences, of which Max Weber was the chief protagonist, has been demonstrated with especial clarity in the work of the late Alfred Schütz. See especially his "Common-Sense and the Scientific Interpretation of Human Action," *Philosophy and Phenomenological Research,* Vol. XIV (1953), pp. 1-37.

II. The Alleged Superiority
of Macro-Theory

We shall now discuss a number of misconceptions which occasionally arise in the arguments over the comparative advantages of micro-theory and macro-theory. Our discussion is not aimed at any of the leading writers—most of whom do not run afoul of these misconceptions—but is designed to clarify problems which regularly perplex students and lead many of them astray.

The Superior Strength of Macro-Forces

The miniature precision work of micro-theory is sometimes held to be superfluous because micro-relations must give way in the face of the greater strength of macro-economic forces. If macro-relations will in the end dominate over micro-relations, why waste time and effort on the complications of the micro-theory?

Assume that we know the investment and production plans of all firms, and assume further that we know that these plans exceed what is possible with the given supply of capital or labour. We then conclude that not all of the plans can be fulfilled, and that sooner or later some of them will have to be abandoned as impracticable or cut down to a more moderate size. Why should we then analyze what turns out to be impossible, why should we not immediately move on to a discussion of what is practicable? The answer to this question is not difficult. Among the most important tasks of economic theory is to explain why and under what circumstances expectations will be disappointed and decision-makers will be forced to change their plans. The theory must explain the limits that are set to the execution of plans, not only in the aggregate but also in the particular instances, for example by the supply of capital, which in turn has to be explained by principles strongly founded in micro-theory. One might say, perhaps, that the upper limit of the supply of capital can be approximately defined without micro-analysis; and, even more clearly that the limits of the supply of labour could be ascertained without micro-theoretical considerations. There remains, nonetheless, the need for a theory of plan adjustment. This is an inescapable problem, especially since this adjustment of plans is dictated by changes in prices, which in themselves are the primary subject of economic analysis for a market economy.

Consider the similar problem of micro-functions of such shapes and sizes that their aggregation would yield a macro-function which could not possibly prevail in the long run. Assume, for example, that so many individual marginal propensities to consume are greater than 1 that the aggregate marginal propensity to consume would also exceed 1. Such an economy could have only the most unstable equilibrium, for the smallest rise in investment would lead to an explosive increase in the national income, and the slightest decline in investment to a precipitous fall in income. (The explosive increase would presuppose, of course, the help of the banks, including the central bank.) Some macro-theorists conclude from this that the aggregate consumption function simply cannot have the form supposedly determined by the micro-functions, in particular that the aggregate marginal propensity to consume cannot be greater than 1 and that this, therefore, sets a limit to the individual propensities to consume.

This way of thinking runs perilously close to assuming that things are in fact what they ought to be if our theory is to be simple. If it is true that the aggregate marginal propensity to consume in the long run is in actual fact not greater than 1, or if it is true that it cannot be greater than 1, then the economic theorist has the task to explain how it comes about that there are these limits to consumption by individual households. This micro-theoretical task, incidentally, is not very hard. For it is certainly not difficult to understand why most people do not plan in the long run to consume more than their income (even if they do not mind doing so in the short run). No macro-theoretical Procrustean bed is required for this explanation.

A more difficult question is the analysis of the factors determining the functional distribution of income, particularly of the reasons for the approximate stability of the share of wages in the national income, which in the United States amounts to around 65 per cent. The micro-theorist starts out with the consideration of the distribution of a goodly number of variables:

Between production functions and factor-ratios on the one hand, and aggregate distributive shares on the other lies a whole string of intermediate variables: elasticities of substitution, commodity-demand and factor-supply conditions, markets of different degrees of competitiveness and monopoly, far-from-neutral taxes. It is hard to believe that the theory offers any grip at all on the variability of relative shares as the data change . . .[28]

Professor Solow asks whether one really needs a special theory which explains "how a number of unruly micro-economic markets are willy-nilly squeezed into a tight-fitting size 65 straight-jacket."[29] Is there perhaps a macro-theoretical system from which the "magic number" can be deduced? "It would be nice to have a single aggregative bulldozer principle with which to crash through the hedge of micro-economic interconnections and analogies."[30] But this bulldozer has not yet turned up, and Professor Solow is not convinced that it ever will.

Faith in a macro-economic principle of such blunt power that the entire intricate network of micro-theory is pushed firmly aside is not well founded. To be sure, micro-theory has never succeeded in explaining exact numerical values of economic quantities such as the prices of oranges and refrigerators, wage rates and rentals, the velocity of circulation of money and the rate of savings, the growth in the gross national product and the distributive shares. Economists must be satisfied with explaining *why* such quantities in pure theory must in general be taken as determinate and *how* they will react to changes in certain data. Thus, we cannot say why the share of wages in total income works out to around 65 per cent. We rest content if we can point to the kind of changes that might cause this share to fall or to rise, and if we can indicate why the results of many small changes can be mutually offset. When one notices, by the way, that this strange stability is somewhat illusory—the share of American workers' income has in fact fluctuated between 63.6 per cent and 68.9 per cent since 1945, and between 58.2 per cent and 73.4 per cent since 1929— then there is really not quite so much to explain after all.

Equilibrium Theory

For one reason or another, perhaps because the term "equilibrium" is more frequently used in micro-theory or because some writers have

---

[28] Solow, *op. cit.*, p. 628. This brilliant article should not be missed by any student of economic theory.

[29] *Ibid.*, p. 628.

[30] *Ibid.*, p. 626.

spoken of "equilibrium theory" when they evidently referred only to micro-theory, some students do not realize that equilibrium plays the same role in macro-theory; and that macro-theory is therefore as much equilibrium theory as is micro-theory. In the micro-model of the perfect market [31] there is a determinate "equilibrium price" because at higher prices there will be excess supply and at lower prices excess demand; adjustment of the quantities supplied and demanded must go on until the price is reached at which the two quantities are equal. Similarly, in the macro-model of the national accounts there is a determinate "equilibrium income" because at higher incomes there will be excess saving and at lower incomes excess investment; adjustments must continue until the income is reached at which the two magnitudes are equal. Naturally there are differences between the two adjustment mechanisms, but such differences exist also between the adjustment mechanisms of different micromodels. For example, in the model of the individual firm, the entrepreneur adjusts his output of goods to his own cost and market estimates, while in the model of the industry, the adjustment is made to the actions of competitors, etc. In macro-models it is always a group—for example, the group comprising all consumers—whose reactions are involved in the process of adjustment or equilibration. In micro-models it need not be a group but may be an individual decision-maker whose adjustments constitute the equilibration; on the other hand, in the micro-model of the general-equilibrium system (if it is regarded as a micro-model) and in the particular-equilibrium system of the market or the industry, group reactions are the essence of the equilibration.

Both in micro-theory and in macro-theory the equilibrium concept should be understood as nothing but a mental device for conducting mental experiments. It is never quite appropriate to treat any concrete historical situation as an equilibrium, no matter whether it refers to price and output or to aggregate income and consumption. The equilibrium of an abstract model refers to a set of precisely stipulated variables and relationships. Precisely the same imaginary "situation" that is shown to constitute an equilibrium between, say, five or six stipulated variables would immediately become a disequilibrium if one other variable were

---

[31] The concept of the "perfect market" should not be confused with the various concepts of competition. See Fritz Machlup, *The Economics of Sellers' Competition* (Baltimore: Johns Hopkins University Press, 1952), pp. 116-124.

introduced into the model. In the real world there are an immense number of variables, which are neither stipulated nor known, and it is therefore absurd to treat any real economic situation as an equilibrium state of affairs.

Neither in micro-theory nor in macro-theory is it admissible to smuggle value judgments into the equilibrium concept. If certain states of affairs that are widely regarded as politically desirable are described as "equilibrium conditions," students are misled about the positive findings, that is, the causal connections; normative points of view are then concealed in a presumably exact theory. It should be categorically stated that equilibrium is neither a Good Thing nor a Bad Thing; it is nothing other than the imaginary point at which the results deduced from a presupposed cause (that has operated under presupposed conditions) can be regarded as complete—and this holds for macro-models as for micro-models.[32]

All things considered, macro-models and micro-models use the equilibrium concept in exactly the same way and to the same extent; no difference can be found between macro- and micro-theory in this respect.

Statics and Dynamics

The notion that micro-theory is "static" whereas macro-theory is "dynamic," or at least "more dynamic" or "more easily dynamized," seems to persist in the minds of the less sophisticated students of economics. Even though "static" and "dynamic" are kaleidoscopic words with shifting meanings,[33] this notion is wrong, no matter which of the countless meanings of the words are accepted. To be sure, the victims of this misconception can defend themselves by pointing to the fact that Keynes himself presented his macro-model as "dynamic theory."[34] Yet, not only the critics of Keynes but also his most convinced supporters have rejected

---

[32] For a more careful exposition of these ideas about the equilibrium concept see my essay, "Equilibrium and Disequilibrium: Misplaced Concreteness and Disguised Politics," *Economic Journal*, Vol. LVXIII (1958), pp. 1-24. Reproduced in the present volume, pp. 43-72.

[33] See my essay, "Statics and Dynamics: Kaleidoscopic Words," *Southern Economic Journal*, Vol. XXVI (1959), pp. 91-110. Reproduced in the present volume, pp. 9-42.

[34] John Maynard Keynes, *op. cit.*, pp. vi-vii.

the idea.[35] The original form of the Keynesian macro-model was static in every sense of the word.

In recent literature most writers have called a theory "dynamic" if variables of different periods of time are assumed to be causally related so that, for example, a variable dated today is determined, or partly determined, by one of yesterday and can in turn influence the value of a variable of tomorrow. The macro-model of Keynes contains only undated variables and his own definitions prescribe that processes are timeless or causes and effects simultaneous. Only later reconstructions of his model by other "architects" have produced process models adapted to period analysis in which, for example, the income of yesterday is connected with the consumption of today, which will then influence the output of tomorrow. (The time intervals are usually not specified but merely the time sequences, although sometimes a quarter-year interval is spoken of.[36])

Such a process model shows not only the position of the new equilibrium but also the stages on the way to the new equilibrium. To the enlightened equilibrium theorist it has always been clear that the equilibrium position is no more than the fictitious terminal point of a process of adjustment and that the practical significance of equilibrium analysis is found in the movement, not in the final position.[37] For some problems the intermediate points (apart from the direction of the movement) are more interesting than the fictitious destination. This is particularly true with respect to the successive changes of aggregate quantities such as income and saving, and therefore dynamic macro-theory is as a rule more useful than static macro-theory which, ignoring the stages passed through

---

[35] Gottfried Haberler, *Prosperity and Depression* (Geneva: League of Nations, 3rd ed., 1941), p. 473; Joseph A. Schumpeter, *op. cit.*, p. 1183. Cf. also Paul Samuelson, Oskar Lange, Arthur Smithies, *et al.*

[36] As an example I may refer to my model of income propagation presented in 1939. See "Period Analysis and Multiplier Theory," *Quarterly Journal of Economics*, Vol. LIV (1939), pp. 1-27. Reproduced in *Readings on Business Cycle Theory*, ed. Gottfried Haberler (Philadelphia: Blakiston, 1944), pp. 203-234.

[37] The fact that economic statics describes only the fictitious terminal points, not the path of the movement, must not make us forget that statics too serves to explain change. If "comparative statics" shows the equilibrium positions for two different constellations of data, this is to explain the movement from one position to the other as the effect of the respective change in data. On the close connection between dynamics and comparative statics, see Paul A. Samuelson, "The Stability of Equilibrium: Comparative Statics and Dynamics," *Econometrica*, Vol. IX (1941), pp. 97-120.

during the process of adjustment, jumps immediately to the imaginary end point.

Of course there are also process models in micro-theory. Probably the best known of these is the so-called cobweb theorem for markets with lagged adjustments of the quantity supplied. In this model the amount supplied at any one time is a function of a market price ruling at an earlier period; the market price of today will determine the quantities of goods which at some future point will come on the market. The purpose of this dynamic micro-model is to explain the conspicuous fluctuations in prices and quantities in markets for products which are produced under particular types of circumstances.

In one of my books I presented a dynamic micro-model that was designed to explain the pricing and selling policies adopted by certain sellers. The problem was to show that the *sequence* in which changes in prices and in expenditures on advertising were made was decisive for the volume of sales. It takes a process model to make this clear.[38]

One must not fall into the error of assuming that dynamic theory is in general better than static theory. Dynamics is no more superior to statics than a hammer is superior to a drill or a screwdriver. Each of these tools has its own use and is less suitable for other uses. If the time-processes and exact sequences of adjustment are not important in a theoretical problem in economics, the use of dynamic theory is superfluous; if they are important, static theory is inadequate. Perhaps it is true that there are more problems in micro-theory for which the static technique is sufficient than there are in macro-theory. But this need not remain true in the future. In time it may well happen that building activity in micro-dynamics will increase and large numbers of micro-dynamic models will be constructed.

Some writers have held that static theory is characterized by models containing only a few variables of which only one is independent, and dynamic theory by models containing a larger number of independent variables. This meaning of statics and dynamics is now obsolete, but even if one adhered to it, the assertion that macro-models are in general "more dynamic" than micro-models would still be untenable. For there are a good

---

[38] Fritz Machlup, *The Economics of Sellers' Competition* (Baltimore: Johns Hopkins University Press, 1952), pp. 185-189.

many macro-models that work with only a single independent variable, to wit, aggregate investment.

When all is said and done, it is clear that micro-dynamics and macro-statics, if this jargon must be retained, have fundamentally the same claim to methodological respectability as have micro-statics and macro-dynamics, no matter what may be the relative frequency with which each type of theory is currently used.

Ex Ante and Ex Post

A widespread misconception, in the propagation of which some well-known authors are implicated, relates to the distinction between *ex post* and *ex ante* magnitudes and is based on the belief that macro-theory permits and fosters the use of *ex post* magnitudes while micro-theory deals only with *ex ante* magnitudes. This notion rests upon a number of fallacies, and we must start at the beginning to get the matter clear. The somewhat dubious *ex post* magnitudes involved are usually contained in so-called identity equations; consequently we must start by clarifying the function of such equations in a theoretical system.

If one writes an equation such as $M=N$, where M and N may each be composed of several parts, the equation can have a number of very different meanings. For example, the equation may mean that (1) the two magnitudes are accidentally equal *(coincidence)*; (2) the two magnitudes are assumed to be equal for the purposes of hypothetical reasoning *(hypothetical assumption)*; (3) the two magnitudes are equal because somebody does something to make them equal in response either to an inner compulsion or an external order *(policy, norm)*; (4) the two magnitudes are equal because there is some force of an anonymous nature that will come into operation to make them equal *(tendency)*; (5) the equality of the two magnitudes is a condition for something to occur or not to occur, that is, for the existence of some situation or event *(equilibrium condition)*; (6) the two magnitudes are equal by definition, that is, they measure the same thing and cannot logically be different *(identity)*.

It is a sin of omission if a mathematically inclined writer leaves his readers unclear about the meaning of his equations. Fortunately, it is becoming customary for model-builders to indicate for each equation whether it represents a personal attitude, a behavior, a policy norm, a technical necessity, an equilibrium condition, or an identity (definition). To confuse a definition with an equilibrium condition is a bad mistake. For example, if one defines saving and investment so that they are the same, he cannot at the same time say that there is some force operating to adjust saving to investment. On the other hand, if one describes such an adjustment process, he must not at the same time define the two quantities to be the same by definition. A proposition concerning an occurrence or process can never be derived as the "consequence" of a definitional identity.

Many identity equations are essentially classifications. For example, suppose we divide the number of births (B) into live births (L) and stillborn (S). We then get the identity $B = L + S$. These symbols do not represent three independent quantities but only two, for one counts live births and stillbirths and adds them. If L and S are already established facts, then we speak of *ex post* magnitudes. Of course, a mistake may have been made and a recount or check of some sort may show that the number of stillborn was actually larger than was originally reported; in this case, the sum, B, must be larger too. The conclusion, that B is larger if S is larger, must surely not lead one to assert that the number of births will be larger if more children are killed at or before birth. This sort of increase of S would not be a consequence of a correction of a report on an already established fact—i.e. *ex post*—but it would be the consequence of actions taken, a measure carried out, a process occurring. In this case one speaks of *ex ante* because the actions precede the consequences, the results are effected by an antecedent cause. The increase in S is *ex post* if it constitutes the correction of a statistical error; it must raise B, provided L had been correctly reported. On the other hand, the increase in S is *ex ante* if it is brought about by some event or act; it must reduce L, since it cannot affect B.

Ex ante relationships can of course be much more complicated. Assume that many parents want a certain number of children and that they therefore seek to induce or prevent pregnancy. Then the actual relationship between L and S during any given period of time may influence the number of births at a later period. Thus, an increase in S_1 may lead to an increase in B_2 and, indeed, to an increase in both S_2 and L_2, because parents who were disappointed as a result of stillbirths in Year 1 may plan to have children in Year 2. This kind of relationship is expressed by means of the lagged variables of dynamic equations.[39]

Macro-theory is full of this sort of thing. For example, think of the identity equation that says that profits (P) are either paid out as dividends (D) or reinvested in the firm (R); thus $P = D + R$. If, in any period, the dividends paid turn out to be higher than was originally reported, while retained earnings were correctly reported, then P must increase along with D. These are *ex post* magnitudes. If, however, corporations just before the end of the year decide to distribute extra dividends, then of course R will be decreased by the same amount that D is increased. This is a statement *ex ante* about the consequences of actions. If one further assumes that corporations do not use their retained earnings for real investments but rather for increasing their liquid cash holdings, whereas share holders spend their dividends for consumption, then an increase of D may, through the consequent increase in effective demand, lead to an increase in profits, P, which in turn involves an increase in D or R, or both. This last *ex ante* possibility should, however, be expressed by an equation with lagged variables, since D does not raise P at the same time; D_1 raises P_2, and with it D_2 and R_2.

The described sequence of events is by no means "necessary" or even the most probable of several alternatives. The outcome may be the exact opposite. Assume that share holders prefer to keep their dividends in the form of liquid balances while the firms would have invested the undistributed profits in real assets. Under these circumstances, increased dividend payments would diminish the profits of the next period: D_1 decreases P_2, and with it $D_2 + R_2$. From the simple equation $P = D + R$ none of this follows.

And now for one more example, this time relating to saving and investment. Let S_P and I_P represent planned saving and investment, and S_r and I_r the actually realized amounts saved and invested, respectively. From the identity $S_r = I_r$ nothing follows. If we divide the realized *(ex post)* quantities into planned and unplanned amounts, then the identity becomes $S_p + S_u = I_p + I_u$. Again, nothing follows from this equation. Yet, if the same equation is interpreted *ex ante*, and $S_p = I_p$ is

---

[39] Not all equations containing dated variables pertaining to different dates are for that matter necessarily composed of *ex ante* magnitudes. For example, the two terms in Robertson's definition of savings, $S_t = Y_{t-1} - C_t$, are determined *ex post*.

stated as an equilibrium condition, then the set of equations acquires implications concerning occurrences to be expected. If the equilibrium condition was originally fulfilled and then S_p suddenly increases, what will happen? The equations themselves give no answer; one needs to add behavior functions which show how producers will react to a market decline and what savers will do with their savings. If the new saving does not reduce interest rates or improve liquidity conditions or otherwise induce higher investment, then sales will fall and producers will find themselves with smaller profits, greater inventories, reduced cash, or perhaps more debts. The *ex post* equation will be realized partly through unplanned saving (negative S_u) and partly through unplanned accumulation of inventories (I_u); but without behavior functions one can say nothing about the further course of events, and this is what really matters. Will there be induced decreases in production, declining prices, changes in interest rates, unemployment, unemployment benefits, budget deficit, or what? About these matters the equation has nothing to tell us. Nevertheless, the little trick of dividing saving and investment into their planned and unplanned components is useful because it invites the more thoughtful to think about the relevant *ex ante* relationships, especially about the probable reactions to unplanned events.

Now we are in a better position to appreciate the role of *ex post* magnitudes in macro-models: they are part of definitions and as such have nothing to say about causal relationships. Naturally one needs definitions as much in micro- as in macro-theory; but the micro-theorists have, as a rule, been more careful in dealing with them and have seldom made the mistake of attempting to derive statements about cause-and-effect from definitions alone. Macro-theorists have not always been careful and have repeatedly been misled into thinking that they could deduce consequences from an *ex post* definition, for example, that they could deduce the effects of an increase in investment from the definitional equation $Y = C + I$. This is logically impossible, and therefore equally inadmissible in macro-theory and in micro-theory.

Measurability

Perhaps it was the inclusion in macro-theory of *ex post* aggregate economic magnitudes that led to the close association between macro-theory and statistical social accounting and econometric research. In any event, it is often asserted that the magnitudes and relationships which make up the macro-models are measurable while the magnitudes and relationships of micro-models are not measurable. Behind this assertion lies, if not a misconception, at least an exaggeration of differences.

It is undoubtedly incorrect to say that the development of social accounting was a consequence of Keynesian macro-theory. The pioneering, conceptual, methodological, and statistical work of measuring the national income and its components preceded the work of Keynes.[40] Perhaps one can fairly agree that increased interest in statistical data was aroused because the new macro-models cried out for statistical testing. And it is true that the econometricians have for the most part worked with macro-models. However, this was the natural consequence of the fact that in quick succession economic statistics provided for the first time reliable data for social accounting and economic theory created macro-models suitable for the new kinds of problems that had arisen during the depression of the 1930's.

Before we can judge the measurability of the variables and relationships in a theoretical model, it is necessary to clarify the distinction between mental constructs and operational concepts. An operational definition describes the operations used in determining or measuring an observed state or event.[41]. If there are a variety of operations, then there

---

[40] The National Bureau of Economic Research, in New York, began its activities with measurements of national income and published its first work on this subject in 1921: Wesley C. Mitchell, Willford I. King, Frederick R. Macaulay, Oswald W. Knauth, *Income in the United States: Its Amount and Distribution, 1909-1919* (New York: National Bureau of Economic Research, 1921). A respectable series of similar investigations followed, among others those by W. I. King and by Maurice Leven, cultimating in the work of Kuznets. See especially, Simon Kuznets, *National Income and Capital Formation, 1919-1935* (New York: National Bureau of Economic Research, 1937), and *National Income and Its Composition, 1919-1938* (New York: National Bureau of Economic Research, 1941).

[41] The notion of the "operational concept" comes from the American physicist Percy W. Bridgman, in his *The Logic of Modern Physics* (New York: Macmillan & Co., 1927). The idea, and the demand that all empirical disciplines employ only operational concepts, were accepted and energetically expounded by many neopositivists. To give Bridgman's own example, the concept "length" is defined by the operation of repeatedly "laying on" a measuring rod to the object measured. Distance between two planets is, therefore, something quite different, since for this measuring operations must be employed.

will be a variety of concepts. If, for example, we endeavor to discover the price of a good, we can ask sellers what their prices are, or perhaps what their net proceeds are, or we can ask the buyers what they have paid, or we can look into the trade journals. Each of these is a different operational concept of price and it would be sheer accident if the figures obtained by these different methods for the same good at the same time actually coincided. A theoretical model of price determination contains, on the contrary, an idealized construct of price which is an imagined not an observed (reported or recorded) price. This is a fundamental difference. A mental construction is not measurable, though it is often so devised that it corresponds to something observable, perhaps measurable, or to some thing derived from observations; or that something observable, perhaps measurable, corresponds to deduced consequences of a conjunction of constructs. One usually says that operational concepts are the empirical "counterparts" of mental constructs; a "pure" (unreal, fictitious) construct in an abstract model may have one or more operational (empirical) counterparts in reality. (The construct is "pure" in that it is free from the "impurities," the countless side-phenomena existing in coarse reality. The essence of a thing in its ideal purity can only be displayed by a fiction.[42])

---

[42] Several scholars have put great importance on the difference between abstraction and construction and have insisted that the epistemological value of abstractions "derived from reality" was higher than that of "arbitrary constructions." Walter Eucken argued that the latter merely involve playing mental games and he stated: "Correctly derived models are not 'constructed models,' as they are called, but quite the contrary." *Die Grundlagen der Nationalökonomie* (Berlin-Göttingen-Heidelberg: 6th ed., 1950), p. 270. My own position, in brief, is this: The fact that a model is designed to help in the explanation of observed reality sets, of course, a limit to the whims of its builders. In order to succeed in explaining reality the model must be so designed that it contains the variables and relations presumed to be relevant. Hence it makes little difference whether one interprets it as a useful "construction" or as the result of a useful "abstraction" from reality. Consider, for example, a model of an economy without transport costs—a most important and useful model. One can say that it is derived from reality and that one has merely abstracted from transportation costs, which are not relevant for the given problem and would unnecessarily complicate the relationships. Or one can say that one has constructed an imaginary model of a spaceless economy and that the construction permits simplified mental experiments adequate for the purposes of the problem. It makes little difference in essence which method of expression one uses. From a pedagogical point of view I find it advantageous to speak of constructions, for if one works with models which contain only five or six

The question therefore is not whether the constructs built into macro-models are more easily measurable than are those of micro-models—since abstractions and constructions can never be measured at all—but whether they have better operational counterparts than the constructs of micro-models. The models of economic theory usually contain two types of construct: *variables,* for example, prices, outputs, costs, quantities demanded, income, consumption, saving, investment, etc., and *relations* (between two or more variables), for example, cost functions, demand functions, consumption functions, investment functions, etc. With respect to *variables* it seems to me that our question permits a relatively unambiguous answer: one can find for micro-variables just as easily observable and measurable operational counterparts as for macro-variables.

Indeed, prices, output, and sales of a good are more easily established than are national income, aggregate consumption, and aggregate investment. The different kinds of statistical procedures and techniques for calculating national income are well known; according to the different operations and manipulations used by statisticians there are numerous different operational concepts of national income. (Different results, for example, are obtained according to whether tax statistics, production statistics, trade statistics, etc., are used to estimate the incomes of individual groups, and according to what prices are used—factor cost or market prices—if and how changed valuations of inventories or foreign-exchange reserves are treated, if and how residential properties and durable consumer goods are depreciated, etc.) The pure construct of national income is untouched by most of these operational travails; it simply has a number of different operational concepts as alternative counterparts. The operational concepts which represent the counterparts of the pure constructs of

---

variables it sounds somewhat forced to say that one has merely abstracted from a reality which contains thousands of variables.

From an epistemological standpoint the difference may perhaps be significant, for if one is analyzing the origin of knowledge, one asks whether the concepts that serve as explanations are freely invented or are derived from observation. The psychological origin of knowledge is, however, irrelevant from a logical point of view, and the explanatory value does not depend on the origin. Of course, the invention which lies behind a construct must be useful for its purpose, that is the construct must do its job of helping in an explanation. Abstractions "distilled from experience" and constructions "freely invented" have the same status as far as the joint verification of sets of hypotheses is concerned.

micro-variables are also numerous and diverse but, at least for partial analysis, they require less cumbersome and intricate operations (computations). Of course, the more qualities and types of product that are manufactured by an industry the more difficult problems are presented in the calculation of price and output for the "product" of the industry; but these same problems must also be solved for the aggregate quantities in social accounting, which contain the values of the products of all separate industries as their components, and hence involve the aggregation of thousands of sub-aggregates resulting from as many intermediate calculations.

But what is the situation with respect to the operational counterparts of the constructs of relationships, the imagined *relations* between variables, such as, say, behavior functions? Is not the measurement of relations in macro-analysis easier and more reliable than in micro-analysis? Have not econometricians been more successful in their attempts to calculate macro-relations, for example, the aggregate consumption function, than they have been in the few attempts to discover micro-relations, for example, the demand functions for certain agricultural products?

If one means by "successful" that a much greater number of statistical macro-functions have been produced which within a year or two proved wrong or inapplicable, then, but only then, can one call the measurement of macro-relations successful. For statistical consumption functions and investment functions have indeed been produced in far greater numbers than statistical supply or demand functions for particular goods. But neither the former nor the latter have stood up to testing against new data.

This is not mentioned with malice or condescension. The effort, ingenuity, and patience of econometricians deserve recognition and respect. Their failures are caused, as I see it, by the very nature of the problem: too many things change in reality which in our abstract models are held unchanged. Indeed it is hard to understand why we should expect behavior functions to remain constant for any long period, let alone forever. Perhaps one may assume that in many cases the changes in many individual behavior functions will offset each other so that one can rely on the law of large numbers to keep the aggregate function reasonably stable. Be this as it may, we have not as yet succeeded in establishing any empirical aggregate relationship that has proved better, over any period, short or long, than the "naive model" which assumes that aggregate quantities will have the same value in any given year as in the previous year.[43]

In the eyes of many, a theory deserves the greater respect the more easily it can be tested—at least in principle—by means of empirical data. It is alleged that macro-theory has this advantage over micro-theory. But this is to some extent a matter of comparative audacity. Macro-econometricians are daring and confident enough to publish numerical hypotheses —which are verifiable, to be sure, but which have never survived a test. Micro-econometricians are not so optimistic as their colleagues, and publish only rarely any numerical hypotheses on micro-relations. Their hypotheses would be just as verifiable—and would have just as little chance to survive. Micro-econometricians could easily construct masses of models and compute the necessary coefficients to predict the prices of cereals, consumption of electricity, sales of textiles, etc. Only their superior insight and caution prevent them from doing so. Many "experts" are employed to prepare such micro-economic forecasts and if they are lucky they may hit the bull's eye, or at least the inner circle. But for the most part their forecasts are projections of trends corrected by a strong admixture of common sense, intuition, and a general feeling for events. Micro-courage, for better or for worse, has not been up to taking the risk of providing econometric models, complete with all accessories, inclusive of regression coefficients and random variables.

To make a long story short, let me state that I do not think much of the measurability of behavior functions and other relations, and I do not believe in the measurability of macro-relations any more than in that of micro-relations. Furthermore, I doubt the constancy of such relations and therefore do not see how it would help much even if we could measure them. What is the point of laboriously calculating an elasticity of demand of last year if all is changed next year?[44] And on what grounds

---

[43] This method of comparison was proposed by Professor Milton Friedman in order to deal with the claims to successful testing put forward by many forecasters whose predictions on the basis of a complicated formula diverged five or ten per cent from the actual values. Friedman recommended the rejection of a formula if the predicted result did not in fact come nearer than the naive prediction of "no change."

[44] The acute remarks of Lionel Robbins on this question deserve to be read and re-read. Lionel Robbins, *An Essay on the Nature and Significance of Economic Science* (London: Macmillan, 2nd ed., 1935), pp. 107-112.

do we dare to assume that the aggregate investment function calculated from data of past years will hold in future years?

The law of large numbers, it bears repeating, might make it appear more plausible to assume somewhat greater stability of certain macro-relations. It is also conceivable that for similar reasons a macro-model could do without some variables and some relationships between variables which would seem indispensable in a micro-model. These are the only arguments which, in my opinion, can support the proposition that the problems of measurability may be more easily solved in macro-analysis than in micro-analysis.

Applicability

The last of the misconceptions I want to treat here relates to the question of the relative applicability of the theories. One often hears it said that macro-theory is more applicable than micro-theory. It this true?

First we must be clear that the problems of measurability and of applicability are not the same. It is quite easy to see that a purely qualitative theory, a theory which merely concerns itself with the direction of change or movement, does not involve measurement (in the strict sense) but may still be applicable. The greater part of economic theory is of this kind. Even if it is "quantitative" and can be formulated with the aid of algebraic or geometric models, it may not be "numerical." "Larger" and "smaller," "rising" and "falling," are applicable judgments without the necessity of measurement (at least in the strict sense of the word).

The application of a theory can be attempted on three levels: the course of events can, with the help of a theory, be (a) explained, (b) predicted, or (c) controlled. These three objectives of science—"savoir pour prévoir pour pourvoir," as Comte has neatly put it—are here ordered according to the size of the task. We can often explain after the event but not predict; we can often predict but not control. Explanation of the past, if it is of recognized importance, is called history. Attempts to control the future, especially if undertaken by the State, are called policy. Thus the three levels on which economic theory is applicable are (a) economic history; (b) economic forecasting, and (c) economic policy. (This is perhaps a little superficial, but it will do for our purposes.)

Economic history is quite impartial in the rivalry between micro- and macro-theory and makes use of each. If one wants to explain the greater prosperity of coastal cities and states in antiquity, one immediately thinks of merchant ships and of the importance of transport costs; if one wants to explain the trade routes of the Middle Ages or the development of markets, towns, and guilds, one relies on models of exchange, costs, prices, monopoly, and competition; and if one wants to explain the effects of the continental blockade, the Zollverein, or the growth of railroads, one again turns to the theory of relative prices. If, however, one wants to deal with the debasement of coins in ancient Egypt, the policy of the mercantilists toward the precious metals, the depreciation of the Assignats, the inflations after the war, or the depression of the thirties, one will use aggregative theory. Micro- and macro-theory serve the economic historian with equal readiness.

Similarly, economic forecasting uses macro-theory and micro-theory according to the task in hand. In order to predict that agricultural prices will be low if harvest prospects are good, to conclude that a cold snap in the late spring will cause higher fruit and wine prices, to evaluate the effects of a late thaw in the (North American) Great Lakes on the price spreads in the future market for wheat, one needs micro-models. One needs macro-models to be able to predict that more extensive plans for investment in industry will lead to higher tax revenues, higher customs receipts, lower foreign-exchange reserves, and lower reserves of commercial banks. Of course, there are also predictions for which both macro- and micro-theory are required; for example, if certain actions of an export cartel are expected to have certain effects on the price of the cartellized commodity, on the real terms of trade of the affected countries, and on the level of national income of the exporting country.

It should be clear also that economic policy can dispense with neither micro- nor macro-theory. Agricultural policy, small-business policy, anti-monopoly policy, tariff policy, conservation policy, regulation of transportation, public utilities, etc., must be based almost entirely on micro-theory, while monetary and credit policies must be largely grounded in macro-theory. Social-security measures will be largely founded on micro-theory but may have some important consequences that can only be analyzed with macro-theory; for example, an increase in labor costs may threaten to cause a rise in unemployment and, to avoid it, credit and budget policies resulting in injections of new money into the economy may be demanded. Financial policy is largely founded on macro-theory but may have some important consequences that can only be analyzed with micro-theory; for example, certain turnover taxes may be found to be especially regressive, certain indirect taxes to be shiftable, the treatment of certain corporation-tax deductions to be inducive to uneconomic tax avoidance, etc. It would be interesting to examine governmental memoranda and parliamentary debates to see on what kind of economic theory their arguments rested. (Of course one ought not to expect all members of legislatures and parliamentary committees to be especially expert, and in any event the economic justifications for new or amended statutes will often be merely a pretext for the protection of special interests.)

Our final conclusions on the question of the applicability of the two types of theory can hardly be doubted. It is a misconception to consider macro-theory more applicable in any sense than micro-theory. Micro-theory and macro-theory do not differ so far as their applicability to so-called reality is concerned.

III. Economic Micro-Theory and Managerial Economics

My remarks on the question of the applicability of economic theory to practical problems have so far been limited to the realms of economic history, economic forecasting, and economic policy; I have said nothing about the economics of business management. The examples given of applications of micro-theory have been confined to problems of political economy, that is, problems concerning the economy as a whole, not individual business firms. I have avoided all references to the interrelations between micro-economics and management economics. This omission has probably been noted, and perhaps regretted, by many readers; I shall try now to fill the gap. I offer my comments on this subject with some reservations: they are clearly tentative and if the reader has misgivings about some of what will be said here, let him be assured that the writer has too.

The Economic Theory of the Firm

The two fundamental concepts of micro-economics are the Household and the Firm. Most economic theorists view the theory of the household and the theory of the firm as the foundations of micro-economics, some indeed consider that they encompass the whole of it. Yet, if we consider the "pure" theory of the firm to be an analysis of profit-maximizing behavior, that is, an attempt to discover how the profit-motivated entrepreneur makes rational decisions, how he acts in different situations, and how he reacts to changes in the data that concern him, how then does the task of the micro-theory of the firm differ from that of managerial economists? Are they the same? Are they partly overlapping? Or are they quite different?

It is sometimes said that the essential difference between the micro-theoretical analysis and the managerial or business-oriented analysis of the firm is that the one is a positive science while the other is a normative science or a practical art. I doubt, however, that this would make as much of a difference as is commonly believed. Several textbooks of logic show how normative propositions, prescriptions and imperatives, can with little difficulty be transformed into positive hypothetical propositions. A statement of what one ought or ought not do, can be translated into a statement of the consequences that would follow if he did or did not take the action in question. One may with equal justification regard managerial economics as normative—in that it purports to give advice to the business manager and tells him what the optimal decision would be—or as positive—in that it formulates general statements on the effects which particular types of managerial decisions might have on a firm's profits. In so far as micro-economic theory analyzes profit-maximizing decision-making, there is hardly anything left of the supposedly differentiating criterion between micro-economics and managerial economics.

One distinction sometimes made in years past, is now generally rejected, namely, that managerial or business economics deals with a mass of practical procedures, skills and institutions that have nothing to do with economic theory, for example, bookkeeping and accounting, business statistics and finance, organizational and administrative techniques, marketing and advertising, etc. Managerial economics is a subject, and perhaps

129

the most important subject, within the curriculum of a school of business, but it surely must not be taken as the catchall designation of everything that is taught in a business school.

According to another possible distinction, which has something to it although it is rejected by most managerial economists, micro-theory is concerned only with the abstract formulation of the conditions and effects of profit-maximization—that is to say, with the statement of formal equilibrium conditions in an abstract model featuring assumed cost functions and demand functions—whereas managerial economics is concerned with the practical solution of concrete problems arising in a business firm. Thus, micro-theory is supposed to work on the basis of imaginary cost and revenue functions which are merely assumed as given, whereas one of the chief tasks of managerial economics would be to ascertain the actual cost conditions and selling possibilities from empirical data. According to this view, the study of the techniques of obtaining and interpreting the relevant observational data would belong to managerial economics rather than to the micro-economic theory of the firm.

Operations research, employing modern mathematical techniques, ingenious model constructions, and high-powered mathematical statistics to ascertain the numerical parameters in the algebraic functions used in the model, seems to have become the most important branch (if not all) of management science. Operations research was first used in England and America as an auxiliary science for military strategy; it was later applied to war and defense industries, and eventually to private industry in general. The best-known universities and schools of technology in the United States have established departments or groups for operations analysis, which accept research contracts with the army, navy, and air-force, as well as with private industry. By using their students as apprentices in carrying out these research contracts, they develop new experts in operations research. With the aid of sophisticated mathematical methods and large electronic computers, all sorts of problems are solved for all sorts of industries. (Typical examples are problems of optimal inventory policy; optimal work schedules for machines that have to be adjusted for the production of different qualities, sizes, or calibers; optimal delivery routes in metropolitan areas; optimal use of rolling stock; optimal price differentials for differentiated products.) If managerial economics were to develop chiefly in this direction, this would have the considerable advantage of compelling a stricter selection of the students admitted to business schools, since in this case mathematically untalented applicants would have to be rejected. I have mentioned this particular phase or development of management science because it might prove to be an expedient criterion distinguishing between managerial economics and micro-economic theory of the firm.

One may point to several other differences between what is commonly taught under the name of managerial economics, on the one hand, and micro-economics, on the other. A major part of micro-economics deals with the household, with utility theory, with the pure logic of consumers' choice—subjects which have no place in managerial economics. This, however, would not rule out viewing managerial economics as a part of micro-economics. A serious concern with problems of welfare economics might be mentioned as something that would be appropriate to micro-theory but not to managerial economics. One may think of such problems as the effect of external economies upon optimum allocation; the question of the "ideal output"; the three or more cost curves, inclusive or exclusive of rent; and similar problems that seem to be irrelevant to an exposition of managerial economics.

In all this, we have left aside a difference in methodology, that is, a difference of interest to the student of philosophy of science, which merits a more detailed discussion.

The Imaginary and the Real Firm

The firm in economic micro-theory is a pure abstraction, a mental construction—or, as the Germans would say, an "ideal type"—which has only the function to serve as a connecting link or intervening variable between a change of some data and other changes which are regarded as adjustment to the first change. This mental construct called the firm is merely a heuristic fiction, injected by the theorist between an exogenous change (say a change in cost or demand conditions) and the reaction thereto (change in price and output) for the purpose of explaining—making understood—the reaction as the result of human decisions. The abstraction or pure construct of a firm, that is, of a decision-making unit, prone to think and act in a prescribed manner, can serve its purpose as a link in the

131

causal chain—from the change regarded as cause to the change regarded as effect—no matter whether in reality there exists, or does not exist, anything that looks like a firm. Any similarity between the as-if-firm of an economic micro-model with a historical, legal, or sociological person should be viewed as a mere coincidence.

The firm shares with the household this methodological status as heuristic fiction in economic micro-theory. The theorist injects the micro-economic construct of the household between changes of conditions (price and income changes) and reactions thereto (consumption, labor effort) in order to make the reactions understandable. This idealized household has very little similarity with any real human being, say, with Mr. John Doe, head of the household, a henpecked husband under the combined tyranny of his wife and his children. The fictional householder of pure theory makes all his decisions in perfect rationality, consistency and transitivity, and hence must surely not be confused with any real-world household of our acquaintance.

The good old *homo economicus* was such a pure, mental construction. There have been from time to time so-called experts who complained that this concept was not realistic, that it lacked most of the sentiments and feelings of real human beings. For these literal-minded who cannot well think in abstractions one would have done better to give the concept the name *homunculus economicus*. Perhaps they might then have grasped the idea that it represents not a man born of woman but rather an abstract puppet, artificially produced from a mental test-tube and arbitrarily endowed with only a few human traits selected with a view to their usefulness for certain explanatory purposes.

The confusion of so-called ideal types with so-called real types (as German social scientists like to say, following Max Weber's terminology) or the confusion of mental constructs with operational concepts (as American methodologists prefer to say, following the terminologies of Bridgman and others)[45] is a mistake which few beginners are able to

---

[45] To refer to this pair of methodological concepts by different words in the social and in the natural sciences may be desirable for some epistemological reasons. Many German methodologists of the *Geisteswissenschaften* or *Kulturwissenschaften* firmly believe in this terminological differentiation. But, granted that there is the additional postulate (or precept) of "understandability" (*Verstehbarkeit*) in the social sciences, could one not bear this in mind even without being reminded of it by the use of special terms such as "ideal types" and "real types"?

escape and which some of them can never shake off completely. A well-known American nuclear physicist, a few years ago, wrote a splendid paper about the naive question whether the nuclear particles "really exist." He pointed out that such a question makes no good sense, for it is matter of complete indifference whether or not the electron or the neutrino had an existence outside the theoretical model; and furthermore, that the belief in their real existence—even more than the doubt of it—was a mental obstacle to the progress of theory.[46] These so-called "particles" are pure constructs injected, in the fashion of heuristic model construction, as abstract connecting links between observational data. The names they are given have only the purpose of facilitating discussion, but are not meant to call forth irrelevant associations with things real.

The moral of the story is that the firm in the model world of economic micro-theory ought not to call forth any irrelevant associations with firms in the real world. We know, of course, that there are firms in reality and that they have boards of directors and senior and junior executives, who do, with reference to hundreds of different products, a great many things—which are entirely irrelevant for the micro-theoretical model. The fictitious firm of the model is a "uni-brain," an individual decision-unit that has nothing to do but adjust the output and the prices of one or two imaginary products to very simple imagined changes in data.

The firm in managerial economics is no heuristic fiction. To be sure, the theorist in managerial economics also works with abstract constructs and models, but his subject is the firm itself, not merely the economic results of some "typical" actions attributed to "typical" decisions. It is essential, therefore, that there be operational counterparts to the abstract constructs in the models with which the managerial economist works. Indeed, the practitioners of applied managerial economics work constantly with the operational concept of the firm since one of their major tasks is to investigate concrete problems of the operation of real firms.

Thus, it is possible to see a methodological difference between economic micro-theory and managerial economics in the notion that for managerial economics the firm must really exist, since it is, after all, the very subject of the investigation, whereas for economic theory the firm need be nothing

---

[46] S. M. Dancoff, "Does the Neutrino Really Exist?" *Bulletin of the Atomic Scientists*, Vol. VIII (1952), pp. 139-141.

more than a heuristic fiction, and whether or not it really exists is of secondary importance.

The Dominant Firm

Alas, as it often happens, the most beautiful formulations are not quite tenable in all respects. The story of the purely fictitious firm in economic micro-theory holds up nicely so long as we deal with the theory of competition. For under the pressure of competition the firm does not have much choice in its price and output decisions and, what with the large number of competing firms, it would not make much difference in the end if some of them deviated from the norm and made decisions different from those oriented solely towards maximization of finely calculated profits. If, however, a firm is not just one of many in the same industry but occupies a sheltered or dominant position in the market, and is therefore so much freer in its decisions, then the postulated schema, the heuristic model, will no longer fit. Pareto saw this fifty years ago when he declared that "pure theory" applied only to goods offered under competitive conditions; to explain price and output of monopolies or cartels one would need assumptions which are in closer correspondence with "facts" and therefore transcend "pure" economic theory.[47]

From the assumptions sufficient for the competitive case, one cannot derive the results of the decisions made by a small group of oligopolists. In dealing with polypoly, it is enough to assume that the sellers believe they know how their costs and how their sales will alter in response to small changes in output or in price. In dealing with oligopoly, one needs more: the sellers will be concerned with how their competitors will react; the considerations and expectations of the sellers will depend on what kind of past experiences they have had; whether they have agreements or understandings with one another, and whether they will faithfully observe them; whether a cartel supervises their prices or sales; whether they fear that outsiders might break into their markets, etc. In these circumstances, the simple general construct of profit-maximizing decision-making will no longer be sufficient.

---

[47] Vilfredo Pareto, *Manuel d'économie politique* (Paris, 1909, 2nd ed., 1927), p. 601.

The case of monopoly is free from most of these complications, but there are other considerations that prevent the use of the simple construct of the firm. So long as there are large numbers in any group, deviations from the norm can be disregarded without significant impairment of the deduced results. In the case of only one individual, however, one cannot know whether he acts typically or atypically. A firm in a monopoly position, moreover, can usually afford not to maximize its profits and not to do the things that would be the typical reactions of a profit-maximizer to certain changes in data; it may react in rather different ways, or may not react at all.

This does not mean that the theorist must remain idly resigned and have nothing at all to say about price and output under monopolistic or oligopolistic conditions. But in order to have something to say he must equip himself with a larger collection of models; and in order to know how to construe them and when to apply them he must look around and find out what real firms really try to do in various situations. In these cases, it is obviously no longer a matter of indifference whether or not firms exist in reality. Special knowledge of management behavior is necessary if relevant models are to be constructed. This does not mean, of course, that the constructs and models should be "realistic." Realism and relevance are very different qualities. In a realistic model the relevant factors may be swamped by all sorts of nonessential details, whereas in a relevant model everything is left out that in a series of mental experiments has proved nonessential, that is, has been shown to have little or no influence upon the deduced end-results.

The models in the economic micro-theorist's collection, with which he must work when he analyzes the effects of changes in data upon prices and outputs under oligopoly or monopoly, will also contain idealized and abstract constructs, not empirical concepts of the firm. The point is—and this bears repetition—that the mental constructs of the theorist's thought-world will have real-world counterparts, and their observation will guide the economist in selecting the constructs and models from his mental tool box. Whether and to what extent the economic theorist must, in this task, enlist the cooperation of the managerial economist is an issue still under debate.

IV. The Star of the Piece
and the Supporting Role

The first two parts of this essay gave equal billing to micro- and macro-theory, and cast the floodlights on both so that the contrasts, actual or alleged, could be judged by the audience. In the third part, however, macro-theory hovered in the wings and never came on the stage. Nevertheless, the discourse on the relations between micro-theory and managerial economics has, I submit, contributed to the main theme in that it helped clarify some of the functions of micro-theory and pointed to a range of problems that fall exclusively in the domain of micro-theory and on which macro-theory has nothing to say.

Underemployment and Growth as Timely Problems

There was a time when price theory was almost coterminous with economic theory, when price theory was not only in the center of the theorist's interest but absorbed it almost entirely. The neo-classical school of economics treated the problem of "optimal allocation of scarce resources among a multiplicity of ends" as *the* economic problem and *defined* the "economic principle" in terms of the optimal use of scarce means. Inasmuch as the use of resources is governed by the relative prices of products and means of production, price theory naturally became the foundation of the analysis of economic behavior.

During the depression of the 1930's the widespread existence of unemployment and of unused productive capacity led to a shift of emphasis in economic thinking. Why should economists rack their brains analyzing the economical use of resources most of which were not being used at all? Obviously, then, the most important problem was to find uses for factors of production not scarce but overabundant. The problem of finding the most economical uses for scarce resources was no longer timely.

The depression years were succeeded by the years of armament and of war and, although the means of production were once again scarce, priorities in their use were not governed by the price mechanism but determined by the decisions of administrative officials, by central authorities. Why should one take time and effort to study the operation of the price mechanism if, in distrust of its effectiveness, one has decided to suspend its working so far as possible?

The postwar years were characterized by a new *leitmotif*—the rate of economic growth. The most economic use of productive resources will not guarantee the fastest growth. It is quite conceivable that the available productive resources are used fully and as economically as possible without leading to any growth in the national product per capita. On the other hand, it is possible to obtain a high rate of growth in per capita output without using the means of production in the most economical way. Among the important factors making for fast growth are rapid capital formation, rapid technological progress with prompt application of the new techniques, good organization, active enterprise, improved skill and discipline of the labor force. The optimal use of productive resources, and the functioning of the price mechanism which is to secure it, are, in contrast, of secondary importance if one accepts the view of the "growth specialists," their policy objectives, and their macro-economic growth theory.[48]

Growth Theory and Micro-Analysis

The theory of relative prices and of the allocation of productive resources has thus lost, in many universities, its dominant position, first to the theory of underemployment, then to the theory of governmental planning and control, and finally to the theory of economic growth. The question now is whether growth theory is likely to retain its dominant role in the future and whether it will remain exclusively macro-economic in its orientation.

I doubt that growth theory will forever be the star on the economic

---

[48] Let us assume that the distortions in the "right" price relations caused by government intervention, monopolistic restrictions, or defective functioning of the price mechanism so impair the economic allocation of the available productive resources that the per capita national product is some 5 to 10 per cent below the level possible with optimum use. Let us assume further that the greatest possible insight and circumspection could reduce this loss by half. Even then the result would not exceed that attained in one or two years' normal growth. An increase in the rate of growth would therefore in the long run be incomparably more desirable. To be sure, this ignores the fact that by avoiding a misallocation of resources improvements could be obtained both in the level of output and consumption and in the annual rate of growth.

stage and I believe that its exclusively macro-economic orientation is on the way out. Analysis of the factors promoting growth has largely been responsible for this incipient change in orientation. Capital formation, technological progress, entrepreneurial drive, improvement of human resources—all these have aspects that are accessible chiefly, if not only, to micro-theoretical analysis. In a free-market economy the direct and indirect effects of government measures designed to affect the aggregate rate of saving cannot be satisfactorily analyzed with macro-models alone; often, depending on the type of policy measures proposed, the effects cannot be analyzed at all without resorting to the theory of relative prices. The production of technological knowledge, crucial for technical progress, requires the employment of specific talents and skills which have to be steered away from other uses; again, it takes micro-theory to analyze the problems bound up with this reallocation. Where entrepreneurial drive is lacking or where the willingness to undertake risky industrial investment is inadequate, a micro-theoretical analysis of the pecuniary incentives, for example, of the effects of differential tax treatment of income from different sources, must come to the aid of growth and development policy. Problems of the development of labor efficiency through increased allocations for training and education are also largely micro-economic in nature.

My skepticism regarding the enduring dominance of growth theory within economics springs from the conviction that such one-sidedness cannot last when pressing problems of the day demand other approaches. Economics is being given plenty of tasks which call for the services of specialists of all kinds, not just specialists on economic growth. Probably one will also need "generalists" in economics, experts who have a grasp of the whole field—though it sometimes looks as if these generalists were becoming quite rare, and perhaps extinct.

In any event, micro-theory remains an indispensable keystone of economic science.

V. Summary and Judgment

We shall now attempt a brief summary of our main theses and then, if possible, a judgment about the conflicting claims of superiority of micro- and macro-theory.

Twenty Main Theses

The concise formulation of theses recapitulating the most essential propositions presented has an advantage for those who listen to a lecture, but is dangerous for readers of a printed page. The advantage for the listener is that what he has heard can once again be called to mind in a few sentences and the connections between various parts become clearer thereby. The danger for the reader is that he may by a cursory glance through the essay discover the short summary at the end and, trying to save himself the trouble of pursuing the longer argument, limit his reading to the summary. The compressed theses, separated from their supporting argument and justification, may prove incomprehensible or unacceptable. Let me, therefore, urge the reader to treat this summary as a complement to, and not a substitute for, the foregoing discussion.

1. Large models may either contain small models as component parts or they may merely, by means of aggregation of the variables and relations employed in the small models, present aggregated quantities and aggregative relations.
2. Coordination or integration of small models gives us the system of general equilibrium, whereas cumulation or aggregation of variables and relations employed in small models gives us the basis for systems of aggregative equilibrium.
3. The term macro-theory is most widely understood as synonymous with aggregative theory, and the system of general equilibrium as belonging to micro-theory.
4. It would in principle be possible to call a theory "macro-economic" as soon as it focuses on the behavior functions of whole groups, rather than on the choices of individual decision-units, such as households and firms. With this delimitation, however, almost all theories of partial equilibrium (*e.g.,* the industry), including the equilibrium of a single market, would become "macro-theories," since supply and demand functions, though resultants of individual choices, no longer display these choices as component forces. It is not customary to draw the boundary line of micro-theory so narrowly.
5. The boundary line most often drawn between micro- and macro-theory follows the principle that micro-theory deals with magnitudes that

are obtained by adding together quasi-homogeneous units, whereas macro-theory deals with magnitudes obtained by aggregation of heterogeneous units.

6. A perhaps simpler distinction can be found in the role assigned to price relationships between different goods or types of goods in the models of analysis: in macro-theory they usually play no role.

7. In the history of economic thought macro-theory appears in the very beginning, especially in the theory of money—Davanzati (1588)— and later in the theories of production, distribution, and capital— Quesnay, Ricardo, Böhm-Bawerk, Wicksell—long before Keynes' theory of employment.

8. While it is, of course, possible to concentrate on macro-theory, taking the macro-relations as given without being concerned about their composition, the macro-theorist wanting to understand his subject more profoundly will proceed to study the micro-theoretical underpinning of his macro-models.

9. The decision to seek micro-economic explanations of macro-economic generalizations, that is, to search for the micro-theoretical foundations of macro-theoretical propositions, can be interpreted as a recognition of "methodological individualism" and of the methodological primacy of micro-theory.

10. The notion that several aggregative behavior functions have relatively fixed limits in an aggregative system of the economy as a whole ought not to lead to the belief that the macro-relations are of such overriding power that the behavior functions of individual decision-makers become uninteresting. It is especially in such instances that one must search out what determines the micro-functions and what forces them to adjust to particular circumstances. If we know first the shape or the limits of an aggregative function, this does not relieve us of the responsibility for analyzing its components.

11. The equilibrium concept plays fundamentally the same role in macro-theory as in micro-theory: it is an indispensable mental tool in the analysis of causal connections.

12. It is quite wrong to think that macro-theory is always dynamic and micro-theory is always static. We can have static macro-theory and dynamic micro-theory. Perhaps it may be said that for most problems of relative prices static micro-theory may prove sufficient, while for

most aggregative problems, such as those concerning national income, dynamic macro-theory may be needed.

13. One of the worst mistakes an economic theorist can make is to "derive" causal connections from equations that express definitional identities. In equations with *ex post* magnitudes there can be corrections of incorrectly reported data, but there can be no "effects" of one magnitude upon others. Such effects can be derived only from dynamic functions between *ex ante* magnitudes. The confusion between *ex ante* and *ex post* is especially common in macro-theory.

14. All variables as well as relations in theoretical models are idealized or mental constructs, for which operational counterparts may or may not exist. For the most part, the operational counterparts of the theoretical variables are measurable, and those of micro-variables are often more easily measurable than those of macro-variables. The operational counterparts of many theoretical relations cannot, unfortunately, be reliably measured either for micro-behavior functions or for macro-behavior functions. Of the many measurements of macro-behavior functions that have been presented, not a single one has stood up to testing. Perhaps this is because one cannot expect these functions to remain unchanged from one year to the next. It is true, however, that one can plausibly expect aggregative behavior functions to remain more stable than individual behavior functions.

15. Economic theory is "applied to reality" in economic history, economic forecasting, and economic policy. There is no fundamental difference between micro- and macro-theory, however, in the frequency or in the success with which each is so applied.

16. In one of its parts, to wit, the theory of the firm, micro-theory overlaps managerial economics. An essential difference may be seen in the fact that economic micro-theory concerns itself merely with the abstract formulation of the conditions of profit-maximization in imaginary situations regarding costs and sales, whereas managerial economics attempts to ascertain and interpret the relevant empirical data in concrete cases and to solve practical problems of business operation. Modern operations research, mathematically oriented and employed to solve practical problems, may bring out most sharply the contrast between managerial economics and abstract economic micro-theory.

141

17. A methodological difference between managerial economics and economic micro-theory of the firm may be seen in the notion that for managerial economics the firm must really exist, since it is the subject of the investigation, whereas for economic micro-theory the firm may remain a pure fiction, since the subject of study is only the causal connection between changes of prices and quantities (interpreted as adjustments) and changes in environmental data (interpreted as causes).

18. In the theories of monopoly and oligopoly, however, adequate model construction presupposes that there actually are firms of various sorts. If the theorist did not know anything about firms in reality, he would not know how to build his models and in what situations he should apply them.

19. The long-lasting predominance of price theory came to an end when during the great depression the question of the optimal allocation of scarce productive resources became uninteresting, and the question of underemployment alone seemed important. Later, the postwar years brought with them the great interest in economic growth, and the largely macro-economic orientation of growth theory delayed the restoration of micro-theory in general and price theory in particular.

20. Inasmuch as growth theory requires micro-theory for its further development, and inasmuch as many important problems of the day need micro-analysis, the balance is likely to be restored. In any event, micro-theory remains an essential keystone of economic science.

Concluding Judgment

Contests have always been popular. Yet, the spectators are usually disappointed if a contest does not end with a final decision for one side but, instead, in a draw with no one to cheer. And so, likewise, some readers may be disappointed if neither micro- nor macro-theory lies stretched out on the mat. Even so, my decision must be: no winner, no loser.

Ever since the beginning of economics, macro- and micro-theory have existed side by side; they will continue to do so in the future. Each is needed, neither is expendable.

We have had to reject a number of assertions that claimed the superiority of macro-theory. Moreover, we have had to recognize, in matters of philosophy of science, a certain primacy for micro-theory in that the sound curiosity of the scientist will not let him be satisfied with macro-economic behavior functions but will force him to advance to investigations of the underlying choices of individuals.[49]

A tentative speculation may be ventured, suggesting the possibility of a subtle association between modes of economic theorizing and political philosophy. I have not previously alluded to it, but may venture a comment before I conclude this essay.[50]

Micro-economics is firmly based on methodological individualism, on the principle of starting all theoretical deductions from generalizations about choices, decisions and actions of the individual. There is no logical link between methodological individualism and ethical or political individualism, but there are psychological associations between them. An economist who has become accustomed to assign great importance to individual choices as elements in the explanation of economic phenomena may easily have developed a bent of mind hospitable to ideas of individual freedom of choice in economic, political, and social affairs in general.

Macro-economics, on the other hand, deals with aggregates and collectives, usually without regard to individual decision-units and individual choices. Although this disregard is meant to hold only for purposes of theoretical explanation and prediction, it may dispose the specialist in macro-economics towards a disrespect for the scope of free individual choice. In addition, the selection of macro-variables, including policy variables and policy-induced parameters, may make him increasingly inclined to place the chief emphasis upon government activity in economic life, to blame "unsatisfactory" results on "insufficient" government contributions to national income, and to expect "better" results from stepped-up government activity.

---

[49] M. H. Peston writes that "economic variables are not to be judged in terms of which are of logically primary importance and which are secondary;" and that "macro-theory and micro-theory are seen to be complements not substitutes," *op. cit.,* p. 61. I can accept this position without fear of inconsistency. The logical primacy (or, more correctly, methodological primacy) of micro-variables and micro-relations has no bearing on their importance. Which are more important in a particular instance depends on the problem before us and on the model selected.

[50] This paragraph and the next four were not included in the original German version.

If these speculations are right, one would expect the student concentrating on micro-theory to be influenced in favor of economic and political individualism, and the student concentrating on macro-theory to be influenced in favor of economic collectivism or at least of a larger role of government in the nation's economic affairs. The influence, to be sure, may also be the other way 'round: economic libertarians may be attracted chiefly by micro-theory, and interventionists chiefly by macro-theory. All these tendencies, in both directions, may exist, but one should not even suggest their prevalence without making proper qualifications. After all, the quantity theory of money is macro-economic in nature, and so is virtually any type of capital theory; yet, surely no collectivist influences can be attributed to them. If the mentioned associations are effective, they apparently hold only for particular kinds of models within the two general modes of economic theorizing.

Needless to say, no claims of superiority can be made on the grounds of the political "conditioning" that may be associated with micro- and macro-economic theory, except on the basis of political value judgments. Partisans of either political philosophy may of course, if they care to, pronounce that one of the two types of theory is "superior" in instilling the "right attitude" in the student. Such pronouncements have no scientific standing.

There is one point only on which one might concede superiority to macro-theory—though it would not be very "scientific" either—namely, that most students find macro-theory easier to learn. The study of micro-theory makes greater demands on the intelligence and concentration of the student. Macro-theory, so far as it is not econometric, seems simpler, and the intellectually under-equipped student is more likely to pass examinations successfully if he has only macro-theoretical questions to answer.

Section Three

Semantic Issues
in Value Theory

MARGINAL ANALYSIS AND EMPIRICAL RESEARCH

Reprinted with permission from *The American Economic Review*, Vol. XXXVI, No. 4, Part 1, Sept., 1946.

Certain critics of "conventional" economic theory from time to time voice surprise at the general acceptance of marginalism and at "the confidence of the textbook writers in the validity of the marginal analysis."[1] They disapprove of allowing the principle of marginalism to play the role of a fundamental postulate in the teaching of economics.

Marginalism Implied in the Economic Principle

These critics would probably revolt against all those definitions of economics which contain marginalism as an implicit criterion. Marginalism, as the logical process of "finding a maximum," is clearly implied in the so-called *economic principle*—striving to achieve with given means a maximum of ends.

Economics in a narrow sense is confined to such aspects of conduct as can be explained with reference to the principles of maximizing satisfaction, income, or profit. Under definitions of this sort any deviations from the marginal principle would be extra-economic. Yet, to refuse to deal

---

[1] Richard A. Lester, "Shortcomings of Marginal Analysis for Wage-Employment Problems," *Am. Econ. Rev.*, Vol. XXXVI, No. 1 (Mar., 1946), p. 63.

with any type of business conduct that cannot qualify by the strict standards of marginalism may justly be regarded as a lazy man's excuse. If certain types of business conduct can be found in reality with regularity and consistency, it is undoubtedly desirable to analyze them regardless of their "economic rationale."[2] And if some of these allegedly "non-economic" aspects of conduct can be explained within the conceptual framework of economics, one may prefer definitions which admit behavior types not strictly subject to marginal analysis among the proper subject matter of economic theory.

Interpretation of Business Behavior

To recognize the study of certain types of merely "traditional" conduct as legitimately within the province of economic theory is one thing; it is another to accept as correct the interpretations of business behavior offered by the critics of marginal analysis. Unable to see how marginal analysis can be applied to their material, these critics have concluded that marginalism should be discarded. It can be shown, however, that the alleged "inapplicability" of marginal analysis is often due to a failure to understand it, to faulty research techniques, or to mistaken interpretations of "findings."

This is not to deny that a goodly portion of all business behavior may be non-rational, thoughtless, blindly repetitive, deliberately traditional, or motivated by extra-economic objectives. But the material thus far presented as the result of empirical research has not proved what the analysts intended to prove. In some instances their findings were the result of careful research, based on a thorough knowledge of economic theory, but their interpretations were still questionable. In other instances the whole approach of the research project was so faulty that the findings as well as the interpretations are all but worthless except as targets for critical discussion.

---

[2] *Cf.* the admonition that "if an economist finds a procedure widely established in fact, he ought to regard it with more respect than he would be inclined to give in the light of his own analytic method." R. F. Harrod, "Price and Cost in Entrepreneurs' Policy," *Oxford Economic Papers,* No. 2 (1939), p. 7.

I. MARGINAL ANALYSIS OF THE SINGLE FIRM

Any attempt to "test" marginalist theory through empirical research presupposes full understanding of the theory. It is necessary to know precisely what the theory says, what it implies, and what it intends to do. Since it has been developed gradually over a period of more than a century,[3] it will not suffice to take any particular writer as one's authority or any particular exposition as one's text. Earlier versions lack the necessary refinements and methodological foundations; later formulations often take for granted necessary assumptions or qualifications made in previous expositions. To criticize the theory because of the errors and omissions in any treatise, however representative, is unfair.

The following statement of essential elements in the marginalist analysis of the single business firm attempts merely to give major emphasis to points often overlooked or misunderstood.

The Determination of Output and Employment

The theory of the "equilibrium of the single firm" is not as ambitious as is often believed. It does not attempt to give all the reasons why a given firm makes the type or quality of product which it makes; why it produces the output that it produces; why it employs the workers that it employs; or why it charges the prices that it charges. It is probably an understatement of the importance of the historical situation when Hall and Hitch modestly remark: "There is usually some element in the prices ruling at any time which can only be explained in the light of the history of the industry."[4] The phrase "usually some element" does not do justice to the part played by historical antecedents in the determination of product, output, employment, and prices. The role of the past in shaping the actual conditions under which the firm operates, in developing the routine of its responses to changes in conditions, and in

---

[3] Cournot was among the earlier expositors of marginal analysis of the single firm.
[4] R. L. Hall and C. J. Hitch, "Price Theory and Business Behavior," *Oxford Economic Papers*, No. 2 (1939), p. 33.

impressing it with experiences which have taught it to size up and anticipate these changes as the basis for its decisions—this role is by no means denied by marginal analysis. The role of the past in the process of adjusting the present to the anticipated future is essential in all theory of human conduct. It is implied in the very attempt of constructing a pattern of behavior of the single firm.

Instead of giving a complete explanation of the "determination" of output, prices, and employment by the firm, marginal analysis really intends to explain the effects which certain *changes* in conditions may have upon the actions of the firm. What kind of changes may cause the firm to raise prices? to increase output? to reduce employment? What conditions may influence the firm to continue with the same prices, output, employment, in the face of actual or anticipated changes? Economic theory, static as well as dynamic, is essentially a theory of adjustment to change. The concept of equilibrium is a tool in this theory of change; the marginal calculus is its dominating principle.

A. Marginal Revenue and Cost of Output

Subjectivity of Cost and Revenue

The proposition that the firm will attempt to equate marginal cost and marginal revenue is logically implied in the assumption that the firm will attempt to maximize its profit (or minimize its losses). It should hardly be necessary to mention that all the relevant magnitudes involved—cost, revenue, profit—are subjective— that is, perceived or fancied by the men whose decisions or actions are to be explained (the business men)—rather than "objective"—that is, calculated by disinterested men who are observing these actions from the outside and are explaining them (statisticians and economists as theorists— not as consultants).

The marginal cost that guides the producer is the addition to his total cost which he expects would be caused by added production. An outside observer, if he had expert knowledge of the production techniques and full insight into the cost situation of the producing firm, might arrive at a different, "objective" figure of the firm's marginal cost; but what the observer thinks is not necessarily the same as what the producer thinks. The producer's actual decision is based on what he himself thinks; it is based on "subjective" cost expectations.

One may perhaps assume that the producer is intensely interested in knowing his cost and that, in general, he has the experience which enables him to know it. Yet, one must not assume that all producers "really" know their cost in the sense in which an efficiency expert would determine it; several of them may lack the interest or experience; they may not find it worth their while to dig too deeply into the mysteries of their business. (After all, we know that there are good business men and bad, and that the majority is somewhere between good and bad.) But this does not invalidate the proposition that the producer is guided by marginal cost.[5]

The same thing is true with regard to price expectations and sales expectations. It is the "demand as seen by the seller" from which his revenue expectations stem. The increase in demand which is relevant in the analysis of the firm need not be "the real thing"; it may precede an "actual" increase in demand, lag behind it, or be entirely imaginary. The business man does what he does on the basis of what *he* thinks, regardless of whether you agree with him or not.

Marginal analysis of the firm should not be understood to imply anything but subjective estimates, guesses and hunches.

The Range of Price and Output Variations

Beginning students of economics who watch their instructor draw demand and cost curves covering half the blackboard may be misled into believing that the business man is supposed to visualize the possibilities of producing and selling amounts of output ranging from almost zero up to two or three times the amount that he is currently producing and selling; that the business man is supposed to figure out how much he might be able to sell at prices several times as high as the

---

[5] One may wish, of course, to qualify any social implications of the proposition once the subjective character of the relevant cost data is recognized.

current price, and how much at prices only one-half or one-third as high. The curve draftsman, indeed, seems to ascribe extraordinary powers of imagination to the business wizards.

Misunderstandings of this sort, and erroneous criticisms of marginal analysis, could be avoided if it were made clear to the students that the length of the curves, *i.e.*, the wide range they cover, was chiefly designed to enable those in the back rows of the class room to make out what goes on on the blackboard; and to permit them to practice curve analysis without using magnifying glasses. The range of possibilities—prices, sales, outputs—which a business man may have in mind is probably quite narrow. Rarely will a business man bother pondering the probable effects of a price increase or cut by 50 per cent; but he may easily think about what a 10 or 15 per cent price change might do to his sales; or what discount it might take to land some additional orders.

The principles of analysis are not altered by the realization that the alternatives which business men weigh concerning prices or production volumes cover a much more moderate range than the curves which teachers of economics draw to depict the pattern of marginal calculus.

The Time-Range of Anticipations

In view of the known attempts to derive statistical cost curves from accounting data—which of necessity refer to conditions of the past—it is important to mention that the marginal cost and marginal revenue concepts in the analysis of the equilibrium of the firm refer to expectations of future conditions. To be sure, past experience is always in the background of anticipations of the future, and past accounting records may form a firm point of departure for evaluating prospective and hypothetical cost and revenue figures. But anticipations alone are the relevant variables in the marginal calculus of the firm.

What is the time-range of the significant anticipations? How far into the future do they reach, and what period, if any, is given special emphasis? Is tomorrow more important than next year or several years hence? Is it the "short run" or the "long run" which controls current action?

When a firm wishes to increase production, it usually has a choice of expanding the equipment and productive capacity of its plant or of stepping up the output of the existing plant with unchanged equipment. If productive capacity is already well utilized, the marginal cost of producing larger outputs will be higher in the existing establishment with unchanged equipment than in an establishment with adjusted, increased equipment. If several degrees of adjustment in the productive equipment are possible, several marginal cost functions will be "given" and several different outputs will be the "equilibrium output" under given sales expectations.

To cope with these problems economists have made the distinction between the "short period," assuming no adaptation of equipment, and the "long period," assuming complete adaptation of equipment. Students often believe that the latter period is called "long" because it takes a long time to expand the plant. This need not be the case. A better understanding of the concepts might be achieved by associating the degree of planned plant adjustment with the length of time for which the changed production volume is expected to be maintained. If an increased demand is expected to prevail for a short period only, it will not pay to invest in plant expansion, and "short-run cost" will determine output. On the other hand, if demand is expected to continue at the higher level for a sufficiently long period, an expansion of the establishment will be considered a profitable investment, and "long-run cost" will determine output. Needless to say, many intermediate periods, that is, several degrees of plant adjustment with different marginal cost conditions, may exist.

On the basis of this reasoning one will recognize it as a misunderstanding to argue that short-run cost is of controlling influence on the ground that we always live and work in the short period. The duration for which demand conditions are expected to prevail will determine the relevant "period" of cost anticipations. Of course, this relevance is again subjectively determined, not by the "objective" judgment of the economist.

The time-range of the anticipations with regard to the demand and selling outlook is subject to similar considerations. It is a mistake to think that the relevant "period" for demand and marginal revenue expectations is determined by the length of time it takes for today's production to reach the market.[6] If a price reduction is apt to spoil the market for a long time to come, or a price increase to harm customer loyalty, the effects on future profits will hardly be neglected in considering current actions. If a firm were to regard a certain price change as a desirable step for the time being, but feared that a later reversal might be difficult or costly, it would weigh this anticipated future cost or loss against the short-run benefit.

Anticipations of this sort, complementary or competing with one another, are not exceptions to marginal analysis but are part and parcel of it. To be sure, when an instructor teaches graphical analysis, he will do well to abstract from complicated cost and revenue anticipations and to concentrate on those that can be neatly packed away in geometric curves.

The Numerical Definiteness of the Estimates

The geometric curves and arithmetic schedules by which the instructor presents marginal cost and marginal revenue of the firm seem to leave no room for doubt that these anticipations take the form of estimates of definite numerical values. While this may be necessary for teaching purposes, it should not mislead the student into believing that every action of the business man is in fact the result of a conscious decision, made after careful calculations of differential revenue and cost.

Businessmen do not always "calculate" before they make decisions, and they do not always "decide" before they act. For they think that they know their business well enough without having to make repeated calculations; and their actions are frequently routine.[7] But routine is based on principles which were once considered and decided upon and have then been frequently applied with decreased need for conscious choices.[8] The feeling that calculations are not always necessary is usu-

---

[6] Richard A. Lester, *Economics of Labor* (New York: Macmillan, 1941), p. 181.

[7] See George Katona, "Psychological Analysis of Business Decisions and Expectations," *Am. Econ. Rev.*, Vol. XXXVI, No. 1 (Mar., 1946), p. 53.

[8] Discussing the difference between "routine behavior" and "genuine decisions," Dr. Katona explains with regard to routine actions that "principles, well understood in their original context, tend to be carried over from one situation to another." *Ibid.*, p. 49. Genuine decisions are made when expectations "change radically." *Ibid.*, p. 53.

ally based upon an ability to size up a situation without reducing its dimensions to define numerical values.[9]

The business man who is persuaded to accept a large order with a price discount or some other concession usually weighs the probability that he will have to make the same concession to his other customers. This is one of the business man's considerations included in the "calculation" or marginal revenue. In order to explain this to the student, or to reduce it to curves and schedules, the economics teacher makes "exact" calculations; in order to make up his mind whether to take or reject the order, the business man ordinarily needs no arithmetic, mental or written, and indeed needs no concrete figures. Yet his reasoning or his routine behavior is most conveniently analyzed in terms of marginal revenue.

Where the marginal revenue is negative, that is to say, where gross receipts on accepting the additional order (with the price concession) would be smaller than without it, no further consideration is necessary. But if the dollar volume of sales can be increased by accepting the order (taking full account of all repercussions on future marketing possibilities), the business man must take another step in his reasoning: will it pay to make more sales in view of the additional cost of producing the larger output? If conditions have not changed, he will not have to make new calculations; if changes have occurred or are expected, some figuring may be required. But it is a type of figuring for which usually no accounting records are consulted, no memoranda prepared and of which no records are made. Often the business man can do this "figuring" in his head; if not, he may take a piece of scrap paper, jot down a few round numbers, reach his conclusion, and throw the paper in the waste basket.

The theorist's contention that such reasoning is typically based either on additional cost or on total cost—and hence most conveniently described in terms of marginal cost—is contradicted by certain empirical researchers who claim that most business men calculate on the basis of average cost even if they lose money by doing so. With this contradiction we shall deal later.

---

[9] Although I do not know either the width or length of my automobile, I am quite capable of making adequate comparisons between these magnitudes and the space between two parked cars, which I estimate again without thinking of feet, inches, or any numbers.

Non-Pecuniary Considerations

Marginal analysis of the equilibrium of the single firm rests on the assumption that the business firm attempts to maximize its profits. To make this assumption is not to deny that the men who run a business may be motivated also by other considerations.

That a business man is motivated by considerations other than the maximization of money profits does not necessarily make his conduct "uneconomic." The economic theorist finds no difficulty in fitting into the pattern of "economic" conduct (that is, into the conceptual scheme of consistent maximization of satisfaction within a given preference system) the householder and consumer who makes donations to friends or the church; or the seller of labor services who chooses a badly-paying but less strenuous job in preference to one that pays more but calls for more exertion. Likewise, there is nothing essentially "uneconomic" in the conduct of a business man who chooses to pay higher prices for raw material purchased from a fraternity brother, or to sell at a special discount to members of his church, or who refrains from embarking on a promising expansion of his business because he prefers an easier life.

There are economic theorists who would include considerations of this sort among the data for the marginal calculus of the firm. The satisfaction from favoring his friends through higher purchase prices or lower selling prices is a special reward or "revenue" to the business man; he may ask himself how much it is worth to him, and we may conceivably add it to his revenue curve. To give up an easier life, expend greater efforts and increase his worries are among the business man's "cost" when he considers an expansion of his business; we may conceivably add it to his "cost" curve. Any number and type of non-pecuniary sacrifices and rewards could thus be included, at some sort of "money equivalent," among the costs and revenues that make up the profits of the firm; the marginal calculus of the firm would become all-inclusive.

It seems to be methodologically sounder if we do not reduce the non-pecuniary satisfactions and dissatisfactions (utilities and disutilities) of the business man to money terms and do not try to make them part of the profit maximization scheme of the firm. If *whatever* a business man does is explained by the principle of profit maximization—because he does what he likes to do, and he likes to do what maximizes the sum of his pecuniary and non-pecuniary profits—the analysis acquires the character of a system of definitions and tautologies, and loses much of its value as an explanation of reality. It is preferable to separate the non-pecuniary factors of business conduct from those which are regular items in the formation of money profits.

This methodological controversy is not too important. Not much depends on whether non-pecuniary considerations of the business man are translated into money terms or, instead, treated as exceptions and qualifications in the explanation of typical business conduct. The purpose of the analysis of the firm is not to explain all actions of each and every firm in existence; we are satisfied if we can explain certain strong tendencies in a representative sector of business. The chief aim of the analysis, moreover, is to show the probable effects of certain changes; if the direction in which output or price is likely to move as a result of a certain change in "data" is not affected by the existence and strength of non-pecuniary factors in business conduct, their inclusion in or exclusion from the marginal analysis of the firm is not a crucial matter.

As a matter of fact, the nature, strength and effects of non-pecuniary considerations in business behavior are problems that need to be investigated. One may presume that producing larger production volumes, paying higher wage rates, or charging lower product prices than would be compatible with a maximum of money profits may involve for the business man a gain in social prestige or a certain measure of inner satisfaction.[10] It is not impossible that considerations of this sort substantially weaken the forces believed to be at work on the basis of a strictly pecuniary marginal calculus.

During the war we were able to observe that patriotism was a strong force in the production policy of American business. There can be no doubt that many firms produced far beyond the point of highest money profits. To be sure, they made large profits, but in many instances they could have made still more money without the last, particularly expen-

---

[10] A gain in social prestige may sometimes increase the good will of a firm on which it expects to cash in later. If such a gain is an aim of the firm's policy, it should be treated as a part of its pecuniary considerations. For example, a firm may grant extraordinarily high wage rates as a part of its selling and advertising expense; that is to say, it may hope that its "generous labor policy" will make its products more popular. A portion of current labor cost of the firm would then properly be allocated to future rather than current output.

sive, portions of output. Their conduct was not defined by the principle of maximization of money profits.[11]

Another of the possibly important qualifications in the analysis of the firm refers to the conflict of interests between the hired managers and the owners of the business. The interest of the former in inordinately large outlays or investments may be capable of descriptions in terms of a pecuniary calculus, but it is not maximization of the firm's profits which serves here as the standard of conduct. Maximization of salaries and bonuses of professional managers may constitute a standard of business conduct different from that implied in the customary marginal analysis of the firm. The extent to which the two standards would result in sharply different action under otherwise similar conditions is another open question in need of investigation. At this juncture we know only that a qualification must be made. How much it may modify the results of marginal analysis of the single firm we do not know.

B. Marginal Productivity

and Cost of Input

The Firm, the Industry, the Economy

Marginal productivity has different meanings in the equilibrium theories of the single firm, the industry, and the whole economy. In the theories of demand for particular "factors of production" (productive services) by the industry or economy as a whole marginal productivity analysis is of another methodological character than in the theory of

---

[11] Observance of laws and regulations presents a special problem for the analysis of business conduct. It will depend on business morals whether prohibited, unlawful alternatives may be regarded as definitely excluded and therefore non-existent; or whether they may be considered as possibilities subject only to certain peculiar risks. Assume, for example, that a price ceiling is fixed for the sale of a product, and fines are provided for violations. To the business man who is unconditionally law-abiding the ceiling price is the only possible price, regardless of how insistently some of his customers may tempt him with higher bids. To the business man, however, who abides by the law only because of the risk of being found out and fined, "demand prices" above the ceiling are real possibilities and the risks of penalties are additions to cost or deductions from revenue. If the sanctions for violations include jail sentences, the risk becomes largely non-pecuniary and it is up to the potential violator, or to the theorizing economist, whether or not that risk will be "converted" into money terms. Black-market prices are in part the result of such risk conversions.

factor employment by the individual firm: the level of abstraction and the frame of reference are different.

In this article we are concerned only with the analysis of the single firm. Like marginal product cost and marginal revenue in the theory of the firm's output, marginal factor cost and marginal productivity are the variables in the theory of the firm's input.

Determination of Input and Output

In a sense, the determination of input on the basis of factor cost and factor product is merely the reverse side of the determination of output on the basis of product cost and revenue. In the former, the cost of and revenue from employing additional factors are balanced; in the latter, the cost of and revenue from producing additional product are balanced. Before we draw curves for the cost of production of a good, we must assume that the supply curves of the factors of production are known, because the buying prices of factors are among the things that make up production cost. Before we draw curves for the revenue productivity of a factor we must assume that the demand curves for the products made with the help of this factor are known, because the selling prices of products are among the things that make up factor productivity. Hence, in each pair of curves one of the curves comprises the data shown in one curve of the other pair.

The interrelationship among the four curves (or functions) can be shown schematically as follows:

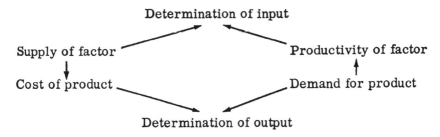

A fifth set of data, the production function, showing the technological transformation of factors into products, is implied in both pairs of curves: in the analysis of output it is among the data determining the cost of production; in the analysis of input it is among the data determining the productivity of the factor.[12]

These remarks should make it clear that neither of the two analyses is prior to the other. They are of strictly equal rank, merely two ways of looking at the same thing, namely, the conduct of a single firm maximizing its profits. The only difference is that the significant magnitudes of the analysis are, on the one side, units of factors (such as labor hours) and, on the other side, units of product.

Marginal Net Revenue Productivity

When we speak in the analysis of the firm of "marginal productivity" of a factor, this is an abbreviation for longer but synonymous expressions such as "marginal value productivity" or "marginal net revenue productivity."

The following steps are pedagogically expedient in explaining the concept of marginal net revenue productivity:

(1) Determine by how much a given physical volume of production, X, is increased if the employment of a particular factor is increased slightly (*e.g.*, by one unit), and call the output increase the factor's "marginal physical product," *MPP*.

(2) Determine the selling price, P, at which *MPP* can be sold.

(3) Multiply *MPP* by P in order to obtain the "value of the marginal physical product," *VMPP*.

(4) Determine whether X, because of the sale of *MPP*, has to be sold at a price lower than it would sell if *MPP* were not sold; if so, multiply this price reduction, $\triangle P$, by X, and obtain the "revenue loss on sales because of price cut," $X \triangle P$.

(5) Deduct $X \triangle P$ from *VMPP* in order to obtain the "marginal gross revenue product," *MGRP*.

---

[12] This shows that the customary analysis lacks elegance. Production cost and factor productivity are "derived" rather than "original" data. One could do more elegantly with only three sets of data: (a) the possibilities of buying productive services (the factor supply function), (b) the possibilities of transforming them into products (the production function), and (c) the possibilities of selling the products (the product demand function).

(6) Determine whether the production of *MPP* was connected with increased or decreased outlays for any other complementary or substitutable means of production (materials, fuel, lubricants, labor of any sort, capital funds, wear and tear of equipment, etc.), exclusive of the factor in question, and call them (positive or negative) "incidental expenses," $\triangle C$.

(7) Deduct $\triangle C$ from *MGRP* in order to obtain the "marginal net revenue product," *MNRP*.

The use of the word "revenue" as an adjectival modifier is preferred by many writers in order to stress (a) the distinction between physical product and money product, and (b) the fact that marginal revenue is less than selling price if it takes a price cut to dispose of additional output. The use of the word "net" is preferred in order to stress the fact that additional output will rarely be produced efficiently by increasing the employment of one particular factor while leaving all other outlays unchanged; as a rule, some other adjustments will be appropriate. That "marginal productivity" refers regularly to a net revenue product has been clear to economic theorists for over fifty years.[13]

Technology, Market and Supply Conditions

The marginal net revenue product of a factor, at some level of employment, becomes zero or negative. This may be due to technological difficulties—shown in step (1) of the above scheme—or to difficulties in marketing—shown in step (4)—or to difficulties with other supplies and expenses—shown in step (6).

On the other hand, it is possible that both the marginal physical product and the marginal gross revenue product are zero and, nevertheless, the marginal net revenue product is positive. This will be the case if additional units of factor are used only to secure "incidental reductions in expenses" for other means of production (*i.e.*, substitution) rather

---

[13] *E.g.*, "the net product . . . is the net increase in the money value of . . . total output after allowing for incidental expenses." (Alfred Marshall, *Principles of Economics,* 8th Edition, p. 521.) For a more detailed discussion of the concept, see my essay, "On the Meaning of the Marginal Product," *Explorations in Economics,* Contributed in Honor of F. W. Taussig (New York and London, 1936), pp. 250-63. Reproduced in the present volume, pp. 191-206.

than an increased production volume. For example, an additional un-skilled laborer may be employed as another watchman to reduce the "use" of certain materials which are in heavy demand outside of the plant. Or he may be employed to dust or cleanse certain valuable equip-ment and thus reduce outlays for repairs or replacements. Substitution of this sort is nearly always possible[14] and will usually make for positive marginal net revenue productivities even when marginal gross revenue productivities are negative because of limitations in the demand for the product.

Marginal productivity reflects all sorts of technological possibilities. An increased amount of the factor may be used (a) for reducing other expenses without increasing total output (substitution in the narrow sense), (b) for increasing total output with no or few adjustments in the use of other factors (substitution in a wider sense), and (c) for increasing total output with corresponding increases in the use of other factors (inclusive of long-run adjustments, possibly without any substitution). In the last case the incidental expenses will certainly absorb the major portion of the marginal gross revenue product.

Marginal productivity reflects also all possible situations in the demand for the product. If demand is completely inelastic beyond a certain volume, that is, if additional output is not saleable at all, the effect upon marginal productivity is not any worse than if larger outputs can be marketed at severely reduced prices. For whenever the elasticity of demand is less than unity, gross revenue from larger outputs would be lower than from smaller outputs. Hence, the marginal gross revenue product of the factor would become negative. Possibilities of landing additional orders at a price discount but without affecting the rest of the business (that is, possibili-ties of price discrimination) would show in the fact that no deduction for revenue loss would have to be made from the value of the marginal

---

[14] The assumption of fixed coefficients of production sometimes affords convenient and permissible simplifications of analysis. But in actual fact, substitution is a practical possibility in almost any production. Beginners sometimes think that substitution of labor for capital must mean the scrapping of machines and shifting of their functions to hand labor. Better care or maintenance work for equipment, postponing the need for replacement, constitutes a clear case of substitution of labor for capital. Increased utilization of plant capacity with increased employment and output also raises the ratio of labor to capital and is another form of substitution.

physical product. Whatever views the firm may have concerning the market for its product are fully reflected in the marginal productivity of the factors employed.

Marginal productivity, finally, reflects all possible conditions of supply of complementary and substitutable factors. Extreme scarcity of a complementary factor may cause a most rapid decline in marginal productivity. Increased supply of substitutable factor may drastically reduce the whole marginal productivity schedule.

While the conditions of supply of complementary and substitutable factors are among the data determining the marginal productivity of a particular factor of production, the conditions of its own supply are regarded as a separate matter. The "incidental expenses" of increased employment of the factor do not include any of the cost of that factor. The cost of the factor itself is not a part of its marginal net productivity but, instead, is the counterpart with which a balance is sought.

Marginal Factor Cost

Where the supply of the factor is perfectly elastic at a given point, that is, where the firm may be able to employ an additional amount without having to pay for it a higher price per unit, the "marginal factor cost" is equal to the price of the factor (wage rate). If, however, by purchasing or employing more of a factor the firm bids up the price not only of the additional units of the factor but also of the units previously employed, this increase in outlay is a part of the cost of the additional employment. The additionally employed factors would cost the firm not only what they themselves are paid but also the incidental increase in the pay of their fellow factors.

Marginal factor cost, in other words, is the total increase in payment for the particular type of productive service: it consists of (1) the price (wage) paid to the additionally employed, and (2) the price increase (wage increase) paid for the amount of services employed before the addition. In the case of labor, these increases may be due to union action anticipated because of the increased demand for labor, or to the impossibility of discriminating against older employees when new ones can be attracted only at higher rates of pay.

In considering any increase in employment the employer will ask himself whether the additional services will "pay for themselves," that is, what they will cost him and what they will be worth to him. This is all that the economist means when he says that the employer, maximizing his profits, equates marginal factor cost with marginal productivity.

Monopoly, Monopsony, Discontinuities

Neither the existence of monopoly nor of monopsony need invalidate the proposition that the firm will equate marginal productivity and marginal cost of input. For any degree of monopoly is fully reflected in marginal net revenue productivity, and any degree of monopsony is fully reflected in marginal factor cost.[15]

Discontinuity of the marginal productivity and marginal factor cost curves, however, may make it impossible for the two magnitudes to be equal. If marginal factor cost at a certain level of employment is below marginal productivity but would be above it at the next higher possible level of employment, the firm will stop short of the latter. Moderate jerks from "marginal cost below revenue" to marginal cost above revenue" are nothing unusual in arithmetic illustrations; in geometric curves they occur only under special assumptions.

For example, marginal net revenue productivity may precipitously drop at a given employment if the product is sold under certain oligopoly conditions (involving high elasticity of demand in the case of a price increase and low elasticity in the case of a price reduction[16]) and if the

---

[15] To be sure, there may be a large difference between the price of the factor and the value of its marginal physical product. This difference is due to (a) the reduction in product price that the firm must grant to its customers in order to dispose of an increased output and (b) the increase in factor price that the firm must grant to its suppliers or employees in order to acquire an increased input. These two parts of the spread between the price of the factor and the value of its marginal physical product have been called (a) "monopolistic exploitation" and (b) "monopsonistic exploitation" of the factor. These terms, misleading in several respects, are merely to remind the student of the fact that the spread would not exist if the firm were (a) selling its products under pure competition and (b) buying its factors under pure competition.

[16] Under such oligopoly conditions the firm will maximize profits at a volume of output at which marginal revenue is above marginal cost.

factor is not easily substitutable for other factors. The marginal factor cost curve might intersect this marginal productivity curve in its vertical portion. Likewise, marginal factor cost may precipitously rise at a given employment if the factor is bought or hired under certain oligopsony conditions (involving high elasticity of supply in the case of a reduction in the factor price and low elasticity in the case of a raise[17]). The marginal productivity curve might intersect this marginal factor cost curve in its vertical portion. Under such circumstances the firm would be in equilibrium, with its profits maximized, at a volume of input (employment) at which marginal factor cost is below marginal productivity.

Subjectivity, Range, Concreteness

Almost everything that has been said in earlier sections concerning the meaning of marginal revenue and marginal cost of output holds true, *mutatis mutandis*, in regard of the meaning of marginal productivity and marginal cost of input. More specifically, we should emphasize that

(1) the concepts are to be understood as referring to subjective estimates and conjectures;

(2) the range of imagined variations of the magnitudes in question may be rather narrow;

(3) the time-range of the relevant anticipations will depend on the circumstances of each case and will rarely be confined to the short run;

(4) the estimates need not be reduced to definite numerical values;

(5) non-pecuniary considerations may effectively compete with those pertaining to the maximization of money profits.

It is probably unnecessary to expatiate again on these points in connection with marginal productivity analysis. Only on the subject of numerical definiteness does further discussion seem advisable, especially in view of what was said above about the concept of marginal net revenue productivity. The process by which this magnitude may be derived, involving seven separate "steps" and at least as many variables, is rather

---

[17] Oligopsony in the labor market is probably not as frequent as oligopoly in the product marker.

formidable. If this analytical pattern were taken as a realistic description in photographic likeness of the actual reasoning of the typical employer, the employer would have to be endowed with talents which only few possess in reality.

An analogy may explain the apparent contradiction.

The "Extreme Difficulty of Calculating"

What sort of considerations are behind the routine decision of the driver of an automobile to overtake a truck proceeding ahead of him at slower speed? What factors influence his decision? Assume that he is faced with the alternative of either slowing down and staying behind the truck or of passing it before a car which is approaching from the opposite direction will have reached the spot. As an experienced driver he somehow takes into acount (a) the speed at which the truck is going, (b) the remaining distance between himself and the truck, (c) the speed at which he is proceeding, (d) the possible acceleration of his speed, (e) the distance between him and the car approaching from the opposite direction, (f) the speed at which that car is approaching; and probably also the condition of the road (concrete or dirt, wet or dry, straight or winding, level or uphill), the degree of visibility (light or dark, clear or foggy), the condition of the tires and brakes of his car, and—let us hope—his own condition (fresh or tired, sober or alcoholized) permitting him to judge the enumerated factors.

Clearly, the driver of the automobile will not "measure" the variables; he will not "calculate" the time needed for the vehicles to cover the estimated distances at the estimated rates of speed; and, of course, none of the "estimates" will be expressed in numerical values. Even so, without measurements, numerical estimates or calculations, he will in a routine way do the indicated "sizing-up" of the total situation. He will not break it down into its elements. Yet a "theory of overtaking" would have to include all these elements (and perhaps others besides) and would have to state how changes in any of the factors were likely to affect the decision or actions of the driver.[18] The "extreme difficulty of cal-

---

[18] Very cautious drivers are apt to work with so wide safety margins that small changes in the "variables" may not affect the actions. Timid souls may refuse to pass at all when another car is in sight.

culating,"[19] the fact that "it would be utterly impractical"[20] to attempt to work out and ascertain the exact magnitudes of the variables which the theorist alleges to be significant, show merely that the *explanation* of an action must often include steps of reasoning which the acting individual himself does not *consciously* perform (because the action has become routine) and which perhaps he would never be *able* to perform in scientific exactness (because such exactness is not necessary in everyday life). To call, on these grounds, the theory "invalid," "unrealistic" or "inapplicable" is to reveal failure to understand the basic methodological constitution of most social sciences.

Imagine an empirical researcher attempting to test by a naïve questionnaire method the "theory of overtaking," questioning hundreds of drivers about their ability to estimate distances and speed, and to calculate the relevant time intervals and the degrees in which a small change in any one of the variables affected the result. Would he not obtain the most hopeless assortment of answers? Would not these answers support the conclusion that the assumptions of the theorists had been wrong and that one must look for other explanations? Yet I can hardly believe that any sensible person would deny the relevance of the enumerated variables and would contend, for example, that speed and distance of the approaching automobile could not have been taken into account by the driver passing the truck, because he was not good in mathematics.[21]

The Analysis of Change Needs No Exactness

The business man who equates marginal net revenue productivity and marginal factor cost when he decides how many to employ need not engage in higher mathematics, geometry, or clairvoyance. Ordinarily he would not even consult with his accountant or efficiency expert in order to arrive at his decision; he would not make any tests or formal

---

[19] Lester, *Am. Econ. Rev.,* Vol XXXVI, No. 1, p. 72.

[20] *Ibid.,* p. 75.

[21] Driving at night, when he has nothing to go by except the size and brilliance of the headlights of the approaching cars, the experienced driver becomes conscious of the fact that in daytime he has better ways of sizing up their speed and distance. With reduced visibility he will "calculate" with greater safety margins.

calculations; he would simply rely on his sense or his "feel" of the situation. There is nothing very exact about this sort of estimate. On the basis of hundreds of previous experiences of a similar nature the business man would "just know," in a vague and rough way, whether or not it would pay him to hire more men.

The subjectivity of his judgments is obvious. Just as different drivers may reach different conclusions about the advisability of passing another car under given "objective" conditions, different business men will have different "hunches" in a given situation. The subordinates or partners of the man who makes a decision may sharply disagree with him; they may see the situation quite differently. They may be more optimistic about the possibilities of obtaining more orders with only slight price concessions or through increased sales efforts (which would raise both the marginal revenue and marginal productivity curves drawn by the theorist to characterize their considerations). Or they may be more certain about the technical possibility of achieving a larger output by certain production methods (which would lower the marginal cost curve, and could raise or lower the marginal productivity curves). Some decision, usually a routine decision without debate, is made, or at least some action is taken; and the decision or action is necessarily affected by the business man's conjectures concerning sales possibilities and production possibilities.

The way in which changes in the essential variables will affect the probable decisions and actions of business men is not much different if the curves which the theorist draws to depict their conjectures are a little higher or lower, steeper or flatter. These curves are helpful to the student of economics in figuring out the probable effects of change—in learning in what direction output, prices and employment are likely to be altered, and under what circumstances increases or decreases are likely to affect business men of different vision or daring in rather similar ways; and any differences can be conveniently "typed" in terms of shapes, positions and shifts of the curves into which the theorist condenses the business men's conjectures.

Equipped with this understanding of the meaning and purposes of marginal analysis, we may proceed to a discussion of the findings of empirical research which purportedly failed to verify it—or by which it was deemed to be contradicted and disproved.

II. EMPIRICAL RESEARCH ON THE SINGLE FIRM

There is not as yet available any large amount of material derived from systematic empirical research on the business conduct of the single firm. But almost everybody interested in these questions has had occasional conversations with business men, and the impressions gained from such inquiries into the business men's experiences often form an empirical basis for the doubts which so-called "realistic" critics entertain of "theoretical" analysis.

I submit that the few systematic and the many casual researchers have often been misled by pitfalls of semantics and terminology and by a naïve acceptance of rationalizations in lieu of genuine explanations of actions.

Economists' Vocabulary and Business Language

The vast majority of business men have never heard of expressions such as elasticity of demand or supply, sloping demand curves, marginal revenue, marginal cost. If they do not know the words or the concepts how can they be supposed to think in these terms? A scattered few of the men may have been exposed to such words and ideas in half-forgotten college courses, but they have found in practice they had no use for a vocabulary unknown to their associates, superiors, subordinates, and fellow business men. Thus the most essential terms in which economists explain business conduct do not exist in the business man's vocabulary. Does this not prove that the explanations are unrealistic or definitely false?

Only an inexperienced researcher could draw such a conclusion. The technical terms used in the explanation of an action need not have any part in the thinking of the acting individual. A mental process in everyday life may often be most conveniently described for scientific purposes in a language which is quite foreign to the process itself.

To ask a business man about the "elasticity of demand" for his product is just as helpful as inquiring into the customs of an indigenous Fiji Islander by interviewing him in the King's English. But with a little ingenuity it is possible to translate ideas from the business man's language into that of the economist, and *vice versa*. Questions such as "Do you think you might sell more of this product if you cut the price by 10 per cent?" or "How much business do you think you would lose if you raised your price by 10 per cent?" will evoke intelligent answers in most cases provided the questions are readily reformulated and adapted to the peculiarities of the particular man and his business. Often it will be necessary to know a good deal of the technology, customs and jargon of the trade, and even of the personal idiosyncrasies of the men, before one can ask the right questions. A set formulation of questions will hardly fit any large number of business men in different fields and, hence, questionnaires to be filled out by them will rarely yield useful results.

Rationalizations of Decisions or Actions

Psychologists will readily confirm that statements by interviewed individuals about the motives and reasons for their actions are unreliable or at least incomplete. Even if a person tries to reconstruct for himself in his memory the motives and reasons for one of his past actions, he will usually end up with a rationalization full of afterthoughts that may make his actions appear more plausible to himself. Explanations given to an interviewer or investigator are still more likely to be rationalizations in terms that may make the particular actions appear plausible and justified to the inquirer. In order to be understood (and respected) the interviewed person will often choose for his "explanations" patterns of reasoning which he believes to be recognized as "sound" and "fair" by others. Most of these rationalizations may be subjectively honest and truthful. It takes an experienced analyst to disentangle actual from imaginary reasons, and to separate relevant from irrelevant data, and essential from decorative bits of the information furnished. Written replies to questionnaires are hopelessly inadequate for such purposes.[22]

Questions of business policy are particularly difficult objects of inquiry because the business man usually is anxious to show by his answers

---

[22] *Cf.* George Katona, *Price Control and Business* (Bloomington, Ind., 1945), p. 210. He states that "only detailed interviews can probe into the motives behind business decisions."

that he is intelligent, well informed, and fair. The standards of fairness and business ethics to which he wishes to conform are often those which he believes are accepted by his lawyers, accountants, customers, competitors, fellow citizens, economists and whatnot. Only through detailed discussions of different situations and decisions, actual as well as hypothetical, will an investigator succeed in bringing out true patterns of conduct of the individual business man.[23]

A. Average Cost and Price

One of the conclusions of casual or systematic empirical research on the business firm is that business men do not pursue a policy of maximizing profits, and of pricing according to the marginal cost and marginal revenue principle, but instead follow rules of pricing on the basis of average cost calculations even where this is inconsistent with profit maximization.

We shall attempt to reinterpret the findings of systematic research along these lines. For this purpose we must first clear up some misunderstandings which appear to have contributed to the support for the average-cost theory of pricing.[24]

---

[23] For further comments on the difficulties of good empirical research on business conduct, see my paper "Evaluation of the Practical Significance of the Theory of Monopolistic Competition," *Am. Econ. Rev.*, Vol XXIX (1939), p. 233. After discussing the policies of my former business partners I concluded (p. 234): "An investigator who would have based his findings on their answers to questionnaires or even on personal interviews, would have come to erroneous results. An investigator who could have seen all the actually or potentially available statistics would have come to no results at all. The only possibility for a fruitful empirical inquiry into these problems lies, I think, in the more subtle technique of analyzing a series of single business decisions through close personal contact with those responsible for the decisions."

[24] According to modern theory price equals average cost (inclusive of normal profit) chiefly under the pressure of competition. The individual firm will charge a price above or below average cost depending on the situation and in line with the marginal calculus. However, when price has risen above average cost, other firms will expand production and new firms will enter the industry and their competition tends to reduce price to the average cost level. Thus it is not the price policy of the individual firm but the pressure of actual or potential competition which makes prices equal to average cost. In contrast with this, the theory advanced by the critics of marginal analysis asserts that firms set their prices according to average cost regardless of the state of competition and regardless of the market situation.

171

Averaging Fluctuating Costs and Prices

In discussions with business men I have found that two different types of averages must be distinguished: averages over time and averages as a function of the volume of output.

Selling prices frequently fluctuate over time, not only cyclically and seasonally but during the week or the day. In calculations for investment, cyclical price fluctuations will be taken into account and average prices will be estimated. In planning the production of seasonally demanded goods—summer dresses, swimming suits, winter sport clothes, Christmas toys—price discounts for off-season sales will be counted into the average selling price. Hotels in resorts may charge preferential rates for guests arriving on Tuesdays and leaving on Thursdays; wholesale grocers will dispose of over-ripe fruit and vegetables at reduced prices; public utilities may charge lower rates to industrial off-peak customers; in all these cases the firms will have to figure out their average revenue or average price.

Costs may show similar fluctuations over time. Raw—material and fuel prices may vary cyclically and seasonally, electric–power rates even over different hours of the day. Seasonal changes of the weather may cause cost differences in several technical processes—natural instead of artificial heat for drying when wind, temperature and humidity are favorable; hydroelectric instead of steam-generated power when rivers carry sufficient water; and so on. These and hundreds of other reasons call for calculations of average costs by the affected business firms.

The average revenues and average costs which must be calculated to take care of such variations over time are not in the least inconsistent with the marginal revenue and marginal cost principles. Indeed, if increases in output are under consideration, the marginal changes of revenue and cost as functions of output will have to comprise any changes over time that will affect revenue or cost. That the firm figures with these averages over time does not mean that it makes its decisions concerning price policies on the basis of an average-cost rule rather than the maximum-profit rule.

Actual versus Potential Average Costs

The absence of the expressions "marginal cost" and "marginal revenue" from the business man's vocabulary and the fact that he usually explains his price policy in terms of "average cost" account for a good part of the skepticism of the empiricists. Yet, the words used are not indicative of the lines of thinking; the marginal calculus may be followed ·without pronouncing or knowing any of the terms in question.

In the economist's jargon, the business man who considers taking more business is supposed to say to himself: "At the increased volume of output, marginal cost will be this much and marginal revenue that much." (Statement I.) In a literal translation into everyday language, he would say, "The increase in production will cost me this much and will bring in that much." (Statement II.) He could say it also in a different version: "The increase in business will raise total costs from this to this much, and total receipts from that to that much." (Statement III.) These statements are absolutely equivalent, all expressing the marginal calculus of variations.

The same thing can also be expressed in a fourth, much more complicated way: "The increase in business will change average cost from this to this much, and average price from that to that much; it will, therefore, change profits by changing the margin of so and so much, times an output of this much, to a margin of so and so much, times an output of that much." (Statement IV.) With all its complications the statement is still equivalent to the former ones. It is a bit foolish to divide total costs and receipts by the output figures just in order to multiply afterwards the differences again by the output figures; but it is not incorrect. The average cost figures as such are, of course, irrelevant in the calculation.[25]

The average cost figures, in spite of their prominent place in our busi-

---

[25] This can be easily illustrated by assuming any set of figures. Assume that the firm considers taking new orders for 1,000 tons of product, reducing its average price. Statement IV might read: "The increase in business from 10,000 tons to 11,000 tons will raise total cost from $80,000 to $86,900 and, hence, will reduce average cost from $8.00 to $7.90; it will raise total receipts from $99,500 to $107,800 and, hence, will reduce average price from $9.95 to $9.80; it will, therefore, raise profits by changing a margin of $1.95, times an amount of 10,000,

ness man's complicated statement, had no place in his actual decision. The decision was based on the profitableness of the added business. When not only the current but also the potential average cost—that is, the average cost at a different production volume—and also the change in total receipts are considered, then the reasoning is true marginal calculus, not average-cost reasoning as some mistakenly believe.

Average-Cost Pricing as the Lawyer's Ideal

Generations of lawyers have accepted and proclaimed the fairness of the average-cost standard of pricing. Decades of regulatory experiments and arguments, and a long history of court decisions, have emphasized the average-cost principle as the just basis of pricing. Is it then surprising that business men try to explain their pricing methods by average-cost considerations?

Corporations in regulated industries are some times caught in their official price justifications: a change in the market situation may make it wise and profitable to change the selling price, but that price has been anchored to an average-cost calculation which it is now difficult to disavow. The company cannot very well submit to their regulatory commissions revised average-cost calculations every time market conditions change. They have to put up with relatively inflexible prices which, were it not for the regulatory authorities, might be as much against their own interests as against those of the consumers.

More often, however, the business man is not conscious of the fact that he uses average-cost considerations merely as rationalizations or justifications. Selling with high profit margins might indicate monopoly and "squeezing of the consumer"; selling below cost might indicate un-

---

i.e., $19,500, to a margin of $1.90, times an amount of 11,000, *i.e.*, $20,900. Let's take the business."

Statement III would read under the same circumstances: "The increase in business will raise total costs from $80,000 to $86,900, that is by $6,900, and will raise total receipts from $99,500 to $107,800, that is by $8,300. Let's take the business."

Statement II on the same situation would read: "The increase in production will cost me $6,900 and will bring in $8,300. Let's take the business."

Statement I, finally, would read: "At the increased volume of output, marginal cost will be $6.90 and marginal revenue $8.30. Go ahead."

fair competition and "cutting the throat of the competitor." As a good citizen the business man wishes to avoid both these wicked practices. As long as he can justify his prices as covering "average cost plus a fair profit margin" he can say, to others as well as to himself, that he is living up to the accepted standards of law and decency. If this "fair profit margin" is at times a bit generous and at other times rather thin, he can still justify his price. (That such variations betray his "explanation" of this pricing method as incomplete or untenable may escape his attention as well as that of his inquirers.)

Average-Cost Pricing as the Accountant's Ideal

Selling price must cover average cost inclusive of overhead and fair profit margin if the business enterprise is to live and to prosper. A good accountant regards it as his duty to watch over the soundness of the firm's pricing methods and to warn against prices below full cost.

Practical and academic accountants have sometimes attacked the marginal-cost principle as a fallacy conducive to practices that are liable to result in business losses. They have reasoned that a general application of differential cost considerations might mean that firms forget that they ought to recover their overhead in *some* part of their business.

Reasoning of this sort reveals a twofold misunderstanding of the marginal principle. (a) That marginal cost does not "include" fixed overhead charges need not mean that it will always be below average total cost; indeed, marginal cost may equal or exceed average cost. (This will always be true for volumes of output at or beyond "optimum capacity" of the firm.) (b) To use marginal cost as a pricing factor need not mean that price will be set at the marginal cost level. Indeed, this will never be done. In the exceptional case of pure competition, price cannot be "set" at all but is "given" to the firm and beyond its control; and marginal cost will be equal to price not because of any price policy but only because of adjustments in the firm's production volume. In the normal case of monopolistic competition, the firm will never charge a price as low as marginal cost; it will charge a price at which marginal revenue is equal to marginal cost, and this price must therefore be above both.

It is a stupid misunderstanding to believe that the use of marginal cost in the business man's pricing technique implies an advice that selling price should be set at the marginal cost level. Marginal cost and marginal revenue considerations mean nothing else but what a business man means when he asks himself: "Could I get some more business and would I want it under the conditions under which I could get it?"

The idea, held by some accountants, that pricing on the basis of the marginal principle would sacrifice profits is the opposite of the truth—except in one very special sense; where the average-cost rule has been used as a monopolistic device, resort to the marginal principle might be taken to mean abandonment of a cartel arrangement in the industry and "outbreak" of unrestricted competition.

Average-Cost Pricing as a Cartel Device

In times of depression business men often discover that it is wiser to lose only a part rather than all of their overhead cost; that it is better to sell at prices below full cost than to stick to prices which would cover all costs but at which they cannot sell. They usually deplore these deviations from the full-cost principle of pricing and argue that nobody would *have* to sell below cost if nobody *did* sell below cost.

Price fixing among producers or official price codes may in such situations succeed in the maintenance of a monopolistic level of price in spite of strong temptations for competitive price cutting. Tacit understandings about the observation of average-cost rules of pricing sometimes constitute an alternative way of achieving price maintenance in a declining market. Moral suasion in the direction of "good accounting" and of "sound pricing" on the basis of "full cost" may be an effective device of domestic price cartels (through trade associations or in the form of tacit understandings).

Outright price fixing, just as any other cartel agreement, is a device to affect the estimates of demand conditions for the products of the individual firms. Only if demand as seen by the individual seller is effectively changed through his anticipations of serious reactions on the part of his competitors and fellow cartel members will he find it advantageous to restrict his output to the extent necessary for the maintenance of the agreed price. The essential effect of the agreement is upon the elasticity of the expected demand. As a rule, elasticity becomes absolutely zero (that is, the demand curve breaks off abruptly) at the largest volume of output which the individual cartel member thinks he can sell at the fixed price. If he considers price cutting in contravention of the agreement as a practical alternative, the demand curve will not break off but continue downward with reduced elasticity—reduced because of the risk of penalizing or retaliatory actions.

The general adoption of an average-cost rule is in effect a price agreement among the members of the particular industry. Where a trade association announces a representative "average cost," the announced value need not tally at all with the average cost of an individual firm. Where cost conditions are believed to be very similar throughout the industry, the understanding may be informal and tacit. It may be made entirely a matter of "business ethics" not to sell below average cost plus fair profit margin. For the firm which strictly observes this ethical code the demand curve breaks off abruptly at the output it can sell at that price. The average-cost calculation of that firm takes the place of the fixed cartel price and is the essential determinant of its demand and marginal-revenue considerations.

If a business man believes that the best policy for him in the long run is to stick to the cartel, this does not mean that he disregards the marginal principle. On the contrary, the feared consequences of breaking away from the cartel, its probable effects upon long-run demand and revenue, dictate his continued adherence. Likewise, if violations of the ethical code of average-cost pricing are feared to have adverse consequences, continued membership in this "ethical cartel" is not a departure from the marginal principle. The average-cost rule and the sanctions for violating it have the same sort of effects upon demand elasticity and marginal revenue which other types of price agreements have been shown to have.

Average Cost as a Clue to Demand Elasticity

Even without any ethical or unethical code prescribing an average-cost rule of pricing, average cost may be the most important datum for the estimate of demand elasticity. The elasticity of demand for any particular product is determined by the availability of substitutes. In order to estimate how much business a firm may lose if it raises its price, it will consider whether existing or potential competitors can supply competing products at the particular price. The elasticity of supply from competing sources determines the elasticity of demand for the firm's product. The supply from competing sources will depend on their actual or potential cost of production. And usually the best clue that a firm has to the production cost of competitors is its own production cost, corrected for any known differences of conditions.

Assuming that competitors have the same access to production factors, materials and technology, their production cost can not be much different from that of a particular producer who may just be weighing the chances of a price increase. In the absence of any cartel arrangements he will have to count on his competitors to expand their business at his expense if he ventures to raise his selling price above average cost. Where he need not fear the capacity of existing competitors, but entry into the industry is relatively easy, he will have to reckon with newcomers' competition if he makes the business too attractive by allowing himself too generous a profit margin above average cost. Under such circumstances he will know that he stands to lose too much business and had better stick fairly close to a price based on average cost.

Notwithstanding any rationalizations of this price policy, the reasons for it lie in the competitiveness of the industry resulting in a high elasticity of demand visualized by individual sellers.[26] To "explain" this price by reference to some emotional attachment to the average–cost principle is to miss the mark. The role of average cost in the firm's pricing process in this case is to aid in gauging the elasticity of the long-run demand for its product.

Reasons and Variables

Seeing how many different roles average cost may play in the pricing process without in the least contradicting the statement that marginal

---

[26] Where the average-cost rule is a cartel device, the elasticity of demand will be small or zero from the actually realized point on *downward*. When average cost is a clue to sizing up potential competition, the elasticity of demand will be high from the actually realized point on *upward*. The former prevents price reductions, the latter price increases.

cost and marginal revenue determine output and price, one should realize the dangers of attempts to use utterances of business men as evidence against the correctness of marginal analysis.

Business men's answers to direct questions about the reasons for charging the prices they are charging are almost certainly worthless. Every single fact or act has probably hundreds of "reasons"; the selection of a few of them for presentation to the inquirer is influenced by the prejudices or old theories which the informant had impressed upon him by school, radio, newspapers, etc.

Except in the case of a genuine decision leading to a recent change of policy, one may say that an approach much more fruitful than that of asking about reasons *for* some policy is to ask about reasons *against* its alternatives. Instead of asking for explanations of the price actually charged or the output volume actually produced, questions about "why not more" and "why not less' are likely to yield more revealing results. But even these answers must be checked and double-checked through a network of cross-examination, segregating and isolating certain variables in a manner familiar to the scientist working with the calculus of variations and with the determination of partial derivatives.

Research on Actual Pricing Methods

On the basis of marginal analysis of the firm and the industry, we should expect for most industries that price in the long run would not deviate too much from average cost, yet that the firm would attempt to get better prices when it could safely get them and would not refrain from cutting prices when it believed that this would increase its profits or reduce its losses.

Now let us compare with this the findings of one of the empirical research undertakings which shook the researchers' confidence in the marginal principle and convinced them that business men followed the "full-cost principle" of pricing regardless of profit maximization. Inquiry was made through interview of 38 "entrepreneurs." [27] A large majority of them explained that they charged the "full cost" price. Some, however, admitted "that they might charge more in periods of exceptionally high

---

[27] R. L. Hall and C. J. Hitch, *op. cit.*, p. 12.

demand"; and a greater number reported "that they might charge less in periods of exceptionally depressed demand."[28] Competition seemed to induce "firms to modify the margin for profits which could be added to direct costs and overheads."[29] Moreover, "the conventional addition for profit varies from firm to firm and even within firms for different products."[30]

This is precisely what one should have expected to hear. Do these findings support the theory of the average-cost principle of pricing? I submit that they give little or no support to it. The margins above average cost are different from firm to firm and, within firms, from period to period and from product to product. These differences and variations strongly suggest that the firms consult other data besides or instead of their average costs. And, as a matter of fact, the reported findings include some that indicate what other considerations were pertinent to the price determinations by the questioned business men.

Of 24 firms which gave reasons for not charging higher prices, 17 were tabulated as admitting that it was "fear of competitors or potential competitors" and a "belief that others would not follow an increase." Another two stated that "they prefer a large turnover."[31] To me the 19 answers indicate that these business men were estimating the risk of losing business if they raised prices or, in other words, that they were concerned about the elasticity of demand.

Of 35 firms which gave reasons for not charging lower prices, 4 firms explained that they were members of price-fixing combinations; 2 stated that it was "difficult to raise prices once lowered"; and 21 referred directly or implicitly to their estimates of demand elasticity. (Nine firms: "Demand unresponsive to price"; one firm: "Price cuts not passed on by retailers"; eleven firms: "Competitors would follow cuts.") Only 8 firms gave reasons other than monopolistic price fixing or monopolistic elasticity considerations; these 8 were listed as having "quasi-moral objections to selling below cost."[32] Unfortunately the interviewers did not find out what these conscientious objectors to price cutting thought

---

[28] *Ibid.*, p. 19.
[29] *Ibid.*
[30] R. L. Hall and C. J. Hitch, *op. cit.*, p. 20.
[31] *Ibid.*, p. 21.
[32] *Ibid.*

about the responsiveness of demand; and whether they would remain adamant if they were sure that a small price concession would produce a large increase in sales. I suspect that a cross-examination would have brought out the fact that the moral or quasi-moral views on price maintenance were regularly coupled with a very strong opinion that a price reduction would not produce sufficiently more business and, thus, would constitute useless sacrifice of profits.

In any event, there is little or nothing in the findings of this inquiry that would indicate that the business men observed an average-cost rule of pricing when such observance was inconsistent with the maximum-profit principle. On the other hand, there is plenty of evidence in the findings that the business men paid much attention to demand elasticities—which to the economist is equivalent to marginal–revenue considerations.

The Absence of Numerically Expressed Estimates

Why should others in the face of this evidence have come to the conclusion that the marginal principle was not applied and profit maximization not attempted by the group of business men studied? How could others have failed to be impressed by the facts just recited?

It seems that their confidence in the conventional analysis was lost when they found to their surprise that the business man had no definite numerical estimates of the magnitudes relevant to the application of the marginal principle. They had assumed that a business man should "know" the elasticity of demand for his product, and now they were shocked to find "that the great majority of entrepreneurs were in profound ignorance with regard to its value."[33] A student who had expected to find exact estimates must indeed have been disappointed when most of his informants "were vague about anything so precise as elasticity."[34]

The inquirers found the same vagueness with regard to marginal–cost estimates. While the entrepreneurs usually computed direct cost and total overhead "with some pains at accuracy,"[35] they could not furnish

---

[33] R. F. Harrod, *op. cit.*, p. 4. Concerning this discovery Mr. Harrod remarks emphatically: "This, indeed, must be regarded as one notable result of our inquiry."

[34] R. L. Hall and C. J. Hitch, *op. cit.*, p. 18.

[35] R. F. Harrod, *op. cit.*, p. 4.

any data on marginal cost. He who expected that marginal cost and marginal revenue were equated on the basis of precise calculations must feel stultified. The student who had to do homework computing marginal cost and revenue figures to the second or third decimal point may feel befooled when he learns that the business man does not do anything of the sort. But to conclude from the absence of definite numerical estimates that the magnitudes in question were irrelevant in the conduct of the firms is a *non sequitur.* On the basis of the previous discussion of this subject (see above pp. 166 ff.) we should understand that the construction of a pattern for the analytical description of a process is not the same thing as the actual process in everyday life; and we should not expect to find in everyday life the definite numerical estimates that are part of the scientific pattern.

Apart from the absence of numerical estimates of marginal revenue and marginal cost it is difficult to see what other findings of the inquiry could have persuaded the researchers that they had disproved the theory of marginalism in the conduct of the firm. There is not a single proposition in the tabulated results of the inquiry that can not be fully harmonized with marginal analysis. The "Analysis of Replies to Questionnaire on Costs and Prices," which the researchers presented as an appendix to their report,[36] contains a wealth of illustrative material— illustrative, as I see it, of the application of the marginal principle to business decisions of the single firm.

B. Marginal Productivity and Wage

Empirical research designed to verify or disprove marginal productivity theory in the analysis of input of the individual firm is beset with difficulties. Few systematic endeavors have been made and none has led to any suggestion, however vague or tentative, of an alternative theory. Whereas in certain price research projects those who felt compelled to reject the marginal theory have advanced the average-cost theory of pricing as a substitute, no substitute theory has been forthcoming from those who decried marginal–productivity theory.

---

[36] R. L. Hall and C. J. Hitch, *op. cit.,* pp. 33-45.

Statistical Research

Empirical research on cost, price and output of the individual firm has resulted in several interesting attempts to derive marginal cost functions from statistical data; and also in one or two attempts to derive price elasticities of demand for a firm's products. But nobody, to my knowledge, has ever undertaken to construct from actual data a marginal net revenue productivity curve for a given type of labor employed by a firm. The difficulties are formidable and, since the raw material for the calculations could not come from any records or documents but merely from respondents' guesses of a purely hypothetical nature, the results might not be much more "authentic" than the schedules made up by textbook writers for arithmetical illustrations.

Statistical studies of the relationship between wage rates and employment in large samples of individual firms or industries would be nearly useless because we have no way of eliminating the simultaneous effects of several other significant variables, especially those of a psychological nature. An increase in wage rates may have very different effects depending on whether the employer (1) (a) has foreseen it, (b) is surprised by it; (2) (a) reacts quickly to it, (b) reacts slowly to it; (3) (a) expects it to be reversed soon, (b) expects it to be maintained, (c) expects it to be followed by further increases; (4) (a) assumes it to be confined to his firm, (b) assumes it to affect also his competitors, (c) believes it to be part of a nation-wide trend; (5) connects it with an inflationary development; or is influenced by any other sort and number of anticipations. Most of these moods and anticipations can be translated by the economist into certain shapes or shifts of the marginal productivity functions of the firms; but since the researchers cannot ascertain or evaluate these conjectural "data" for the large number of firms contained in a representative sample, statistical investigations of the wage-employment relation of individual firms are not likely to yield useful results.

Questionnaire on Employment

It has been pointed out above (p. 170) why the method of mailed questionnaires without supporting interviews is hopelessly inadequate for

183

empirical studies of business conduct. Even the most intelligently devised set of questions would not assure reliable and significant answers. Questions designed to achieve the necessary separation of variables would be so complicated and call for so high a degree of "abstract thinking" on the part of the questioned business men that questionnaires of this sort would be too much of an imposition, and cooperation would be too small. Although the questions in Professor Lester's research project on employment did not even approach these standards, he received only 56 usable replies from 430 manufacturers whom he had asked to fill out his questionnaires.[37]

Professor Lester's questionnaires suffered not merely from the inherent weaknesses of the method but also from defects in formulation. These defects were so serious that even the most complete, reliable and intelligent answers could not have yielded significant findings. The business men were asked to rate the "importance" of several factors determining the volume of employment in their firms. No explanation was given whether this importance of a variable—that is, I presume, its responsibility for changes in the employment volume—should refer to (a) the frequency of its variations, (b) the extent of its variations, or (c) the effects of its variations. Surely, the variable rated as least important—perhaps because it varied less frequently than the others—may be just as strategic as any of those with higher importance ratings. What we really need to know, however, is not the *comparative* importance of several factors but rather the effects of variations of each factor separately while the others remain unchanged.

If I want to know by how much an increase in the price of spinach may affect its consumption in an individual household, I shall not get very far by asking the householders to give a percentage rating to each of several listed factors that are believed to be "important" influences on spinach consumption. If it were tried, we should not be surprised to find changes in family income, the number of children and guests at dinner, and the notoriety of Popeye the Sailor's gusto for spinach, receiving much higher percentage ratings than changes in the price of spinach. (In a number of households price may not be a factor at all.) Nobody,

---

[37] R. A. Lester, *Am. Econ. Rev.*, Vol. XXXVI, No. 1, pp. 64-65.

I hope, would conclude from such a poll that price is an unimportant factor in the consumption of spinach.

Yet Professor Lester followed just this procedure when he wanted to find out how important wage rates were in determining the volume of employment in the individual firm. He asked the executives of the companies to "rate" the following factors "in terms of the percentage of importance of each":

   a. Present and prospective market demand (sales for your products, including seasonal fluctuations in demand).

   b. The level of wage rates or changes in the level of wages.

   c. The level of material costs and other non-wage costs and changes in the level of such non-labor costs.

   d. Variations in profits or losses of the firm.

   e. New techniques, equipment, and production methods.

   f. Other factors (please specify).

Of these items the first unquestionably excels all others in frequency and extent of variations. That it won first prize in Professor Lester's importance contest is therefore not surprising. If several respondents gave ratings to item d (variations in profits or losses) and at the same time also to other items, they obviously did not realize that this variable comprised all the others. Professor Lester does not explain why he listed it when he knew that it was not "completely independent" and that "for example, wages affect profits."[38] Nor does he state whether the 43 firms which failed to mention changes in wage rates as an important factor meant that they would continue in business and continue to employ the same number of workers regardless of any degree of wage increase. If this is what they meant, they can hardly be taken seriously. If they meant something else, then it is not clear just what the replies should indicate about the probable effects of wage increases upon employment.

The strangest thing about Professor Lester's list of possibly important variables is that all—except f, the unspecified, and d, the all-inclusive profit-and-loss item—are essential variables of the very analysis which he means to disprove. The prize-winning item, a, the demand for the product, is certainly a most crucial determinant of marginal productivity. (See above pp. 160 and 162.) Items c, non-labor cost, and e, production

---

[38] *Ibid.*, p. 66.

techniques, are two other determinants of marginal productivity. How Professor Lester came to think that the results of this poll would in any sense disprove or shake marginal-productivity analysis remains a mystery.

Questionnaire on Variable Cost

Professor Lester asked his business men also some questions on unit variable costs and profits at various rates of output. The information obtained in answer to these questions might have been useful had it not been based on an undefined concept of "plant capacity." Unfortunately, it must be suspected that not all firms meant the same thing when they referred to "100 per cent of capacity."

Economic theorists use different definitions of capacity. One widely-used definition marks as 100 per cent of capacity that volume of output at which short-run total cost per unit is a minimum; another definition fixes the 100 per cent mark at the output at which variable cost per unit is a minimum. The former definition implies decreasing average total cost, the latter decreasing average variable cost, up to "100 per cent capacity." Professor Lester after painstaking empirical research arrives at the following finding:

The significant conclusion from the data in this section is that most of the manufacturing firms in the industries covered by this survey apparently have decreasing unit variable costs within the range of 70 to 100 per cent of capacity production. . . . [39]

Has Professor Lester asked himself whether this is not merely a self-evident conclusion implied in the definition of capacity used by his respondents?

The steepness of the reported decline in unit variable cost, however, would be an interesting observation—if the data were reliable. (Few of Professor Lester's firms had "constant unit variable costs," or anything approaching this situation, over a considerable range of output.[40]) It is rather peculiar that unit variable costs should decrease steeply (at an increasing rate!) down to a certain point and then abruptly start rising —as one must infer from the term "100 per cent capacity." Where

[39] *Ibid.*, p. 71.
[40] *Ibid.*, p. 70.

186

equipment is not utilized for 24 hours a day, the steep decline and abrupt rise of the unit cost are somewhat questionable.

Professor Lester, nevertheless, has sufficient confidence in his findings to draw conclusions—conclusions, moreover, which could not even be supported if the findings were of unquestionable validity. He states:

> If company output and employment policies are based on the assumption of decreasing marginal variable cost up to full capacity operations, much of the economic reasoning on company employment adjustments to increases and decreases in wage rates is invalid, and a new theory of wage-employment relationships for the individual firm must be developed.[41]

This deduction simply does not follow from the premises. There is no reason why decreasing marginal costs should invalidate the conventional propositions on factor cost and input. Professor Lester could have found dozens of textbook examples demonstrating the firm's reactions under conditions of decreasing marginal cost.

Professor Lester may have been deluded by a rather common confusion between related concepts: from decreasing marginal cost he may have jumped to the assumption of increasing labor returns,[42] and from increasing physical returns he may have jumped to the assumption of increasing marginal productivity of labor. Both these jumps are serious mistakes. For instance, the very conditions which may cause a firm to restrict the employment of labor to a volume still within the phase of increasing physical productivity per unit of labor are likely to result in decreasing marginal net revenue productivity of labor. These conditions are:

(a) an indivisibility of the firm's physical plant facilities,[43] combined with either (or both),

(b) a low elasticity of the demand for the firm's products[44] or (and)

(c) a low elasticity of the supply of labor to the firm.[45]

The first condition, (a), makes a phase of increasing physical produc-

---

[41] *Ibid.*, p. 71.

[42] *Ibid.*, p. 68.

[43] *I.e.*, the firm cannot adjust the number of machines or production units to smaller production volumes but must instead produce small outputs with an inefficiently large productive apparatus.

[44] *I.e.*, the firm realizes that it can charge much higher prices for smaller outputs or cannot dispose of larger outputs except with substantial price reductions.

[45] *I.e.*, the firm realizes that it can enjoy much lower wage rates at lower employment levels or cannot obtain more labor except with substantial wage increases.

tivity of labor in the firm a practical possibility; the other conditions, (b) or (c), make that phase relevant for actual operations by providing the pecuniary incentive to operate the plant inefficiently. Condition (b), the low elasticity of demand for the product, will cause marginal net revenue productivity of labor to be diminishing in a range of employment in which average or even marginal physical productivity of labor is still increasing.

It is not possible from Professor Lester's exposition to find out whether his failure to see these relationships was at the bottom of his faulty theorizing on this point. In any event, his findings on variable costs contain nothing that would even vaguely bear on the validity of marginal analysis.

Questionnaire on Adjustments

Professor Lester's fact-finding and theorizing on substitution between labor and capital and on other adjustments of the firm to changes in wage rates are also marred by inconsistencies and misunderstandings.

After trying to make the most of increasing returns to labor and only a few lines after referring to "unused plant capacity," Professor Lester asserts that "most industrial plants are designed and equipped for a certain output, requiring a certain work force. Often effective operation of the plant involves a work force of a given size."[46] To operate within the phase of increasing returns is to operate inefficiently, that is, with an employment of less labor with a given plant than would be compatible with efficient operations. (Because an increase in employment would raise output more than proportionately.) "Effective operation," on the other hand, logically implies employment at or beyond the point where diminishing returns set in. Professor Lester does not seem to be clear which way he wants to argue.[47]

Professor Lester seems to think that substitution between capital and labor can occur only in the form of installation of new or scrapping of

---

[46] *Amer. Econ. Rev.*, Vol. XXXVI, No. 1, p. 72.

[47] Absolutely fixed proportions between factors of production would imply that short-run marginal productivity of labor drops precipitously to zero at the full capacity level of employment.

existing machinery[48] and that it is supposed to occur "readily" and would, therefore, be "timed" with the wage changes.[49] These are rather common but nevertheless mistaken views.

Professor Lester does not discuss a glaring contradiction in his findings: On the basis of replies to one questionnaire he states that his data indicate "that industry does not adapt its plant and processes to varying wage rates in the manner assumed by marginalists."[50] But on the basis of another questionnaire about adjustments to increases in relative wages, he reports that the introduction of "labor-saving machinery" was given the highest rating in relative importance by the questioned firms whose labor costs were more than 29 per cent of total cost.[51]

The last-mentioned questionnaire apparently was designed to show that wage increases had no important effects upon employment. Six alternative adjustments to increases in relative wages were listed and manufacturers had to give percentage ratings for relative importance. In this popularity contest an item called "deliberate curtailment of output" got the booby prize. Quite apart from the fact that the words were loaded against this item, the result is not in the least surprising. For it is a well-known fact that where competition is not pure (as it rarely is in industrial products), output adjustments to higher production costs take place by way of changes in selling price. Price and product adjustments were another of the alternative items and scored rather well in the poll. If all employment-reducing adjustments—labor-saving machinery, price increases, and deliberate output curtailment—are taken together, they clearly dominate in the importance ratings by the firms.[52] This, or anything else, may not mean much in such an "opinion poll," but it certainly does not prove what Professor Lester wanted to prove. Nevertheless, he contends that "it is especially noteworthy that deliberate curtailment of output, an adjustment stressed by conventional marginal theory, is mentioned by only four of the 43 firms."[53] And he concludes that marginal analysis is all but done for, that "there can be little doubt

---

[48] *Am. Econ. Rev.*, Vol. XXXVI, No. 1, p. 73. See my comments, above, pp. 161—62

[49] *Ibid.*, pp. 73 and 74.

[50] *Ibid.*, p. 73.

[51] *Ibid.*, p. 78.

[52] *Ibid.*, p. 78.

[53] *Ibid.*, p. 79.

about the correctness of the general results" of his test,[54] and that "a new direction for investigations of employment relationships and equilibrating adjustments in individual firms" is indicated.[55]

C. Conclusions

I conclude that the marginal theory of business conduct of the firm has not been shaken, discredited or disproved by the empirical tests discussed in this paper. I conclude, furthermore, that empirical research on business policies cannot assure useful results if it employs the method of mailed questionnaires, if it is confined to direct questions without carefully devised checks, and if it aims at testing too broad and formal principles rather than more narrowly defined hypotheses.

The critical tone of my comments on the research projects discussed in this paper may give the impression of a hostile attitude towards empirical research as such. I wish to guard against such an impression. There should be no doubt that empirical research on the economics of the single firm is badly needed, no less than in many other fields. The correctness, applicability and relevance of economic theory constantly need testing through empirical research; such research may yield results of great significance.

Sharp criticism of bad research can be constructive in two respects: it may save some of the waste of time which the published research findings are apt to cause if they remain undisputed and are allowed to confuse hosts of students of economics; and it may contribute to the improvement of research. The chief condition for improved research is a thorough understanding of the theories to be tested. Supplementary conditions are a certain degree of familiarity with the technological and institutional peculiarities of the fields or cases on which the research is undertaken and a grasp of the research techniques employed.

---

[54] *Ibid.*, p. 81.
[55] *Ibid.*, p. 82.

ON THE
MEANING OF
THE MARGINAL PRODUCT

Reprinted with permission from *Explorations in Economics*, McGraw-Hill Book Company, 1937.

The marginal productivity of a "factor of production" is usually defined as the schedule of the increments in total "product" obtainable through application of additional units of the "factor." As the quotation marks enclosing "factor" and "product" may indicate, there is no unanimity as to the appropriateness of these words or as to their meaning and definition. Nothing will be said here about the comparative advantage of terminologies; the word factor of production, for example, will be used interchangeably with productive agent, productive service of resources, and the like. It is with the meaning of the terms employed, especially with the units in which factor and product are expressed or measured, that we shall be concerned. Space will not be allocated to the various problems in proportion to their significance; problems of secondary, or even minor, importance may be given a greater (unearned) share of space, partly in order to prove their unimportance, partly because it is the "small things" that invite the interest of the "disinterested" student.

I

Physical Units of Factors

The units of services, the application of which leads to a change in "product," are mostly taken as physical units. They have to be conceived as two-dimensional: as the services of some physical or natural unit of resource through some unit of time. The choice both of the unit of *resource* and of the unit of *time* must be governed by considerations of divisibility and technical or economic relevance, that is to say, it "is not an arbitrary matter of methodology, but a question of fact."[1] We must not take a minute of the labor of an eighth of a man as our unit of labor; nor ordinarily will we take "a year-laborer,"[2] although this may be the smallest unit in which some highly qualified labor services can be bought. The divisibility with respect to time of highly qualified labor deviates particularly from that of the more common types of labor—inasmuch as certain qualified services may be bought by the minute at the one extreme, by five-year contracts only at the other. Organization and other institutional factors (legal provisions, tradition, rules adopted in collective bargaining) may in some trades or industries make quite ordinary labor indivisible below a week.[3] But differences in the length of the labor-week make the hour a more convenient time dimension and the habit of the market has accepted the labor-hour as the customary physical unit.

The unit of land, of course, is any traditional measure of area—not quite so "natural" a one, thus, as the "human unit." If some definite size is taken as "the smallest" unit, it is done so, not because of any limited divisibility of land, but because of the limited divisibility of its complementary factors. The time extension, likewise, depends upon the technique of production—in farming it is a year.

To decide on the unit of capital is to open (or to prolong) a very lively discussion. What resource, first, is spoken of as capital? Some authors choose to speak in terms of particular capital goods (steam engines, power looms, shovels), others in terms of money capital (dollars, francs), others in terms of "abstract disposal over resources," which last can hardly be considered a physical unit. However capital may be defined, its time dimension is perfectly divisible, though rarely is it divided into smaller parts than a day. The market has adopted the year as the basic time unit ("per annum") for expressing the price but the day as the smallest time

---

[1] F. H. Knight, *Risk, Uncertainty and Profit* (Boston: Houghton Mifflin, 1921) p. 111.

[2] As does A. C. Pigou, *Economics of Welfare* (London: Macmillan, 1932) 4th ed., p. 772.

[3] J. R. Hicks, *The Theory of Wages* (London: Macmillan, 1932) p. 27.

unit for actual exchanges. "Time proper" has been suggested as the only dimension, and unit, of the factor capital; this has no meaning, it seems to me, unless what is meant is that "waiting time" or "investment period" is to be conceived of as *a third dimension* of any other (otherwise two-dimensional) factor. This third dimension is, then, the time interval between the application of any productive service, say a labor-hour, and the enjoyment of its product. It is, for certain purposes, more convenient to take waiting time and the value of productive services invested for this time as the two dimensions of capital. Capital, in this case, is no longer amenable to expression in terms of physical units. In the sphere of purely physical units, however, such waiting time can refer only to a concrete physical resource.[4]

"Marginal" productivity of factors has sense only if the units of factors are homogeneous in respect of "efficiency."[5] This must be taken into account in a puristic definition of "factor" by including only productive services of perfect substitutability (interchangeability), while services which are not perfectly substitutable for one another are considered as different factors. If this strict definition of factor is employed, the traditional classification, enumerating three or four factors of production, is definitely abandoned; there is a multitude of productive factors.

Efficiency Units

Many theoretical problems can be simplified if one may assume full homogeneity of factors, *e.g.*, equal efficiency of all laborers or uniform grade or quality of land. (This should not be done for "capital in general" if that is expressed in "physical units.") But often writers are tempted to proceed from this convenient assumption to such statements as that a labor-hour of a certain efficiency is equal to two labor-hours of half the

---

[4] When K. Wicksell discusses "the marginal productivity of waiting" (*Lectures on Political Economy*, London: Routledge, 1934 p. 177), he assumes, at first, a certain number of physically defined resources which receive their value in a process of capitalization at the rate given by the marginal productivity of waiting.

[5] Hicks (*op. cit.*, p. 28) says: "If the labourers in a given trade are not of equal efficiency, then, strictly speaking, they have no marginal product. We cannot tell what would be the difference to the product if one man were removed from employment; for it all depends on which man is removed."

efficiency or to half an hour of double efficiency. Such conversion of units of different efficiencies into uniform efficiency units sometimes involves the danger of circularity in reasoning.

The efficiency of any physical or natural unit of a factor can be measured only by its "effect" on the product; if natural units are then corrected for their different effects on product and, thus, converted into efficiency units, the further examination of the relationship between those units and marginal product may be badly distorted—especially if the different causes of efficiency disparity are not clearly distinguished, and, still more, if the efficiency in producing value,[6] rather than physical efficiency, is taken as a base.

Differences in physical efficiency of physical units of factors may be due to various causes: (*a*) differences by constitution, *i.e.*, natural heterogeneity as to potential performance in definite activities; (*b*) differences in energy and effort expended on the work; (*c*) differences through economies from the larger size of the productive combination, due to specialization or organization of lumpy elements (*i e.*, increasing returns from proportional additions of all factors); (*d*) differences through varied proportions in the factor's cooperation with other factors (*i.e.*, increasing or decreasing returns with changes in the proportion of factors); (*e*) differences due to different techniques. It seems that only the first two[7] of these five causes have been in the minds of recent writers, when they tried, by eliminating them, to construct efficiency units.[8]

---

[6] It is just in this way that Professor Pigou wishes to construct efficiency units. He makes (*op. cit.*, p. 775) the following suggestion. "In order to render this procedure legitimate, all that we need do is to select in an arbitrary manner some particular sort of labor as our fundamental unit, and to express quantities of other sorts of labor in terms of this unit on the basis of their comparative values in the market." Thus, "all the various sorts of labor . . . can be expressed in a single figure, as the equivalent of so much labor of a particular arbitrarily chosen grade."

[7] Joan Robinson distinguished "corrected natural units," which were the "natural units of the factors corrected for their idiosyncrasies" (*Economics of Imperfect Competition*, p. 332), from "efficiency units," which were corrected for variations in efficiency due to increasing returns. When the units were corrected for these differences (type *c* from above list) only constant physical returns would be got (*op. cit.*, p. 345). In a later article on "Euler's Theorem and the Problem of Distribution" (*Economic Journal*, Vol. XLIV [1934], p. 402), Mrs. Robinson admits "that the device suggested . . . for getting over the difficulty by constructing 'corrected natural units' is completely worthless."

[8] Marx, of course, got his "homogeneous mass of human labor-power" by cor-

Even these two kinds of efficiency disparity could usefully be corrected for by construction of efficiency units only if the differences in efficiency of the natural units of the factors involved were the same in respect of all the various uses to which the units may be put. (Then, and only then, could one expect wage differences to take exact account of efficiency disparities.) But if the differences are different in respect of different occupations, then indeed the case is different.

On first thought, one might imagine that labor is grouped in several efficiency classes—each then constituting a group of homogeneous factors —and that degrees of substitutability are established between the various classes. But this device breaks down when we realize that the members of one group, while uniform within their group and perfectly substitutable with respect to a certain occupation, are not equally suitable for other jobs. Some members of the group may be almost perfectly substitutable for those of another group, others very little. In view of the different efficiency in other kinds of work of laborers who are homogeneous only concerning one occupation, it is not possible to express the substitutability of the different groups (factors) for one another by a single definite figure. There would be, instead, a whole range or schedule of figures from almost infinite to almost zero substitutability, and these schedules would be different between the groups F_1 and F_2, F_1 and F_3, F_1 and F_4, . . . F_1 and F_n. The substitutabilities of factor F_1 for factor F_2 could perhaps be represented as a positive function of the number of members still working in the F_1 group; for the more units that are still employed as factor F_1, the greater will be the number of the more versatile units included; the greater the number of units from the group F_1 who have been called upon as substitutes for other factors, the smaller will be the "marginal substitutability" for factor F_2 of the rest of factor F_1.

The complications due to the fact that the versatility of a factor is

---

recting all the "innumerable individual units" for their deviations from what he called the labor "socially necessary . . . under the normal conditions of production, and with average degree of skill and intensity prevalent at the time." Thus, after the invention of the power loom, one labor-hour of a hand-loom weaver was "only half an hour's social labor." See *Capital*, Vol I (ed. Kerr, 1909), p. 46. The great difference between the (however questionable) efficiency units employed by modern writers and those employed by Marx lies in that the former do not try to deduce the value of the products from the quantity of labor after they had deduced the quantity of labor from the value of the products.

not universal for all types of work but differentiated with respect to different types are bad enough. They are multiplied if one tries to take account of the further fact that the substitutability of services for one another is also an increasing function of time. (Skill is increased, abilities acquired, resistances overcome, etc.) This is true not only of substitutability between different grades of labor, but also between labor and "capital." The very definition of capital, indeed, depends on the length of time allowed for rearrangements to be carried through. If capital is referred to as *one* factor of production, it is because of its efficiency in allowing time-taking processes to be undertaken. This efficiency is different according to the length of time allowed for the forms to be changed.

Apart from these special properties of "the factor" capital, the complications are dire enough to make us well understand how much more convenient it is to assume homogeneity of factors, or to assume a moderate number of non-competing groups, or to reason, with Marshall, about factors of "normal" or "representative" efficiency.[9] Such assumptions are not only more convenient but "realistic" enough to permit of first, and higher, approximations to the solution of most problems. Mr. Hicks's conclusions in his *Theory of Wages* are not appreciably damaged by the fact that he assumed "average unskilled labor" to be of uniform efficiency in all industries.[10]

A most peculiar species of efficiency unit is Professor Pigou's "unit of uncertainty-bearing," which is defined as "the exposure of a £ to a given scheme of uncertainty, or . . . to a succession of like schemes of uncertainty during a year . . . by a man of representative temperament and with representative knowledge."[11] Having recognized that uncertainty-bearing and waiting were "generally found together" but "analytically quite distinct from" each other, Professor Pigou tries to establish uncer-

---

[9] Alfred Marshall, *Principles of Economics,* 8th ed., p. 516. Whether J. B. Clark's "social unit of labor" (*Distribution of Wealth,* p. 63) is an efficiency unit or a value unit, or some still more mythical unit, I have not been able to find out.

[10] *Op. cit.,* p. 33. In drawing marginal productivity curves for a particular firm one need not be disturbed by considerations of whether or not additional units of factors of equal efficiency will be obtainable; the lowest quality of additional units may be taken care of by a decreased elasticity of the factor supply curve to the firm (Robinson, *Imperfect Competition,* p. 345); that is to say, the slope of the factor supply curve may express the decreasing efficiency of the units which have to be drawn from other groups or grades.

[11] Pigou, *op. cit.,* p. 772.

tainty–bearing as "an independent and elementary factor of production standing on the same level as any of the better-known factors." For want of a natural unit of uncertainty-bearing he constructs ingeniously an efficiency unit by reducing the uncertainties involved in different exposures "on the basis of comparative market values" to an equivalent in terms of an arbitrarily selected "fundamental unit" of uncertainty-bearing.[12] That through modern developments, especially through the pooling of certain uncertainties, a number of undertakings have become less uncertain than in former times leads Professor Pigou to the statement that "the factor uncertainty-bearing has been made technically more efficient."[13]

As we have said above, efficiency units as natural units corrected for differences in physical performance in well-defined activities are *toto caelo* different from efficiency units with market values taken as the measure of efficiency. These latter are more correctly regarded, and frowned upon, as "value units" of factors.

Units of Factors in Terms of Value

By measuring units of factors in terms of their market value, marginal productivity analysis is, to my mind, reduced *ad absurdum*. One must bear in mind that marginal–productivity analysis as a part of the theory of distribution is to serve as explanation of the market values of factors or services. To define these services in terms of their market values is to give up the task of explaining them. Indeed, to use Professor Knight's words, "we cannot discuss the valuation of things without knowing what it is that is being evaluated."[14] After all, the marginal productivity curve is to be the substance behind, and under certain assumptions the same as, the demand curves for factors, *i.e.*, for definite (physically defined) services, not for units of value.[15]

---

[12] *Ibid.*, p. 775.

[13] *Ibid.*, p. 778.

[14] Knight, *op. cit.*, p. 125.

[15] Mrs. Robinson's "marginal product per unit of outlay" was an attempt at getting a marginal productivity curve which constituted the entrepreneur's demand curve not only under most but under all assumptions. In these terms, wage will equal "marginal product" even for employers who are monopsonistic buyers of labor. See "Euler's Theorem," p. 412.

Value units of factors are what Professor Pigou once called a "Pound Sterling worth of resources." He used this concept not in the theory of distribution but in an analysis of the national dividend, and he has withdrawn it from the later editions of his *Economics of Welfare*. One could never explain the exchange ratio between productive services of different kinds, if one measured their units in value terms. That a hundred dollars worth of labor services equals a hundred dollars worth of uncertainty bearing, and equals a hundred dollars worth of land services would be all our wisdom.

When it has, thus, been made clear that the units of a factor must not be measured in value terms, it becomes twice as difficult to show that "units of capital" in terms of value are of a different stuff from those units which we have just solemnly condemned. Capital, when conceived as associated with waiting time, or investment period, or consumption distance of something, needs, of course, a fuller designation of this "something," be it a commodity or a service of a (human or man-made) resource. Under quite particular assumptions it is possible to remain in the sphere of purely physical units, but we should have, then, as many different factors as we have different "somethings," and, to be sure, just as many different marginal productivity schedules. But if we choose to conceive of capital[16] as the total stock of non-permanent resources at a given time which enables us to use a part of the available productive services for the production of future outputs, then the aggregate of such resources cannot be expressed but in value terms. They are "homogeneous" only in the one respect that they permit the undertaking of time-consuming methods of production. The value of the resources (bundles of services) is the result of a choice between a great number of alternative uses of their services of which some are devoted to immediate consumptive satisfaction. The valuation of these services is, therefore, to some extent determined by opportunities other than their use in "capitalistic" (time-taking) production. More about these value units of capital will be said at later points of our analysis.

---

[16] I should like to express my indebtedness to Professor von Hayek, whose unpublished manuscripts helped me greatly in arriving at my views on capital theory.

Units of Factors in Terms of Money

Measurement in units of value is a highly abstract conception as long as value is thought of "in real terms." To make it more realistic, one may think in terms of money. It is only in the case of one factor that units may properly be measured in terms of money, the case, namely, of capital, or, more appropriately termed, money capital. In a sense, we may regard units of money capital as natural units.[17] It is units of money that are the object of the producers' demand. That money is demanded by entrepreneurs because it gives command over resources does not impair the argument. This demand—for *money to invest*—is not to be confused with the concept of a demand for money—*money to hold*—employed in monetary theory. Observations about the marginal productivity schedule of money capital may be deferred to a later point when we discuss the units of return.

The problem of correcting money units of capital for changes in efficiency (namely in the efficiency to provide command over resources) forces itself on one's mind when one considers that the supply of money capital may originate from credit creation through an elastic banking system or through dishoarding—with ensuing changes of prices. All these price changes would, of course, find their expression in changes of the marginal productivity curves. But some writers wish to eliminate certain price changes (of cost elements) by means of corrected units. That is to say, they wish to deflate the money-capital units with reference to particular price indices. Examples of "units of capital in terms of buying-power" so devised are Mr. Keynes's "wage-units" and "cost-units," which relate the money units respectively to the wage level and to the level of all prime-cost factors.[18]

II

Physical Units of Product

That the schedule of marginal products in terms of physical units is fundamental for all other productivity schedules can be stated without

---

[17] *Cf.* Robinson, *Economics of Imperfect Competition*, p. 343.

[18] J. M. Keynes, *The General Theory of Employment, Interest and Money* (London: Macmillan, 1936), pp. 40 *et seq.*

fear of contradiction. It is also true that serious points of analysis arise in connection with physical productivity: problems such as increasing and diminishing returns as phases of the "law of proportions of the factors," the quite different increasing returns due to specialization of factors and similar "economies," questions concerning divisible, indivisible, limitational factors, and what not. Indeed, the widespread discussion of this range of problems makes it excusable, or even imperative, to leave them aside here in favor of other matters.

Value of the Marginal Physical Product

It is only in terms of value that different types and qualities of product become comparable and economic problems arise. But the particular concept of the "value of the marginal physical product" is not the all-important one; it is, in fact, relevant for but two special cases.

The one is the case of a producer who sells his goods on a market so perfectly competitive that he does not expect any price changes to result from an increase or decrease of his output. In such a producer's expectations, the value of an addition to his physical product would be the same as an addition to the total value of his output. This is the meaning of the proposition that, to the competitive seller, the value of the marginal physical product is equal to the marginal product of value.

The second case is that of an economist, like Professor Pigou, who reflects upon the national dividend and its measurement. For his purpose it is not relevant whether an addition to the physical product of a particular kind does or does not cause the value of all such goods to fall; he considers relevant nothing but the value of the physical marginal (social) net product.[19]

Marginal Value Product

"Marginal product" without other adjectival qualification should be understood to mean, not marginal physical product, but marginal value

---

[19] Pigou, *op. cit.*, p. 135.

product.[20] Synonyms are marginal product in value, or marginal product of value. Value productivity, and nothing but value productivity, is what matters in distribution theory.

The marginal value product is the composite effect of a number of elements, or changes of elements; how many and which of those elements have to be taken into account in making up the marginal productivity schedule depends entirely on the problem in hand. In an analysis of the equilibrium of the single firm all those "dependent changes" have to be included in the economist's reasoning which are held to be included in the entrepreneur's reasoning. And what these changes are will, of course, depend on the particular entrepreneur's estimate of his position in the markets in which he deals. The pure competitor will not anticipate any price changes to follow from his actions; a monopolistic competitor will anticipate certain reactions on the part of consumers, and perhaps also certain reactions on the part of his competitors, in framing his own policy of pricing and output; a producer who faces imperfect competition in the markets where he buys will anticipate changes of the factor prices to result from his actions. And this is but a small list of "dependent changes." On another plane, anticipations of more or less future, more or less lasting, price changes, anticipations of political forces, of monetary policy, and the like, may enter. Turning from the single firm to problems of the industry or the economy as a whole, still more "dependent changes" must be taken into account.[21]

Discounted Marginal Product

Just as products of different kinds or qualities can be compared only in terms of value so products available at different moments of time can

---

[20] It is perhaps worth emphasizing that the founders of modern theory regarded, either implicitly or explicitly, the marginal product as value product: thus the "marginal contribution to value" in the theory of imputation of Menger and Wieser, Wicksteed's "marginal worth of services," Marshall's "net increase in the money value of total output." These writers, of course, did not see the differences in value product arising out of different degrees of competition.

[21] The problem of selecting those "other things being changed " the reactions of which may be shown by the shape of the curve, and those "other things" the reactions of which may be shown by a shift of the curve, calls for separate treatment.

be compared only in terms of present or discounted value. That the rate of discount may depend in turn on the marginal productivity of capital no more invalidates the argument than does the fact that the prices of other factors are data for the productivity schedule of the factor under view.[22]

Thus, it is perfectly correct to explain wages "by the discounted marginal product of labor,"[23] or, in a recent formulation, by the equalization of the "cost of any unit of current labor" to "the discounted value of every alternative output that could be gotten from it."[24]

Uncertain Marginal Product

It should be clear that all these marginal products are not realized but expected products, that is to say, they are the resultants of a number of estimates in somebody's mind. Such estimates are made with more or less confidence in one's own foresight and more or less uncertainty about the probabilities of the anticipated outcomes. The entrepreneur whose business process is "complicated, long-stretched-out, and uncertain as to its outcome . . . not only discounts, he speculates."[25] And, as has been shown convincingly by Knight, he will, in his demand prices for factors, take account of the uncertainty involved in his undertaking—so that, in case his estimates should all be proved right in the course of events, a profit would be left for him.

The marginal productivity schedule for any factor will therefore be in terms of discounted, and more or less "safely" estimated value. (That is to say, with some "safety margin" because of the uncertainty involved.) Are now these marginal products conceived as value "in real terms" or in terms of money?

---

[22] The discussion of "marginal net productivity" in Section III will dwell upon this point.

[23] F. W. Taussig, *Principles of Economics*, Chap. LII. (New York: The Macmillan Co., 1937).

[24] Hicks, "Wages and Interest: The Dynamic Problem," *Economic Journal*, Vol. XLV (1935), p. 461.

[25] Taussig, *ob. cit.*, Vol. 2, p. 200.

Marginal Product in Terms of Money

There cannot be any doubt that the marginal productivity schedule within the single firm runs in terms of money and nothing but money. Whether the marginal productivity schedules for factors in the industry or in the economy as a whole are conceived in real terms or in money terms depends on—the economist concerned. Such marginal productivity schedules are nothing but a convenient method of depicting anticipated reactions of the most complicated sort in the form of a simple functional relation. It is a matter of technique, habit, and predilection (of the economist, of course) whether he wishes to lead his train of reasoning in the one way or the other. Logically the two are equally legitimate. Marginal productivity analysis in terms of money has the advantage of appearing more realistic, and of copying more nearly the way of thinking of economic individuals; but it has the disadvantage of requiring allowance for changes in the supply of money and for changes in "price levels." Marginal productivity analysis in real terms has the advantage of yielding more direct results about the factors' shares in the national dividend;[26] the necessary allowance for changes in relative prices is in this case not much less than that in the case of the schedule in money terms; one distinct disadvantage of the schedule in real terms is that it calls for a supply schedule in real terms, which for short periods is meaningless. This point has been stressed by Mr. Keynes on the ground that, owing to the prevalent significance of money wages in wage bargaining, the labor supply may be determinate in money terms but not in real terms.[27]

---

[26] I suggest that Mr. Hicks's distinction between "labor-saving" and "very labor-saving" inventions (*Theory of Wages,* p. 123) may be represented as follows. Labor-saving inventions may raise the marginal productivity of labor (though relatively less than the marginal productivity of the other factors) in real terms, but must lower it in terms of money. "Very labor-saving inventions" lower it in both real and money terms.

[27] Keynes, *op. cit.,* p. 8. Mr. Keynes overemphasizes this point. If money wages are fixed, the lower and left part of the labor supply curve becomes irrelevant. Changes in employment take place in a range of the graph above and to the left of the labor supply curve.

Marginal Product of Capital in Terms of Ratios

From our discussion of the units of the factor "capital," one would rightly expect that special allowances would have to be made also in the measurement of its units of product. For certain of its meanings, we allowed capital to be measured in value terms or money terms rather than in terms of physical units. If the product, as well as the factor, is measured in value or money, it will be most convenient to express the one as a ratio of the other. The most concise definition of the productivity of capital is Professor Fisher's "rate of return over cost";[28] cost, in turn, is the value of all invested services with respect to their alternative uses. In a sense, the ratio or rate in which the marginal product of capital is expressed is determined by the "time substitutabilities" between the alternative consumptive services that can be obtained at different future points of time from present productive services.[29]

III

The strict definition of the marginal productivity of a factor, as the schedule of increments in product due to additional units of the factor *used with a given (unchanged) amount of other factors,* raises problems which we have so far neglected. To apply the principle of "unchanged amounts of other factors" to the economy as a whole is one thing; to apply it to each single establishment is another. The application to the economy as a whole allows reapportionment of all factors with respect to their combinations in different groups or establishments. The application to a single establishment breaks down in those cases where the

---

[28] Irving Fisher, *The Theory of Interest* (New York: The Macmillan Co., 1930) p. 155. Mr. Keynes (*op. cit.,* p. 135) presents the following definition of the "marginal efficiency of capital in general." It is defined as equal to the greatest of those rates of discount "which would make the present value of the series of annuities given by the returns expected from the capital-asset during its life just equal to its supply price." As I understand it, this definition is not meant to exclude small investments in working capital, like the investment in a few labor-hours; such investment is fully covered by the term "capital-asset."

[29] *Cf.* Hicks's article on "Wages and Interest," in the *Economic Journal,* Vol. XLV (1935), and my article on "Professor Knight and the Period of Production" in the *Journal of Political Economy,* Vol. XLIII (1935).

proportion in which the different factors cooperate cannot be varied with continuous and small effects on the amount of product. Imagine the proportion between all or some of the factors within a group to be rigidly fixed, owing to technical conditions (like the proportion of elements in chemical compounds); then the increase in the amount of one of these factors without accompanying increase in its complementary factors would yield a zero addition to the product, while the decrease in the amount of the same factor would cause a considerable loss of product. For these reasons, a number of authors (foremost, Wieser and Pareto) raised strong objections against the application of the marginal productivity principle to single groups or single firms, and derived the value of the factors from their alternative uses through transfer of factors between different groups within the economy. Even with rigidly fixed proportions of factors *within* all given groups, an increase (or decrease) in the supply of a certain factor in the economy as a whole can be taken care of through changes in the proportion *of* the different groups, that is to say, through an increase (or decrease) in the number of these groups which employ more of this factor and a decrease (or increase) in the number of those groups which employ less of this factor.

Principle of net productivity is the name by which Mr. Hicks denoted this chain of reasoning.[30] Its counterpart is the *principle of variation,* which is to give us marginal products through assuming variability of the proportion of factors within each combination. It is, as Hicks has shown, the principle appropriate to long-run considerations, while the net productivity principle is that appropriate to the short period, during which some proportions are likely to be rigid.

For the marginal productivity schedules (as substance behind the demand for factors) of single firms or industries, the marginal *net* product is the fundamental concept. "The net product," said Marshall, " . . . is the net increase in the money value of . . . total output after allowing for incidental expenses."[31] The incidental expenses, *i.e.,* the payments to

---

[30] *Theory of Wages,* p. 14; "Marginal Productivity and the Principle of Variation," *Economica,* Vol. XII (1932). Marshall's "marginal net product" supplied the term, though Marshall himself did not separate it from the marginal product where full variability of factors was given. Remember the marginal shepherd who did not call for any new complementary factors to be added to the establishment.

[31] *Op. cit.,* p. 521.

other factors newly employed together with the factor under consideration, are anticipated on the basis of these other factors' prices, which are
given for the single firm and determinate for the economy as a
whole. It is capital that is nearly always in complementary demand with other factors. If it were possible to employ one more unit
of labor in a given plant, with given machinery, given raw material, and
given intermediate products, it still would not be a "given amount of
other factors," since the application of more capital is involved in the
investment of more labor-hours over a certain period. The net productivity
principle may be considered as another support—if it were needed—
for the legitimacy of using given rates of interest for finding the marginal net product of labor (the discounted marginal product), and of
using given prices of invested services for measuring the units of capital.

The principle of variation and the principle of net productivity yield
the same results, if enough time is allowed for the former to come into
full play. But also in the short run one may consider the strict marginality
principle as fully satisfied[32] by the net productivity principle. For it
secures, for the economy as a whole, through factor transfers between
different establishments, the perfect variability of proportions which is
postulated by the clause that "additional units of one factor are used
with a given (unchanged) amount of other factors." The schedule of a
factor's marginal productivity in the economy as a whole will, of course,
be quite different from an aggregate of all marginal productivity curves
in all single enterprises of the economy. The former will take account
of the necessary changes of the latter due to the conservative changes in
prices of the complementary factors in the course of their reapportionment among competing uses.

---

[32] This was recognized by Professor F. M. Taylor, *Principles of Economics*, Chap.
IV (New York: Ronald Press, 1925) See on this point Knight, *op. cit.* pp. 102-
114, and Hicks, "Marginal Productivity and the Principle of Variation," *Economica*,
Vol. XII (1932).

REPLY TO
PROFESSOR TAKATA

Reprinted by permission from *Osaka Economic Papers,* Vol. IV, No. 2, Sept. 1955.

I. Introduction

Every year, for the last 28 years, I told the students in my classes, perhaps very wrongly but with sincere conviction, the following story about the marginal productivity theory.

There are many teachers who present what they call the marginal productivity theory as a theory of wages. I believe that this should not be done, because (1) there is not one "marginal productivity theory" but there are several, so that it would be preferable to speak of a "marginal productivity principle" which can be used in different theories, and (2) the marginal productivity principle is not used as a "theory of wages," or a theory of factor prices, but only as a theory of demand for factors of production.

(1) The marginal productivity principle is used in at least four different theories:

(a) in the theory of input determination by the individual firm;

(b) in the theory of factor employment by the particular industry;

(c) in the theory of the factor market; and

(d) in the theory of general equilibrium.

In these different theories the m. p. principle is combined with several different sets of assumptions; for example, in the theory of the firm we are not constrained to assume either pure or perfect competition, but may assume any kind of monopoly or oligopoly, monopsony or oligopsony. In the theory of the industry we must assume pure competition among the firms, but there may well be monopoly on the factor supply side; moreover, it is not necessary to assume perfect newcomers' competition (pliopoly in my terminology) but we may assume an industry closed to new entrants. In the theory of the factor market we are confined to more stringent assumptions; we shall have to assume pure insiders' competition as well as perfect newcomers' competition in the industries which compose the demand for the factor; we are still free to assume a monopolistic supply of the factor. In the general equilibrium theory of the Walrasian form we are limited to assumptions of pure and perfect competition all around. There are some recent attempts to expand general equilibrium theory enough to permit imperfection of competition among the assumptions but this is still controversial among the theorists.

(2) The marginal productivity principle alone can never explain the wage rate, because a demand curve alone can never explain a price. A supply curve must furnish the other blade of the theoretical scissors. In the limiting case of a "perfect market" with "perfect competition" it is sometimes said that, given the supply curve of labor, the marginal productivity curve will determine the wage rate; but with equal justification one could say in this case that, given the marginal productivity curve of labor, the supply curve will determine the wage rate. Both expressions had better be avoided.

(3) We should avoid expressions such as "marginal productivity" rises or falls, or is raised or lowered, because it is never clear whether we mean
   (a) marginal productivity at the given volume of employment,
   (b) marginal productivity at an adjusted smaller or larger volume of employment,
   (c) marginal productivity at a volume of employment at which the factor supply is fully employed, or
   (d) marginal productivity at any volume of employment, that is, the whole curve.

It is usually possible by proper safeguards to make clear which of these four meanings we have in mind.

(4) Since we must distinguish
  (a) the marginal physical product,
  (b) the value of the marginal physical product,
  (c) the marginal value product (or marginal revenue product), and
  (d) the marginal net revenue product,

we should use such language as would avoid confusions among these four concepts of marginal productivity.

II. Terminology

I hope you will forgive me for troubling you with this long introduction. I did it in order to explain to you some of my oral comments on your paper. Now it will be easy to see that there is no *real* difference of opinion between us, but only a difference in the meaning we have attached to our terms. You mean by "marginal productivity theory" what I mean by the "limiting case."

I concede readily that "marginal productivity theory of wages" (in your language) has broken down and must be discarded. Using my language, however, we must regard the marginal productivity theory of demand for labor as a highly useful tool. For example, it helps us explain why, if (in the absence of unlimited competition among workers for jobs and through the exercise of union power or state power) the wage rate is set above the level which marginal productivity (marginal net revenue product) would have at full employment, the actual volume of employment will be smaller. Indeed, it is only the marginal productivity theory of demand that can help explain by how much the actual volume of employment will be reduced at the wage rate so fixed. The wage rate itself can be explained only by applying some additional principle, such as your power theory.

While, I believe, there is no disagreement between us on the essential points, we may ask whether my terminology is permissible. An analogy may help us in the answer. Would we ever say that the marginal utility theory breaks down and must be discarded when commodity prices are fixed by monopolists or by the government? Surely "marginal utility" will not in these cases explain the prices, but it will explain the quantities demanded at the prices fixed by monopoly or state power. What the marginal *utility* principle does in the theory of demand for consumers goods,

209

the marginal *productivity* principle does in the theory of demand for productive factors. Thus I submit that there is a good justification for my terminology. Please forget or disregard what John Bates Clark wrote about marginal productivity, and do not blame modern theorists for what our predecessors may have "intended." The intention of marginal productivity theories in modern theory is *not* the explanation of factor prices.

III. Real Issues

To make sure that we really agree on the real issues, I shall confirm my agreement on specific points:

(1) There may be, and usually is, wage rigidity even in the absence of labor monopoly.

(2) The monopoly power of unions cannot be explained entirely by their market position; a large part of the explanation will be in terms of sociological and political factors.

(3) In the course of technological progress, many changes in production technique will reduce, rather than increase, the marginal productivity of labor both at the actual employment level and the full employment level. This reduction may well be so drastic that even a large increase in the supply of capital may not suffice to offset it.

(4) Actual wage rates are often above the level which marginal productivity would have at the point of full employment; unemployment will arise as a result.

(5) To explain how wage rates can be raised to and maintained at such levels, we must resort to explanations outside "pure economic theory"; the power theory probably provides the principle for these explanations.

I may have missed some other real issues, but I have not noticed any point of essence on which I would disagree with you.

Section Four

Semantic Issues

in Macro-economics

and Economic Policy

FORCED

OR

INDUCED SAVING:

An Exploration Into Its Synonyms And Homonyms

Reprinted with permission from *The Review of Economics and Statistics,* Vol. XXV, No. 1, February 1943.

Concepts and Terms in Flux

Concepts and terms, in every-day use as well as in scientific use, have often peculiar histories. A "new" concept is usually an adaptation of an old one which suggests itself to observers of a phenomenon as they attempt its interpretation. If the new concept is still unnamed, they name it after some other idea that appears to them as an appropriate simile or metaphor. The chosen name, however, may suggest to others some slightly different associations and, therefore, altered concepts. Moreover, changes of the frame of reference, or of the angle from which the phenomenon is looked upon, may require remodeling of a concept. But the remodeled concept may still pass under the old name. Other observers come along, dislike the name, and suggest different ones. Synonyms develop. Most or all of the terms which are then used for the growing family of concepts have had previous uses, and many of the terms are again put to new uses. Homonyms and equivocations grow in number. Makers of dictionaries must list more and more meanings under each name and must give more and more synonyms for each meaning.

To complain about the continuous change of concepts and terms, about the conversion of ideas and names, is to misunderstand the nature of growth of a body of knowledge—at least in the social sciences. Attempts to halt the development (for example, through the establishment of "committees on nomenclature and terminology") are in vain and often deplorable. To be sure, wilful innovators sometimes suggest change merely for the sake of change. If concepts and terms shift like women's fashions, the change may confuse discussion and become a nuisance.[1] But otherwise, we must accept it as a fact that new problems and new treatments of old problems may require changes in concepts and in terms.

When the family of related concepts—related by meaning or by name or both—is large, an occasional examination of the family record and a probing of the relationships is helpful. Old confusions may be clarified, and new confusions avoided, through such an examination. And better understanding of the concepts usually results in better understanding of the phenomena whose explanation they are to serve.

This article will survey and briefly analyze the various concepts connoted by the term "forced saving," and the various terms assigned to its basic idea.

The Basic Idea of Forced Saving

Many—though not all—of the concepts which passed under the name of forced saving can be reduced to a fairly simple idea. Imagine that the total amount of money spent for goods and services remains absolutely the same from "day" to "day," and that the degree of financial integration (the number of hands or accounts through which money has to pass

---

[1] Jacob Viner once made the accusation that in J. M. Keynes' *General Theory* "no old term for an old concept is used when a new one can be coined, and if old terms are used new meanings are generally assigned to them." (Jacob Viner, "Mr. Keynes on the Causes of Unemployment," *Quarterly Journal of Economics.* LI, 1936, p. 147.) However, many of the Keynesian concepts and terms have proved useful, and current writings on fiscal and monetary economic problems have largely adopted Keynes' conceptual schemes as well as his terms.

on its way from income disburser to income recipient) remains also unchanged. Under these circumstances, total investment outlays can increase if, and only if, income disbursers have decided to increase their savings out of their given money incomes. The condition of the absolutely constant income stream implies an equality between saving and investment, an equality in which the saving is the "autonomous" variable and investment the "adjusted" one. For, on the one hand, no funds are available for investment outlays other than the moneys made available by savers; and, on the other hand, all these available funds are actually used for investments, or the income flow would not remain constant. If now, in contradistinction to the described conditions, an increase in the money and income flow is staged—either through creation and disbursement of new money or through activation of idle money—investment outlays are no longer limited by preceding decisions of income recipients to save. Investment can now exceed intended saving; that is to say, capital formation can be in excess of what people saved out of their previous income; the extra capital formation is "forced," so to speak, upon the community through monetary witchcraft.

This is the basic idea which underlies most of the concepts of forced saving. The basic, simple theme, however, undergoes many complicated variations. It is linked up with other themes, such as the reallocation of resources, movements of prices, changes in income distribution, reaping of windfall profits, adjustments of cash reserves, adaptations of savings to increased incomes, etc. The combination of the basic theme with these supplementary ones is the chief reason for the confusing variety of concepts.

The Role of Forced Saving in Modern Theory

The history of the idea of forced or unintended saving is almost as old as the history of economic doctrines in general; the conception can be traced back at least to 1802. But age is not what makes the idea important. What gives it real significance is the role which it plays in the theory of economic fluctuations and in the theory of economic development.

The strictly "Neo-Wicksellian" theorists saw in the phenomenon of forced saving a mechanism that explained "over-investment" as well as crisis and contraction (Mises, Strigl, Hayek, Robbins, etc.). In the theories of other writers, forced saving played its role only in the explanation of the prosperity phase of the cycle (Schumpeter, Pigou, Robertson, Keynes, etc.). It is interesting to reread in this connection a famous footnote in Lord Keynes' *Treatise on Money:*

> The notion of the distinction which I have made between Savings and Investment has been gradually creeping into economic literature in quite recent years. The first author to introduce it was, according to the German authorities, Ludwig Mises in his *Theorie des Geldes und der Umlaufsmittel* . . . published in 1912. Later on the idea was adopted in a more explicit form by Schumpeter, and "Forced Saving" *(i.e.,* the difference between Savings and Value of Investment as defined by me, though without there being attached to the idea, . . .) has become almost a familiar feature of the very newest German writings on Money. But so far as I am concerned . . . my indebtedness for clues which have set my mind working in the right direction is to Mr. D. H. Robertson's *Banking Policy and the Price Level* published in 1926.[2]

While Professor Mises disclaimed authorship of the term "forced saving"—which actually had been used by Wicksell—he admitted that he had "described the phenomenon."[3] The notion, as we said before, was really not so novel as Lord Keynes first believed. But nowhere was the idea of forced saving as an element of expansion more colorfully employed than in the picture which Professor Schumpeter painted of the tides of trade. Professors Ellis,[4] Haberler,[5] and Marget,[6] in the accounts which they give of Professor Schumpeter's theory, all agree that in it forced saving is "given a prominent place" as "an essential element."

Undoubtedly, the forced-saving idea got its greatest boost in Schumpeterian theory, because here it was promoted from the rank of a cyclical phenomenon to the rank of a secular phenomenon. Forced saving—not the term but the concept—became an essential element in Professor

---

[2] J. M. Keynes, *A Treatise on Money* (London: Macmillan, 1930), Vol. I, pp. 171-72.

[3] Ludwig v. Mises, *Geldwertstabilisierung und Konjunkturpolitik* (Jena: Fischer, 1928), p. 45.

[4] Howard S. Ellis, *German Monetary Theory, 1905-1933* (Cambridge: Harvard University Press, 1934), p. 402.

[5] Gottfried Haberler, *Prosperity and Depression* (3rd edition, Geneva and New York, 1941), p. 42.

[6] Arthur W. Marget, *The Theory of Prices* (Englewood Cliffs, N. J.: Prentice-Hall, Inc., 1938), Vol. I, p. 498.

Schumpeter's *Theory of Economic Development.*[7] For, according to Schumpeter, only credit expansion can finance on a large scale the "new combinations of productive factors" which constitute "development," while whatever contribution to the financing of innovations can be gotten from voluntary saving owes its existence to the high profits derived from previous "development."[8] Thus, in the end, all economic development must be regarded as the result of forced saving.

Professor Schumpeter did not use the term, forced saving, in the first edition of his *Theory of Economic Development,* but only later in a famous German article published in 1918.[9] But the term did not secure permanent favor with Professor Schumpeter. What he once called an "extremely happy expression"[10] he considered later a "misleading phrase" which "it is better to avoid."[11] In this rejection of the term Professor Schumpeter is certainly not alone. If a term has come to connote so many different meanings as is the case with "forced saving," it has lost its usefulness. But the usefulness of the concepts need not be affected by the depreciation of the term under which they were first introduced.

The History of the Idea

Professor Hayek has given us an extremely interesting note on the history of the doctrine of forced saving.[12] I may be permitted to present here a chronological list, based on Professor Hayek's studies, which points to the highlights in this history.

1802: Henry Thornton (Saving arising from "defalcation of revenue")
1804: Jeremy Bentham ("Forced frugality")
1811: T. Robert Malthus ("Augmentation of capital through changed distribution of the circulating medium")

---

[7] First German edition, Munich, 1912; English edition, Cambridge, Mass., 1934.

[8] *Ibid.,* English edition, pp. 72 ff.

[9] "Das Sozialprodukt und die Rechenpfennige," *Archiv für Sozialwissenschaft und Sozialpolitik,* XLIV (1917-18), pp. 627-715, especially p. 706.

[10] *The Theory of Economic Development,* English edition, p. 109.

[11] J. A. Schumpeter, *Business Cycles* (New York: McGraw-Hill Book Co., Inc., 1939), Vol. I, p. 112, fn. 1.

[12] F. A. v. Hayek, "A Note on the Development of the Doctrine of Forced Saving," *Quarterly Journal of Economics,* XLVII (1932-33), pp. 123-33. See also his *Prices and Production* (London: Routledge, 1931), Ch. 1.

1811: Dugald Stewart ("Fictitious capital")
1823: Thomas Joplin ("Pressure and anti-pressure of capital upon currency")
1829: John Stuart Mill ("Forced accumulation")
1879: Leon Walras ("Increase of capital by the issue of bank notes")
1898: Knut Wicksell ("Enforced saving")
1912: Ludwig v. Mises (Credit expansion causing "more capitalistic production" and "increased saving")
1912: Joseph Schumpeter (Credit creation directing resources into "development," generating profits and saving)
1920: Albert Hahn ("Capital formation through credit extension")
1921: Alvin H. Hansen ("Compulsory saving" through "reducing real purchasing power of income recipients")

All the writers included in our brief "history" had the basic idea in common: that investors were furnished money (credit) which was not actually or virtually transferred from money recipients who refrained from using it, but, instead, was additional to the money funds in use; and, thus, that the investment outlays financed by the additional funds were in excess of the investment outlays which could have been made with the funds made available by those who refrained from re-spending all of their receipts. This is, however, merely the immediate monetary aspect of a phenomenon which may assume different real forms. To the real substance behind the monetary screen we must now turn.

Five Extreme Cases

The "real" situation resulting from the excess of investment outlays over "intended saving out of received income" does not conform to a definite pattern; a variety of patterns is possible, depending on a number of conditions. Even if we consider merely the more "immediate" effects of the additional investment outlays (and disregard what may follow in subsequent periods), several possibilities can be visualized. I propose to look into some which, therefore, cover and limit the more probable possibilities.

(A) To start with a very fantastic case, let us assume complete occupational immobility of all productive resources inclusive of labor, with no unemployed reserves available at places where they are needed. Hence, production cannot be increased in any field. The investment goods which are purchased with the additional investment funds are "bidden away" from other investors. Prices of investment goods and incomes of their producers are, of course, increased. The increase in investment outlays is not materialized in any increase in "real" investment. (Looking some steps ahead, one may observe what will be done with the increased incomes of the producers of the higher-priced investment goods. The income increments may in part be saved and the rest may bid consumption goods away from other consumers.)

(B) Going to the opposite extreme, let us assume that unemployed reserves of all productive factors are available in equal efficiency at given prices or wage rates. The investment goods which are purchased with the additional funds are readily produced; the real purchasing power of other investors or consumers is not encroached upon. The increased use of resources is at the expense of leisure only. With prices unchanged, the additional investment outlays are fully materialized in additional real investment. (Looking some steps ahead, the new incomes of the newly-employed factors will be partly saved and partly spent for consumption goods. With all resources available, the production of consumers' goods also can be readily increased to satisfy the new demand.)

(C) Let us assume now that unused resources are available for an expansion of the production of investment goods but not for an expansion of the production of consumption goods, mobility of resources being nil.' The investment goods demanded by the disbursers of the additional funds are readily produced with resources withdrawn only from idleness. Prices of investment goods remaining unchanged, the investment outlay in excess of voluntary saving is fully materialized in additionl real investment. (Looking some steps ahead, the new incomes of the newly employed factors will in part be saved and in part be spent for consumption goods. Since the production of consumption goods cannot be expanded, their prices must rise, the recipients of new incomes bidding away consumption goods from those whose incomes are unchanged.)

(D) For the sake of completeness let us assume now the opposite of the preceding case, namely, that unused resources are available for expanded production of consumers' goods but not for that of producers' goods, mobility still being excluded. The investment goods demanded by the disbursers of the additional investment funds must be bidden away from other investors. Prices of investment goods are increased, and the additional investment outlays are not materialized in additional real investment. (Looking some steps ahead, one may see that parts of the increased incomes of the producers of producers' goods are saved, but other parts spent for consumption goods. With the production of consumers' goods expansible, the "investment in excess of intended saving" would result this time in an increase of real consumption and in no change of real investment.)

(E) Now we come to what was probably the standard case of most writers on forced saving, the case of practically full employment of resources, with reasonable mobility of resources between industries. The additional demand for investment goods on the part of the disbursers of new funds leads to higher prices of investment goods. This means that some amounts of investment goods are bidden away from other investors, but also that the production of investment goods is expanded, productive resources being withdrawn from the production of consumption goods. The additional investment outlay is thus not fully, but to some extent, materialized in additional real investment. (Looking some steps ahead, one may observe the incremental incomes of producers of investment goods partly saved and partly spent for consumers' goods. Prices of consumers' goods will rise for two reasons; first, because of the increased cost of resources; second, because of the increased consumption demand out of increased money incomes. As the consumption demand rises the competition for resources increases and a retransfer of resources from the production of investment goods to that of consumption goods may set in.)

Real Investment and Real Consumption

Summarizing these five cases, all of which started with increased investment outlays and subsequently brought forth increased consumption outlays, we find that the effects upon real investment and real consumption were different in each case.

	Real Investment	Real Consumption
Case (A)	unchanged	unchanged
Case (B)	increased	increased
Case (C)	increased	unchanged
Case (D)	unchanged	increased
Case (E)	increased	decreased

We must distinguish, however, investment as an accumulated stock from investment as a flow, *i.e.*, as a rate per period of time. This distinction may be of importance in the outcome of case (E). For it is not impossible that, in consequence of the increased consumption outlays, the retransfer of resources from the production of investment goods to that of consumption goods eventually leaves the flow of real investment below the level at which it was in the beginning. Nevertheless, in terms of real resources sunk into construction, accumulated investment has increased and, under the particular assumptions, it can have increased only at the expense of consumption. There seems to be little doubt that the writers on forced saving were thinking chiefly of this accumulation of real capital during the transition period.

A few of the writers are anxious to find out at whose expense the real capital was accumulated; that is to say, who it was who did ("was forced to do") the real saving (the "foregoing of consumption") which was embodied in the increased investment. For purposes of such analyses, the concepts of forced saving had to be particularly refined. Specimens of these refined concepts will be discussed after this more general orientation.

Encroachment on Potential Consumption

The conception becomes rather slippery when the implicit assumptions of a given state of the industrial arts and a given supply of productive resources are dropped. If technical progress results in higher efficiencies of productive factors, or if additional amounts of factors are drawn into the productive system, any reduction of real consumption, which otherwise might be associated with forced capital accumulation, becomes unnecessary. Real consumption may even increase. In this case one may be tempted to speak of the encroachment which the forced capital formation makes upon potential consumption or leisure. An advance in technology or a larger supply of resources, in absence of forced saving, would result in larger consumption or more leisure or both; with investment outlays financed by additional credit, some of the resources that would have gone into the production of consumption goods (or into the "enjoyment" of leisure) can be "directed" into the production of capital goods. Professor Schumpeter places much emphasis on this encroachment upon potential alternatives by innovations financed through credit creation: "Even with respect to those quantities of factors which currently accrue . . . and can be used for the new purposes without having previously served any old ones, it is more correct to say that they are shifted from the uses they would have served had the new purposes not been decided on, than simply to say that they go to the new uses directly."[13]

If unemployment is the practical alternative to investment, and if the additional investment outlay and the re-spending of these funds by the recipients of the additional income result in increased production of investment goods as well as of consumption goods, it becomes difficult to insist that the investment constitutes an "encroachment upon potential consumption." Involuntary leisure is not customarily regarded as a part of consumption; it would be too odd to put the label "forced saving" on the "forced reduction of involuntary leisure." This, however, does not mean that in this case the label cannot be used at all. For several other things to which the idea of forced saving may apply are in the picture: that through the additional funds productive resources are "directed" into capital formation; that investment outlays exceed the amounts which voluntary savers intended to set aside from their received incomes; that the additional money sums are accepted by the people and absorbed into their cash balances; that incomes rise and are propagated (passed on and on) until their recipients are induced to save enough to match the additional investment outlays; etc. In other words, the idea of an actual or potential reduction of consumption forced by the additional capital accumulation is only one of a number of ideas connected with the notion of forced saving.

Stinting, Lacking, and Doctored Contracts

The sharpest set of tools for the dissection of some sorts of forced saving was prepared by Professor D. H. Robertson.[14] Indeed, they are so

---

[13] *Business Cycles,* Vol. I, p. 111, fn. 1.
[14] D. H. Robertson, *Banking Policy and the Price Level* (Cambridge, England: Macmillan, 1926) ; "Saving and Hoarding," *Economic Journal,* XLIII (1933), pp. 399-413. Some of the definitions given in the 1926 book were slightly modified in the 1933 article. I am using the latter.

sharp that few writers dare to handle them lest they cut themselves. Therefore, with timid apprehension do I undertake to exhibit the Robertsonian set of concepts.

This set of concepts may be expressed in one sentence, to be explained presently: "Automatic stinting" and "induced saving" will under certain conditions entail "automatic lacking" and "induced lacking," respectively, which together are "imposed lacking"; this, in combination with saving resulting from a "doctoring of past contracts" (a Pigovian creation) and other "windfalls," is what may result from an excess of investment over "spontaneous saving."

Saving, in this conceptual scheme, is the difference between consumption expenditures and "disposable income." Disposable income is the income of the previous "day" (income period). Lacking means consuming less than the value which the disposable income has had at the time of its receipt. Saving refers merely to money amounts; lacking, on the other hand, refers to "real" quantities. I "lack" if I consume today less than yesterday's income was worth yesterday.

Automatic stinting means "consuming less . . . than one would have done if other people had not altered [increased] their expenditures," *e.g.*, their investment outlays, the encroachment upon one's real consumption being the result of actual price increases or of prevented price reductions. Automatic stinting need not involve lacking. For example, one may have decided to dissave, and the intended "dislacking" may just be offset by the automatic stinting. But, if there was no spontaneous dissaving (and no simultaneous change in productivity), automatic stinting entails automatic lacking.

The automatic effects on real consumption—through price increases or prevented price falls—are not the only effects which the increase of other people's expenditures has upon consumers. The increase in the rate of expenditure by other people is liable to disturb "the proportion of money stock to disposable income" of firms and individuals; and they will try to build up their money stocks. This designed building-up of cash balances, in consequence of higher prices and/or higher incomes, is indirectly induced by the additional investment outlays and is, therefore, called induced saving. The induced saving is likely to involve lack-

223

ing, lacking which is voluntary rather than automatic, but certainly not spontaneous: it is induced lacking.[15]

Automatic lacking and induced lacking are the two component parts of imposed lacking, that is, of the lacking which results from the current investment in excess of spontaneous saving. But if such additional investments were undertaken not merely today and yesterday but also on preceding days, and have caused certain shifts in relative prices, we must not fail to look into the changes in income distribution which were implied in the price movements and may have affected the ability and willingness to save. (This is one of the "social consequences of variations in the value of money,"which"may well lead to increased saving," as was emphasized by Professor Mises.[16]) Since these price movements were probably in favor of wealthier income groups, total saving may thereby be substantially enhanced.

Of the relative changes in income distribution, two types were singled out because of the major importance they may have in this connection: profits due to the fact that past contracts fix certain costs while product prices rise—the "doctoring of past contracts"[17]—and profits due to the appreciation of inventories and other assets—capital gains. (The "past contracts" are, of course, merely one particular cause for the much more general fact that prices do not rise simultaneously and proportionately.) Since larger corporate and entrepreneurial savings and investments result from these profits, and since the profits can be attributed to the previous excess of investment over spontaneous saving, one may detect here another species of secondary (or "forced") saving, quite apart from the imposed lacking which results from the same cause.

---

[15] That a man with rising income should be said to be "lacking" may appear paradoxical. But since the lacking is not relative to the income he had some day back in the past but merely relative to the real income of "yesterday," he may "lack" when he uses a part of his increased income for building up his cash reserve.

[16] Ludwig v. Mises, *Theory of Money and Credit* (London: H. E. Batson, 1934), pp. 195 ff and 361. (First German edition, 1912.)

[17] In Pigou's phrase, "business men, who are, in the main, borrowers and wage payers, find themselves in times of prosperity in receipt of a windfall gain, consequent upon what is, in effect, a doctoring in their favor of past contracts. They are thus in a position to add to the stream of floating capital to be turned into industry." A. C. Pigou, *Industrial Fluctuations* (London: Macmillan, 1927), p. 122.

Automatic, Induced, and Secondary

At the risk of being quite unprecise, I may attempt to get the three main distinctions of the Robertsonian exhibit into the simplest possible form:

(a) In consequence of the additional investment outlays, prices are increased and the real purchasing power of consumers is reduced. (Automatic lacking.)

(b) In consequence of the additional investment outlays, transactions, incomes, and prices are increased and consumers feel impelled to use parts of their incomes for building up their cash reserves. (Induced hoarding.)

(c) In consequence of the additional investment outlays, relative prices and the distribution of income are altered in favor of entrepreneurs, who can and will increase their voluntary saving. (Secondary saving.)

It should be understood, however, that these three species of forced saving are interrelated more closely than merely as effects of a common cause. The price increase which is supposed to perform the "expropriation" of the consumer[18] is inversely related to the extent of the induced hoarding. If in the course of an expansion of investment outlays the income recipients allow the real value of their cash reserves to decline and do not withhold income from re-spending, consumers' demand rises more strongly and the ratio of consumers' expenditures to investment outlays is less reduced than it would be with large induced hoarding. But the rise of prices of consumers' goods may be greater than it would be with large induced hoarding. The price increase alone is, therefore, a poor measure of the "expropriation." Even with a more drastic price rise, that is to say, with a larger reduction of the purchasing power of the monetary unit, aggregate real consumption during the transition period will be —if at all—less reduced when induced hoarding by income recipients is slight (and, hence, slow).[19]

---

[18] Howard S. Ellis, *op. cit.,* p. 425.

[19] Cf. A. C. Pigou, *op . cit.,* Ch. XIII ("Credit Creations and the Associated Real Levies"), pp. 135-46.

Abstinence, Accumulation, and Generated Savings

The idea "that the contribution of banks to capital accumulation rests upon expropriation" of the consumer,[20] is linked, of course, with the assumption of scarce, or even fully employed, resources. But in fact the forced capital formation, financed through credit expansion, need not at all be at the expense of the consumer.[21] In order to comprise more general conditions, the forced-saving concept had to be widened, although this widening cannot be traced to any single author. To many writers the forced reduction of consumption was only one, and perhaps only a secondary, phase of the problem of forced capital formation.

The notion that the extension of bank credit confiscates part of the consumers' purchasing power was still present in Lord Keynes' *Treatise on Money*. There it is stated, for example, that "the new investment in excess of the volume of saving will be made possible, not by voluntary abstention from consumption by refraining from spending money-income, but by involuntary abstention as the result of money-incomes being worth less."[22] But, to be sure, this was not a major point in the cycle theory expounded by Lord Keynes in the *Treatise*.

Forced reduction of real consumption was not the major point either in the theory of Professor Mises. He placed major emphasis on two other points. One was the change in income distribution which accompanies the expansion process and favors the entrepreneurs, who thus can use large parts of their incomes for saving and investment: secondary or generated saving. [23] The other point was the encouragement which artificially low interest rates are apt to give to "more capitalistic" enterprise, resulting in a formation of capital which may involve excessively long periods of production.[24]

The forced compression of consumers' purchasing power was no more

---

[20] Howard S. Ellis, *op. cit.*, p. 425.

[21] "An expanding bank currency during periods of business recovery will provide funds for new capital formation without a curtailment of consumption." H. G. Moulton, "Commercial Banking and Capital Formation," *Journal of Political Economy*, XXVI (1918), p. 878.

[22] *A Treatise on Money*, Vol. I, p. 175.

[23] This point was also stressed by Hawtrey.

[24] See *The Theory of Money and Credit*, pp. 360 ff., and *Geldwertstabilisierung und Konjunkturpolitik*, p. 45.

than a side-line in Professor Schumpeter's theory. Only in a few places did he refer to this idea, as, for example, in the following statement: "The price-boosting effects of bank money give rise to the phenomenon of 'forced saving.' People, without intending to save, are forced to do so by having their real incomes reduced because of increased prices. In this way the means of production and the stocks of goods which are disposable for productive purposes in the economy are increased, and the fund available for immediate consumption is diminished."[25] In most other places Professor Schumpeter relegated the competition between capital formation and consumption to second place, assigning primary importance to the competition between innovation and "static" production. The innovating entrepreneur is furnished purchasing power, enabling him to carry out his new combinations, and if he draws productive resources away from other uses, it is the less "dynamic" producer who is chiefly affected.[26]

What I have called before "secondary" or "generated" saving , that is, the saving on the part of the recipients of increased incomes, particularly profits, is also featured in Professor Schumpeter's theory. The idea is advanced that the additional investments generate profits, out of which emerge the savings which eventually pay for the enterprises first financed by "banking resources." According to Schumpeter's 1912 version, the "shares and bonds"of the new enterprises "gradually are paid for" out of these generated savings, thus "are resorbed by the community's savings."[27] Although these savings are voluntary, the significant fact is that they are themselves a result of the expansionary investment, and thus, in a sense, forced into being by the credit expansion.

Saving Must Equal Investment

The most general forced–saving theory is that of Lord Keynes. Although he insists that all saving is "equally genuine" and "voluntary," he

---

[25] "Das Sozialprodukt und die Rechenpfennige," *op. cit.*, p. 706.

[26] In his most recent exposition (*Business Cycles,* p. 112, fn. 1), Professor Schumpeter restates "that it is primarily the purchasing power of other *firms* that is reduced in order to make room for the requirements of entrepreneurs, and that the reduction of the 'real' purchasing power of some *households* is a secondary phenomenon which, moreover, is compensated in part by the increase in the real purchasing power of others."

[27] *Theory of Economic Development,* p. 111.

chooses to define it so that it can never deviate from investment. Without anybody changing his wishes and desires, every increase in investment makes people save more. Investment is the determining variable, saving is "necessarily" equal to it.

In Keynesian theory, however, saving is equal to investment in at least four different senses. (1) If one accepts the Keynesian definitions, he need not ask what *makes* saving equal to investment, because the two are merely different terms for one identical concept (*viz.,* the difference between current income and current consumption). On the other hand, if one takes the act of saving and the act of investment as two different things, so that saving and investment are no longer identical by definition but merely equal by means of some reliable mechanism, then one must ask just what this mechanism is. The different answers that one can get to this question suggest the three other senses in which saving is equal to investment.[28] (2) The money disbursed today as additional investment outlay must be held by somebody to whom it is income. Even if the income recipient intends to spend all his income tomorrow, as soon as the stores open, he has not spent it today; hence, today he has "saved." (3) If the funds disbursed in one single dose of additional investment outlay are observed on their course through the economy, passing from hand to hand (account to account), one will see them appear again and again as income of different people, each probably saving a part of the funds and spending another part for consumption. If you follow the chain of spending and re-spending long enough, the savings of the consecutive income recipients will eventually add up to the original investment outlay; hence, saving (the sum of the series) will have become equal to investment (the single dose). (4) If the additional investment is not a single dose but a rate per period, that is to say, if the additional investment is repeated period after period, aggregate incomes per period will rise, and will continue to rise until the income recipients increase their rate of saving enough to offset fully the rate of additional investment. In other words, investments generate income and, under the influence of increased incomes, people are induced to higher saving; hence saving

---

[28] One other sense of equality was refuted by Keynes: the "classical" theory that investment becomes equal to saving through the functioning of the interest-rate mechanism in the capital markets.

(the eventually reached and then maintained level) becomes equal to investment (the initially started and then maintained level).

In none of these senses is saving the result of spontaneous decisions on the part of savers. In one case, (2), we did not give the alleged "saver" enough time to go shopping. In another case, (3), we simply waited long enough until a series of consecutive acts of saving added up to the sum of an original investment outlay. In the last case, (4), we saw the level of additional investment force the level of income up to a point where people felt induced to save enough. This last sense is the really essential one for Keynesian theory; and in this sense, the "forced" or "generated" character of the saving is most apparent.[29]

Income-Induced Saving

The nature of this saving as "forced," or not spontaneous, is fairly explicitly stated by Lord Keynes in several places. "It is the increased output which produces the increased saving." [30] And "it is . . . impossible for the community as a whole to save *less* than the amount of current investment, since the attempt to do so will necessarily raise incomes to a level at which the sums which individuals choose to save add up to a figure exactly equal to the amount of investment." [31] The Robertsonian "induced saving" is reformulated by Lord Keynes in the following proposition: "No one can be compelled to own the additional money corresponding to the new bank-credit, unless he deliberately prefers to hold more money rather than some other form of wealth. Yet employment, incomes and prices *cannot help* moving in such a way that in the new situation *someone does* choose to hold the additional money." [32]

Now, the forced saving in Keynesian theory is, of course, not the same as the forced saving in the theories which elaborated upon forced reductions of consumption. The very essence of the Keynesian theory is to

---

[29] The Keynesian definition of saving is not needed for the proof of this equality of saving to investment. See my *International Trade and the National Income Multiplier* (Philadelphia: Blakiston, 1943).

[30] J. M. Keynes, *The General Theory of Employment, Interest and Money* (London and New York: Macmillan, 1938), p. 328.

[31] *Ibid.*, p. 84. (Italics in the original.)

[32] *Ibid.*, p. 83. (Italics are mine.)

show how additional investment, as a rule, is associated with increased, rather than reduced, consumption. And as he took "forced saving" as equivalent to "forced frugality," Lord Keynes was justifiably critical of the concept. His criticism, however, went further than that. According to him, " 'forced saving' has no meaning until we have specified some standard rate of saving. If we select (as might be reasonable) the rate of saving which corresponds to an established state of full employment the definition would become: 'Forced saving is the excess of actual saving [read: investment] over what would be saved if there were full employment in a position of long-period equilibrium.' " [33] And he concludes that "an attempt to extend this perfectly clear notion to conditions of less than full employment involves difficulties." [34]

This conclusion is not justified. For, certainly, full employment is not the only "reasonable standard" for the rate of saving. It is just as reasonable to take for the analysis of any given situation the current income level as the standard and, thus, to take as the standard rate of saving that which corresponds to a given level of income. The definition, formulated after the above pattern, would then become "Forced saving is the excess of actual saving [read: investment] over what would be saved if the level of income were unchanged." This definition tallies well with what many writers have in mind when they speak of forced or unintended (unintentional) saving. "Excess of *ex post* over *ex ante* saving," or "excess of realized over expected saving," is another term in use for this concept of forced saving.

Investment which equals intended saving leaves money income unchanged. [35] Increased investment outlays with unchanged money income obviously imply reduced consumption outlays. To distinguish such a situation from another one, where an increase in investment outlays is not offset by a decrease in consumption expenditures, is perfectly good sense; whether one refers to the latter situation by speaking of an excess of investment over intended saving, or by speaking of forced saving, or money-income-increasing investment, or simply expansionary disbursement, is not of great importance.

---

[33] *Ibid.*, p. 80.

[34] *Ibid.*, p. 81.

[35] This is not an empirical statement but follows from the definitions of the terms involved.

Temporary Abnormal Saving

The concept of forced saving puts in an *incognito* appearance at the Keynesian exposition under a very strange disguise. Professor Robertson was the first to discover [36] it there: it was called "temporary reduction of the marginal propensity to consume." [37]

A reduction of the marginal propensity to consume is obviously an increase in the marginal propensity to save. But an increased "propensity" to save sounds very much like something spontaneous and not at all like something induced or even forced. But we know that "propensity," in Lord Keynes' theory, does not always mean propensity — the psychological concept — but means in some places a ratio between *ex post* (realized) quantities — the tautological concept. [38] Thus we can understand that the "temporary increase of the marginal propensity to save" need not mean that people wish or desire or are inclined to save more; it may simply mean that the ratio between actual investment and income rises for a while. Additional investment creates additional income, and additional income generates more income as well as saving out of income in the course of time rather than at a stroke. He who understands this will be clear about the fact that, with an unchanged desire to save a certain portion out of received income, the ratio of investment to income must appear temporarily increased and will go back to "normal" only when income and saving have adjusted themselves to the increased level of investment. In the meantime, that is to say, during the transition to the new equilibrium levels, investment exceeds the rate of saving which would correspond to the "normal marginal propensity to save."

The words "normal savings" and "abnormal savings" were used by Professor Arthur Smithies in an article in which he explicitly adopts the "Keynesian method" of analysis. [39] Discussing a particular kind of invest-

---

[36] D. H. Robertson, "Some Notes on Mr. Keynes' General Theory of Employment," *Quarterly Journal of Economics,* LI (1936-37), p. 178.

[37] J. M. Keynes, *op. cit.,* p. 123.

[38] See Gottfried Haberler, "Mr. Keynes' Theory of the 'Multiplier': A Methodological Criticism," *Zeitschrift für Nationalökonomie,* VII (1936), pp. 299-305; or Fritz Machlup, "Period Analysis and Multiplier Theory," *Quarterly Journal of Economics,* LIV (1939-40), p. 14.

[39] Arthur Smithies, "The Behavior of Money National Income under Inflationary Conditions," *Quarterly Journal of Economics,* LVII (1942-43), p. 115.

ment expenditures, *viz.* war expenditures, he speaks of a "gap between war expenditure and normal savings, which must be bridged by abnormal savings induced by" the higher rate of war expenditures.[40] Clearly, this "abnormal saving" is the 1942 Model of forced saving.

Socialistic Saving

When Professor Schumpeter explained how with the newly created bank-credit productive resources could be "directed" into new uses, withdrawn from the "static" circular flow and "allotted" to new enterprise, he made his picture of this forced capital formation clearer by pointing, as an analogy, to capital formation in a socialistic community. New credits, issued by the banking system, do, in a capitalistic economy, what new orders, issued by the central planning authority, would do in a socialistic economy.

Professor Röpke, comparing the types of "coercion" which are employed "to free the tempo and extent of investment from the limitations imposed by the rate of [voluntary] savings," stated: "The difference may perhaps be expressed by saying that in our economic system it is *monetary 'forced saving'* which sets the wheels of over-investment in motion, while in Soviet Russia it is *authoritarian 'forced saving.'* Whereas in Russia the coercive machinery is represented by the G.P.U. . . . , in capitalism it is represented by the banking system. . . ."[41]

Incidentally, the technique of socialistic "forced saving" need not be that of direct commandeering of resources, but may also be monetary in character. If a socialistic commonwealth were organized in conformance

---

[40] *Ibid.*, p. 117. On p. 116 we read "that under the impact of additional war expenditure the marginal propensity to save is temporarily increased, and it is only after time has been allowed for the multiplier effect to work itself out fully that the marginal propensity to save returns to its normal level. In fact, it is this distortion of the marginal propensity to save that, if nothing else does, will ensure the identity of war expenditure and saving at every point of time." It is, in fact, not a distortion of real propensities but only a distortion of concepts which becomes manifest at this point. An "identity"—established by definition—need not be "ensured" by anything. But if "normal saving" is less than investment or war expenditures, and saving is defined as identical with investment or war expenditures, the difference must be "abnormal" or "forced" saving.

[41] Wilhelm Röpke, *Crises and Cycles* (London: Hodge, 1936), p. 107. (Italics are in the original.)

with the blueprint of Professor Lange,[42] the allocation of resources would not be planned by the authorities and executed upon their direct orders, but would instead be left to the working of the money mechanism, just as in a capitalist system. But, since the voluntary saving on the part of income recipients would be fairly slim under a system without large private incomes from capital, the bulk of the saving would have to be "forced saving." It would be done either through planned additions to the money flow or, more commonly, through planned distribution of the state income (from profits, rent, interest, and taxes) between capital formation and "social dividend."[43]

Fiscal Saving

The term "authoritarian forced saving" was used also for certain fiscal policies in capitalistic economies. If the government raised funds from would-be consumers and then allocated these funds to the construction of capital, the case would be one of involuntary abstinence and capital accumulation. Professor Röpke himself, who had first used the term authoritarian forced saving with reference to the method of direct commandeering of resources (and in contradistinction to "monetary forced saving"), used it later for what might be called "fiscal forced saving." Discussing the case where government trust funds (social security reserves, which are raised at the expense of consumption expenditures) are used for investment purposes during a boom period, he said that "this sort of budget policy might make things even worse by adding to the monetary forced saving, which is the concomitant of the boom, the additional investment facilities of authoritarian forced savings."[44]

---

[42] Oscar Lange and F. M. Taylor, *On the Economic Theory of Socialism* (Minnesota: University of Minnesota Press, 1939).

[43] In a review of H. D. Dickinson's *Economics of Socialism* by Lange in the *Journal of Political Economy*, L (1942), pp. 299-303, Lange revised his previous statement about the government–controlled rate of capital accumulation in the socialistic state. He now considers it possible to adjust the rate of investment to the "ex-ante saving" of the consumers; and he states that it is thus "possible, in theory, to remove from the socialist economy the 'arbitrariness' in the determination of the rate of capital accumulation." But, still, "through 'corporate' saving or dissaving done by the Social Fund the rate of capital accumulation can be made, as a piece of deliberate planning by the authorities, to diverge from that set by consumers' preferences." (*Ibid.*, p. 303.)

[44] Röpke, *op. cit.*, p. 158.

Fiscal saving, however, may again mean several things. First of all, it may be thought of in the sense in which it has just been used, namely in the sense that the government raises funds from consumers — reducing their consumption expenditures — and puts these funds to real investment purposes. But, secondly, one may think of fiscal saving in the sense that the government uses funds, raised at the expense of consumption outlays, for the retirement (reduction) of the public debt. The effects of these two types of "fiscal saving" may certainly be different. But there is still a third sense: the "government net saving," as it is listed in national income statistics. This refers to the use of ordinary government revenue for debt reduction, irrespective of whether the revenue (taxation) was at the expense of consumption or at the expense of private saving. Of course, only in the former, not in the latter, case would "government net saving" really constitute forced saving.

Forced Loans, Taxes, Rationing

In the set of concepts reviewed in the preceding two sections, the phenomenon of forced saving was seen either in the character of the government expenditure (capital construction) or in the double condition of consumption-reducing revenue and asset-increasing (or debt-reducing) disbursement. In recent discussions of war finance, however, the term forced saving has been used with no reference to the character of the government expenditure and exclusively with reference to the way in which funds were raised.

The term has again been used rather indiscriminately, though some attempts have been made to distinguish between "compulsory loans" and "refundable taxes." [45] These words are not self-explanatory, but the idea is to apply the former to forced loans out of saved funds and the latter to post-war credits for taxes paid by low-income groups. A more thorough distinction would separate loans out of "past savings," *i.e.,* out of inactive funds; refundable taxes out of "current savings," *i.e.,* out of current in-

---

[45] This distinction was made, for example, in the "Memorandum on Adequate War Taxation," prepared by economists of Iowa State College, and signed by many prominent members of the profession, to be submitted to administration agencies and congressional committees.

come which would have been saved had it not been taxed away; and refundable taxes cutting into consumers' expenditures, *i.e.,* out of current income which would have been consumed had it not been taxed away.

Only the last of these forced loans could really be called forced saving, and even then the transaction should be understood to constitute forced saving only from the individual's point of view — because he gets a claim against the government — but hardly from the point of view of society — unless one wishes to regard war expenditures as capital formation.

Forced saving in the sense of individual consumers' involuntary abstinence may also be seen in the proposed system of general expenditure rationing. In order to "control" war-time inflation, governments may resort to general expenditure rationing, making it impossible for consumers to spend more than certain amounts, fixed either absolutely or in some relation to income or to expenditures in the past. If this rationing makes it impossible for consumers to spend as much as they otherwise would, the resulting saving is certainly a type of forced saving from the point of view of the individual. The saving may take the form of hoarded cash or deposits, or of securities purchased, especially government bonds. Whether or not any "national saving," *i.e.,* capital formation, is associated with the forced individual saving is again a matter of appraising the nature of the government expenditure.

Even ordinary commodity rationing may result in induced saving if the rationing is very comprehensive. If the greater part of the necessities and semi-luxuries is rationed, consumers will hardly spend on non-rationed luxuries all the additional money with which they would have liked to buy more of the rationed articles if they could get them. If the consumers are prevented from spending as much as they wish on food and clothing, they may decide not to invest all the spare money in liquor and movies but instead to put a part of it in government bonds or to leave it idle. These savings of the individual consumers are "forced" by the rationing of the desired commodities. (Without rationing and price fixing, consumers would spend the money sums in question in higher prices of the scarce goods. The aggregate abstinence of the consumers in real terms would be the same under inflated prices as it would be under rationing and saving; but the distribution of the abstinence would be different and the abstinence would not be rewarded by the claims on future real income which the individual saver has embodied in the savings — provided prices do not rise after all, cheating the saver of some portion of his savings.)

Corporate Saving

Another saver against his will may be found in the stockholder of a corporation. The stockholder may like to receive his share in all the net earnings of the firm in the form of cash dividends and to use them for consumption. If the corporation decides not to distribute all its net earnings, the stockholder is forced to save against his will unless he is willing to sell some of his stocks.

The practice of "ploughing back" parts of corporate profits has become almost universal in the United States. Undistributed profits are used to finance plant expansions, to pay off funded or unfunded debts, or to accumulate liquid assets (securities) or even idle cash balances. This practice of "self-financing" deprives the stockholders of the free choice to consume their earnings or to save them, and, in the latter case, to invest them in the same enterprise or elsewhere. A number of evil consequences are attributed to this type of "forced saving": that investible funds are misallocated, because the self-financing corporation avoids the probing by the capital market and the selective test of the interest rate; that the directors, disposing of this easy money, put prestige considerations ahead of profit calculations; that the corporations hoard the undistributed funds and thus may aggravate a depression; that the corporations invest the funds and thus may cause overinvestment booms which are apt to be followed by crises and depressions.

By the last-mentioned theory of overinvestment, which was advanced by Professor Vito,[46] the concept of forced saving through corporate saving is merged with the original concept of forced saving through credit expansion. For, according to this theory, forced saving in the sense of undistributed profits of corporations and forced saving in the sense of credit expansions are jointly and severally held responsible for financing business upswings and creating unhealthy booms.

---

[46] Francesco Vito, "Il risparmio forzato e la teoria di cicli economici," *Rivista Internazionale de Scienze Sociali* (1934).

Summary

Our survey of concepts connected with the term forced saving, and of terms connected with the main concepts of forced saving, may be conveniently concluded with a list of all these related concepts and terms. In this list, however, the promiscuous expression forced saving itself shall be avoided and shall be replaced by synonyms or circumscriptions.

1. Involuntary absolute frugality — or absolute reduction of the real purchasing power of the consumers — in consequence of increased prices of consumers' goods, the price increase being the result of additional investment outlays, which are financed through newly created or activated funds and compete for intermediate goods and services.

2. Involuntary relative frugality — or prevented increase of the real purchasing power of the consumers — in consequence of the avoidance of an otherwise occurring decline in prices of consumers' goods; this decline in prices would have come about through technical improvements or a more plentiful supply of productive resources, but is prevented from taking its (full) course, because additional investment outlays, financed through newly created or activated funds, compete for intermediate goods and services.

3. Involuntary abstinence of groups of consumers with fixed or insufficiently rising money incomes — but not a reduction of total real consumption — in consequence of higher prices of consumers' goods, this price rise being the result of expansionary investment outlays and of expanded incomes of other consumer groups.

4. Automatic stinting, or consuming less than one would have done if other people had not increased their expenditure, the encroachment upon one's real consumption being the automatic result of actual price increases or prevented price reductions.

5. Automatic lacking, or uncompensated automatic stinting, being the automatic (price-effected) reduction of one's consumption below the value which the disposable income had at the time of its receipt.

6. Induced hoarding, or the building up of one's cash reserves in order to adjust them to the increase in prices or income or transactions which was caused by the increased disbursements by others.

7. Induced lacking, or the voluntary, but not spontaneous, reduction

of one's consumption below the value which the disposable income had at the time of its receipt, the reduction being the "real" counterpart of the induced hoarding (mentioned under 6).

8. Imposed lacking, or the sum of automatic lacking (mentioned under 5) and of induced lacking (mentioned under 7).

9. Secondary saving due to the doctoring of past contracts; that is to say, saving by those—usually entrepreneurs—who have gained by having to pay contractually fixed rates and prices while they receive prices which have increased in consequence of (previous) expansionary investment.

10. Secondary saving due to windfall profits through asset appreciation; that is to say, saving by those who have gained through appreciated inventories, and who receive for their products, made on existing equipment, prices which have increased in consequence of (previous) expansionary investment.

11. Secondary saving due to the shifts in income distribution which, as a rule, accompany expansionary investments and favor groups — usually entrepreneurs — with higher ability and willingness to save. (This concept includes those mentioned under 9 and 10.)

12. Profit-generated saving by the recipients of profits which arise from economic development initiated by innovators and financed by credit creation.

13. Automatic increase in money-holding by the recipients of income disbursed through expansionary investment, this "saving" or cash accumulation not being the result of thriftiness (mentioned under 15 and 16) or of induced hoarding (mentioned under 6) but simply the inevitable consequence of the fact that one cannot spend money before he receives it. (This is one sense in which "saving" always equals investment.)

14. Unintentional corporate saving, in the form of increased cash, inventories, and other assets, or reduced debts, subsequent to the receipt of increased net profits and prior to their distribution as dividends.

15. Successive income-induced saving out of an additional income stream which was created through a single dose of additional investment, the series of savings by successive income recipients eventually adding up to the amount of initial investment, and the additional income thus dwindling down to zero because of the "leakages" through saving. (This is another sense in which saving must equal investment.)

16. Income-induced saving by the recipients of additional income which is created through a continuous or periodic outlay of additional investment, the income-induced saving per period eventually reaching the level of the investment per period. (This is probably the most significant sense in which the rate of saving is equal — forced up — to the rate of investment.)

17. Excess of investment over what would be saved if there were full employment in a position of long-period equilibrium.

18. Excess of investment over "saving," saving being defined as the difference between current "normal" income and current consumption, thus "creating" "windfall profits" in the amount of the excessive investment.

19. Excess of investment over saving out of disposable income, or over what would be saved if the level of income remained unchanged.

20. Excess of realized saving over anticipated (expected, intentional) saving.

21. Excess of *ex post* over *ex ante* saving.

22. Temporary reduction of the marginal propensity to consume during the transition period before income and consumption adjust themselves to an increased investment level.

23. Abnormal saving, or the excess of investment over what would be saved on the basis of the normal marginal propensity to save.

24. Directing productive resources into the production of more capital goods, the directing achieved through the disbursement of additional credit.

25. Directing productive resources into the production of more capital goods, the directing achieved through direct allocation or commandeering.

26. Socialistic compulsory saving, achieved through disbursement of additional money (mentioned under 22) or through the planned distribution of the "social fund" between "dividend" and capital formation or through direct allocation of resources (mentioned under 23).

27. Fiscal compulsory saving, or spending on real investment purposes the proceeds from taxes that reduce consumption expenditures.

28. Fiscal saving through reducing the government debt out of taxes which reduce consumption expenditures.

29. Compulsory old-age insurance, forcing individuals to pay premiums that they would not have paid otherwise.

30. Refundable taxes.

31. Refundable taxes that reduce consumption expenditures.

32. Expenditure rationing, making it impossible for the income recipient to spend more than a permitted amount.

33. Rationing-induced saving, or the reduction of consumption expenditures which results from the fact that most of the desired commodities are rationed.

34. Corporate saving, or the non-distribution of corporate profits which, if distributed to the shareholders, would be used for consumption purposes.

This list of related concepts and terms is probably far from complete. There is little doubt that it will be still more incomplete in a few years, when the family of concepts and terms will have grown further.

ANOTHER VIEW
OF COST-PUSH AND
DEMAND-PULL INFLATION

Reprinted with permission from *The Review of Economics and Statistics,* Vol. XLII, No. 2, May, 1960.

It is with some hesitation that I join the discussion and thus contribute to the galloping inflation of the literature on the creeping inflation of prices. My excuse is probably the same as that of most of my fellow writers: dissatisfied with much of what others have written, I have, perhaps presumptuously, decided that my way of thinking would be more successful. Hence, I am presenting another view of cost-push and demand-pull inflation.

The Current Debate

Before I set forth the controversial issue and the most widely held views, I shall indulge in a few preliminaries by referring briefly to the old squabble about what should be meant by inflation.

Inflation of What?

Some people regard "inflation" as a *cause* (explanation) of a general rise in prices (and of some other things too), while others use the word as a *synonym* (equivalent) for a general rise in prices. In times when governments undertake to control prices by prohibitions with threats of sanctions against unauthorized price raising, many writers realize how awkward it is to use the term inflation to signify price increase, because then they want to discuss the "latent" or "repressed" inflation — one that does not show up in a general price index, or does not show up adequately. Also when one talks about inflation and deflation as apparent opposites, a definition in terms of general prices is quite inconvenient, inasmuch as the problem of deflation is so serious largely because it shows up in falling volumes of production and employment instead of falling prices.

One solution would be to use the word inflation always with a modifying word that tells exactly *what* is blown up: currency, credit, spending, demand, wages, prices, etc. This would be a great help; indeed some controversial problems would disappear, because the disputants would find out that they were talking about different things, and other problems would be greatly clarified. The most lively issue of our times, whether "our" inflation in the last four years has been due to a demand-pull or to a cost-push, would lose some of its muddiness if the analysts had to qualify all their pronouncements with regard to the inflation of credit, spending, demand, wholesale prices, consumer prices, and so forth.

A search of the learned literature would yield scores of definitions of inflation, differing from one another in essentials or in nuances. A search of the popular literature, however, reveals no realization of the differences in the meanings experts give to the term. The differences apparently have been reserved for the treatises and the quarterlies; the daily papers and the weeklies were not to be encumbered with "technicalities." Now that inflation has become such a widely debated topic, with many scholars participating in the debates, the popular meaning of inflation, denoting an increase in the consumer price index, has been increasingly adopted by the professional economists. Although this is probably bad for analysis, we may have to accept it. But at the risk of appearing pedantic I shall continue to speak of various kinds of inflation and to specify which I happen to be speaking about.

The Controversial Issue

Opinion is divided on whether consumer prices in recent years have increased chiefly (1) because industry has invested too much and government has spent too much (relative to the nation's thrift) or (2) because big business has raised material prices and/or big labor has raised wage rates too high (relative to the nation's increase in productivity). The issue is partly who is to be "blamed" for the past rise in consumer prices, and partly what policies should be pursued to avoid a continued increase.

If demand-pull inflation is the correct diagnosis, the Treasury is to be blamed for spending too much and taxing too little, and the Federal Reserve Banks are to be blamed for keeping interest rates too low and for creating or tolerating too large a volume of free reserves, which enable member banks to extend too much credit.

If cost-push inflation is the correct diagnosis, trade unions are to be blamed for demanding excessive wage increases, and industry is to be blamed for granting them, big business may be blamed for raising "administered prices" of materials and other producers goods to yield ever-increasing profit rates, and government may be assigned the task of persuading or forcing labor unions and industry to abstain from attempts to raise their incomes, or at least to be more moderate.

Not everybody draws the appropriate conclusions from the theory which he espouses. And not everybody is willing to adopt policies to correct the undesirable situation. (Nor does everybody find the situation sufficiently undesirable to get seriously worried.) [1] The ambivalent position of many partisans of labor unions is noteworthy. They reject the wage-push diagnosis because, understandably, they do not wish to take the blame for the inflation. But they also reject the demand-pull diagnosis, because this diagnosis would militate against the use of fiscal and monetary policies to bolster employment. They want effective demand to be increased at a rate fast enough to permit full employment at rapidly increasing wage rates; but they do not want to attribute increasing prices either to the increase in demand or to the increase in wage rates. The only way out of this logical squeeze is to blame the consumer-price increase on prices "administered" by big business; but in order to support

---

[1] Cf. "Argument for Creeping Inflation," *New York Times,* March 3, 1959; "Slow Inflation: An Inescapable Cost of Maximum Growth Rate," *Commercial and Financial Chronicle,* March 26, 1959; "Inflation—A Problem of Shrinking Importance," *Commercial and Financial Chronicle,* April 23, 1959—all by Sumner H. Slichter.

this hypothesis one would have to prove that the profit margins and profit rates of the industries in question have been rising year after year — which they have not. [2] But we shall see later that matters are not quite so simple and cannot be analyzed exclusively in these terms.

Our first task is to deal with the contention that the distinction between cost-push and demand-pull inflation is unworkable, irrelevant, or even meaningless.

"Cost-Push No Cause of Inflation"

There is a group of outstanding economists contending that there cannot be such a thing as a cost-push inflation because, without an increase in purchasing power and demand, cost increases would lead to unemployment and depression, not to inflation.

On their own terms, these economists are correct. The rules of inductive logic say that if A and B together cause M; and if A without B cannot cause M, whereas B without A can cause M; then B, and not A, should be called the cause of M. Make A the wage-raising power of the unions and the price-raising power of the corporations; make B the credit-creating and money-creating power of the monetary system; make M the successive price increases. It should be quite clear that without the creation of new purchasing power a continuing price increase would be impossible. Hold the amount of money and bank credit constant (relative to real national product) and all that the most powerful unions and corporations can do is to price themselves out of the market.

Having admitted all this to the economists who reject the possibility of cost-push inflation, we can shift the weight of the argument to the question whether, given the power of the monetary system to create money and credit, this power would be exercised to the same extent if strong trade unions and strong corporations desisted from raising wages

---

[2] "The period 1947 to 1958 was a time of decreasing profit margins. This fact is important because it shows that the initiative in raising prices was not being taken by employers. In the four years 1947 to 1950 inclusive the net income of non-financial corporations after taxes per dollar of sales averaged 4.45 cents. In the next four years the average net income was 4.10 [cents] per dollar of sales; and in the three years 1955 to 1957 inclusive, it was about 3.3 cents per dollar of sales." Slichter, *Commercial and Financial Chronicle*, April 23, 1959.

and prices as it actually is exercised when wages and prices are being pushed up. There would probably be quick agreement that, given our present system, the exercise of the wage-raising power of strong unions and the price-raising power of strong corporations induces, or adds impetus to, the exercise of the ability of the banking system to create purchasing power.

The point then is that an increase in effective demand is a necessary condition for a continuing increase in general prices, but that a cost-push under present conditions will regularly lead to an expansion of credit and to that increase in effective demand which will permit the increase in consumer prices.

There remains, however, an important question of fact. Assume it is decided not to exercise the power to create money and credit — more than is needed to maintain a constant ratio to real national product — even at the risk of severe unemployment that might result if wages and prices increased; would we then have to expect that the strong unions and corporations would continue to make use of their wage-raising and price-raising powers? Some economists are convinced that unions and business firms would adopt much more moderate policies if they had to fear that any lack of moderation would lead to unemployment and stagnation. This does not mean that a considerable level of unemployment would be required to impress industry and unions with the desirability of moderation. Industrial firms would know that, under an unyielding monetary policy, they could not hope to pass increases in labor cost on to consumers and they would therefore refuse to yield to union pressure. Unions, in turn, would not strike for higher wages if they were sure that industry could not afford to give in. Hence, no cost-push and no extra unemployment.

Acceptance of this view by any number of economists would not yet make it a practicable policy. It could not work unless the monetary authorities embraced it without reservation, since any indication of a lack of faith and determination on the part of the authorities would remove the premise: unions could hope that industries would hope that an eventual relaxation of the monetary brake would "bail them out" and by means of an expansion of demand avert the business losses and the unemployment that would threaten to arise in consequence of wage and price increases.

"Demand-Pull No Cause of Inflation"

Having shown that there is a sense in which the contention is correct that "cost-push is no cause of inflation, it takes a demand-pull to produce it," we shall now attempt to show that the opposite contention may likewise be correct. There are indeed assumptions for which it would be appropriate to say that "demand-pull is no cause of inflation, it takes a cost-push to produce it." What are these assumptions and how do they differ from those of the traditional model?

In the traditional model, prices rise or fall under the impact of anonymous market forces. They rise when at their existing level the quantity of goods demanded exceeds the quantity supplied. Not that producers, noticing the increased demand, would decide that they could do better if they "charged" more; rather the mechanism of a "perfect market" would automatically lift prices to the level where the consumers would not want to purchase any more than was supplied. Sellers, in this model, don't ask higher prices, they just get them. The same thing happens in the model of the perfect labor market. When the demand for labor increases, workers don't ask for higher wages, they just get them as a result of competition.

In a large part of our present economy, prices and wages do not "rise" as if lifted by the invisible hand, but are "raised" by formal and explicit managerial decisions. Assume now that prices and wage rates are administered everywhere in the economy in such a way that changes in demand are not taken into account; instead, they are set in accordance with some "rules of thumb." Prices and wages may then be so high (relative to demand) that inventories accumulate, production is cut, and labor is unemployed; or they may be so low (relative to demand) that inven tories are depleted, production is raised, customers must patiently wait for delivery or their orders are rejected, and there are plenty of vacancies, but no workers to fill them. If the rules of thumb are universally observed by producers, distributors, and labor unions and take full account of increased cost of production and increased cost of living, but disregard all changes in demand, then there can be no demand-pull upon prices. In

246

such circumstances an increase in effective demand leads to unfilled orders and unfilled vacancies, but not to higher prices.[3]

One may object, of course, that such a model cannot possibly apply to all markets; that there exist numerous competitive markets in which no producer has enough power to "set" or "charge" a price; that in many markets in which prices are administered the would-be buyers, in periods of increased demand, offer higher prices in order to be served and sellers are glad to accept them even though they exceed their list prices; and that this regularly happens when the demand for labor is brisk, so that wages paid can be higher than the rates agreed in collective bargaining. Thus, demand-pull is likely to work despite the existence of administered prices and wages.

Although the objection may be sustained on practical grounds, this does not destroy the value of the model. If there are, in actual fact, *many* industries where backlogs of orders accumulate while prices fail to rise and where job vacancies grow in number while wages fail to rise, then the model has some relevance, and it is legitimate to speculate about the functioning of an economic system in which *all* prices and wages are administered on the basis of cost calculations and held at the set levels even in the face of excess demand. It is not easy to decide whether on balance the institutions in our economy are such that a model featuring "market-clearing prices" or a model featuring "cost-plus prices" fits better the purposes of speculating about the over-all performance of the entire economy.

In any case, the contention must be granted that there may be conditions under which "effective demand" is not effective and won't pull up prices, and when it takes a cost-push to produce price inflation. But this position disregards an important distinction, namely, whether the cost-push is "equilibrating" in the sense that it "absorbs" a previously existing excess demand or whether it is "disequilibrating" in the sense that it creates an excess supply (of labor and productive capacity) that will have to be prevented or removed by an increase in effective demand. Thus we are back at the crucial issue; a "monistic" interpretation cannot do justice to it.

---

[3] ". . . if all prices were administered on the basis of markup over direct cost—then excess demand might exist in all markets, yet without effect on the price level." Gardner Ackley, "Administered Prices and the Inflationary Process," *American Economic Review,* Papers and Proceedings, XLIX (May 1959), 421.

Statistical Tests

It is possible to grant the usefulness of the distinction between cost-push and demand-pull in building theoretical models for speculative reasoning, and yet to deny its usefulness in identifying the causes of general price increases in concrete situations. It may be that the concepts are not operational, that statistical tests are either unavailable or unreliable.

Some have proposed to answer the question, whether wage-push or demand-pull had "initiated" the upward movement of prices, by looking to see which has *increased first,* prices or wages. But "first" since what time? If prices and wages have risen in turn, in successive steps, the choice of a base period is quite arbitrary, and a conclusion assigning the leading or initiating role to one factor or the other would be equally arbitrary. (This is especially so if our statistical information is limited to annual data.)

Not much better is the idea of looking to see which of the two, money-wage rates or consumer prices, has *increased more.* The arbitrary choice of the base period for this comparison is again a serious difficulty. But even more important is the fact that the annual rise in productivity (output per labor hour) normally secures increases in real wages over the years. Hence it is to be expected that wage rates increase relative to consumer prices regardless of whether there is inflation, and regardless of whether prices are pulled up by demand or pushed up by wages.

Even some highly-seasoned economists have fallen victim to another logical snare: that any increase in money-wage rates that *exceeded the increase in labor productivity* was a sure sign of a wage-push. Yet, even if there were no labor union in the country and no worker ever asked for higher wages, a demand-pull inflation would eventually pull up the wage level; and if the demand-pull were such that prices and wages rose by any percentage above two or three a year — and it may well be five or ten or twenty per cent — money-wage rates would be up by more than the rate of increase in productivity. This, then, would have been the result of demand-pull only, without any wage-push at all. Hence the proposed statistical test is completely inconclusive.

A test which is based on a fundamentally correct chain of reasoning would compare profit rates with wage rates, and diagnose demand-pull when *profit rates increase faster than wage rates.* A slight variant of this test uses the relative shares of profits and wages in national income. The theory behind these tests is simply this: when an expansion of effective demand — without a wage-push — pulls up product prices, an increase in profits and profit rates would result until wage rates are pulled up by the derived demand for labor. On this theory, an increase in consumer prices associated with increased profit rates, but with wage rates lagging, would reliably indicate the existence of a demand-pull inflation. The operational difficulties with a test based on this theory are the same as those connected with other statistical tests: the arbitrary selection of the time periods. The theory, moreover, applies to an economy in which most prices are the result of anonymous market forces, not of administrative decisions. If most prices were administered and the price setters decided to raise their "profit targets" (perhaps at the same time that trade unions were out to engineer a wage boost, but a little faster or by a bigger jump) we could find — given the present monetary regime guided by the high-level-employment goal — that prices and profit rates increase ahead of wage rates even though the movement was not started by an autonomous expansion of demand. Hence, the lead of profit rates is not a reliable indication of demand-pull; it may occur also in conjunction with a cost-push in which price setters take a leading part.

Widely accepted as reliable symptoms of demand-pull inflation are over-employment and over-time payments. The statistical operations proposed to establish these symptoms are, for over-employment, to see whether *job vacancies exceed job applications* and, for over-time pay, to see whether *average hourly earnings have increased faster than wage rates.* Some critics rightly point out that the presence of these symptoms does not rule out that some cost-push has contributed to the inflation of prices. Indeed it would have been possible that a cost-push actually initiated the process and that the compensatory monetary injection, expanding demand to avoid the threatening unemployment, turned out to be heavier than necessary. Thus while these tests can verify the existence of an inflation of demand, they cannot prove that it was excess demand that precipitated the inflation of consumer prices.

Proposed Concepts and Distinctions

The diversity of expert opinion and the absence of any good statistical tests to support a diagnosis may in part be due to the lack of precise definitions. It is clear than an inflation of effective demand is a necessary condition not only for a demand-pull inflation of consumer prices but also for a cost-push inflation. Without an expansion of demand the cost boost would result in less production and less employment, not in a continuing rise of the level of consumer prices. Should one then speak of a demand-pull inflation only when the expansion in demand is clearly the initiating factor and any administrative cost increases are clearly induced? Or should one also speak of a demand-pull inflation if administrative wage and material-price increases start and lead the procession of events, but are then joined and overtaken by induced or compensatory expansions of demand?

Autonomous, Induced, and Supportive Demand Inflation

It is useful to distinguish autonomous from induced and supportive expansions of demand. *Autonomous* would be expansions which are not linked to previous or to expected cost increases; hence, disbursements which would also occur if no cost increases had been experienced or anticipated. *Induced* expansions of demand are direct consequences of a cost increase, in that those who receive the increased cost-prices or those who pay them will make larger disbursements than they would have made otherwise. For example, the industrial firms yielding to union pressure for a wage increase may borrow from banks (or dig into cash reserves) in order to pay the higher wage bill; or the recipients of higher wages may increase installment purchases and induce an expansion of consumer credit. *Supportive* (compensatory) expansions of demand would be those which are engineered by monetary or fiscal policy designed to reduce the unemployment arising, or threatening to arise, from cost increases. For example, the monetary authorities may reduce reserve requirements or create reserves in order to allow banks to extend loans, or the fiscal authorities may increase government expenditures in an attempt to expand effective demand and employment.

Without wishing to restrict the freedom of choice of those who formulate definitions, I submit that the choice should be appropriate to the purposes for which the concept is used. If the concept of a demand-induced inflation, or demand-pull inflation, is to serve for diagnostic and prognostic purposes in the development of economic policies, it would seem preferable to confine it to autonomous expansions of demand. This would not obstruct but rather aid the analysis of instances in which cost-induced expansions or supportive expansions of demand should turn out to be excessive in the sense that they create more employment opportunities than are destroyed by the cost increases, and hence give rise to some of the symptoms of a demand-induced inflation.

Aggressive, Defensive, and Responsive Cost Inflation

Similar obscurities due to a lack of essential distinctions surrounded the concept of the cost-induced inflation. Perhaps so much is clear that the term refers to increases in consumer prices that are the (direct or indirect) result of cost increases—labor cost, material cost, or any other cost. But it is not clear whether these cost increases have to be *autonomous* in the sense that they would not have come about in the absence of any monopoly power (price-making power), merely as a result of competitive demand. For it is quite possible that formal administrative decisions are behind cost increases which, however, do not go beyond what would have occurred without such decisions. For example, a trade union may achieve a "victory" in its negotiations with an employer group, bringing home the same raise in pay which the individual employers would have offered (without collective bargaining) in trying to get or keep the labor force they want. Let us decide to call these cost increases *responsive* (or competitive) to distinguish them from those that could *not* be obtained in a purely competitive market.

It would be misleading to denote all non-responsive (non-competitive) price or wage increases as "autonomous," since they may well be "induced" by some changes in the economic situation. (And the adjectives "autonomous" and "induced" are usually used as opposites.) A wage-

251

rate increase, for example, is not responsive unless it is in response to an excess demand (short supply) in the particular labor market; but an increase which is not "demand-induced" (and which therefore presupposes some "autonomy" with respect to competitive market forces) may yet be induced by (a) an increase in the employer's profits, (b) an increase in wage rates obtained by other labor groups, or (c) an increase in the cost of living. I propose to call (a) a "profit-induced" wage increase, (b) an "imitative"(or "spill-over") wage increase, and (c) a "defensive" wage increase. Any one of these increases may act as either an "impulse" or a "propagation" factor in the inflationary process.

Profit-induced and imitative increases as well as spontaneous increases may be called *aggressive* because they are designed to achieve a net advance in the real wage rate. A *defensive* increase merely restores real earnings which the group in question has long been enjoying; an aggressive increase raises real earnings above that level. The specification of a time interval is necessary in the definition so that one avoids calling "defensive" what really is a battle to defend the ground just gained in an aggressive action. For example, an aggressive wage-rate increase of ten per cent is likely to be partially eroded within less than a year through the resulting cost-push inflation (aided by induced and supportive expansions of demand). If the same trade unions then demand "cost-of-living raises" to restore their real wages, it would be somewhat ironic to call these new wage adjustments "defensive." But there will always be a wide range in which cost increases may as legitimately be considered defensive as aggressive, especially since trade unions take turns in their actions, each defending the real earnings of its own members that have suffered in consequence of the aggressive actions of other unions, and at the same time attempting to obtain a net improvement.

Administrative price increases by industries producing materials and other producers goods which enter as significant cost items into the prices of many other products can likewise be characterized as responsive (competitive), defensive, or aggressive. Purely responsive increases cannot occur in an industry with much unused productive capacity; only when plants are working at capacity and orders are piling up can administrative price increases be merely responsive; in such circumstances it is economically irrelevant that these prices are administered. Defensive increases leave real profit rates substantially unchanged; these increases take account of increased production cost and no more. Needless to say, the rates of return must be calculated on the basis of the reproduction cost of the required capacity; that is to say, the book values of the fixed capital may be too low if reproduction cost of buildings and equipment is higher than at the time of their acquisition, or too high if assets are included which are not required for current production. Thus, price increases designed to defend, in periods of falling production, a profit rate that is calculated on the basis of the value of assets inclusive of unused capacity are really aggressive; and price increases designed to raise the money rate of return on capital just enough to take care of increased replacement costs are really defensive.

Should all kinds of wage increase and price increase be included in the concept of a cost-push inflation whenever they are collectively negotiated, unilaterally announced, or otherwise the result of administrative action? I submit that increases which are merely responsive (competitive) do not belong there at all. Defensive increases do of course play an important role in the process of price inflation and the economist will surely not leave them out of his analysis. But in an explanation of an inflationary process going on year-in year-out the aggressive increases have a more substantive role to play than defensive increases; and when it comes to assigning "blame" for an inflation of consumer prices, the aggressive cost boosts will obviously be the more eligible candidates.

The Basic Model Sequences

With the help of the proposed concepts the two basic model sequences of consumer-price inflation can be easily described.

(A) *Demand-pull infla-tion:*	Autonomous expansions of demand (government spending, business spending, consumer spending) are followed by responsive (competitive) price and wage increases.
(B) *Cost-push inflation:*	Aggressive increases of wage rates and/or material prices are followed by induced and/or supportive (compensatory) demand expansions.

Cost-push models are relatively simple as long as they contain only a single impulse—either wage or price increases—with all sequential changes in the nature of adjustments.

(B-1)	*"Pure" wage-push inflation:*	Aggressive increases of wage rates are followed by induced and/or supportive demand expansions, and by responsive increases of material prices and other wage rates.
(B-2)	*"Pure" price-push inflation:*	Aggressive increases of material prices are followed by induced and/or supportive demand expansions, and by responsive increases of other material prices and wage rates.

Models become more complicated as more discretionary actions are included in the sequence of events, especially imitative and defensive increases of cost elements, or even aggressive increases, requiring further adjustments. For example, an autonomous demand expansion may be followed by administered wage and price increases more drastic than merely competitive increases would be; thus, the increases would be partly responsive and partly aggressive, requiring further demand expansions, induced or supportive, if unemployment is to be avoided. Or, aggressive wage and price increases may be followed by excessive demand expansions, perhaps because a nervous government rushes in with overdoses of supportive injections of buying power; some of the effective demand thus created would then be in the nature of an autonomous expansion, resulting in further (responsive) upward adjustments of costs.

Attempted Application

Even the most complicated model sequence will probably still be much simpler than the actual course of events as reflected in the data at our disposal. Since reality is so messy that no neat and simple model will fit at all closely, whereas various complex models will fit approximately, it is not surprising that even impartial analysts arrive at divergent interpretations of the so-called facts.

The Postwar Inflation

In the narrow scope of this article no attempt can be made to sift the data, to assess the comparative applicability of the various models, and to award first prize to the best-fitting model. But I shall not dodge this question and shall indicate briefly what impressions I have derived from the data presented by governmental and private researchers.

I believe that for an explanation of the consumer-price inflation from 1945 to 1948, and from 1950 to 1952, the basic model of the demand-pull inflation does as well as, or better than, any of the other models, simple or complicated. On the other hand, for the period 1955-59 several cost-push models appear to do better, and I am prepared to regard the consumer-price increases of these four years as a result of a cost-push inflation.

The choice among the various cost-push models is a hard one, especially in view of the controversy about the behavior of administered material prices. The periodic increases in steel prices have sometimes been regarded as the most strategic impulse factor in the inflationary process. A special theory of "profit-target pricing" assuming "periodic raising of the target" has been devised in support of this diagnosis and an array of empirical material has been added in its support.

Wage or Profit Push?

Neither this theory nor the statistical data seem to me to make the model of the "material-price-push inflation" a plausible explanation of the period in question. While many of the administered price increases may have hampered the performance of our economy and accelerated the inflationary process, I doubt that all or most of them have been "aggressive" in the sense defined. The reported data on profit rates and profit margins do not, in my judgment, indicate that the price increases were aggressive. Of course, few, if any, of the increases since 1955 have been in the nature of responsive adjustments to excess demand—but probably most of them were defensive in nature, taking account of cost increases without raising real profit rates. I cannot verify this impression of mine to everybody's satisfaction, and perhaps not even to my own. But my impression is strengthened by the deduced consequences of certain assumptions, which I consider plausible, concerning the policies and objectives of business managers.

There is, in my opinion, nothing invidious in contending that there are essential differences between most wage increases obtained by strong labor unions and most increases of material prices announced by strong corporations. Nor is it meant to be critical of union policies or uncritical of business policies if many wage increases are held to be aggressive, and many administered price increases defensive. The point is that the situation of most businesses is such that a series of aggressive price increases would be either injurious to them in the long run or downright impossible. A series of aggressive wage increases, on the other hand, may be both possible and beneficial to the labor groups concerned.

To hold that most administered price increases have been defensive rather than aggressive, does not mean (a) that the prices in question were not too high—they probably were, (b) that the increases did not speed up the inflationary process—they certainly did, or (c) that they were "justified"—which they were not if a competitive market model is used as the standard. But if the question is only whether these price increases were the "impulse factors," the "initiating forces" of the price inflation, then I believe the answer is negative.

Wage Increases and Productivity

I do not expect serious exception to the proposition that most of the wage increases obtained by strong trade unions in the last four years, whether spontaneous or profit-induced or imitative, have been aggressive in the sense defined. (This is in contrast to most wage increases between 1945 and 1952, which were responsive.) We must now inquire whether aggressive wage increases are inflationary if they do not exceed the relative rate at which productivity increases.

Aggressive Wage Increases to Capture Average Productivity Gains

According to accepted doctrine, the consumer price level can be held approximately stable, and full employment maintained, if the average increase in money-wage rates does not exceed the average increase in productivity in the economy as a whole. Some of the necessary qualifications to this proposition are not relevant to the issues under discussion. For interested readers they are presented in a footnote.[4] One qualification, however, that may matter here to some extent concerns the additional profits needed as returns on the additional investments required for the increase in national product. It is sometimes possible for total product per worker to increase, thanks to a progress of technology, organization, or skills, without any increase in capital investment. More often, however, it takes some additional investment to achieve an increase in productivity. If such investments were not allowed to earn a return, prog-

---

[4] There is first the qualification for the sacrifice of fixed-income recipients. The existence of contractual payments in fixed money amounts makes it possible for wage rates to increase a little more than productivity. Assume, for the sake of a simple arithmetical illustration, that of a national product of $1000 a share of $700 is distributed in the form of wages, $100 in the form of profits, and $200 in the form of fixed interest, rent, and pension payments. If now net national product rises by $20 (or 2 per cent) and the recipients of fixed money incomes get no share in the increased product (because prices are held stable), 20 per cent of the increased product, i.e., $4 becomes available as a possible bonus for labor in addition to their 70 per cent share, or $14. Total wage payments can thus increase by $18, or 2.57 per cent.

A second qualification relates to possible improvements in the terms of trade. Assume that the price of imports (relative to the price of exports) falls by 2 per cent and that imports had amounted to 10 per cent of the net national product, or $100. If the entire gain of $2 is seized as another bonus for labor, wages can rise by $20, or 2.86 per cent.

A third qualification concerns the possible effects of increased tax revenues. Assume that the effective tax rate on profits (distributed plus undistributed) is 50 per cent while the marginal tax rate on wages is 20 per cent. The additional profits are (10 per cent of $20=) $2, and the taxes on this are $1. The taxes on additional wages are (20 per cent of $20=) $4. If the government kept expenditures constant despite increased revenues, another bonus of $5 could be distributed in the form of wages, bringing the total addition to $25 before taxes, or more than the entire increase in net national product. (We neglect now the tax on the third bonus.) Wages before taxes could with all three bonuses be increased by 3.57 per cent, compared with a 2 per cent increase in national income.

The second and third bonuses, however, cannot be counted upon; the second bonus may just as likely be negative, since the terms of trade may deteriorate rather than improve. Even the first bonus is likely to disappear in an economy with perpetual inflation, because contractual incomes might gradually be made subject to automatic cost-of-living adjustments. All three qualifications are probably less important than the one presented in the text and this one works in the opposite direction.

This exposition has been freely adapted from Friedrich A. Lutz, "Cost- and Demand-Induced Inflation," *Banca Nazionale del Lavoro,* No. 44 (March 1958), 9-10. The adaptations were necessary because I believe Lutz's argument to be partly erroneous.

ress might be stopped short; but if they are to earn a return, total profits must increase lest the rates of return on capital are cut, which could lead to reduced investment and employment. Hence, as a rule, wage increases must not absorb the entire increase in output. And if the additional investments were so large that capital per worker has increased at a percentage rate greater than that of output per worker, wage rates cannot even increase by as much as output per worker and still allow price stability with full employment.[5]

The following formulation will steer clear of such technicalities and express the essential points. Apart from a few modifying influences, such as a squeezing of quasi-rents in stagnant industries, a whittling down of the real claims of recipients of contractual incomes, or a lucky improvement in the terms of foreign trade, real wages per worker cannot increase faster than product per worker. If *money*-wage rates are raised faster than productivity, and the monetary authorities supply the money needed to pay the increased wages without unemployment, prices will rise enough to keep *real*-wage rates from rising faster than productivity. To say that the price inflation has the "function" of keeping the increase in real wages down to the rate at which productivity increases may help some to understand the mechanism. But it is not really an appropriate expression, for nothing has to "function" to "prevent from occurring" what cannot occur anyway. Either prices rise (with the help of supportive expansion of demand) to cut the real wage rates to the level made possible by the productivity increase, or unemployment occurs (if demand expansion is prevented or restrained) and cuts total real wages even lower.

If money wages were not increased at all and all increments to the net national product that are due to technological progress were distributed to consumers in the form of lower prices, *all* income recipients—wage earners, business owners, and fixed-income recipients—would share in the increased product. If money wages all over the economy are increased approximately by the rate at which average productivity has increased, prices on the average will neither fall nor rise and hence the fixed-income recipients (bondholders, landlords, pensioners, perhaps also civil servants,

---

[5] If wage rates were to increase as much as output per worker while prices were kept from rising, total output would not be large enough to allow any return to be earned by the new capital; employers, then, might not want to maintain the level of investment and employment. See Lutz, *loc. cit.,* 4.

teachers, etc.) will be cut out of their share in the increment. Thus, aggressive money-wage increases which, on the average, equal the average increase in productivity in the economy will improve the relative income share of labor at the expense of the receivers of contractual income.

Aggressive Wage Increases to Capture Individual Productivity Gains

The "rule" that price stability and full employment can be maintained if all money wage rates are increased by the same percentage by which average productivity has increased in the economy as a whole is frequently misunderstood and mistakenly applied to advocate increases in money-wage rates in individual firms or industries by the same percentage by which productivity has increased in these firms or industries. In other words, the rule is perverted to the proposal that the benefits of advancing productivity should accrue to the workers in the industries in which the advances take place. It is twisted into a proposition justifying

. . . union demands in those industries, which, because of improved technology and consequent cost reductions, can afford to pay higher wages without charging higher prices for their products. This proposition is thoroughly unsound. It misses completely the economic function of prices and wages; its realization would sabotage the economic allocation of resources without serving any purpose that could be justified from any ethical or political point of view.[6]

A sensible allocation of resources requires that the same factors of production are offered at the same prices to all industries. It causes misallocations if industries in which technology has improved are forced to pay higher wages for the same type of labor that gets lower pay in industries where technology has not changed. Wage rates should be temporarily higher in fields into which labor is to be attracted, not in fields where labor is released by labor-saving techniques. It is economic nonsense to advocate that wage rates should be forced up precisely where labor becomes relatively abundant.

---

[6] Fritz Machlup, *The Political Economy of Monopoly* (Baltimore: Johns Hopkins University Press, 1952), 403.

259

One might accept an economically unsound arrangement if it were ethically much superior. But no one could claim that the proposition in question satisfied any ethical norm. If five industries, let us call them A, B, C, D, and E, employ the same type of labor; if any of them, say Industry A, develops a new production process and is now able to make the same product as before with half the amount of labor; then this Industry A could afford to raise its wage rates without raising its selling prices. Should now workers in Industry A get a wage increase of 100 per cent while their fellow workers in Industries B, C, D, and E get nothing? Should the coincidence that the technological advance took place in A give the workers there the windfall of the entire benefit, raising them above the rest of the people? I can see no ethical argument that could be made in favor of such a scheme.

But as a matter of practical fact, apart from economics and ethics, the scheme could never be consistently applied, because the workers in other industries would not stand for it, . . . similar wage increases would have to be given in all . . . firms and industries regardless of their ability to pay, regardless of whether their selling prices would remain stable or go up slightly or a great deal. It simply would not be fair if a favored group were to be the sole beneficiary of progress while the rest of the population would have to sit back and wait for better luck.[7]

No fair-minded person would ask them to sit back and wait; every labor union with any power at all would press the claims of its members, and where no unions existed workers would eventually appeal to their employers and to the public to end the injustice. Yet, any "equalizing" wage increases would be clearly of the cost-push type and would, if unemployment is prevented, lead to consumer-price increases which take away from the originally privileged worker groups some of the real gains they were first awarded (with the approval of short-sighted commentators and politicians).

This spill-over of money-wage increases and the cost-push inflation which it produces (with the help of a supportive demand inflation) serve to redistribute some of the productivity gains first captured by the workers in the industries where the gains occurred. This redistribution by means of consumer-price inflation cuts back the real wages of the first-successful labor groups, whose unions will then complain about the erosion of their incomes and will call for seemingly defensive wage increases to regain the ground lost through inflation (though they rarely lose all of their gain in real income and often keep a large part of it).

---

[7] *Ibid.*, 404-405.

In short, a policy that condones wage increases in industries which, because of increased productivity, can afford to pay increased wages without charging increased prices, is actually a policy that accepts a rising cost-price spiral without end.

Price Reductions Essential
for Stability

A wage increase obtained by a particular labor group may initiate an inflationary process, but the speed of this process will depend largely on the incidence of defensive price increases and of imitative and defensive wage increases. If nothing but responsive (competitive) price and wage increases were to occur, the rate of inflation initiated by an isolated wage boost would be very small, perhaps negligible. It is, nevertheless, interesting to examine models of price inflation that include neither defensive nor imitative increases.

Inflation Without Spill-Over Wage-Push

In the inflationary process described in the last section, the industries that were forced to pay the increased wages (out of the economies provided by improved techniques) were assumed, for the sake of the argument, not to increase their selling prices. The price inflation was chiefly the work of a spill-over of the wage increases into fields where productivity had increased less or not at all. But even in the absence of any spill-over, even if no worker in the country were to receive a raise that did not come from economies in production, some degree of consumer-price inflation would be inevitable in an economy in which (a) wage rates are never reduced in any sector, even in the face of unemployment, (b) wage rates are increased to capture productivity gains entirely in the industries where they accrue, and (c) full employment is secured, if necessary, through expansion of effective demand. Now when workers are released in the industries where productivity increases, but production, with unchanged prices and unchanged demand, is not increased, it will take an inflation of demand to create employment for the workers set free by the advance of technology. In other words, the "technological unemployment" will have to be cured by an expansion of demand, which in turn will cause a rise in consumer prices.

Does not this argument overlook the increase in demand on the part of workers who receive wage increases? It does not. Since the wage increases were granted just to offset the cost reduction made possible by the increase in output per worker, the workers who stay employed receive their raise out of funds no longer paid out as wages to the workers who lost their jobs. A little arithmetic may clarify this point. If 90 workers can now produce the output previously produced by 100, and are now paid the total wage that was previously paid to 100, the total purchasing power in the hands of the workers stays the same. The 10 workers who were released get nothing, and what was saved on them is being paid to the "more productive" 90. The firm, paying the same wage bill (though to fewer workers), finds its costs neither increased nor reduced and keeps its selling prices unchanged. Since at these prices demand is the same as before, the firm has no use for the 10 workers; nor has anybody else if wages rates are nowhere reduced. If the authorities want them re-employed, a demand inflation has to be engineered. True, the 10 workers will produce something once they are employed, but only after increased prices have created incentives for employers to use more labor; or they will have to be employed (and paid for with new money) in the production of public services not sold in the market.

The assumptions built into the model underlying this chain of reasoning have excluded growth (of labor force and capital stock) and excess capacity. If there were adequate excess capacity in each and every line of production, the demand created (in order to re-employ the labor released by the more productive industries) could be satisfied without price increases anywhere. But no inflation model can reasonably include the assumption of ubiquitous excess capacity; limited facilities (bottlenecks) are implied in any explanation of inflation. Thus, no exception should be taken to the assumption that the new wages paid to the re-employed workers will not all be spent for their own products, but largely for other things, and that prices will be bid up in the process.

The exclusions of a growing labor force and a growing capital stock have served merely to simplify the reasoning. When inputs and outputs are increasing, a certain increase in the money supply and in aggregate spending will be required to manage the increase in output and trade at given prices. An expansion of money demand to effect a re-absorption of technological unemployment would be over and above the money demand required to take care of the growth in labor force and capital stock. To combine the analyses of such growth and of technological unemployment would be an unnecessary complication; the other growth factors can be disregarded without vitiating the conclusions derived in an isolated treatment of technological unemployment.

The price inflation to be expected from a demand inflation engineered to absorb "technological unemployment" will of course be quite moderate in this case, where all the spill-over wage increases are ruled out. Here is a type of inflation that cannot be characterized as a cost-push inflation, and not as a demand-pull inflation either, if that term is reserved for autonomous expansions of demand. To be sure, aggressive wage increases are involved in the process, but these increases, merely offsetting the growth of productivity, will push up only the cost per labor hour, not the cost per unit of output, and thus no price increases can be said to result from cost increases.

Inflation Without Any Wage Increases

One may easily jump to the conclusion that technological unemployment, and the need to resort to demand inflation as its only cure, is entirely due to the aggressive wage increases, giving to the workers in the technically advancing industries the entire benefit of the productivity gain. This conclusion would be wrong. The consequences will be the same if in the absence of any wage increase the firms in question find their profits increased but for some reason fail to let consumers benefit in the form of lower selling prices.

Does this argument rely on lower marginal propensities to spend, or on insufficient investment opportunities, or on excessive liquidity preferences? It does not. Even if it is assumed that corporations spend all of their retained profits and stockholders spend all their dividends—just as the workers would have spent their wages—the workers released in the industries where technology has advanced will not be re-employed without the help of demand inflation unless prices to consumers are lowered. The case is almost the same as that in which the workers cap-

263

tured the productivity gain, except that now the corporations and their owners pocket the entire benefit.

Why "almost" the same, why not exactly the same? Because there is the possibility that an increase in retained earnings, as an increase in capital supply, raises the marginal productivity of labor and thus the demand for labor at given wage rates. But it would be absurd to expect that this would suffice to re-employ all the released labor. Assume that the entire amount saved on the wage bill is spent on new machinery; this new demand for machinery (and indirectly for the labor that goes into its manufacture) merely takes the place of the former workers' demand for consumer goods (and indirectly for the labor that went into their production). Thus the spending of the retained profits—earned by reducing the wage bill—constitutes no increased demand for labor. Only the resulting increase in productive facilities may eventually help the demand for labor to the extent of a small fraction of the technological unemployment created by the (labor-saving) increase in productivity. Hence the conclusion is the same as it was in the case of wage increase: only if consumers get a chance through lower prices to buy more products with their given money incomes will the released workers get a chance to find jobs in the absence of demand inflation.[8]

But why should firms refuse to lower their prices when production costs fall? The well-known theoretical models of a monopolist responding to a lowering of his cost curve show, with no reasonable exceptions, that he would reduce his selling price and increase his output. If firms can be observed acting otherwise, what is wrong with the model or what is wrong with the firms? One possible hypothesis would be that the firms of the real world had been in "disequilibrium," charging less than profit-maximizing monopoly prices and waiting for a good occasion to adjust their position. If now their costs are reduced, inaction, failure to reduce their prices, may be an easy way to adjust. Another hypothesis would be that

---

[8] This does not mean that the entire increase in productivity must be passed on to consumers in the form of reduced prices. Technological unemployment will neither be perpetuated nor require a price-inflating demand expansion for its cure if wage rates are raised by the national average increase in productivity. This will still permit price reductions in the industries where productivity has increased. The money the consumers save in buying these products at reduced prices will be spent on other goods and will drive up some other prices, without however raising consumer prices on the average.

the firms of the real world are in positions of not firmly coordinated oligopoly, where the safest rule is always "not to rock the boat," that is, never to reduce prices lest a rival mistake it for an outbreak of price competition. A third hypothesis would be that the "administered" prices in modern business cannot be explained by any models based on intelligent considerations, but are set by some fixed rules of thumb, and that one of these rules is never to reduce a price. There are perhaps still other hypotheses to explain the fact of "downward inflexibility" of prices—if indeed it is a fact. But no matter which hypothesis is accepted, the conclusion remains valid that if prices are not reduced when productivity has increased, technological unemployment arises and cannot be absorbed except through demand inflation and consequent consumer-price inflation.

Stabilization of Individual Prices Necessitates Inflation

The argument of the preceding pages was designed to demonstrate that the failure to reduce prices in industries where productivity has increased will result in an inflationary increase of general prices, which

(a) will be most rapid if the productivity gains are captured by the workers of these industries by way of wage–rate increases—because of the practically inevitable spill-over of the wage increases to other worker groups; but

(b) will also occur, though much more slowly, in the absence of such spill-over, because it will take a demand expansion to re-employ the workers released when the wage bill of the progressive industries is distributed over fewer workers; and

(c) will not be avoided even in the absence of any wage increases, because a demand expansion will be required to re-employ the workers released when the entire part of the wage bill that is saved through the technological advance is transformed into profits without giving consumers a chance to buy more product.

An economist willing to rely on the most abstract and general principles of economic theory can derive this "inevitability" of inflation from a simple set of theorems. He can deduce from the equilibrium conditions in a system of general equilibrium that general prices must rise if individual prices are maintained in industries where productivity increases. For a fall of production cost in one industry will call forth a reduction of the price of its product relative to the prices of all other products; this adjustment of relative prices will, in a money economy, proceed either through a fall in the money price of the product that now requires less labor per unit than before or through an increase in all other money prices (or through a combination of both); hence, stabilization of the money price of the more economically produced product implies that equilibrium will be restored through a general increase in money prices.

I do not propose to use this technical way of reasoning to convince trade–union leaders, business executives, or members of Congress. But the previous argument was, I trust, understandable before I added the sophisticated demonstration of its conclusion.

The O'Mahoney Plan to Check Inflation

It should now be clear that the only way to prevent inflation of consumer prices, and prevent unemployment too, is to make prices more flexible in the downward direction and, in particular, to encourage price reductions in industries where productivity has increased. Senator O'Mahoney's plan, partly incorporated in Senate Bill 215 of April 1959, and receiving serious consideration by several members of Congress, would achieve exactly the opposite. According to the preamble of the Bill, its author believes that "inflation will be checked if the pricing policies of these [dominant] corporations are publicly reviewed before increased prices may be made effective." On this theory the Bill provides for public hearings and investigations of large corporations whenever they want to raise prices. But the harder it is made for firms to raise prices the more surely will they avoid ever reducing their prices.

If a nation is committed to a full-employment policy, that is, to a policy of using demand inflation to create employment, it can avoid inflation only by avoiding anything that may create unemployment. Since economic growth proceeds chiefly through technological progress, and technological unemployment can only be avoided through price reductions, the prime requirement of a non-inflationary full-employment policy is to prevent the workers, owners, and managers of the progressing industries from capturing all the productivity gains accruing in these industries in the form of increased money wages and increased profits, respectively, and to encourage the dispersion of most of these gains to consumers in the form of reduced prices.

The O'Mahoney policy in effect encourages the trade unions in the industries in question to get out and capture the entire productivity gains for their workers. It does so implicitly because, if the firms are prevented from raising prices after the aggressive wage increases have absorbed "only" the new economies, the labor unions will no longer be blamed by the public for causing or precipitating higher prices. The "visible link" between these wage increases and price inflation is removed, and the union leaders will have even less compunction in pressing for these supposedly non-inflationary wage increases. The firms, losing all or most of the productivity gains to their workers, will hardly be eager to reduce prices. But even if they should, by means of tough bargaining, succeed in keeping a good deal of the gains, they will surely not dream of sharing any part of them with the consumers, because they would consider it foolish to reduce prices that cannot be raised again except after expensive, cumbersome, and perhaps embarrassing public inquisitions.

The O'Mahoney plan to check inflation would actually tend to make inflation perennial and perpetual. The only thing that can be said for the proposed policy is that it might in the short run, perhaps for a couple of years, slow down the progress of the price inflation. But even this is doubtful since, apart from encouraging trade unions to fight for the productivity gains accruing in their industries, it does nothing to check the spill-over wage increases, which in genuine cost-push fashion engender many chains of defensive, "approvable" price increases and necessitate continual resort to supportive demand inflation.

Conclusion

It was not the purpose of this article to lead up to a critique of a proposed policy; this was a mere by-product. The intention was to examine the conceptual framework employed in recent discussions and, in view of its inadequacies, to propose some improved theoretical tools that may serve better in the analysis of the inflationary process of our time.

Analysis requires the following distinctions: an administered cost increase may be "equilibrating" in the sense that it merely "absorbs" a previously existing excess demand, or it may be "disequilibrating" in the sense that it creates an excess supply that may be prevented or removed only by an expansion of demand. To facilitate the analysis, three kinds of demand expansion are distinguished: *autonomous, induced,* and *supportive.* Likewise, three kinds of cost increase are distinguished: *responsive, defensive,* and *aggressive.* Any one of these cost increases may be "administered"; but the responsive ones would also occur in a fully competitive market. Neither defensive nor aggressive increases are in response to excess demand, and both therefore presuppose monopolistic power; defensive increases, however, attempt merely to restore previous real earnings of the group concerned, while aggressive increases raise real earnings above previous levels.

With the aid of these new concepts one can construct models of the inflationary process of various degrees of complexity. It may be possible to develop empirical tests for the choice of the model that fits best the recorded data of particular periods. The author believes that the price inflations of the periods 1945-48 and 1950-52 were of the demand-pull type, but that for 1955-59 a cost-push model would fit better. He tentatively suggests that wage-push was more effective than profit-push.

Finally the relation of inflation to increases in productivity was examined. The popular idea of a "non-inflationary" distribution of productivity gains by way of wage increases to the workers employed in the industries in which technology has advanced was found to be untenable. Imitative wage increases would lead to a brisk inflation. But some degree of inflation would occur even without such "spill-over" wage increases, because the distribution of the productivity gains to the workers or owners in the progressing industries would result in technological unemployment, and remedial full-employment measures would inflate the price level. The only way of avoiding inflation is through price reductions in industries where productivity has improved.

DISPUTES, PARADOXES, AND DILEMMAS CONCERNING ECONOMIC DEVELOPMENT

Reprinted with permission from *Rivista Internazionale di Scienze Economiche e Commerciali* Anno IV (1957), N. 9.

A dispute is a verbal expression of a difference of opinion, a controversy in which conflicting contentions are argued.

A paradox is a seemingly self-contradictory statement, or just any unexplained or surprising contradiction, sometimes merely an apparent contradiction which disappears upon closer inspection or reflection, sometimes a statement or "phenomenon that exhibits some conflict with preconceived notions of what is reasonable or possible." (For some of these definitions I am indebted to the *Oxford Dictionary*.)

A dilemma is a choice between equally unfavorable alternatives. It may be the conflict involved in a difficult choice, where the decision in favor of one alternative implies the sacrifice of the other, especially when there are moral commitments to favor both.

Such contradictions and conflicts, real or apparent, can be found in the meaning, theory, and programs of economic development. We shall attempt to take an inventory of them and shall sort them out under four headings: A. Definitions, B. Objectives, C. Recommendations, and D. Theories. Such an inventory has, I believe, more than entertainment value. Its chief value is to get in the shortest possible time a good idea of a good many of the problems of economic development, problems which at present occupy larger numbers of economists than does any other single complex of economic problems.[1]

A. Conflicting Definitions

1. If development is a process leading from a less developed to a more developed stage, economic development implies the idea of a " less developed" and perhaps of an "underdeveloped economy." But the term "underdeveloped economy" has been applied to at least three different kinds of situation: (a) where there exist *underdeveloped productive resources,* potentialities waiting to be utilized; (b) where the people are *poor,* relative to people elsewhere and perhaps also relative to physiological (chiefly nutritional) needs; and (c) where the people have *"Malthusian trouble,"* that is, any increase in total production tends to be more than taken up by an increase in population so that the plane of living cannot be raised.

Several combinations of these three conditions are possible. Using the customary logical symbol a' for the non-existence of condition a, and similarly b' and c,' we find the following five combinations possible: a b' c'; a b c' ; a b c; a' b c'; and a' b c. (The other three combinations are ruled out: a b' c and a' b' c, because the presence of Malthusian troubles presupposes poverty and, hence, cannot exist in the absence of poverty; and a' b' c' means that none of the possible conditions making for an underdeveloped economy is present.)

The existence of undeveloped resources[2] in an economy not troubled by poverty (a b' c') is a most desirable state of affairs. It means that there is a good possibility of further development, and since the people are not poor and thus can save if they want to, this development potential is likely to be realized in the course of time. How splendid to be rich and yet underdeveloped! In this sense the United States, paradoxical

---

[1] The author abstains from blaming or crediting any particular writers for any of the opinions surveyed in this essay—no names will be cited. As far as he can, he also attempts to conceal his own opinions by hiding them as those of "some theorists," "some critics," "some opponents," and so forth. At some points he could not resist stating his opinion.

[2] Perhaps it should be said that it depends on the state of technology and on relative prices whether or not certain factors are regarded as "productive resources."

though it sounds, is an undeveloped country; it has more undeveloped resources, absolutely and relative to its population than most countries whose development is now being considered or undertaken. According to United Nations terminology, rich undeveloped countries are not called "undeveloped," because this term is really used as a euphemism for "poor."

Undeveloped resources in a country where people are poor but not under Malthusian pressures (a b c') make for promising development programs. Foreign grants or loans and investments may achieve good results in these circumstances where the domestic ability to save is initially small or nil. It does not necessarily mean that the marginal efficiency of capital will be greater in poor countries, when the rate of investment is stepped up, than in rich countries with undeveloped resources, but the productivity of labor may be significantly increased—which seems to be more essential for poor countries than for rich.

Prospects are poor in countries where poverty is combined with Malthusian troubles, even if there are undeveloped resources—(a b c)—and their development is pushed vigorously. If, because of increased birth and survival rates and a consequent upsurge in population, average income cannot be improved for good, should the development of undeveloped resources be called "economic development"? After all, poverty would not be alleviated and, if relative living standards measure the state of "underdevelopment," no progress will be achieved by a development program that does not reduce the Malthusian pressures.

The absence of undeveloped resources in a poor country, even without Malthusian problems (a' b c'), makes it difficult to promote development. Of course, capital equipment can almost always improve the productivity of land and labor, but the development potential is not great where every square foot of land is in use, every member of the labor force is occupied, and no unexploited mineral deposits or water resources exist. The only kind of investment in such an economy is "capital-intensive," as some writers, rather paradoxically, have called the more intensive use of labor and land through the employment of larger amounts of capital. From the point of view of the world as a whole this is a rather wasteful use of capital in view of the better investment opportunities elsewhere where idle resources are waiting to be used as soon as enough capital becomes available.

The worst of all possible situations seems to be that of a country

271

without undeveloped resources, with great poverty, and with Malthusian pressures preventing any improvement (a' b c). There is another paradox in such a situation, however, in that the very existence of Malthusian pressures points to the existence of undeveloped "labor resources." We shall not try to examine whether this eventual supply of labor makes the possible development of the country less or rather more illusory.

The basic paradox in the definition of an "underdeveloped economy" lies in the fact that the term is not used for the economies with the greatest "development potential," but chiefly for those which would *not* be regarded as seriously underdeveloped in a world without barriers, political or otherwise, to the movement of goods, capital, and people.[3] But even if we are taking the world as it is, the contradictions in the concept of "underdeveloped economies" are serious enough to suggest dropping the term for the sake of clearer analysis.

2. In juxtaposition to the normative concept "progress," to the quantitative or dimensional concept "increase," and to the biological or organic concept "growth," the role of the term "development" is not clear cut by any means. It is, of course, possible to forget subtle distinctions and use all these terms interchangeably. But some economists have insisted on their differentiated use. "Increases" in total output that were somehow associated with "natural population growth" have been referred to as "economic *growth*" whereas the term "economic *development*" has been reserved for processes of institutional change instrumental in accelerating the rate of increase of average output. But there is no consistency in the use of the terms and many apparent contradictions disappear when the meanings of words used by particular writers are clarified.

For many purposes it is essential to make clear whether "development" *is* the increase of income (per capita) or *leads* to such an increase. Since certain causes or conditions of income creation, such as changes in legal, political, or economic institutions, cannot be measured, it should be clear that a "rate of development" cannot be stated in numerical terms if development is understood as a process of institutional change. Still, if a (measurable) increase in the rate of increase of income is attributed to (non-measurable) institutional changes which are regarded as "economic

---

[3] Without such barriers, people would leave the "bad lands" and migrate to the better-endowed regions, in which the use of capital would yield much greater increases of output.

development," it would be perfectly meaningful to speak of a "slow" or "fast" development. By and large, most writers have discussed economic development as if it were measurable; indeed, most of them have identified it with the rate of increase in income per head.

3. A statistically operational definition of economic development must contain directions for measurement. But several conflicts are possible concerning the choice of the essential magnitudes. Should *national income* or only *consumption* be considered as essential? Should we look at *total* income, or *per capita* income, or income *per worker,* or at the *level of living of the masses?*

Think of a nation where total income is increasing, whereas income per worker stays constant, and income per head declines. One may not wish to regard this as economic development.—Think of a society where total income is increasing, where even income per head is increasing, but where all this increase takes the form of additional gold hoards of some wealthy princes, while the masses stay as poor as before. One may prefer not to speak of economic development in this case—Think of a country which uses a large part of the annual increase in its labor force for investment in office buildings, mansions, race tracks and auto roads, while consumption per head is barely maintained at a subsistence level. Is this economic development?—Think of a nation whose oil resources are developed by a corporation owned partly by foreigners who contribute capital funds and partly by nationals who contribute land. All the oil is exported. National income per head increases, but only because of profits accruing to domestic stockholders and of tax revenues accruing to the government; the incomes of the masses may not be affected by the development.—Think of a country, and this is purely imaginary, where a part of a large excess population is wiped out (by an epidemic) and, as a result, national income and consumption per head increases.

All these examples are given here in order to show the conflicts involved in measurements of economic development on the basis of formulas prescribed in various definitions. Probably no definition can avoid paradoxical applications. For many analytical purposes I have found it useful to define economic development as those changes in the use of productive resources that result in a potentially continuing growth of national income per head in a society with increasing or stable population. But

273

we should not be surprised if we were shown that this definition runs into unforeseen snags.

B. Conflicting Objectives

4. Some of the conflicts of definition and measurement of economic development reflect fundamental conflicts of social objectives. We must not take it for granted that the objective of increasing *total* income is always ranked below the objective of increasing income *per head*. If they had a choice between either a faster increase in per capita income of an unchanged (or slowly rising) population, or a faster increase in population with an unchanged (or slowly rising) per capita income, some governments and some social philosophers would choose the latter. The old utilitarians speculated which would make for higher social utility: increased individual welfare for a given number of people or a given individual welfare for an increased number of people. And I have heard it said of some governments, for example of Egypt, that their ambitions lie in increased military and political power for their nation, and this requires less that people be fed better than that more people can be fed.

5. The choice between either *consumption* or *total income* including investment as the relevant criterion in the definition or measurement of economic development reflects also a conflict of objectives. In many instances this can be expressed as a conflict between long-range and short-range objectives of society. The longer an increase in consumption can be repressed in favor of an increased saving ratio, the higher may be the consumption level in the future: the *next generation* may benefit from the sacrifices of the present one.

Difficult ethical problems are involved in this choice between short or long periods of waiting for the fruits of development, especially where it is not the individual who freely chooses to sacrifice for the benefit of his children but where it is the government that imposes upon its subjects a sacrifice for the benefit of the unknown people of later generations. The conflict is aggravated by the possibility of misjudgments on a much larger scale for longer-range development programs.

6. A closely related conflict of objectives concerns the size distribution of income. If income equality, or at least less inequality, is a recog-

nized social objective, to what extent is a faster increase in total and average income desired if it can be had only at the price of less equality, and to what extent is *more equality* desired if it can be had only at the price of a *slower increase* in total and average income? Since the savings ratio is reduced when increments of income are more widely and more thinly distributed, the rate of development becomes a function of the concentration of income, either in the hands of private capitalists or of the government.

What then is a "good" development program? Should it soon provide for increased income distributions to the poorest strata of the population or should it rather provide for the capture of most of the income increase and for its reinvestment in order to secure a rate of *capital formation* that would accelerate *further increases* in productivity? In an important sense the problem of income distribution is coextensive with the problem of the time horizon of the development program: to reduce quickly the plight of the poorest is to favor early consumption at the expense of long-range development at a faster rate.

7. Other "distributive" objectives influencing the development plans of many countries relate to favored positions of some social groups, or some religious, racial, or ethnic groups, in the politics of these countries. Sometimes the interest in improving the economic status of a *favored group* prevails over the interest in increasing *total* or *average* national income.

In the development policies of countries which have only recently acquired national independence, such as Burma and Malaya, the indigenous ethnic groups are some times given preferential treatment as against the immigrant and immigrant-descended Chinese and Indians, who under the previous colonial rule, neutral between different parts of the dominated people, had succeeded in achieving higher economic positions than the native Burmese and Malayans, respectively. A rise in total or average national income that would not include the favored group is apparently regarded as undesirable. To achieve an increase in the incomes of the favored group seems to be a major objective of the economic development policy, which may be pursued even if the less-favored groups should suffer a decline in incomes serious enough to reduce the average income of the population. There are probably no official announcements to this effect, but indications that this hierarchy of values prevails can be detected when actual policies are analyzed. (The nationalization of the rice trade in Burma, in the belief that the elimination of the ethnic Chinese from that trade would aid the ethnic Burmese rice growers, is sometimes cited as a case in point,—though such an interpretation may be erroneous.)

8. In the hierarchy of conflicting values some *extra-economic objectives* may be given higher ranks than the "materialistic" improvements of income or consumption measured in goods and services. The establishment or maintenance of a particular political, social, or economic organization may be such an "overriding" consideration.

There are some who would reject any increase in material welfare if it could be had only at the price of weakening the democratic system by giving more power to central authorities; there are others who would renounce an income increase that could be had only by giving freer scope to private enterprise. In some countries the official development plan contains an open declaration to the effect that development should proceed along socialistic lines and that the plan is based on that premise. In certain countries any program that would afford more social equality among different racial groups, or would reduce the degree of "apartheid" between whites and non-whites, would be rejected no matter how much it would promise by way of material benefits. There are some avowed "primitivists" who would oppose development, however promising economically, if it meant drastic changes in the traditions, customs and mores of the people; and there are some avowed "progressives" who would not mind forcing development upon people content with their existing living standard, not interested in any unlift, and averse to a change in their ways of life.

The conflicts between objectives of purely economic improvement and objectives regarding the social and political organization of society cannot be easily resolved. The psychic incomes from living under a particular kind of social or political system cannot be estimated in the same terms as the national product. Moreover, the pleasures which the governing group derive from pursuing what they regard as "national" and "social" goals may be paid for largely by the governed in reduced economic and extra-economic well-being.

9. Of certain objectives which figure heavily in some development programs it is hard to say whether they are economic or extra-economic.

This is especially true of the objectives pursued by "economic nationalism." The demands for greater "independence" of the developing nation from essential imports and from foreign capital are sometimes pressed on economic grounds, though most of the arguments used in such attempts are judged, by competent theorists, to be specious or fallacious.

Several countries which have only recently gained their national independence in the political sphere, believe that they must achieve *"economic independence"* as well, and that this requires that they establish their own industries making the things regarded as strategic for their development—such as steel—even if they could obtain them much more cheaply from abroad in exchange for exports which they can produce with comparative advantage.

Many countries have a horror of foreign capital and foreign enterprise. While they may be conscious of their own lack of capital and enterprise and of the need of both for accelerated development, they do their best to keep out foreign investment, especially in the form of direct investment. Political slogans are employed to harangue the people against tolerating what is called "domination by foreign capitalists" and "exploitation by imperialists."

If some professional economists join the "nationalists" in the advocacy of barriers against the import of strategic goods, capital, or enterprise, they do so, of course, on the basis of long-run considerations. They could not possibly deny the important short-run benefits to economic development through the availability of cheaper capital goods, more capital funds, and more enterprise. Thus, depending on whether the arguments for "economic independence" are economic or political, the conflict is either between the present and the future, or between material improvement and ideology.

10. Whereas total output, as a rule, varies with employment, this is not so under all circumstances, and there may be conflicts between the objective of full employment, let alone maximum employment,[4] and the objective of *maximum total output* at any time and, even more so, over a long period of time.

With a given stock of resources, natural and man-made, and given

---

[4] Full employment permits some unemployment, and is therefore smaller than "maximum employment."

technology, there is a volume of employment at which total output is a maximum (and the marginal product of labor is zero). If the labor force is much greater than that, its full employment would yield less than maximum total output; a maximum of output would be produced only with a part of the labor force unemployed. Where the labor force has increased faster than the capital resources, this conflict between maximum output and full employment is not unlikely.

If fast economic development requires a transfer of labor to new fields, the existence of some pool of unemployed will be an aid to development; for it will be easier to recruit the workers needed in new industries if they do not have to be pried loose from jobs in other places and occupations. It is of course possible that the amount of unemployment that is consistent with "full employment" (in most of its meanings) is sufficient to achieve the labor mobility required for the highest possible rate of economic development. But it may be that "underemployment," at least at times, will permit a rate of development well above the rate achievable under "full employment."

Perhaps one should distinguish four possible "optimum" volumes of employment: one that would permit the *fastest development*; a higher one that would produce the *largest current output*; a still higher one called "full employment," which could be sustained without inflationary pressure and would leave no more workers unemployed than jobs unfilled; and the highest, called *"over-employment,"* achievable only at times of monetary inflation and therefore not permanently sustainable. Development plans in countries with serious underemployment, open or disguised, may be designed to pursue employment objectives inconsistent with the highest possible rate of development as well as with the largest volume of current output.

11. The possibility that the objectives of full employment and faster development may be alternatives is probably widely recognized. But I expect vigorous denials if I submit that there may be a conflict also between the objective of *full employment* and the supposed method of achieving it, the so-called "full-employment *policy*." If this conflict exists, there will be an equally serious conflict between the "full-employment policy" and the objective of fast development.

The suggestion that a "full-employment policy" is often an ill-suited means to the chosen end rests on the fact that an expansion of monetary (effective) demand may in certain circumstances have consequences which compel the government either to discontinue monetary expansion or to adopt policies of direct control which in the course of time reduce the volume of employment below that which could have been reached and sustained under a policy of monetary and fiscal moderation. I cannot here attempt a theoretical analysis of this contention. I confine myself to the hint that the long and remarkable period of high-level employment and fast growth of output in Germany and in Austria in recent years may be attributed to the rejection by their governments of so-called full-employment policies and to the adoption of policies characterized as orthodox, disinflationary, and even deflationary. These old-fashioned policies were adopted against the advice of "modern" economic experts, and the actual achievements were contrary to the expectations and predictions of these experts.

Strong beliefs in particular economic theories have given certain policies — which should of course be nothing but means to ends — the status of ends in themselves. This has occurred not only with regard to full-employment policy but also regarding the maintenance of fixed exchange rates through import and payments restrictions. The development programs of several countries announce, besides the goal of a high rate of growth, a strong advocacy of full-employment policies and of direct controls of imports and payments at fixed exchange rates. I suspect that this (highly popular) combination of monetary expansion with unadjusted exchange rates and direct controls is in the long run a drag on economic development, although it is recommended as an integral part of development planning and as an efficient instrument of accelerated growth.

I readily grant that my position sounds off-hand more paradoxical than the position which it questions. For it is evident that a full-employment policy provides finance for development projects for which it might otherwise be hard to find the necessary funds. How can a policy which manifestly speeds up the start of such projects be suspected as a retarding influence? The answer to this paradox lies in the difference between the short and the long run: an immediate advance — for all to see — with subsequent troubles and difficulties — not seen as a consequence of the "successful" program but, instead, attributed to some "structural" malaise. A slower start might avoid the difficulties and permit sustained growth.

C. Conflicting Recommendations

12. Many of the conflicts apparent in the different programs and recommendations formulated by development experts are implied in the conflicts of objectives. That the pursuit of different objectives calls for different recommendations goes without saying. We shall not repeat under the new heading the issues discussed or mentioned before. But there are also conflicts in recommendations not due to differences in objectives; they may reflect differences of judgment about underlying conditions or expected results, which may also be described as differences in "assumptions" concerning either the initial situation or the probable reactions to policy measures.

The most fundamental of the conflicts concern the direction in which the development ought to proceed: assuming that a high and sustained rate of growth is the predominant objective, should chief emphasis be placed on improvements in *agriculture*, on development of *"cottage industries,"* or on *outright industrialization?*

Each of these possibilities has found strong advocates in many "underdeveloped" countries. Improvements in agriculture might yield the quickest increase in total output with the smallest total capital requirements and the largest impact on the food supply for a notoriously undernourished people. Development of cottage industries might yield remarkable increases in value added through fabrication of goods exportable or import-replacing, and might, without raising problems of migration, housing, and urbanization, permit the utilization of labor resources now obviously underemployed in agriculture. Industrialization might be the most effective way of creating productive employment for large masses of a people suffering from actual unemployment as well as from concealed agricultural unemployment.

A compromise, to pursue all three development policies, is of course possible, but would not remove the problem. A decision to allocate scarce capital resources in equal parts among the competing uses does not get around the fact that a dollar invested in one project is a dollar withdrawn from another project possibly contributing to steadier or faster growth.

13. If, for good reasons or bad, a decision has been made in favor of industrialization, the conflict is not removed but merely shifted to another stage. The question now is: which industries, or what kind of industries,

should be promoted? And the answers are far from unanimous; expert advice contradicts expert advice even where there is no conflict concerning the country or region to which it is to be applied and concerning the objectives to be served.

One conflict, perhaps more fundamental than the others with respect to industrialization, refers to the scope of the industrial development plan; should the plan be so comprehensive as to include *many branches of manufacturing industry* or should it be confined to *public-utility* industries and to the installations sometimes described as constituting the *"social-overhead plant?"* The difference of opinion on this point is probably determined largely by trust or distrust in the wisdom and efficiency of comprehensive planning. [5]

Even those who are most skeptical concerning comprehensive planning have less objections, if any, to public development plans for public utilities — electricity, gas, water, sewage and garbage removal, communication, highways, waterways, railroads, harbor facilities — and for social-overhead services — schools, hospitals, sanitation, etc. Public planning of these projects may create great investment opportunities for private capital and enterprise and thus lead to the maximum rate of development. But to extend the scope of public planning and operation to a large number of branches in manufacturing industry is to invite, in the opinion of this school of thought, wasteful misallocations of resources which would inevitably retard economic development.

On the other side there are those skeptical of free enterprise and confident of the superior efficiency of government planning of all investment. Naturally, they recommend comprehensive development programs, in-

---

[5] This seems to reopen the question of possible conflicts between political objectives and the objective of securing the highest rate of increase of national output per head; yet it is possible to separate the issues. *A collectivist* on political or moral grounds would prefer a collectivist society even if it produced less than a free-enterprise society. A *libertarian-individualist* on political or moral grounds would prefer a competitive free-enterprise society even if it produced less than a socialist one. Conceivably, the conviction that productivity would be greater under one system or another is quite separate from political or moral preferences. In actual fact, however, convictions about such "positive" matters as rates of output are probably in some measure influenced by "normative" judgments, though the experts who entertain these convictions may be absolutely unconscious of any bias. They may be perfectly honest in believing and asserting that their advice is not affected by any moral or political judgments.

cluding a detailed planning of projects in mining, manufacturing, as well as public utility industries.

14. The decision to plan all industrial investment requires a selection of the industries to be established or expanded. Experts disagree on the principles of selection, though many seem to agree on rejecting as undesirable or inapplicable the criterion of profitability on the basis of free-market prices.

Since development programs usually rely to some extent on foreign capital funds and often thereby involve the undertaking of obligations to pay interest and repay principal to foreign countries, and furthermore since development programs usually rely to some extent on the expansion of domestic bank credit and thereby create an excess demand for foreign money (at given exchange rates), many experts recommend investment projects in industries whose eventual operation would in some way "alleviate the balance-of-payments" of the country. This alleviation is supposed to be achieved by an increase in the supply of export goods or a decrease in the demand for import goods; in other words the new output of the new or expanded industries should be exportable or substitutable for imports.

The recommendation that high priority in the development program be given to industries producing either *additional exports or import-substitutes* is contradicted by other experts who hold that considerations of *productivity, employment creation,* or other social benefits should override the proposed criterion of balance-of-payments alleviation. It stands to reason, moveover, that investments in industries which will produce neither exports nor import replacements (for example an electric utility) may, by eventually reducing the production cost of export industries, import-competing industries, as well as non-foreign-trade industries, contribute more to an increase in the supply of exports and to a reduction in the demand for imports than an investment directly in a foreign-trade industry. The conflict is, at least in part, a disagreement between experts who believe only "what they can see" and those who rely on "speculative theories."

15. An underdeveloped country embarking on industrialization with a predominantly agricultural population and a serious scarcity of capital is advised for some time to confine itself to the establishment of *"light*

industries," according to one school of thought. According to another, it should immediately start to establish *"heavy industry."*

All sorts of reasons are advanced in support of these contradictory recommendations. Questions of differences in human adjustment to new conditions of work; questions of geographic dispersion or concentration; questions of "balanced growth" and "strategic sequences" in industrial development; questions of the capital-labor ratio and, consequently, of the volume of industrial employment provided by the available investment funds; questions of the capital turnover; and probably several other controversial questions are brought up in arguing the case for "light industry only" or the case of "heavy industry right now." One or another of these questions may be examined later under the heading of conflicts of theory. The question concerning capital turnover may be discussed in the present context because the preference for investments with "quick capital turnover" has been announced as a major principle for the selection of projects in the development programs of poor countries.

16. There is more confusion than conflict involved in this issue of "quick turnover of capital." Sometimes it is not even clear why a "quick turnover" is desired. The vague idea seems to be like this: "If you have only very little capital, don't freeze it in investments which cannot be liquidated except after or over many years; put it in quickly liquidating investments so that you may have larger funds for re-investment." But why should we care about the size of funds for re-investment if we expect to re-invest in the same production facilities? Should a short "investment period" with low returns be preferred to a longer one with much larger returns? Does quick capital turnover mean that the assets depreciate quickly? Or that the investment quickly pays for itself by virtue of the high profits it can yield?

The recommendation that the development program should promote industries with fast capital turnover makes especially little sense in view of the fact that there is a difference between the accounting definition of "capital turnover" and the concepts which the development experts apparently have in mind. On the accounting definition, capital turnover is the ratio of *annual sales* to capital invested; what the development experts probably mean is either the ratio of *annual depreciation earned* to capital invested or the ratio of *annual gross earnings* (*i.e.*, net income plus depreciation) to capital invested. That the first of these ratios has little connection with the other two is readily seen if it is remembered that sales proceeds may or may not contain large earnings or any earnings at all; it is a sad story, but an enterprise may fail to earn the depreciation of its assets — in which case a fast turnover in the first meaning could go together with a zero turnover in the other meanings.

This confusion does not indicate that the underlying ideas are pointless. A rational allocation of scarce capital, a rational selection of the "best" investment projects from among the vast number of "possible" projects, requires calculations which make implicit or explicit use of the rate of interest. The rate of interest as selecting and allocating device works to exclude certain *projects with long investment periods* in favor of projects with short ones, but these investment periods cannot be taken as a separate selection criterion independent from others which compare alternative uses of resources. Longer investment periods imply the use of more capital relative to other productive resources. But all resources are scarce in some measure. To give preference to short investments over long investments is like favoring investments using less aluminum or less lumber over investments using more of these materials, without taking account of all the other opportunity costs involved.

If the confusion over this issue is cleared up, there remains a conflict of judgment of the relative scarcities, a conflict which the market can solve through an impersonal price system but which a planning authority can "solve" only by listening to one expert rather than to others.

17. In many underdeveloped countries there is little doubt concerning the relative scarcities of two kinds of resources: capital and labor. If capital shortage and labor abundance can be taken as established facts, does it not follow that industrial development projects with *low capital–labor ratios* should be preferred over those with *high* capital–labor ratios? Some experts do indeed draw this conclusion. But other experts do not, and recommend instead that the planning commissions favor projects using plenty of capital per worker.

The recommendation of labor-saving, capital-using investments in countries with abundant labor and scarce capital is a genuine paradox. But the advocates of such a program believe that their theories can resolve the apparent contradiction. We shall have to return to these theories before we get through.

18. Development policy goes beyond the selection of investment proj-

ects and allocation of capital by planning authorities. Among the strategic factors in industrial development are the wages paid to industrial workers relative to the earnings of labor in agriculture and other non-industrial occupations. There is usually a wage differential in favor of industrial labor. But is the differential that exists in a particular country at the present time the "correct" one in the sense of being consistent with the fastest possible increase of total or average national product?

Development experts often advise that the wage differentials be adjusted. Unfortunately, their recommendations conflict. Some argue for an *increase in industrial wage rates,* others for a *reduction.* An increase may be favored in order to make industrial wages more attractive and stimulate more migration of labor into industry; in order to make industry pay for all the "social overhead costs" caused by the migration and concentration of labor through the need of providing additional housing, sanitary and civic facilities; in order to cause industry to use more "modern" production techniques, to employ more capital, and increase the productivity of industrial labor; in order to create large concentrations of capital, facilitating the prevention of dissipation of earnings; in order to create an "élite" within the labor class which would lead the masses in adopting higher standards of civilization, including planned parenthood; and perhaps for several other reasons. On the other hand, a reduction of industrial wage rates relative to the earnings of labor in other pursuits may be favored in order to permit increased employment of labor in industry; in order to raise thereby the total and average productivity of labor in the economy as a whole; in order to reduce a monopoly position of industrial labor unions which keep out a large hypothetical supply of labor anxious to move into industrial occupations if job opportunities were created; and perhaps for other reasons.

Since both the cases for raising and for lowering industrial wages are argued in the interest of faster economic development, the conflict of recommendations is not easily resolved. Some of the conflicts of theory which underlie the conflict of recommendations remain to be examined.

19. Measures to restrict or discourage the inflow of foreign capital were mentioned earlier when we discussed the objective of "national independence" — which these measures were supposed to serve — and its conflict with the objective of fast development. But we added that such measures are sometimes urged also in the interest of fast development in

the long run on the theory that the increasing obligations to pay interest and dividends and to repay foreign capital would eventually bring on serious "balance-of-payments difficulties" which would hamper the continued development of the debtor country so severely that it would have been better to do with *less foreign capital* in the first place. Hence the advice: "take less foreign funds and you will develop faster."

Other development experts have no objections to foreign loans, especially at reasonable interest rates. Their advice is to take all the cheap loans that can be obtained, but to go easy on *direct investment by foreigners.* One point is that dividends are usually higher than interest on the capital obtained, and profits still higher. But the great danger, we are warned, lies not in the higher cost of equity capital but in the impact of and repercussions from the large transfers which the industrializing country will eventually have to make to foreign countries, particularly if the profits of foreign-owned companies are plowed back, the foreign equity is thereby increased, and the earnings from the accumulated capital are increasing cumulatively, until profits paid out reach amounts which will shock the foreign-exchange control authorities out of their wits.

A third group of development experts advises *welcoming any amount of foreign capital,* be it in the form of grants, loans, stock purchases, or direct investment, — provided of course that the funds are used productively. The possibility of a period of strain in the money and foreign–exchange markets at the time of large payments of dividend or principal is not denied; but it *is* held that the use, up to that time, of the capital and reinvested earnings will surely — in the absence of monopolistic distortion or exploitation — have raised the productivity of the economy sufficiently to warrant the judgment that the accrued benefits from the in-payments are far greater than the costs and losses connected with the out-payments. With all the complaints about the burden of paying interest, dividends and debts, it is easy to forget the benefits accomplished and hardships alleviated at the time the foreign loans and investments were received.

Where the inflow of foreign capital is discouraged or restricted for political reasons, the conflict is between objectives and cannot be resolved by economic reasoning. But where both the advocates of restrictive measures and the advocates of unrestricted capital inflow pursue the same major objective — maximum rate of development in the long run — the conflict, one should think, ought to be capable of being resolved on the basis of economic theory and information. Yet, the controversy is continuing.

D. Conflicting Theories

20. The first of the conflicts of recommendations discussed in the preceding section related to the direction which the development program should be given in order to achieve the highest possible sustained rate of growth. One group of advisers strongly urge industrialization of almost any underdeveloped country even if its comparative advantages lie definitely in agriculture and other primary productions. In support of this advocacy of industrialization a variety of theories are advanced, everyone of which is controversial; some are held by a respected avant-garde, others are accepted by the majority, others are rejected by most professional economists but enjoy a loyal following of lay-economists.

An example of the last group is the theory of the economic benefits of *autarky*. This theory maintains that it is in the economic interest of each nation to produce domestically all the goods it needs and to import none. Whereas other theories of industrialization claim exceptions to the "law" of comparative advantages or attempt to show some offsetting benefits of disregarding that law, the theory of the economic benefits of autarky simply denies the law. This conflict cannot be resolved by reasoned argument; it is hopeless to argue where one side flouts logic.

One of the respectable theories stresses the fact that the present comparative-cost relations may drastically change in a foreseen way after a few years of operating an industry which under the law of comparative advantages would not be established, at least not at the present time. The followers of this theory refuse to take the present cost relations as relevant for determining which goods a nation should produce domestically and which it should procure in exchange for exports; instead, they advise the nation to take the temporary loss of producing a good which it can now produce only at a comparative disadvantage but which after a period of practice it will be able to produce with advantage.

This is the *infant-industry argument* for temporary tariff protection or temporary subsidization; it is generally accepted as valid, except that many economists question the ability of economic advisers to forecast correctly the changes in cost conditions induced by production. The empirical evidence at our disposal does not support any optimism concerning the correct selection of genuine infant industries able to compete on the basis of the improved cost conditions, without subsidies or tariffs.

Under the infant–industry argument society is called upon to assume the losses that would be incurred during the period of infancy of the new industry, that is, during a few years of transition until its production cost comes down. Different from this is the *external–economies argument.* Here too society is called upon to initiate action leading to the establishment or expansion of industries that would not occur otherwise; but no loss to society is involved here. As soon at she industry is established or expanded, production costs would be lower; the point is that this cost reduction cannot be brought about (and perhaps not even anticipated) by any individual firm acting by itself. This is why the economies are called external to the firms, or beyond their control. The present cost conditions as seen by entrepreneurs or industrial managers would be no guide to the socially most favorable allocation of resources, according to this theory.

The two arguments just mentioned rest on anticipations of changes in production cost: in one case cost reductions are to be induced in the course of years as a result of practice, learning and other concomitants of "growing up," in the other case the cost reductions are to be realized "as a function of the scale of output produced by the industry." [6] Another somewhat similar argument rests not on changes in cost but on differences between costs to society and costs paid by the producer: if *social cost is less than private cost* of production, the competitive output without government planning and intervention will be below the social optimum, and perhaps even zero. An analogous discrepancy may exist between benefits to society and benefits to the producer; if private benefits are less than social benefits, the competitive output will be too small and perhaps zero. If the law of comparative advantages dictates the international division of labor on the basis of competitive market prices, and thus on the basis of (too low) private benefits and (too high) private costs, the

---

[6] These cost reductions of the second type are not "functions of time," strictly speaking. The lapse of time has no role in the theory of external economies as developed by Marshall.

economy will not produce all that it could advantageously produce.

None of these four theories, which are invoked in support of the establishment of industries unprofitable by competitive–market–price criteria, is particularly germane to the basic idea of economic development or growth. The infant-industry argument is the only one that has any "dynamic" features, in that it involves a process in time. The autarky argument, the external-economies argument, and the excessive-private-cost argument, they are all basically "static" in nature, as is the comparative-cost argument which they are designed to disqualify as either invalid or inapplicable. This is not to suggest that a "static" (timeless) theory is deficient, inferior, or less applicable to the explanation of actual processes in time; it is stated here only in order to stress the contrast with the theories next in this review.

21. The theoretical case for industrialization of an underdeveloped economy is more convincingly bolstered by a thesis that may be characterized as the *"infant–economy" argument.* Just as the infant-industry argument rests on the "growing up" of a particular new industry and on the implications which this process has for the cost of this industry, the infant-economy argument rests on the growth of the economy as a whole, or of its industrial sector, and on the implications which this has for the cost and demand conditions of the entire industry.

In a way, the infant-economy argument for industrialization is again designed as a counter-weight to the comparative-cost argument against the industrialization of a country whose present comparative advantage lies heavily in primary products. The point is that present costs and prices should not count, because they will all change in the process of industrial development — which will not take place without "artificial" inducement. No single industry can look profitable at present costs and prices, but a whole array of industries established and expanded together will be profitable, with some of them supplying the intermediate products for the others, and the latter constituting the demand for the former, and all of them using the services of transportation, communication and other public-utility systems established and expanded simultaneously.

There is probably very little difference between this thesis and the theory of *"balanced growth."* The central point, apparently, is that the establishment or expansion of many an industry would look unwarranted by itself, but fully justified in the context of all the other industrial developments being engineered at the same time. Each industry requires materials, intermediate products, and machines, and the workers employed need consumers goods and services. Hence, the growth of any one industry provides the necessary demand for a host of other industries, and if all of them grow simultaneously the conditions for a healthy development are created; "balanced growth" can succeed where piece-meal industrial development might fail.

This sounds plausible and encouraging, yet to other theorists it appears to conflict sadly with a simple common-sense consideration. While the argument is certainly valid for the world as a whole, does it really hold for each country, each province? If it did, would it not be equivalent to an argument for autarky for every area, however small? Would it not contradict one of the most significant economic insights, the recognition of the advantages of division of labor between regions and countries? To hold that growth should be "balanced" within a country — in the sense that side by side with any industry the supplying industries and the customer industries, indeed all stages of production, be developed simultaneously within the country — seems to be a relapse into crude mercantilist fallacies.

There is an irreconcilable conflict between the extreme thesis of balanced growth and the static law of comparative advantage. However, if the former is modified to exclude the development of industries which would continue to operate under relative disadvantage, and if the latter is qualified to include changes in comparative cost in the course of economic development, then a reconciliation between the two points of view is possible. But no criteria for the practical harmonization have as yet been formulated.

22. Industrialization in the face of clear comparative advantages for primary, not industrial production has been urged also on a very different principle: *to anticipate changes in the net terms of trade* in the course of time.

On the basis of present costs and prices it might be advantageous for a country to produce primary products and exchange them against industrial goods; even on the basis of the different costs and prices anticipated to prevail in the future as a result of developmental adjustments it might still appear advantageous to expand primary production and to exchange this output for industrial imports; but if the marginal cost paid for imports and the marginal revenue received for exports are taken into account, rather than the average prices paid and received, the country might be shown to be better off if it shifted from primary to industrial production. In other words, the differences in the terms of trade for increased volumes of exports and imports and the terms obtainable if less exports are supplied and less imports demanded may be important enough to outweigh the losses from disregarding the relative efficiencies in production.

The principle involved is the same as that observed by a producer who buys as a monopsonist and sells as a monopolist; he will maximize his income by restricting his purchases and sales in accordance with the estimated elasticities of the supply and demand he faces. Instead of taking buying prices and selling prices as guides for his actions he will consider by how much he could influence these prices in his favor by "holding back" in his buying and in his selling.[7] A national economy in which many people act this way will suffer in productivity. Likewise, a world economy in which many countries act in such a fashion will be less productive.

A nation that succeeds in depressing its import prices or raising its export prices by taking up the production of industrial goods hitherto imported — that is, in effect, by switching from the production of exportables to the production of import-substitutes — can gain at the expense of other nations, provided other nations do not play the same game. If many do, their combined output will be lower. Each nation, nevertheless, may hope or illude itself that it will win the squeeze play; and many economists encourage their governments to try. Other economists deplore the neglect of the universally beneficial effects of international division of labor.

The conflict has strong ethical implications since it may be regarded as immoral to try to gain at the expense of others with a net loss for all.

---

[7]In order to illustrate this way of acting in an example which permits a closer analogy between an individual firm and a country, let us assume a firm calculating whether it should buy a certain intermediate product or produce it itself. If it could purchase it for $1.00 or produce it at a constant cost of $1.30 per unit, the decision would be obvious—except if the firm believed it could press down the buying price from $1.00 to $0.90 by cutting back its purchases by 25 per cent. In this case it would just pay the firm to produce 25 per cent of its requirements at $1.30 in its own shops.

But even from the point of view of strictly national interests measured by increasing income, the conflict between *greater productive efficiency* and *more favorable terms of trade* cannot be decided by even the most complete information on production costs and elasticities in international markets, because the actions and reactions of foreign governments would still be unpredictable.

23. Even where there is no hope that comparative cost conditions will change in the foreseeable future so that initially inefficient industries would become efficient and profitable; nor any hope that the output of these industries will, by depressing the prices of imports and bolstering export prices, affect the terms of trade so favorably that the establishment of the industries would be warranted despite their inefficiency — there are still other theories advanced in support of the establishment of large-scale industries with excessive comparative costs. One of these theories holds that the returns from industrial investment, though smaller than the returns from alternative investments, will provide *larger flows of funds for re-investment.*

If an investment of a given magnitude were to yield an additional income of 100 in one project and only of 60 in another, but if most or all of the 100 would be used for consumption whereas a large part of the 60 would be saved and plowed back, choosing the "inferior" investment project may secure a faster long-run rate of development. The additional income derived annually from a capital investment may take several forms: additional wages (because the marginal productivity of labor may be increased, and higher wages paid to a given or increased work force), additional rents, interest payments, dividend payments, entrepreneurial withdrawals, taxes, or retained profits. Assume that high-income-yielding investment is in fields where increased distributions will be made to poor workers, small landowners, small tradesmen, people with high marginal propensities to consume; the annual contribution to saving will then be small or nil. On the other hand, inferior investments, if they are in fields where relatively few or no workers are paid increased wages and where almost all the income accrues to the government or to rich capitalists who are willing to re-invest it all, could secure substantial annual contributions to saving.

If the objective of the nation is to maximize the rate of economic growth in the long run, a case can be made for the less productive investment projects with high ratios of retained and reinvested earnings, in preference to more productive projects yielding income of which little is devoted to further investment. Where industrial undertakings are expected to yield *less income paid out but more income plowed back* than any alternative investment outlet, industrialization may be demanded in the name of faster development — regardless of its relatively poor contribution to current national product.

Objectors to this theory question first of all whether the assumed conditions correspond even approximately to conditions actually prevailing, especially whether it is true that so little of the additional income produced in industry is paid out to workers. After all, to some advocates of industrialization industrial development is the best or the only way of taking care of rapidly increasing labor force, the only way of creating income for large masses of people — which amounts to just the opposite of the thesis in question. Secondly, objectors question whether the establishment of large industrial enterprises with concentrated control is the only kind of investment that could prevent undesired increases in disposable consumer income. The argument against allowing investments in agriculture or small-scale business, because the returns of such investments could not possibly be kept from going into consumption, presupposes that it is impossible to collect funds from these groups of "small people." But the profits of industry, after all, are also "collected" from masses of consumers or large numbers of small operators. If it is possible for these profits to be collected as parts of selling prices, it should be equally possible to collect other funds from consumers or operators, however small or poor, be it in the form of rents, excises or sales taxes, and to channel them into re-investment. If this is so, the theory that more savings can be had out of earnings from large-scale enterprises can hardly be a strong argument for adopting inferior industrial development projects.

24. Other theories of industrialization stress employment opportunities and population growth. It is possible that investments in agricultural improvement and in small-scale industries would yield higher returns to capital as well as larger increases in total output than investments in big industrial projects, and yet would do less to increase the marginal productivity of labor. Indeed, agricultural improvements might well reduce the marginal productivity of labor: output per acre and output per worker

would increase, but fewer workers would be required per acre. New and expanded industrial establishments, on the other hand, would require more labor and would open up new employment opportunities. *To produce a much larger output with fewer men employed may be considered less desirable than to employ more men producing a modest increase in output.* This need not be merely a question of different social objectives; even from the point of view of production trends alone, job-creating investments may in the long run be preferable where population will continue to grow and agriculture can provide neither additional productive employment nor additional food. In anticipation of a continuing increase in the labor force, industrialization may be considered as the "best bet."

As it stands, this theory is not convincing enough to make all development experts advise passing up good opportunities for agricultural improvement. Some of the experts would have to be shown that a delay in starting the industries might in the foreseeable future result in losses of potential output much worse than the losses involved in passing up the investment opportunities in agriculture. [8]

Still more effective relief concerning the vexing problem of how to take care of an increasing population is promised by another theory of industrialization and population growth. It is claimed that the change in the social climate that goes with *industrialization,* especially the development of urban habits of life, *will reduce the birth rate* and eventually check the increase in population and labor force. Thus, even if investment in agricultural improvements should be more productive, in terms of total output, than investment in industrial establishments, the latter, if instrumental in an effective reduction in the rate of population growth, could contribute to a faster increase in output per head.

Critics of this theory are not inclined to accept the claim that industrialization is needed if the population growth is to be checked. Although it may be true that historically industrialization and birth control have been associated, this link is not a necessary one. One should neither rely on industrialization to bring about a reduction in the birth rate, nor

---

[8] A simple arithmetical illustration may help us to visualize the problem of choosing between alternatives of the kind discussed here.

should one proceed on the assumption that such a reduction cannot be effected in non-industrial communities.

25. Some of the issues in the conflicting theories of industrialization reappear in the theories of the wage structure and give rise to similar conflicts about the "appropriate" relation of industrial wage rates to the earnings of labor in the rest of the economy. Some of the disputes were mentioned earlier in connection with conflicts of recommendations (see Sections 17 and 18) but their theoretical base has to be re-examined.

	Production Trade and Consumption	Commodities		Real National Income	Labor Force			
		Rice	Cloth		Total	Empl. in Agric.	Empl. in Indus.	Un-empl.
Present situation	Production	100	—		120	100	—	20
	Export	20						
	Import		20					
	Consumption	80	20	100				
Future situation A. *Without any capital investments*	Production	100	—		130	100	—	30
	Export	20						
	Import		20					
	Consumption	80	20	100				
B. *After investment in agriculture*	Production	130	—		130	90	—	40
	Export	30						
	Import		28					
	Consumption	100	28	128				
C. *After investment in industry*	Production	100	15		130	100	30	—
	Export	10						
	Import		13					
	Consumption	90	28	118				

Note that the labor cost of cloth domestically produced is twice that of cloth acquired in exchange for rice; but this need not be relevant since labor is abundant —the social opportunity cost of labor is zero—and domestic production of cloth would use otherwise unemployed labor.

Plan B permits an increase in real income of 28 per cent—or 30 per cent were it not for the adverse change in the terms of trade—whereas Plan C permits only an increase of 18 per cent—or only 15 per cent were it not for the favorable change in the terms of trade. Plan C, though producing so much less, absorbs all unemployed labor. (Foreign trade is balanced, in all cases, in terms of current prices; the apparent surplus in Plan B or deficit in Plan C are merely on the basis of a calculation in base-priced prices).

The basic position of a "pure theory of relative wages" may be stated as follows: In the absence of obstacles to the movement of workers from the non-industrial to the industrial sector of an economy, and in the absence of differences in the unpleasantness" of industrial and non-industrial work, the equilibrium rates of earning would be equal. As long as industry is expanding, however, and the birth rate is greater in non-industrial areas, wage rates in industry will exceed the earning of labor in other occupations. If this wage differential is "too small," industry will be short of labor and will bid up the rates. If the wage differential is "too large," there will be an excess supply of labor in industry and the wage rate will be depressed.

If the inflow of labor into industry is restricted, either directly or through the fixing of wage rates insensitive to an excess supply of labor, the wage differential will be regarded as excessive by those theorists who apply the standard of competitive markets, or the "competitive norm," to the performance of the economy. These theorists will infer from the wage differential and excess supply that the marginal productivity of labor in industry is above that in other occupations and, therefore, that the total output of the economy could be increased by a transfer of labor into industry. Since such a transfer would tend to lower the marginal productivity of labor in industry, it could be accomplished by a reduction of the wage rates paid by industry. To the extent that economic development depends on the movement of labor and other resources from uses which yield less income to uses which yield more income, *development is retarded by relatively excessive wage rates in industry,* and could be accelerated by a lowering of these rates.

Others object to such reasoning, chiefly because they consider it paradoxical to associate reductions in industrial wage rates with faster economic development, and even more paradoxical to associate a lowering of (marginal and average) labor productivity in industry with an increase in national product. To the first point their opponents reply that the historical trend of rising wage rates in the course of economic development was partly a matter of technical progress but also of capital accumulation and of a consequent excess demand for labor (in contrast to the excess supply assumed to prevail in the situation discussed); to the second point they reply that, starting from a situation where too few are employed in industry, there is nothing paradoxical in attempting to increase total product as well as product per head in the economy as a whole by *raising total product and lowering product per worker in industry.*

26. All this is closely connected with the dispute about high or low capital-labor ratios. It has been asked whether, in order to maximize the rate of growth of national product, the available capital should be intensively utilized by *employing as much labor as possible with the given equipment,* or whether a small part of the labor force should be intensively utilized and made especially productive by *using as much capital as possible per unit of labor.*

Most economic theorists regard these questions as quite naive or primitive. They hold that total output in an economy will not be maximized by promoting establishments either with "high" or with "low" capital-labor ratios, but rather by combining capital and labor in such ways as will equalize the marginal productivities of equal services in all uses. If labor earns more in one field than elsewhere, the capital-labor ratio in that field is probably too high and more labor ought to be employed in it — until earnings are no longer out of line.

Since the movement of labor into industry (with given capital stock) will reduce the amount of capital per worker, some will protest and will point to a "lesson from history" to the effect that economic development has always involved increases in the amounts of capital per worker. This is true enough. It has been one of the essential factors in economic development that the supply of capital increased faster than the supply of labor. To use more capital when more becomes available is certainly the correct response; but it is quite another thing to urge using more capital with particular favored groups of high-wage labor when there is no substantial increase in the total supply of capital, and when the rest of the labor force must do with skimpy capital allotments and therefore attains much lower marginal productivities.

Some theorists believe that the ratio of capital to labor in particular industries is more or less fixed by technology and that changes in the capital-labor ratio in the economy as a whole are effected only by expanding industries with especially high or especially low capital coefficients. Other theorists insist that this view exaggerates the uniformity of technology in given industries; but they believe that at any one time the coefficients are "frozen" by the fixed equipment in existence. A third group of theorists regard even this as a serious exaggeration; they hold that in given industries within existing plants changes in actual operations can be accomplished which effect significant alterations in the capital-labor ratios.

These conflicts of theory, which are due chiefly to divergent interpretations of factual observations, explain some of the discrepancies in recommendations. For example, in situations in which experts agreed that it was desirable to employ more labor with a given supply of capital, economists of the first group recommended the *establishment of new industries that had low capital coefficients;* economists of the third group, however, recommended *wage reductions to stimulate industries to employ more workers in existing plants.*

27. A special theory of accelerated industrial development, linking high capital-labor ratios with high savings ratios (with the former as cause and the latter as effect), undertakes to explain why an allocation of capital and labor in accordance with the marginal principle would retard economic development. An increase in the supply of capital, in a competitive economy or in an economy planned and manipulated to conform to the competitive norm, would result in a wide dispersion of the additional capital over a variety of fields, industrial or non-industrial, in an increase in the marginal productivity of labor all around, and in an increase in wage rates in general. In consequence, a *large part of the output increase made possible by the new capital investments would be dissipated in mass consumption.*

If, instead, the *capital is concentrated* at a few points in the economy where it is *combined with as little labor as possible,* the dissipation of the income produced can be avoided. The marginal productivity of labor in the selected industries would of course be greatly enhanced, but would not lead to a general wage increase. Wage rates in these industries with the high capital coefficients would be exceptionally high; indeed their relative height would be a factor in stimulating further substitutions of capital for labor and, thus, further increases in the capital coefficients of these industries. But since only so few workers would be employed there, total wage payments need not be much increased and no "serious" consumption increases need occur. In other words, most of the income increase can be retained and be made available for accelerated accumulation, with the result that national income can increase at a faster rate and even consumption can soon reach higher levels than it could have reached with an equi-marginal allocation of resources and the smaller savings ratio associated with it.

We have encountered this theme several times in our discussions: when we contrasted general conflicts in social objectives, when we reviewed specific recommendations for accelerated development, when we presented particular theories of industrialization, and finally when we examined the theory of capital-labor coefficients. The repetition was not designed as an aid to indoctrination; perhaps it was an incidental effect of the organization adopted for this survey, perhaps it was an unavoidable, integral part of any comprehensive examination of basic problems of economic development.

28. The special theory of high capital-labor ratios as instruments of increasing the savings ratio and thereby the rate of accumulation may be seen as an instance of two more general theories of economic development. One says that the allocation of resources which is regarded as the "most economic" in "static" theory does not matter much in a dynamic theory of growth. The other says that what matters chiefly in achieving fast growth is the repression of consumption. Combined in one statement they tell the poor nations in effect that they need not worry so much about the *relative productivity of their investments* as about the *effectiveness in preventing an early rise of living standards.*

In a nutshell, the old rule "Economize and save!" is to be amended by dropping the first half, concerned with marginal allocation. The old theories had contended that the more you economize the more you can save; some new theories deny this and contend that sometimes in the process of getting the "most economic" allocation of resources the earnings of labor are raised and the ability to save is thereby reduced.

Several illustrations in this survey of conflicts have been furnished to illuminate various theories which minimize the principle of short-run maximization of productivity and income. These illustrations regularly work with figures chosen so that the main points can be driven home impressively. One may question the relevance of such illustrations for problems of the real world. If the income yielded by the most productive investment is actually a very small percentage of the national income, and the income yielded by the alternative investment is actually just a shade above zero, the certainty that all of the latter would be saved and plowed back is not of any great significance for the prospects of growth. Surely, the largest savings ratio means little if it applies to very small yields. Even if the differences in the propensities to consume of different income recipients are very large, the differences in the relative productivities of different investments may be far more significant.

Another doubt relates to the question *whether the uneconomic choice of investment projects is really the best way of securing an income distribution which maximizes the amount of saving.* If it is important to avoid early improvements in the buying power of the masses, there ought to be some ways of doing this other than by channeling investment funds into projects inferior by normal economic standards. Perhaps it should be mentioned that the "new" theory does not command a wide following. But the conflicts in question seem to be fundamental.

29. One of the major forces in the economic development of the Western world has been conspicuously absent from this review of conflicts: technological progress.

Three phases should be distinguished in an examination of the role of technological progress. First, the invention and discovery of technical knowledge; second, the dissemination of such knowledge to all those who might use it; third, the practical application of that knowledge in actual production. In the development of the economically most advanced countries, the first phase of technological progress, the *acquisition of new knowledge,* has been the most emphasized one because, by and large, *dissemination and practical application followed,* perhaps slowly but surely. In the development now wanted in the economically backward countries, the second and third phases of technological progress are stressed as the important ones. This is not in dispute and the recommendations concerning the desirability of *"technical assistance"* are universally supported.

Perhaps there is a bit of "new" knowledge required for industrial development in backward countries inasmuch as the existing technologies may not fit the different conditions and a certain amount of adaptation may be required. The only conflict in this respect would relate to the *claim that the poor countries could profit from a strong patent system.* But this dispute has been carried on more in legal and political than in economic circles. We confine ourselves to mentioning it.

30. Perhaps the most crucial conflict concerning economic development relates to the question *whether development in backward countries*

requires central planning. Twice in this survey have we touched on this issue: once in the review of conflicts of objectives, and again when recommendations regarding the scope of industrialization were discussed. But this issue is too big to be done justice by brief references or by a brief concluding paragraph.

Section Five

Issues in
Methodology

ISSUES IN METHODOLOGY

INTRODUCTORY REMARKS
Fritz Machlup

This is a session on "Issues in Methodology." Methodology is a part of epistemology, the theory of knowledge. Epistemology, along with ontology, cosmology, and theology, is frequently classified as metaphysics. A discussion of metaphysical issues in the Grand Ballroom, with hundreds of keenly interested economists! What has come over all these practical-minded economists?

Usually only a small minority of American economists have professed an interest in methodology. The large majority used to disclaim any interest in such issues. These disclaimers were based on a misunderstanding of a kind different from that underlying the antitheoretical pronouncements of the extreme historicists and institutionalists. The antitheorists were not aware of the fact that they were theorizing or using theory. But while the researcher in economics cannot avoid using a method and implicitly accepting an epistemological position on how to distinguish the knowable from the unknowable, the true from the false, the probable from the improbable, it is possible for him to refrain from talking about methodology. But the very people who said "let's not bother with methodology, let's not waste time talking about it," did talk about it a good deal. These antimethodologists were not aware of the fact that they talked methodology when they said such things as "this is too abstract," "this is more realistic," "this is purely static reasoning," "this is not statistically verified," "there is no historical evidence for this," and so on.

The six men on this platform are going to talk consciously and openly about issues in methodology.

ARE THE
SOCIAL SCIENCES
REALLY
INFERIOR?

Fritz Machlup

If we ask whether the "social sciences" are "really inferior," let us first make sure that we understand each part of the question. *"Inferior"* to what? Of course to the natural sciences. "Inferior" in what respect? It will be my main task to examine all the "respects," all the scores on which such inferiority has been alleged.

The adverb *"really"* which qualifies the adjective *"inferior"* refers to allegations made by some scientists, scholars, and laymen. It refers also to the "inferiority complex" which I have noted among many social scientists. A few years ago I wrote an essay entitled "The Inferiority Complex of the Social Sciences." In that essay I said that "an inferiority complex may or may not be justified by some 'objective' standards," and I went on to discuss the consequences that "the *feeling* of inferiority"—conscious or subconscious—has for the behavior of the social scientists who are suffering from it. I did not then discuss whether the complex has an objective basis, that is, whether the social sciences are "really" inferior. This is our question today.

The subject noun would call for a long disquisition. What is meant by *"social sciences,"* what is included, what is not included? Are they the same as what others have referred to as the "moral sciences," the *"Geisteswissenschaften,"* the "cultural sciences," the "behavioral sciences"? Is geography, or the part of it that is called "human geography," a social science? Is history a social science—or perhaps even *the* social science par excellence, as some philosophers have contended? I shall not spend time on this business of defining and classifying nor bother here with a definition of "social sciences" and with drawing boundary lines around them.

Grounds of Comparison

The social sciences and the natural sciences are compared and contrasted on many scores, and the discussions are often unsystematic. If we try to review them systematically, we shall encounter a good deal of overlap and unavoidable duplication. None the less, it will help if we enumerate some of the grounds of comparison most often mentioned, grounds on which the social sciences are mentioned, grounds on which the social sciences are judged to come out second best: (1) invariability of observations; (2) objectivity of observations and explanations; (3) verifiability of hypotheses; (4) exactness of findings; (5) measurability of phenomena; (6) constancy of numerical relationships; (7) predictability of future events; (8) distance from everyday experience; and (9) standards of admission and requirements.

We cannot have much science unless things recur, unless phenomena repeat themselves. In nature we find many factors and conditions "invariant." Do we in society? Are not conditions in society changing all the time, and so fast that most events are unique, each quite different from anything that has happened before? Or can one rely on the saying that "history repeats itself" with sufficient invariance to permit generalizations about social events?

There is a great deal of truth, and important truth, in this comparison. Some philosophers were so impressed with the invariance of nature and the variability of social phenomena that they used this difference as the criterion in the definitions of natural and cultural sciences. Following Windelband's distinction between generalizing ("nomothetic") and individualizing ("ideographic") propositions, the German philosopher Heinrich Rickert distinguished between the generalizing sciences of nature and the individualizing sciences of cultural phenomena; and by individualizing sciences he meant historical sciences. In order to be right, he redefined both "nature" and "history" by stating that reality is "nature" if we deal with it in terms of the general, but it becomes "history" if we deal with it in terms of the unique. To him, geology was largely history, and economics, most similar to physics, was a natural science. This implies a rejection of the contention that all fields that are normally called social sciences suffer from a lack of invariance; indeed, economics is here considered so much a matter of immutable laws of nature that it is handed over to the natural sciences.

This is not satisfactory, nor does it dispose of the main issue that natural phenomena provide more invariance than social phenomena. The main difference lies probably in the number of factors that must be taken into account in explanations and predictions of natural and social events. Only a small number of reproducible facts will normally be involved in a physical explanation or prediction. A much larger number of facts, some of them probably unique historical events, will be found relevant in an explanation or prediction of economic or other social events. This is true, and methodological devices will not do away with the difference; but it is only a difference in degree.

The physicist Robert Oppenheimer once raised the question whether, if the universe is a unique phenomenon, we may assume that universal or general propositions can be formulated about it. Economists of the Historical School insisted on treating each "stage" or phase of economic society as a completely unique one, not permitting the formulation of universal propositions. Yet, in the physical world, phenomena are not quite so homogeneous as many have liked to think; and in the social world, phenomena are not quite so heterogeneous as many have been afraid they are. (If they were, we could not even have generalized concepts of social events and words naming them.) In any case, where reality seems to show a bewildering number of variations, we construct an ideal world of abstract models in which we create enough homogeneity to permit us to apply reason and deduce the implied consequences of assumed constellations. This artificial homogenization of types of phenomena is carried out in natural and social sciences alike.

There is no difference in invariance in the sequences of events in nature and in society as long as we theorize about them—because in the abstract models homogeneity is assumed. There is only a difference of degree in the variability of phenomena of nature and society if we talk about the real world—as long as heterogeneity is not reduced by means of deliberate "controls." There is a third world, between the abstract world of theory and the real unmanipulated world, namely, the artificial world of the experimental laboratory. In this world there is less variability than in the real world and more than in the model world; but this third world does not exist in most of the social sciences (nor in all natural sciences). The mistake is often made of comparing the artificial laboratory world of manipulated nature with the real world of unmanipulated society.

On this point of comparative invariance, there is indeed a difference between natural and social sciences, and the difference— apart from the possibility of laboratory experiments—lies chiefly in the number of relevant factors, and hence of possible combinations, to be taken into account for explaining or predicting events occurring in the real world.

Observations and Explanations

The idea behind a comparison between the "objectivity" of observations and explorations in the natural and social sciences may be conveyed by an imaginary quotation: "Science must be objective and not affected by value judgments; but the social sciences are inherently concerned with values and, hence, they lack the disinterested objectivity of science." True? Frightfully muddled. The trouble is that the problem of "subjective value," which is at the very root of the social sciences, is quite delicate and has confused many, including some fine scholars.

310

To remove confusion one must separate the different meanings of "value" and the different ways in which they relate to the social sciences, particularly economics. I have distinguished eleven different kinds of value-reference in economics, but have enough sense to spare my readers this exhibition of my pedagogic dissecting zeal. But we cannot dispense entirely with the problem and overlook the danger of confusion. Thus, I shall reduce my distinctions from eleven to four. I ask that we keep apart the following four meanings in which value judgment may come into our present discussion: (1) The analyst's judgment may be biased for one reason or another, perhaps because his views of the social "good" or his personal pecuniary interests in the practical use of his findings interfere with the proper scientific detachment. (2) Some normative issues may be connected with the problem under investigation, perhaps ethical judgments which may color some of the investigator's incidental pronouncements—obiter dicta—without causing a bias in the reported research findings. (3) The interest in solving the problems under investigation is surely affected by values since, after all, the investigator selects problems in the belief that their solution would be of value. (4) The investigator in the social sciences has to explain his observations as results of human actions which can be interpreted only with reference to motives and purposes of the actors, that is, to values entertained by them.

With regard to the first of these possibilities, some authorities have held that the social sciences may more easily succumb to temptation and may show obvious biases. The philosopher Morris Cohen, for example, wrote in *Reason and Nature* of "the subjective difficulty of maintaining scientific detachment in the study of human affairs. Few human beings can calmly and with equal fairness consider both sides of a question such as socialism, free love, or birth-control." This is true, but we should not forget similar difficulties in the natural sciences. Remember the difficulties which, in deference to religious values, biologists had in discussions of evolution and, going further back, the troubles of astronomers in discussions of the heliocentric theory and of geologists in discussions of the age of the earth. Let us also recall that only twenty-five years ago, German mathematicians and physicists rejected "Jewish" theorems and theories, including physical relativity, under the pressure of nationalistic values, and only ten years ago Russian biologists stuck to a mutation theory which was evidently affected by political values. I do not know whether one cannot detect in our own period here in the United States an association between political views and scientific answers to the question of the genetic dangers from fallout and from other nuclear testing.

Apart from political bias, there have been cases of real cheating in science. Think of physical anthropology and its faked Piltdown Man. That the possibility of deception is not entirely beyond the pale of experimental scientists can be gathered from a splendid piece of fiction, a novel, *The Affair,* by C. P. Snow, the well-known Cambridge don.

Having said all this about the possibility of bias existing in the presentation of evidence and findings in the natural sciences, we should hasten to admit that not a few economists, especially when concerned with current problems and the interpretation of recent history, are given to "lying with statistics." It is hardly a coincidence if labor economists choose one base year and business economists choose another base year when they compare wage increases and price increases; or if for their computations of growth rates expert witnesses for different political parties choose different statistical series and different base years. This does not indicate that the social sciences are in this respect "superior" or "inferior" to the natural sciences. Think of physicists, chemists, medical scientists, psychiatrists, and so on, appearing as expert witnesses in court litigation to testify in support of their clients' cases. In these instances the scientists are in the role of analyzing concrete individual events, of interpreting recent history. If there is a difference at all between the natural and social sciences in this respect, it may be that economists these days have more opportunities to present biased findings than their colleagues in the physical sciences; but even this may not be so. I may underestimate the opportunities of scientists and engineeers to submit expert testimonies with paid-for bias.

The second way in which value judgments may affect the investigator does not involve any bias in his findings or his reports on his findings. But ethical judgments may be so closely connected with his problems that he may feel impelled to make evaluative

312

pronouncements on the normative issues in question. For example, scientists may have strong views about vivisection, sterilization, abortion, hydrogen bombs, biological warfare, and other issues, and may express these views in connection with their scientific work. Similarly, social scientists may have strong views about the right to privacy, free enterprise, free markets, equality of income, old-age pensions, socialized medicine, segregation, education, and so on, and they may express these views in connection with the results of their research. This need not imply that their findings are biased. There is no difference on this score between the natural and the social sciences. The research and its results may be closely connected with values of all sorts, and value judgments may be expressed, and yet the objectivity of the research and of the reports on the findings need not be impaired.

The third way value judgments affect research is in the selection of the project, in the choice of the subject for investigation. This is unavoidable, and the only question is what kinds of value and whose values are paramount. If research is financed by foundations or by the government, the values may be those which the chief investigator believes are held by the agencies or committees that pass on the allocation of funds. If the research is not aided by outside funds, the project may be chosen on the basis of what the investigator believes to be "social values," that is, he chooses a project that may yield solutions to problems supposed to be important for society. Society wants to know how to cure cancer, how to prevent hay fever, how to eliminate mosquitoes, how to get rid of crabgrass and weeds, how to restrain juvenile delinquency, how to reduce illegitimacy and other accidents, how to increase employment, to raise real wages, to aid farmers, to avoid price inflation, and so on and so forth. These examples suggest that the value component in the project selection is the same in the natural and in the social sciences. There are instances in which the investigator selects his project out of sheer intellectual curiosity and does not give two hoots about the social importance of his findings. Still, to satisfy curiosity is a value too, and indeed a very potent one. We must not fail to mention the case of the graduate student who lacks imagination as well as intellectual curiosity and undertakes a project just because it is the only one he can think of, though neither he nor anybody else finds it interesting, let alone important. We may accept this case as the exception to the rule. Such exceptions probably are equally rare in the natural and the social sciences.

Now we come to the one real difference, the fourth of our value-references. Social phenomena are defined as results of human action, and all human action is defined as motivated action. Hence, social phenomena are explained only if they are attributed to definite types of action that are "understood" in terms of the values motivating those who decide and act. This concern with values—not values which the investigator entertains but values he understands to be effective in guiding the actions which bring about the events he studies—is the crucial difference between the social sciences and the natural sciences. To explain the motion of molecules, the fusion or fission of atoms, the paths of celestial bodies, the growth or mutation of organic matter, and so on, the scientist will not ask why the molecules want to move about, why atoms decide to merge or to split, why Venus has chosen her particular orbit, why certain cells are anxious to divide. The social scientist is not doing his job unless he explains changes in the circulation of money by going back to the decisions of the spenders and hoarders, explains company mergers by the goals that may have persuaded managements and boards of corporate bodies to take such actions, explains the location of industries by calculations of such things as transportation costs and wage differentials, and economic growth by propensities to save, to invest, to innovate, to procreate or prevent procreation, and so on. My social science examples were all from economics, but I might just as well have taken examples from sociology, cultural anthropology, or political science to show that explanation in the social sciences regularly requires the interpretation of phenomena in terms of idealized motivations of the idealized persons whose idealized actions bring forth the phenomena under investigation.

An example may further elucidate the difference between the explanatory principles in nonhuman nature and human society. A rock does not say to us: "I am a beast," nor does it say: "I came here because I did not like it up there near the glaciers, where I used to live; here I like it fine, especially this nice view of the valley." We do not inquire into value judgments of rocks. But we must not fail to take account of valuations of humans; social phenomena must be explained as the results of motivated human actions.

The greatest authorities on the methodology of the social sciences have referred to this fundamental postulate as the requirement of "subjective interpretation," and all such interpretation of "subjective meanings" implies reference to values motivating actions. This has nothing to do with value judgments impairing the "scientific objectivity" of the investigators or affecting them in any way that would make their findings suspect. Whether the postulate of subjective interpretation which differentiates the social sciences from the natural sciences should be held to make them either "inferior" or "superior" is a matter of taste.

It is said that verification is not easy to come by in the social sciences, while it is the chief business of the investigator in the natural sciences. This is true, although many do not fully understand what is involved and, consequently, are apt to exaggerate the difference.

One should distinguish between what a British philosopher, R. B. Braithwaite in *Scientific Explanation,* has called "high-level hypotheses" and "low-level generalizations." The former are postulated and can never be directly verified; a single high-level hypothesis cannot even be indirectly verified, because from one hypothesis standing alone nothing follows. Only a whole system of hypotheses can be tested by deducing from some set of general postulates and some set of specific assumptions the logical consequences, and comparing these with records of observations regarded as the approximate empirical counterparts of the specific assumptions and specific consequences. This holds for both the natural and the social sciences. (There is no need for direct tests of the fundamental postulates in physics—such as the laws of conservation of energy, of angular momentum, of motion; or of the fundamental postulates in economics—such as the laws of maximizing utility and profits.)

While entire theoretical systems and the low-level generalizations derived from them are tested in the natural sciences, there exist at any one time many unverified hypotheses. This holds especially with regard to theories of creation and evolution in such fields as biology, geology, and cosmogony; for example, of the

315

theory of the expanding universe, of the dust-cloud hypothesis of the formation of stars and planets, of the low temperature or high-temperature theories of the formation of the earth, of the various (conflicting) theories of granitization, and so on. Where the natural sciences deal with nonreproducible occurrences and with sequences for which controlled experiments cannot be devised, they have to work with hypotheses that remain untested for a long time, perhaps forever.

In the social sciences, low-level generalizations about recurring events are being tested all the time. Unfortunately, often several conflicting hypotheses are consistent with the observed facts and there are no crucial experiments to eliminate some of the hypotheses. But every one of us could name dozens of propositions that have been disconfirmed, and this means that the verification process has done what it is supposed to. The impossibility of controlled experiments and the relatively large number of relevant variables are the chief obstacles to more efficient verification in the social sciences. This is not an inefficiency on the part of our investigators, but it lies in the nature of things.

What Is "Exactness"?

Those who claim that the social sciences are "less exact" than the natural sciences often have a very incomplete knowledge of either of them, and a hazy idea of the meaning of "exactness." Some mean by exactness measurability. Others mean accuracy and success in predicting future events, which is something different. Others mean reducibility to mathematical language. The meaning of exactness best founded in intellectual history is the possibility of constructing a theoretical system of idealized models containing abstract constructs of variables and of relations between variables, from which most or all propositions concerning particular connections can be deduced. Such systems do not exist in several of the natural sciences—for example, in several areas of biology—while they do exist in at least one of the social sciences: economics.

We cannot foretell the development of any discipline. We cannot say now whether there will soon or ever be a "unified theory" of political science, or whether the piecemeal generalizations that sociology has yielded thus far can be integrated into one comprehensive theoretical system. In any case, the quality of "exactness," if this is what is meant by it, cannot be attributed to all the natural sciences nor denied to all the social sciences.

If the availability of numerical data were in and of itself an advantage in scientific investigation, economics would be on the top of all sciences. Economics is the only field in which the raw data of experience are already in numerical form. In other fields the analyst must first quantify and measure before he can obtain data in numerical form. The physicist must weigh and count and must invent and build instruments from which numbers can be read, numbers standing for certain relations pertaining to essentially nonnumerical observations. Information which first appears only on some such form as "relatively" large, heavy, hot, fast, is later transformed into numerical data by means of measuring devices such as rods, scales, thermometers, speedometers. The economist can begin with numbers. What he observes are prices and sums of moneys. He can start out with numerical data given to him without the use of measuring devices.

The compilation of masses of data calls for resources that only large organizations, frequently only the government, can muster. This, in my opinion, is unfortunate because it implies that the availability of numerical data is associated with the extent of government intervention in economic affairs, and there is therefore an inverse relation between economic information and individual freedom.

Numbers are not all that is needed. To be useful, the numbers must fit the concepts used in theoretical propositions or in comprehensive theoretical systems. This is rarely the case with regard to the raw data of economics, and thus the economic analyst still has the problem of obtaining comparable figures by transforming his raw data into adjusted and corrected ones, acceptable as the operational counterparts of the abstract constructs in his theoretical models. His success in this respect has been commendable, but very far short of what is needed; it cannot compare with the success of the physicist in developing measurement techniques yielding numerical data that can serve as operational counterparts of constructs in the models of theoretical physics.

Physics does not stand for all natural sciences, nor economics for all social sciences. There are several fields, in both natural and social sciences, in which quantification of relevant factors has not been achieved and may never be achieved. If Lord Kelvin's phrase, "science is measurement," were taken seriously, science might miss some of the most important problems. There is no way of judging whether nonquantifiable factors are more prevalent in nature or in society. The common reference to the "hard" facts of nature and the "soft" facts with which the student of society has to deal seems to imply a judgment about measurability. "Hard" things can be firmly gripped and measured, "soft" things cannot. There may be something to this. The facts of nature are perceived with our "senses," the facts of society are interpreted in terms of the "sense" they make in a motivational analysis. This contrast is not quite to the point because the "sensory" experience of the natural scientist refers to the data, while the "sense" interpretation by the social scientist of the ideal-typical inner experience of the members of society refers to basic postulates and intervening variables. The conclusion, that we cannot be sure about the prevalence of nonquantifiable factors in natural and social sciences, still holds.

On this score there can be no doubt that some of the natural sciences have something which none of the social sciences has: "constants," unchanging numbers expressing unchanging relationships between measurable quantities. The discipline with the largest number of constants is physics. Examples are the velocity of light ($c = 2.99776 \times 10^{10}$ cm/sec), Planck's constant for the smallest increment of spin or angular momentum ($h = 6.624 \times 10^{-27}$ erg sec), the gravitation constant ($G = 6.6 \times 10^{-8}$ dyne cm^2 gram^{-2}), the Coulomb constant ($e = 4.8025 \times 10^{-10}$ units), proton mass ($M = 1.672 \times 10^{-24}$ gram), the ratio of proton mass to electron mass ($M/m = 1836.13$), the fine-structure constant ($\alpha^{-1} = 137.0371$). Some of these constants are postulated (conventional), others (the last two) are empirical, but this makes no difference for our purposes. Max Planck contended, in *Scientific*

Autobiography and Other Papers, that the postulated "universal constants" were not just "invented for reasons of practical convenience, but have forced themselves upon us irresistibly because of the agreement between the results of all relevant measurements."

I know of no numerical constant in any of the social sciences. In economics we have been computing certain ratios which are found to vary relatively widely with time and place. The annual income-velocity of the circulation of money, the marginal propensities to consume, to save, to import, the elasticities of demand for various goods, the saving ratios, capital-output ratios, growth rates—none of these has remained constant over time or is the same for different countries. They all have varied, some by several hundred percent of the lowest value. One has found "limits" of these variations, but what does this mean in comparison with the virtually immutable physical constants? When it was noticed that the ratio between labor income and national income in some countries has varied by "only" ten percent over some twenty years, some economists were so perplexed that they spoke of the "constancy" of the relative shares. (They hardly realized that the 10 percent variation in that ratio was the same as about a 25 percent variation in the ratio between labor income and nonlabor income.) That the income velocity of the circulation of money has rarely risen above 3 or fallen below 1 is surely interesting, but this is anything but a "constant." That the marginal propensity to consume cannot in the long run be above 1 is rather obvious, but in the short run it may vary between .7 and 1.2 or even more. That saving ratios (to national income) have never been above 15 percent in any country regardless of the economic system (communistic or capitalistic, regulated or essentially free) is a very important fact; but saving ratios have been known to be next to zero, or even negative, and the variations from time to time and country to country are very large indeed.

Sociologists and actuaries have reported some "relatively stable" ratios—accident rates, birth rates, crime rates, and so on—but the "stability" is only relative to the extreme variability of other numerical ratios. Indeed, most of these ratios are subject to "human engineering," to governmental policies designed to change them, and hence they are not even thought of as constants. The verdict is confirmed: while there are important numerical constants in the natural sciences, there are none in the social sciences.

Predicting Future Events

Before we try to compare the success that natural and social sciences have had in correctly predicting future events, a few important distinctions should be made. We must distinguish hypothetical or conditional predictions from unconditional predictions or forecasts. Among the former we must distinguish those in which all the stated conditions can be controlled, those in which all the stated conditions can be either controlled or unambiguously ascertained before the event, and those in which some of the stated conditions can neither be controlled nor ascertained early enough, if at all. A conditional prediction of the third kind is such an iffy statement that it may be of no use unless one can know with confidence that it would be highly improbable for these problematic conditions (uncontrollable and not ascertainable before the event) to interfere with the prediction. A different kind of distinction concerns the numerical definiteness of the prediction: one may predict that a certain magnitude will change, will increase, will increase by at least so-and-so much, will increase within definite limits, or will increase by a definite amount. Similarly, the prediction may be more or less definite with respect to the time within which it is supposed to come true. A prediction without any time specification is worthless.

Some people are inclined to believe that the natural sciences can beat the social sciences on any count, in unconditional predictions as well as in conditional predictions fully specified as to definite conditions, exact degree and time of fulfillment. But what they have in mind are the laboratory experiments of the natural sciences, in which predictions have proved so eminently successful; and then they look at the poor record social scientists have had in predicting future events in the social world which they observe but cannot control. This comparison is unfair and unreasonable. The artificial laboratory world in which the experimenter tries to control all conditions as best as he can is different from the real world of nature. If a comparison is made, it must be between predictions of events in the real natural world and in the real social world.

Even for the real world, we should distinguish between predictions of events that we try to bring about by design and predictions of events in which we have no part at all. The teams of physicists and engineers who have been designing and developing machines and apparatuses are not very successful in predicting their performance when the design is still new. The record of predictions of the paths of moon shots and space missiles has been spotty. The so-called bugs that have to be worked out in any new contraption are nothing but predictions gone wrong. After a while predictions become more reliable. The same is true with predictions concerning the performance of organized social institutions. For example, if I take an envelope, put a certain address on it and a certain postage stamp, and deposit it in a certain box on the street, I can predict that after three or four days it will be delivered at a certain house thousands of miles away. This prediction and any number of similar predictions will prove correct with a remarkably high frequency. And you do not have to be a social scientist to make such successful predictions about an organized social machinery, just as you do not have to be a natural scientist to predict the result of your pushing the electric-light switch or of similar manipulations of a well-tried mechanical or electrical apparatus.

There are more misses and fewer hits with regard to predictions of completely unmanipulated and unorganized reality. Meteorologists have a hard time forecasting the weather for the next twenty-four hours or two or three days. There are too many variables involved, and it is too difficult to obtain complete information about some of them. Economists are only slightly better in forecasting employment and income, exports and tax revenues for the next six months or for a year or two. Economists, moreover, have better excuses for their failures because of unpredictable "interferences" by governmental agencies or power groups which may even be influenced by the forecasts of the economists and may operate to defeat their predictions. On the other hand, some of the predictions may be self-fulfilling in that people, learning of the predictions, act in ways that bring about the predicted events. One might say that economists ought to be able to include the "psychological" effects of their communications among the variables of their models and take full account of these influences. There are too many variables, personal and political, involved to make it possible to allow for all effects which anticipations, and anticipations of anticipations, may have upon the end results. To give an example of a simple self-defeating prediction from another social science: traffic experts regularly forecast the number of automobile accidents and fatalities that are going to occur over holiday weekends, and at the same time they hope that their forecasts will influence drivers to be more careful and thus to turn the forecasts into exaggerated fears.

We must not be too sanguine about the success of social scientists in making either unconditional forecasts or conditional preconditions. Let us admit that we are not good in the business of prophecy, and let us be modest in our claims about our ability to predict. After all, it is not our stupidity that hampers us but chiefly our lack of information, and when one has to make do with bad guesses in lieu of information the success cannot be great. But there is a significant difference between the natural sciences and the social sciences in this respect: Experts in the natural sciences usually do not try to do what they know they cannot do; and nobody expects them to do it. They would never undertake to predict the number of fatalities in a train wreck that might happen under certain conditions during the next year. They do not even predict next year's explosions and epidemics, floods and mountain slides, earthquakes and water pollution. Social scientists, for some strange reason, are expected to foretell the future, and they feel bad if they fail.

Science is, almost by definition, what the layman cannot understand. Science is knowledge accessible only to superior minds with great effort. What everybody can know cannot be science. A layman could not undertake to read and grasp a professional article in physics or chemistry or biophysics. He would hardly be able to pronounce many of the words, and he might not have the faintest idea of what the article was all about. It would be out of the question for a layman to pose as an expert in a natural science. On the other hand, a layman might read articles in descriptive economics, sociology, anthropology, social psychology. Although in all these fields technical jargon is used which he could not really understand, he might think that he knows the sense of the words and grasps the meanings of the sentences; he might even be inclined to poke fun at some of the stuff. He believes he is—from his own experience and from his reading of newspapers and popular magazines—familiar with the subject matter of the social sciences. In consequence, he has little respect for the analyses that the social scientists present.

The fact that social scientists use fewer Latin and Greek words and less mathematics than their colleagues in the natural science departments and, instead, use everyday words in special, and often quite technical, meanings may have something to do with the attitude of the layman. The sentences of the sociologist, for example, make little sense if the borrowed words are understood in their non-technical, everyday meaning. But if the layman is told of the special meanings that have been bestowed upon his words, he gets angry or condescendingly amused.

We must not exaggerate this business of language and profes-sional jargon because the problem really lies deeper. The natural sciences talk about nuclei, isotopes, galaxies, benzoids, drosophilas, chromosomes, dodecahedrons, Pleistocene fossils; and the layman marvels that anyone really cares. The social sciences—and the layman usually finds this out—talk about: him. While he never identifies himself with a positron, a pneumococcus, a coenzyme, or a digital computer, he does identify himself with many of the ideal types presented by the social scientist, and he finds that the likeness is poor and the analysis "consequently" wrong.

The fact that the social sciences deal with man in his relations with fellow man brings them so close to man's own everyday experience that he cannot see the analysis of this experience as something above and beyond him. Hence he is suspicious of the analysts and disappointed in what he supposes to be a portrait of him.

High-school physics is taken chiefly by the students with the highest IQs. At college the students majoring in physics, and again at graduate school the students of physics, are reported to have on the average higher IQs than those in other fields. This gives physics and physicists a special prestige in schools and universities, and this prestige carries over to all natural sciences and puts them somehow above the social sciences. This is odd, since the average quality of students in different departments depends chiefly on departmental policies, which may vary from institution to institution. The preeminence of physics is because of the requirement of calculus. In those universities in which the economics department requires calculus, the students of economics rank as high as the students of physics in intelligence, achievement, and prestige.

The lumping of all natural sciences for comparisons of student quality and admission standards is particularly unreasonable in view of the fact that at many colleges some of the natural science departments, such as biology and geology, attract a poor average quality of student. (This is not so in biology at universities with many applicants for a premedical curriculum.) The lumping of all social sciences in this respect is equally wrong, since the differences in admission standards and graduation requirements among departments, say between economics, history, and sociology, may be great. Many sociology departments have been notorious for their role as refuge for mentally underprivileged undergraduates. Given the propensity to overgeneralize, it is no wonder then that the social sciences are being regarded as the poor relations of the natural sciences and as disciplines for which students who cannot qualify for the sciences are still good enough.

Since I address primarily economists, and since economics departments, at least at some of the better colleges and universities, are maintaining standards as high as physics and mathematics departments, it would be unfair to level exhortations at my own colleagues. But perhaps we should try to convince our colleagues in all social science departments of the disservice they are doing to their fields and to the social sciences at large by admitting and keeping inferior students as majors. Even if some of us think that one can study social sciences without knowing higher mathematics, we should insist on making calculus and mathematical statistics absolute requirements—as a device for keeping away the weakest students.

Despite my protest against improper generalizations, I must admit that averages may be indicative of something or other, and that the average IQ of the students in the natural science departments is higher than that of the students in the social science departments.

No field can be better than the people who work in it. On this score, the natural sciences would be superior to the social sciences.

The Score Card

We may now summarize the tallies on the nine scores. With respect to the invariability of recurrence of observations, we found that the greater number of variables—of relevant factors—in the social sciences makes for more variation, for less recurrence of exactly the same sequences of events.

With respect to the objectivity of observations and explanations, we distinguished several ways in which references to values and value judgments enter scientific activity. Whereas the social sciences have a requirement of "subjective interpretation of value-motivated actions" which does not exist in the natural sciences, this does not affect the proper "scientific objectivity" of the social scientist. With respect to the verifiability of hypotheses, we found that the impossibility of controlled experiments combined with the larger number of relative variables does make verification in the social sciences more difficult than in most of the natural sciences.

With respect to the exactness of the findings, we decided to mean by it the existence of a theoretical system from which most propositions concerning particular connections can be deduced. Exactness in this sense exists in physics and in economics, but much less so in other natural and other social sciences. With respect to the measurability of phenomena, we saw an important difference between the availability of an ample supply of numerical data and the availability of such numerical data as can be used as good counterparts of the constructs in theoretical models. On this score, physics is clearly ahead of all other disciplines. It is doubtful that this can be said about the natural sciences in general relative to the social sciences in general.

With respect to the constancy of numerical relationships, we entertained no doubt concerning the existence of constants, postulated or empirical, in physics and in other natural sciences, whereas no numerical constants can be found in the study of society. With respect to the predictability of future events, we ruled out comparisons between the laboratory world of some of the natural sciences and the unmanipulated real world studied by the social sciences. Comparing only the comparable, the real worlds—and excepting the special case of astronomy—we found no essential differences in the predictability of natural and social phenomena.

With respect to the distance of scientific from everyday experience, we saw that in linguistic expression as well as in their main concerns the social sciences are so much closer to prescientific language and thought that they do not command the respect that is accorded to the natural sciences. With respect to the standards of admission and requirements, we found that they are on the average lower in the social than in the natural sciences.

The last of these scores relates to the current practice of colleges and universities, not to the character of the disciplines. The point before the last, although connected with the character of the social sciences, relates only to the popular appreciation of these disciplines; it does not aid in answering the question whether the social sciences are "really" inferior. Thus the last two scores will not be considered relevant to our question. This leaves seven scores to consider. On four of the seven no real differences could be established; but on the other three scores, on "invariance," "verifiability," and "numerical constants," we found the social sciences to be inferior to the natural sciences.

What does it mean if one thing is called "inferior" to another with regard to a particular "quality"? If this "quality" is something that is highly valued in any object, and if the absence of this "quality" is seriously missed regardless of other qualities present, then, but only then, does the noted "inferiority" have any evaluative implications. In order to show that "inferiority" sometimes means very little, I present here several statements about differences in particular qualities:

Champagne is inferior to rubbing alcohol in alcoholic content.
Beef steak is inferior to strawberry jello in sweetness.
A violin is inferior to a violoncello in physical weight.
Chamber music in inferior to band music in loudness.
Hamlet is inferior to Joe Palooka in appeal to children.

Sandpaper is inferior to velvet in smoothness.*

Psychiatry is inferior to surgery in ability to effect quick cures.

Biology is inferior to physics in internal consistency.

It all depends on what you want. Each member in a pair of things is inferior to the other in some respect. In some instances it may be precisely this inferiority that makes the thing desirable. (Sandpaper is wanted because of its inferior smoothness.) In other instances the inferiority in a particular respect may be a matter of indifference. (The violin's inferiority in physical weight neither adds to nor detracts from its relative value.) Again in other instances the particular inferiority may be regrettable, but nothing can be done about it, and the thing in question may be wanted none the less. (We need psychiatry, however much we regret that in general it cannot effect quick cures; and we need biology, no matter how little internal consistency has been attained in its theoretical systems.)

We have stated that the social sciences are inferior to the natural sciences in some respects, for example, in verifiability. This is regrettable. If propositions cannot be readily tested, this calls for more judgment, more patience, more ingenuity. But does it mean much else?

The Crucial Question: "So What?"

What is the pragmatic meaning of the statement in question? If I learn, for example, that drug E is inferior to drug P as a cure for hay fever, this means that, if I want such a cure, I shall not buy drug E. If I am told Mr. A is inferior to Mr. B as an automobile mechanic, I shall avoid using Mr. A when my car needs repair. If I find textbook K inferior to textbook S in accuracy, organization, as well as exposition, I shall not adopt textbook K. In every one of these examples, the statement that one thing is inferior to another makes pragmatic sense. The point is that all these pairs are alternatives between which a choice is to be made.

Are the natural sciences and the social sciences alternatives between which we have to choose? If they were, a claim that the

327

social sciences are "inferior" could have the following meanings: (1) We should not study the social sciences. (2) We should not spend money on teaching and research in the social sciences. (3) We should not permit gifted persons to study social sciences and should steer them toward superior pursuits. (4) We should not respect scholars who so imprudently chose to be social scientists. If one realizes that none of these things could possibly be meant, that every one of these meanings would be preposterous, and that the social sciences and the natural sciences can by no means be regarded as alternatives but, instead, that both are needed and neither can be dispensed with, we can give the inferiority statement perhaps one other meaning: (5) We should do something to improve the social sciences and remedy their defects.

This last interpretation would make sense if the differences that are presented as grounds for the supposed inferiority were "defects" that can be remedied; but they are not. That there are more variety and chance in social phenomena; that, because of the large number of relevant variables and the impossibility of controlled experiments, hypotheses in the social sciences cannot be easily verified; and that no numerical constants can be detected in the social world—these are not defects to be remedied but fundamental properties to be grasped, accepted, and taken into account. Because of these properties research and analysis in the social sciences hold greater complexities and difficulties. If you wish, you may take this to be a greater challenge, rather than a deterrent. Difficulty and complexity alone are not sufficient reasons for studying certain problems; but the problems presented by the social world are certainly not unimportant. If they are also difficult to tackle, they ought to attract ample resources and the best minds. Today they are getting neither. The social sciences are "really inferior" regarding the place they are accorded by society and the priorities with which financial and human resources are allocated. This inferiority is curable.

MATHEMATICS, REALISM AND A TIME FOR SYNTHESIS

Fritz Machlup

I shall address myself to three issues: the use of mathematics, the role of realism, and the time for synthesis. The first two—mathematics and realism—seem almost antithetical. My comments will probably disappoint both those who want more mathematics and those who want more realism in economic analysis.

I do not deny Professor Samuelson's assertion that mathematics is a language and even one which for some purposes is superior to English or German. But for other purposes it is inferior or even altogether unsuitable. There are things that ought to be said but cannot be said in mathematical language.

Perhaps I underestimate the potentialities of mathematics. It is true that Atlas, the mental giant in the Barnaby series whose memory for names is so very poor, manages to translate such simple names as J. J. O'Malley into algebraic formulas and vice versa. This ability need not be confined to the mental giants of the comic strip. But there are definite limits to translatability into mathematics. Thus far, love letters cannot well be written in mathematics and read with a full appreciation of the romantic feelings of the writer. And I challenge Professor Samuelson to translate into mathematics the paper he has just read to us in English and preserve all its qualities, including its fine humor. And, to come to the real issue, I submit that the basic human attitudes that underlie economic conduct—and that must be understood if we are to understand economics—cannot be described and analyzed exclusively in mathematical language.

Professor Samuelson is contemptuous of what he calls the "pseudo problems of qualitative essence." Am I really concerned with a pseudo problem if I wish to get at the essence of a phenomenon or at its merely qualitative aspects? To my mind, it is perfectly good practice, before making statements about anything, to make clear what it is one is talking about; that is, to discuss the essence of the matter. Professor Samuelson makes specific mention of the "sterile" question of the essence of value. I shall not attempt to tell other people in which problems they should be interested and from which problems they should turn away. I for my part continue to be interested and concerned with the problem of the essence of value even if it takes other languages than mathematics to talk about it.

Those who talk only one language are probably barred from the appreciation and understanding of some problems. On the other hand, a problem is sometimes recognized as a mere pseudo problem when its analysis is translated into other languages. All this, I think, adds strength to the argument for polylinguistic scholarship.

There are those who disparage the use of mathematics in economic theory on the ground that it must result in "too unrealistic" models. This complaint, which in my opinion reveals misunderstanding of the fundamentals of scientific methodology, provides me with a welcome transition to the second issue on which to comment: the call for more realism and the rejection of manifestly unrealistic postulates in economic analysis.

No one has ever suggested that a theory of the individual consumer should start, as a first approximation, with a postulate that the consumer seeks to maximize the consumption of food, let alone bread. From the very beginning a "multitude of ends" has been considered the appropriate assumption for a theory of consumer's choice. However, for the sake of graphical demonstrations by indifference curves, a reduction of the possible choices to just two alternatives has proved handy. Of course, this is terribly unrealistic, as those who cannot comprehend such technical things and need an escape are anxious to emphasize, but everybody has been aware of it.

In the theory of the individual seller of labor services, no one believes it would be fruitful to assume that the worker aims to maximize his pecuniary income. It is obvious that not only the alternative opportunity of leisure or the disutility of effort must be taken into account but also such things as differences in working conditions in different employments or differences in living conditions in different places. However, a good deal of insight into the relationship between income and leisure and about the influence of income deductions on the labor supply can be gained by a model which is deliberately unrealistic in omitting the differences in working and living conditions and in isolating the effects of changes in the net rate of pay.

No one would seriously hold that businessmen have no other goal than money profits. It takes no unusual powers of observation to realize that not all businessmen want to get stomach ulcers, that some of them prefer to take it easy, that most of them dislike sleepless nights worrying about risky deals, that some like to gamble, that many are patriots who will want to avoid doing things which the government says are bad for the country, that several like to be "big shots" running big enterprises and being admired for their position, that many have a pride of workmanship and a feeling for sportsmanship. But it is quite apparent that a good many things could be "seen" by operating a much simplified model in which (besides output of a homogeneous product) only pecuniary costs and revenues enter as variables and the maximization of the difference is the basic hypothesis. Unrealistic? Surely. But whenever one can learn something by a simpler method it would be silly to insist on learning it a more complicated way. The addition of "admittedly realistic" variables into analytical models can be defended only if they significantly modify the results.

This means, of course, that models of different degrees of realism and complexity will be adequate for different problems. Certain problems can be adequately analyzed with the maximization of pecuniary profits as the basic working hypothesis; other problems cannot and require much more complicated models. Professor Boulding recognizes this and does not claim that his "asset preference" assumptions are needed for all problems of the economics of the firm. What he does not say, and in my opinion should say, is that there is not one theory of the firm but that there are many. To expect that one theory of the firm should serve all purposes is almost like expecting one all-purpose theory of man or a panacea that cures all ills from sore throats to broken noses. What in our textbooks has been called the theory of the firm is only a part of static price and distribution theory and does not attempt or pretend to be more. Is it not very unreasonable to complain about its inadequacy for other purposes? A model designed to analyze business decisions about the price and output of some particular product or set of products need not be equipped to analyze decisions about the investment of available funds, about the payments of dividends, about the increase in the power of management, and so forth; and if it were equipped for all these purposes, it would be unnecessarily clumsy. Universal tools which, for example, can work as screw drivers, drills, hammers, pincers, and scissors all at once are neither economical nor efficient. A universal theory of the firm which could explain the output of a given product and also the growth of the firm through agglomerative merger and perhaps also any other kind of business conduct would be an uneconomical and inefficient theory.

If I say that the theory of the firm in price analysis is one thing and the theory of the growth of the firm is another—and that the choice of variables is dictated by the problem at issue and not by what to naïve observers appears to be realistic—I should like to acknowledge the benefit of discussions with Dr. Edith Penrose, of Johns Hopkins University, who has been working on the theory of the growth of the size of the firm.

How naïve it is to call for a comprehensive all-purpose theory of the firm becomes particularly clear from Mrs. Penrose's finding that the concept of the firm changes as we switch from one problem to another. The firm in conventional price theory is only a very distant relative of the firm in the legal sense, of the firm in any of the sociological senses, and of the firm in any of the other economic senses. All of these are different kinds of animals—or, perhaps I should say, different kinds of models. The concept of the firm may have its criterion in a balance sheet, or in a particular collection of assets, or in the personality of an entrepreneur, or a set of managers, or in a group of persons in control, or in the people who own the equity, or in a corporate name or charter, or probably still other things. Believe me, the "problem of decay and death" of the firm, which Professor Boulding called "mysterious," looks totally different depending on which of the concepts of the firm is adopted—and on the basis of some of the concepts the problem looks not mysterious but meaningless. This is an important conclusion, especially in view of the recent "survival theories" of the firm (Alchian and Enke) that rest on the distinction of successful firms and failures. But I should not anticipate here too many of the findings of Dr. Penrose's critical analysis of these theories.

Some economic theorists have become excessively enamored of the application of biological concepts to economic problems and, I am afraid, Professor Boulding is among them. "Death and Transfiguration" is a beautiful tone poem; and "The Death of a Salesman" makes an interesting stage play. But before we make much of the "death of a firm" in economic analysis we had better be quite sure how we define the firm and how we ascertain its demise.

If I had to summarize my comments on Professor Boulding's paper in one sentence, I should say this: I agree with his conclusion "that the impact of more realistic theories of the firm on static price analysis is likely to be small," but I am skeptical with regard to his hope that by integrating different models of the firm into a more realistic model we shall progress faster in economic dynamics.

On the problem of integration and realism I should like to add this: It is of course possible that the models of the firm that will prove useful in growth theory will also look more realistic. If they do, this will be so chiefly because of the particular personal experiences of those who pass such judgments, but I do not think there would be any reason to be happy about it. In analysis it is not realism but relevance that counts, as Professor Knight once so cogently demonstrated. As to the eternally popular demand for integration and synthesis, I should like to quote from Professor

Boulding's latest book,[1] where he said that "a synthesis of inadequate parts may be worse than no synthesis at all," which he footnoted by the remark that "institutionalism in economics may be regarded as a premature attempt at synthesis of the social sciences, an attempt to synthesize bad economics, bad sociology, and bad anthropology in a medium of subconscious emotional bias." But underlying these remarks is Professor Boulding's conviction, which he apparently shares with the Walrus of *Alice in Wonderland,* that now "the time has come" to talk of many things at once.

It is not so, I submit, that synthesis can wait until the several parts of systematic knowledge are perfected. Probably we do know more now than thirty years ago; but in another thirty years we shall know more than now. The license to synthesize is not granted only upon a certification of maturity. No matter how imperfect our tools, synthesis is always permissible and necessary whenever we deal with specific cases of reality. But synthesis of different fields of knowledge is never called for while we are engaged in developing or formulating general theories. There is no use for a "general synthesis" because we never know just what mixture of bodies of knowledge—what "knowledge mix"—will be best suited for the concrete case that we may run into. One case may call for a synthesis of social psychology, cultural anthropology, and economics; another for a synthesis of public health, law, and economics; a third may call for a synthesis of criminology, political science, and economics. Hence, we should not scramble our analytical tools before we apply them.

The time to synthesize is when we wish to explain or diagnose particular situations or to predict or control particular events. Reality is complex and no single field of knowledge can suffice for grappling with concrete cases. "Application of theory" means, or should mean, synthesis of the findings of several disciplines. But "synthesis in the abstract" serves no good purpose.

---

[1] *A Reconstruction of Economics* (Wiley, 1950), p. 5.

INSTITUTIONALISM
AND EMPIRICISM
IN ECONOMICS

Frank H. Knight

First, a plea to auditors or eventual readers disposed to be critical: Remember that my real title must be, "A Few Brief and Hasty Observations Suggested by the Topic Printed in the Program."

The word institutionalism recalls a movement in economic thought in this country that was active from a little before World War I until it was largely drowned by discussion of the depression, or perhaps boom and depression, and especially by the literature of the Keynesian revolution. It included three or four main branches, one of which was statistical economics—the obvious connotation of empiricism, and quite remote from any ordinary meaning of institution. And there were other "isms" more or less descriptively called "institutional" or "empirical." An explicitly practical approach, via discussion of social problems, was also prominent, though the name welfare economics is of later vintage. In fact, what the various protagonists had in common was antipathy to orthodoxy or classicism or theory or whatever cussword might be preferred to designate the abstract mechanics of utility, markets, and prices which had formed the primary content of the standard introductory course in economics.

Now, theorizing is a fancy some lean to and others hate. Or more commonly, perhaps, men like their own and abhor or reject that of others—often with a fanfare of being antitheoretical when they are notoriously likely to be most theoretical of all. Or again, they like to be original or interesting and hence "recognized" and more in demand. The psychology of believing and of controversy is at least as important as truth, and tends more and more to predominate over the latter interest, in my own thinking. Anyway, my task here is neither to bury theory nor to praise it, but to try to sketch the relationships between certain points of view that have been proposed for the study of economics. My only prejudice is—parodying what E. B. Wilson once said of mathematics in social science—that if we have theory, it should be correct; and I am sure that we shall always have it with us. (Like the poor, and partly for that reason.) However, I must say that looking at the history and at the present state and prospects of economic thought and of economic policy raises doubts as to how important correct theory actually is. But still I think it somehow ought to be correct, and that the difference might be practically significant.

Let me say, too, that I am not interested, or am negatively interested, in the jurisdictional dispute aspect of the question. I shall contend rather than argue, in view of time limits, that the proper relationship between different approaches is one of complementarity rather than of competition or substitution—using the jargon of consumption theory itself, which fits here. It is not either this or that or the other, but all of them, each in its proper place and proportion—like economic choices themselves. There is a place for abstract price theory, but it is a limited place. As a theorist, I feel as much annoyance at the attackers for not adequately stating these limitations, in their enthusiasm for demolition, as I do for their uncomprehending denunciation. The need in methodology is for a workably clear analysis of the problems and appropriate lines of effort at their solution—the functions of economists in the inclusive sense. Moreover, economics cannot be sharply demarcated from other social and human sciences, or even from the natural sciences, which impinge in manifold ways on the study of man and of human problems.

The appropriate starting point for economists in such a job

analysis seems to me to be the notion of economy or economizing—making resources or means go as far as possible—following one *Oxford Dictionary* definition. It is noteworthy that this general meaning has been attached to the word quite recently, and the idea in any clarity is distinctive of modern thought. Still further, there is a hoary and deep-seated prejudice against the economic interest, which leads to gross misunderstanding—cf. the words stingy and materialistic. Economy applies to the use of any means to the achievement of any end or group of ends, whatever means are available, and whatever ends are actually pursued, idealistic or selfish, in good taste or bad; the means and ends are taken as given. The main qualification, an essential one, is that economics does not deal with technology or techniques, which are also taken as given, but with the apportioning and proportioning aspects of choices, where a plurality of ends are in view and a plurality of resources used. In the problem situation of any individual (including any group which in fact acts as a unit) there is a general principle of correct economy; it is that the total result is maximized by an apportionment which equalizes increments of result for equal increments of any resource. It is an a priori truth, and all general economic dicta are applications under different circumstances. Motives or desires are treated as forces, and the general result is a position of equilibrium. Such a mechanistic view of conduct is subject to sweeping qualifications—which form the basis, such basis as there is, for the attacks upon theory.

However, the whole theory of individual economic behavior is introductory—a preliminary to economics as a social science, which deals with economic organization. In the apportioning and proportioning decisions of a modern economy the ordinary individual plays a quite limited and indirect role. To a much greater extent, they are made by enterprises (individual entrepreneurs or firms), but in the main they result from the interaction of choices in a complicated network of markets. And economics is primarily a study of the system of markets. This in turn centers around a notion of general or simultaneous equilibrium—and of how far and why it is achieved or approximated or fails to be. And always in the background, if not in the foreground, are the practical questions of how far this is a good thing or of what to do about it when the result seems to be subject to improvement. The action in question is chiefly through political measures, presumably under a democratic system of law making and enforcement. We may note in passing that the market economy is far too much criticized because it "doesn't work" in accord with the abstract theory; the theoretical ideal (or model), miscalled "perfect competition," since there is no implication of rivalry, would be quite intolerable. Even at the level of individual choice it would be highly irrational to behave in close accord with the principle of economic rationality, a serious endeavor to maximize a satisfaction function. Competition in the proper psychological meaning is only one of many irrational motives which have both a real and a proper place in individual behavior in markets—not to mention errors of manifold kinds which are inevitably committed. But in varying degree, motives which are not realistically economic can be forced into that mode of description.

Even a Crusoe would not be (and ought not to be) economically rational. But the notion of equilibrium of a market economy is subject to much more sweeping limitations—or at least they are much more obvious. Descriptively speaking (ignoring value judgments), human responses bear no simple quantitative functional relation to their conditions as stimuli. They are subject to (unpredictable) delay, and to arbitrary or capricious variations in the preference functions which causal analysis must take as data, and many of the important conditions cannot be observed, still less measured. There may be thresholds which analysis can and should take into account (as Mr. Boulding's paper suggests), but I think not often. The main limitation lies in the nature and function of mind, which is to anticipate and project. Even consumers' wants and choices are in a large measure anticipatory and hence subject to error. For the entrepreneur, making productive decisions, it would be suicide to respond to the momentary price situation; he must adapt his policies to future conditions, more or less accurately forecast, even when "no change" is the best prediction he can make. Thus he will take account of the apparent direction and velocity of changes in his pilot variables and beyond these of underlying causes and of ideal or normal values, as well as their actual levels. And he himself will have motives other than the desire to maximize the present worth of a future stream of pecuniary profit.

Worst of all, the future situation of any entrepreneur will depend on the predictions and decisions being made by others, extending more or less over the economy, even the world. But mutual prediction and action in accord with prediction are self-contradictory; hence individual decisions cannot be highly rational, not to say accurate, but must include an element of strategy. The parallelism with forces in equilibrium with the method of simultaneous equations is at best an analogy, serving for schematization, and must be used with great caution. A force has to be balanced by a resistance—in mechanics inertia or friction; this relation should be worked through and the concept of frictionless conditions much less carelessly employed, as it often points in quite the wrong direction. But such details, though essential, cannot be followed up here. Nor can the qualities of other analogies, including mechanical governors, the animal body, and others suggested by Mr. Boulding, which I also have used for expository purposes. New and unfamiliar terms, Greek derivatives in place of Latin, like homeostasis and cybernetics, seem to me to serve chiefly the purpose of attracting attention, to *épater le bourgeois,* and to give the profession something to talk about for a time. Closer analogies could be constructed by starting from the distribution of a flow, such as water or electric current, among a plurality of channels; but these would have to be modified in essential respects to fit the basic economic principles of diminishing utility and productivity. We must remember it is all a problem of exposition, and a balance or imbalance of forces making for change in opposite directions is clearly the essential fact.

The final problems of economics, as of any social science or any science, center in two things and the relations between them: first, to understand or explain some set of phenomena; and second, to use knowledge for the guidance of action. Thus we raise the question of the similarity or contrast between social and natural science. Only one main point can be noted here, and it has already been suggested in noting the impossibility of acting on the basis of mutual prediction. (And mutual control is a more palpable contradiction.)

If economists were the hirelings of an absolute dictator, their task would be partly and abstractly analogous to that of science as the basis of technology. Only partly and abstractly, even then; for control of human beings must take account of the fact that they do have minds—opinion and will—as mere physical objects supposedly do not. Hence their manipulation is largely a matter of coercion or persuasion and deception (really forms of coercion) which have no application to the purposive relations of men to physical objects. In a democracy, by contrast, the government is not really a ruler but an intermediary mechanism of group self-control. Consequently, the task of the social scientist in relation to practice is that of an expert and impartial counselor in the making of rules to govern associative life, by those who are to live under the rules. It bears little relation to the problem of prediction in terms of natural causality, for the purpose of interference from without and purposive redirection of the course of events. To be sure, the physical scientist is also a part of the physical universe; but he makes relatively little use of physics in deciding upon a course of action, even in designing an experiment (insofar as he can predict the result it is not an experiment); and much less in, say, a card game, a tea party, or his own market behavior.

The economist is up against special difficulties as soon as he ceases to take his individuals as given, specifically their wants, resources, and technology, and attempts to account for these data. He is up against history, and that is very largely a different sort of problem. And the "very largely" adds to the complication. For the given conditions at any time are in part the result of previous conduct of individuals which more or less fits the concept of effectively using given means to achieve given ends, but only in a limited degree, and no clear line can be drawn. Economizing is less a distinct sector of conduct than it is an aspect of most conduct, more or less the relevant aspect, depending on what one is trying to do. The same items of behavior are typically amenable to interpretation in quite different conceptual frames of reference. The problem of method here is that of the division of intellectual labor, and it clearly has no satisfactory solution. Specialization cannot practically be carried nearly as far as in the case of physical and biological science.

What needs to be said here is that the original purpose of economics on the classical price-theory line was educational or, one might say, propagandist. It was to show that free co-operation of individuals as consumers and producers, under the guidance of prices fixed by free purchase and sale in markets, is a way, and within wide limits a better way, than tradition and authority, to organize the efficient use of resources to achieve the freely chosen ends of individuals. (The philosophical assumption that this is the general end of economic society cannot be examined here.) For this purpose it does not matter what particular wants the individuals have or what concrete resources they possess or what technical processes are known and available. Taking freedom as a fact and as the norm of policy makes these things irrelevant. The purpose of explaining that this comes about, and how, is not less important now than it was in 1776 or at any time in the past. But as the open market organization came into more unrestricted prevalence, unquestioned and even intolerable weaknesses developed; and discovery of the reasons for these and of suitable remedial action became important and then imperative. The matter of suitable action—separating evils reasonably attributable to the economic order from those which belong to the lot of man on earth—is of course more acute now than ever. For these purposes, price theory is in general fairly adequate, at least in the earlier stages of inquiry, without supplementing by other approaches. Institutionalism and the rest are therefore to be viewed as independent studies of the same broad subject matter from the standpoint of different objectives. And the task of methodology is to show what are these other points of view and the corresponding modes of attack. For the most part, they center in the area already suggested, accounting for the wants, resources, and technology which price theory takes as given. Only a few very general observations can be offered here.

I take up empiricism first, because what I have to say can be quite brief. To begin with the aspect of relation to policy, there is nothing it would seem possible to argue about; and in that of explanation, contributing to the understanding of economic phenomena, all that can be done is to indicate the character of a possible treatise. As to policy: As soon as any line of public action is decided on or even is chosen as worth investigating, the need for quantitative data to show the amount of effect to be expected from any amount of interference of a given sort is too obvious to need discussion before an audience of economists. In many cases, however, if not in most, such quantification will involve causal analysis, the inductive separation of different antecedent elements that can be acted upon, and perhaps also correlation of such elements with different elements in a composite effect. The study would call for co-ordination of abstract qualitative analysis with the use of statistical data to reduce the relation to quantitative terms.

Secondly, as to explanation. The sort of analysis just described involves a sort of explanation, the sort which Mill referred to as finding empirical laws, in contrast with causation proper, but which positivists hold to be the only possible type. Critical discussion of the positivist theory of knowledge is out of the question here, but two limitations are obvious. First, the field of investigation to be called "economic" must be defined in some other way. For one cannot tell empirically, by looking at any act, whether it is economic or not; that depends on the intention and how far this is realized up to limits set by the means under command. In fact there are usually preferences in the use of means, also; and the distinction between means and ends is very loosely used. And then, any discussion of policy involves norms beyond subjective individual preferences. A social problem arises out of conflicts of private ends, and some objective comparison is obviously necessary to any adjudication. (This is said in awareness of the common view that interpersonal comparisons are unnecessary for the serious treatment of "welfare.")

The treatment of institutionalism, distinguished from quantitative empiricism, raises vast and difficult problems. As already observed, when we face the task of explaining the "givens" of the first stage of theorizing, we are in the field of history and must deal with behavior forms and social processes that are much less tractable intellectually than are market data or even utility comparisons. In particular, again to repeat, not much is explained by individual acts motivated by the maximizing principle. History is in large part more fruitfully considered in terms of culture patterns or institutions and their changes, or of individual acts motivated by rivalry, conformity and distinction, craving for victory, success, fame, creative self-expression, the crusading spirit—ends which do not realistically fit the formula of balancing marginal utilities. Now the term "institution" has two meanings, though, as usual, they widely and variously overlap. One type is called "crescive" (Sumner and Keller), since they "just grow," Topsy-fashion; they may be said to be created by the "invisible hand." The extreme example is language, in the growth and changes of which deliberate action hardly figures; nor is there much serious effort to do anything about it. It is the fundamental institution, and law is in varying (and disputed) degree of the same kind. The other type is of course the deliberately made, of which our Federal Reserve System and this Association itself are examples. With age, the second type tends to approximate the first.

Accordingly, there are two main branches of institutionalism, properly so called. Of the first, German "historicism" is more or less the ideal type. In the American movement, it is best—but not very well—represented by Veblen, who is venerated, or damned, as the father of the institutionalist gospel. A variant is the legal economics of John R. Commons, in one phase of his work, and of Walton Hamilton and others. It would seem to be the special task of economic (or legal-economic) historians, in the interpretive side of their work; perhaps historical economics can be distinguished from economic history. Marxism and the stage theories are especially in point. The great mystery, to me, is the relation between history as explanation and history as a problem, the thing to be explained. We do get a sense of understanding a situation by tracing its continuous development from some past beginning—which has to be rather arbitrarily chosen. Regarding Veblen, I must say—or "confess," from the standpoint of his admirers—that if he has any intelligible theory of history or specifically economic-institutional history, I cannot find it in his writings. I do not even see the meaning of cumulative change. His insistence on Darwinism as the pattern for all social science would imply a biological struggle for existence as the selective agent, and I cannot think that that carries us far in the interpretation of institutional change. Language would again be a leading case in point. To a limited degree it might apply to technological advance—disregarding much that can hardly be disregarded. The Marxist economic (or materialistic?) interpretation reduces to much the same thing. The idea of selective survival seems abstractly plausible (spontaneous variation much less so), but we surely have to look beyond biological elimination for the main selective principle. As to Veblen, the theory seems inconsistent with his diatribes against any "meliorative trend" and insistence upon colorless mechanism. But he inveighed in terms quite as sarcastic against a static or mechanistic view of human nature—his interpretation of hedonism and of classical economics. And he himself seems more concerned with "inveighing against" than with colorless description. The relations between history (or even evolution) and science as treating of the repetitive aspect of phenomena should also be mentioned as a subject for another treatise.

The second branch of institutionalism proper, as corresponding to the "made" type of institution, is represented by the later work of Commons. He called his main idea the collective control of individual behavior through working rules. He made long and careful firsthand study of certain examples of such institution building, primarily labor organizations and the law-making activities of the courts, culminating in the decisions of the U.S. Supreme Court. His scientific interest centered in reasonable value, decreed by authoritative or forcible action, in contrast with prices fixed in the open competitive market. Such action presupposes monopoly, either natural or contrived, particularly the collusive action of groups of wage earners. Commons was not concerned with the broad social effects of such action, especially with results of price fixing under general consumer and producer freedom—which must obviously result in either shortage or surplus. In fact, he shared the popular "prejudice" exaggerating the extent and social cost of business monopoly and the general ineffectiveness of market competition, though he rather deprecated such violent and sweeping condemnation of classical economics or of capitalism as formed Veblen's most conspicuous interest. In his book, *Institutional Economics* (1934), he discussed at some length the relation between Veblen's position and his own. While cordially praising Veblen's work and frankly recognizing the large common ground between the latter and his own, he was critical of Veblen's methodological concepts. He says that according to Veblen's definition of science, in terms of the tests of validity embodied in modern technology, "there is no science of human nature," for in the human sciences, "the subject-matter itself is a pragmatic being, always looking to the future and therefore motivated by purposes."

In conclusion, let us glance at the philosophical root of the methodological controversies which are so characteristic of the social sciences, in contrast with those dealing with nature. In fact, they are hardly sciences, in the restricted sense which the word increasingly takes on, under the influence of natural science prestige and of positive, or pragmatic, philosophy. (The two are radically different, and their confusion is a major source of fallacy in the controversies over method in the social field.) In fact, any strictly empirical (or logical-empirical) theory of knowledge is largely misapplied in the interpretation of human data. For, to repeat (and as Commons said), human conduct is motivated and anticipatory; and to understand it, or to act intelligently in social situations of any kind, we must take account of beliefs, desires, and objective valuation which are neither directly observed nor at all accurately inferred—or especially predicted—from sense observation of behavior itself. Moreover, it is the motives which often interest us, more than acts in themselves.

Note that we must say "largely" misapplied. The crucial fact is that man exists in several universes of (his own) conceptual thinking, and no intellectual bridges connect these in any satisfactory way. Consequently, the right approach is a plurality of approaches, used in accord with the nature of problems in hand. Men are knowers as well as known, users and used, also liking and liked (and the opposites), individually and mutually and in groups of manifold complexity. We are physical beings, first of all, in which the laws of physics and chemistry hold good as they do outside our bodies, within the limits of measurement. And these sciences claim to yield the complete and only possible explanation of all that happens. Yet they obviously cannot explain the explaining activity itself, our knowing or using, or our divers social attitudes or emotions. This fact cannot be denied without asserting it; for machines do not argue about their own nature and are not involved in error or prejudice, as must be true of at least one side in this as in other disagreements and conflicts. We do and must understand ourselves and other persons and social phenomena, in terms of many different categories, which we cannot logically interrelate.

This is true even of physical artifacts. We understand, say, an automobile, by knowing how it works, including its responses to various controls. Also by knowing what it is for and how it serves its purposes; also by knowing the history of its development, which involves much or all of the history of technology and of mind and civilization. There is some interconnection among these modes of understanding, but that in itself is a profound philosophical problem. In particular, the historical understanding contributes little and very indirectly to the utilitarian problems of using the car or repairing, building, or improving it. That is chiefly a matter of its mechanics, of how it works. History—even biological evolution—is of disappointingly little value for prediction and is not greatly improved when put, as far as possible, in quantitative and statistical terms as a basis for extrapolation. Man is a conventional animal; but he is also unconventional, as well as both rational and romantic in many senses. But all such statements, while true and illuminating, cannot be of much use in predicting or effecting concrete changes.

Many other ways of understanding which we have not mentioned are involved when the subject matter is ourselves and other men and the complex institutional structures into which men build themselves—largely unintentionally, through acts which aim only at adaptive or exploitative reaction to the existing situation. The various and warring psychologies should hardly be ignored, even in a brief survey. Beyond the many forms of causality, at least for the thinking of men themselves, they have a mysterious creative faculty, small but indubitably real, and their most important trait. They can make decisions, as individuals and as groups of various kinds, to change their own nature. This activity, the distinctive meaning of that word, is inherently irreducible to positive uniformity and predictable continuity.

Thus the final word in social science methodology, beyond using all categories of explanation and all figurative analogies, wherever they are helpful (and only there!) is this: that all rational explanation and directive action has serious inherent limits. The social problem is misconceived if viewed as parallel with that of science as the foundation of technology; it is chiefly a matter of agreement upon ends or, rather, establishing unity of purpose. Again we refer to democracy, a society committed to individual freedom as its primary value. With this much given, the fundamental part of economic analysis, both as explanatory and as a guide to social policy, must—in spite of all sweeping limitations—be the mechanics of instrumental choice, demand and supply, and prices. Empirical-quantitative study is indispensable for determining how far to push any policy; but it is subject to much the same limitations, set by the inconstancy of men's desires and motives. Institutional-historical study is illuminating, but practically useful only in a very general way; we cannot, it seems, learn from history what to do or to expect in any present situation, nor even very definitely what not to do. Life and society are orderly, up to a point—which itself cannot be accurately determined. To have a mind means to change it occasionally, hence to act unpredictably—but not too often, too erratically, or too far, or it would cease to be mind. As intelligent beings, we live somewhere between causation and chaos.

ECONOMIC THEORY AND MATHEMATICS —AN APPRAISAL

Paul A. Samuelson

It has been correctly said that mathematical economics is flying high these days. So I come, not to praise mathematics, but rather to slightly debunk its use in economics. I do so out of tenderness for the subject, since I firmly believe in the virtues of understatement and lack of pretension.

I realize that this is a session on methodology. Hence, I must face some basic questions as to the nature of mathematics and of its application. What I have to say on this subject is really very simple—perhaps too brief and simple. The time that I save by brief disposal of the weighty philosophical and epistemological issues of methodology I can put to good use in discussing the tactical and pedagogical issues—or what you might even call the Freudian problems that the mathematical and nonmathematical student of economics must face.

The Strict Equivalence of Mathematical Symbols and Literary Words. On the title page of my *Foundations of Economic Analysis,* I quoted the only speech that the great Willard Gibbs was supposed ever to have made before the Yale Faculty. As professors do at such meetings, they were hotly arguing the question of required subjects: Should certain students be required to take languages or mathematics? Each man had his opinion of the relative worth of these disparate subjects. Finally Gibbs, who was not a loquacious man, got up and made a four-word speech: "Mathematics is a language."

I have only one objection to that statement. I wish he had made it 25 per cent shorter—so as to read as follows: "Mathematics *is* language." Now I mean this entirely literally. In principle, mathematics cannot be worse than prose in economic theory; in principle, it certainly cannot be better than prose. For in deepest logic—and leaving out all tactical and pedagogical questions—the two media are strictly identical.

Irving Fisher put this very well in his great doctoral thesis, written exactly sixty years ago. As slightly improved by my late teacher, Joseph Schumpeter, Fisher's statement was: "There is no place you can go by railroad that you cannot go afoot." And I might add, "Vice versa!"

I do not think we should make too much of the fact that in recent years a number of universities have permitted their graduate students to substitute a reading knowledge of mathematics for a reading knowledge of one foreign language. For after all we run our universities on the principle that Satan will find work for idle hands to do; and the fact that we may permit a student to choose between ROTC and elementary badminton does not mean that these two subjects are methodologically identical. And besides, we all know just what a euphemism the expression "a graduate student's reading knowledge" really is.

Induction and Deduction. Every science is based squarely on induction—on observation of empirical facts. This is true even on the very imperfect sciences, which have none of the good luck of astronomy and classical physics. This is true of meteorology, of medicine, of economics, of biology, and of a number of other fields that have achieved only modest success in their study of reality. It used to be thought that running parallel with induction there runs an equally important process called "Deduction"—spelled with a capital *D*. Indeed, certain misguided methodologists carried their enthusiasm for the latter to such extremes that they regarded

Deduction as in some sense overshadowing mere pedestrian induction.

Now science is only one small part of man's activity—a part that is today given great honorific status, but which I should like to strip of all honorific status for purposes of this discussion. However, to the extent that we do agree to talk about what is ordinarily called science—and not about poetry or theology or something else—it is clear that deduction has the modest linguistic role of translating certain empirical hypotheses into their "logical equivalents." To a really good man, whose IQ is 300 standard deviations above the average, all syllogistic problems of deduction are so obvious and take place so quickly that he is scarcely aware of their existence. Now I believe that I am uttering a correct statement—in fact, it is the only irrefutable and empty truth that I shall waste your time in uttering—when I say that not everybody, nor even half of everybody, can have an IQ 300 standard deviations above the mean. So there is for all of us a psychological problem of making correct deductions. That is why pencils have erasers and electronic calculators have bells and gongs.

I suppose this is what Alfred Marshall must have had in mind when he followed John Stuart Mill in speaking of the dangers involved in *long* chains of logical reasoning. Marshall treated such chains as if their truth content was subject to radioactive decay and leakage—at the end of n propositions only half the truth was left, at the end of a chain of $2n$ propositions, only half of half the truth remained, and so forth in a geometric multiplier series converging to zero truth. Obviously, in making such a statement, Marshall was describing a property of that biological biped or computing machine called *homo sapiens;* for he certainly could not be describing a property of logical implication. Actually, if proposition A correctly implies proposition B, and B correctly implies proposition C, and so forth all the way to Z, then it is necessarily true that A implies Z in every sense that it implies B. There can be no leakage of truth at any stage of a valid deductive syllogism. All such syllogisms are mere translations of the type, "A rose is a rose is a rose."

All this is pretty well understood when it comes to logical processes of the form: Socrates is a man. All men are mortal.

Therefore, Socrates is mortal. What is not always so clearly understood is that a literary statement of this type has its complete equivalent in the symbolism of mathematical logic. If we write it out in such symbolism, we may save paper and ink; we may even make it easier for a seventeen-year-old freshman to arrive at the answer to complex questions of the type: "Is Robinson, who smokes cigarettes and is a non-self shaver, a fascist or is it Jones?" But nonetheless, the mathematical symbolism can be replaced by words. I should hate to put six monkeys in the British Museum and wait until they had typed out in words the equivalent of the mathematical formulas involved in Whitehead and Russell's *Mathematical Principia.* But if we were to wait long enough, it could be done.

The Case of Neoclassical Distribution. Similarly, in economics. The cornerstone of the simplest and most fundamental theory of production and distribution—that of Walras and J. B. Clark—is Euler's theorem on homogeneous functions. Now it is doubtful that Clark—who rather boasted of his mathematical innocence—had ever heard of Euler. Certainly, he cannot have known what is meant by a homogeneous function. But nonetheless, in Clark's theory, there is the implicit assumption that scale does not count; that what does count is the proportions in which the factors combine; and that it does not matter which of the factors of production is the hiring factor and which the hired. If we correctly interpret the implication of all this, we see that Clark—just as he was talking prose and knowing it—was talking the mathematics of homogeneous functions and not knowing it.

I have often heard Clark criticized for not worrying more about the exhaustion-of-the-product problem. He seems never to have worried whether rent, computed as a triangular residual, would be numerically equal—down to the very last decimal place—to rent calculated as a rectangle of marginal product. Like King Canute, he seems simply to have instructed his draftsman to draw the areas so as to be equal.

As I say, Clark has often been criticized for not going into this problem of exhaustion of the product. I myself have joined in such criticism. But I now think differently—at least from the present standpoint of the nature of true logical deductive implication as distinct from the human psychological problem of perceiving truth and cramming it into the heads of one's students or readers. Even if Euler had never lived to perceive his theorem, even if Wicksell, Walras, and Wicksteed had not applied it to economic theory, Clark's doctrine is in the clear. His assumptions of constant-returns-to-scale and viable free-entry ensure for him that total revenue of each competitive firm will be exactly equal to total cost. And with this settled in the realm of cost and demand curves, there is no need for a textbook writer in some later chapter of his book dealing with production to suddenly become assailed by doubts about the "adding-up problem of exhaustion-of-the product."

Now let me linger on this case for a moment. Economists have carefully compared Wicksteed's and Clark's treatment of this problem in order to show that mathematics is certainly not inferior to words in handling such an important element of distribution theory.

What is not so clear is the answer to the reverse question: Is not literary economics, by its very nature, inferior to mathematics in handling such a complex quantitative issue. As one eminent mathematical economist put it to me: "Euler's theorem is absolutely basic to the simplest neoclassical theory of imputation. Yet without mathematics, you simply cannot give a rigorous proof of Euler's theorem."

Now I must concede that the economics literature does abound with false proofs of Euler's theorem on homogeneous functions. But what I cannot admit—unless I am willing to recant on all that I have been saying about the logical identity of words and symbols—I simply cannot admit that a rigorous literary proof of Euler's theorem is in principle impossible.

In fact, I tried a literary proof on my mathematical friend. He quite properly pointed out that it was not rigorous in the way it treated infinitesimals. I fully agree. My argument was heuristic. But I do claim that if my friend and I could spend a week or so talking together, so that I could describe in words the fundamental limit processes involved in the Newton-Leibniz calculus and derivatives, then this problem of lack of rigor could be met. In fact, much more subtle properties of Pfaffian partial differential equations are in principle capable of being stated in basic English. As Professor Leontief has pointed out, the final proof of the identity of mathematics and words is the fact that we teach people mathematics by the use of words, defining each symbol as we go along. It is no accident that the printer of mathematical equations is forced to put commas, periods, and other punctuation in them, for equations are sentences, pure and simple.

Geometry in Relation to Words and Mathematical Analysis. Today when an economic theorist deplores the use of mathematics, he usually speaks up for the virtues of geometrical diagrams as the alternatives. It was not always thus. Seventy years ago, when a man like Cairnes criticized the use of mathematics in economics, probably he meant by the term "mathematics" primarily geometrical diagrams. From the point of view of this lecture, the ancients were more nearly right than the modern critics. Geometry is a branch of mathematics, in exactly the same sense that mathematics is a branch of language. It is easy to understand why a man might have no use at all for economic theory, invoking, instead, a plague on mathematical economics, on diagrammatic textbooks, and on all fine-spun literary theories. It is also easy to understand why some men should want to swallow economic theory in all of its manifestations. But what is not at all clear—except in terms of human frailty—is why a man like Cairnes should be so enamored of literary theory and should then stop short of diagrams and symbols. Or why any modern methodologist should find some virtue in two-dimensional graphs but should draw the line at third or higher dimensions.

I suggest that the reason for such inconsistent methodological views must be found in the psychological and tactical problems which constitute the remaining part of my remarks.

But before leaving the discussion of the logical identity of mathematical symbols and words, I must examine its bearing on a famous utterance of Cairnes. He lived at a time when, as we now know, mathematics was helping bring into birth a great new neoclassical synthesis. Yet Cairnes went so far as to say: "So far as I can see, economic truths are not discoverable through the instrumentality of mathematics. If this view be unsound, there is at hand an easy means of refutation—the production of an economic truth, not before known, which has been thus arrived at." Now this view is the direct opposite of that of Marshall. Marshall in his own way also rather pooh-poohed the use of mathematics. But he regarded it as a way of arriving at truths, but not as a good way of communicating such truths—which is just the opposite of Cairnes's further remarks on the subject.

Well, what are we to think of the crucial experiment proposed by Cairnes? In the first place, he himself was both unable and unwilling to use the mathematical technique; so it might have been possible for us to produce a new truth which Cairnes could never have been capable of recognizing. Indeed, many have cogently argued that Jevons had in fact done so. However, from the methodological viewpoint that I have been expounding, it will be clear that any truth arrived at by way of mathematical manipulation must be translatable into words; and hence, as a matter of logic, could quite possibly have been arrived at by words alone. Reading Cairnes literally, we are not required to produce a truth by mathematics that could not have been proved by words; we are only required to produce one that has not, as a matter of historical fact, been previously produced by words. I suggest that a careful review of the literature since the 1870's will show that a significant part of all truths since arrived at have in fact been the product of theorists who use symbolic techniques. In particular, Walrasian general equilibrium, which is the peak of neoclassical economics, was already enunciated in Walras' first edition of the *Elements* at the time Cairnes was writing.

Jevons, Walras, and Menger each independently arrived at the so-called "theory of subjective value." And I consider it a lucky bonus for my present thesis that Menger did arrive at his formulation without the use of mathematics. But, in all fairness, I should point out that a recent rereading of the excellent English translation of Menger's 1871 work convinces me that it is the least important of the three works cited; and that its relative neglect by modern writers was not simply the result of bad luck or scholarly negligence. I should also add that the important revolution of the 1870's had little really to do with either subjective value and utility or with marginalism; rather it consisted of the perfecting of the general relations of supply and demand. It culminated in Walrasian general equilibrium. And we are forced to agree with Schumpeter's appraisal of Walras as the greatest of theorists—not because he used mathematics, since the methods used are really quite elementary—

but because of the key importance of the concept of general equilibrium itself. We may say of Walras what Lagrange ironically said in praise of Newton: "Newton was assuredly the man of genius *par excellence,* but we must agree that he was also the luckiest: one finds only once the system of the world to be established!" And how lucky he was that "in his time the system of the world still remained to be discovered." Substitute "system of equilibrium" for "system of the world" and Walras for Newton and the equation remains valid.

Summary of Basic Methodology. In leaving my discussion of Methodology with a capital M, let me sum up with a few dogmatic statements. All sciences have the common task of describing and summarizing empirical reality. Economics is no exception. There are no separate methodological problems that face the social scientist different in kind from those that face any other scientist. It is true that the social scientist is part of the reality he describes. The same is true of the physical scientist. It is true that the social scientist in observing a phenomenon may change it. The theory of quantum mechanics, with its Heisenberg uncertainty principle, shows that the same is true of the physical scientist making small-scale observations. Similarly, if we enumerate one by one the alleged differences between the social sciences and other sciences, we find no differences in kind.

Finally, it is clear that no a priori empirical truths can exist in any field. If a thing has a priori irrefutable truth, it must be empty of empirical content. It must be regarded as a meaningless proposition in the technical sense of modern philosophy. At the epistemological frontier, there are certain refined difficulties concerning these matters. But at the rough and ready level that concerns the scientist in his everyday work, the above facts are widely recognized by scientists in every discipline. The only exceptions are to be found in certain backwaters of economics, and I shall not here do more than point the finger of scorn at those who carry into the twentieth century ideas that were not very good even in their earlier heyday.

Differences in Convenience of Languages. I now turn to the really interesting part of the subject. What are the conditions under which one choice of language is more convenient than another? If you are a stenographer required to take rapid dictation, there is no doubt that you will prefer shorthand to old-English lettering. No disinterested third party will ever be in doubt as to whether Roman numerals are less convenient than arabic numerals for the solution of problems in commercial arithmetic; and the same goes for a comparison between a decimal system of coinage and that used by the English.

A comparison between a language like French and one like German or English or Chinese is a little more difficult. We might concede that any proposition in one language is translatable into another. But that is not relevant to the psychological question as to whether one language is intrinsically more convenient for a certain purpose than another. We often hear it said that French is a very clear language, and that German is a very opaque one. This is illustrated by the story that Hegel did not really understand his philosophy until he had read the French translation!

I do not know whether there is anything in this or not. It seems to me that Böhm-Bawerk or Wicksell written in German is quite as straightforward as in English; whereas I find Max Weber or Talcott Parsons difficult to understand in any tongue. I suspect that certain cultures develop certain ways of tackling problems. In nineteenth century German economics it was popular and customary to ask about a problem like interest or value: What is the essence of interest or value? After this qualitative question is answered, then the quantitative level of the rate of interest or price-ratio can be settled. Now I happen to think that this is sterile methodology. But I cannot blame it on the German language.

It is interesting, however, that Menger wrote a letter to Walras on this very subject. As reported by Profesor Jaffe's interesting article *(Journal of Political Economy,* 1936), Menger said that mathematics was all very well for certain descriptive purposes, but that it did not enable you to get at the essence of a phenomenon. I wish I thought it were true that the language of mathematics had some special faculty of drawing attention away from pseudo problems of qualitative essence. For, unlike Menger, I should consider that a great advantage.

Baconian and Newtonian Methods. There are many empirical fields where translation into mathematical symbols would seem to have no advantage. Perhaps immunology is one, since I am told not a single cure for disease—vaccination against smallpox, inoculation for diphtheria, use of penicillin and sulpha, and so forth—has been discovered by anything but the crudest empiricism and with sheer accident playing a great role. Here the pedestrian methods of Francis Bacon show up to much greater advantage than do the exalted methods of a Newton. If true, we must simply accept this as a fact. I am sure that many areas of the social sciences and economics are at present in this stage. It is quite possible that many such areas will always continue to be in this stage.

Pareto regarded sociology as being of this type. But curiously enough, he goes on to argue that the chief virtue of mathematics is in its ability to represent complexly interacting and interdependent phenomena. I think we must accept this with a grain of salt. Analogies with complicated interdependent physical systems are valuable if they alert us to the dangers of theories of unilateral causation. But after mathematical notions have performed the function of reminding us that everything depends upon everything else, they may not add very much more—unless some special hypotheses can be made about the facts.

On the other hand, there are areas which over the years have fallen into the hands of the mathematically annointed. Earlier I mentioned the case of symbolic logic. There are still some girls' seminaries where literary logic rules the roost; but no sensible man expects that in the centuries ahead the field of logic will be deloused of mathematics.

Another field is that of physics. Its capture by mathematics is a fact—as solid and irreversible as the second law of thermodynamics itself.

It is dangerous to prophesy. But I suspect that in some small degree the same will hold of the field of economic theory. For a century mathematics knocked at the door. Even today it has no more than a foot in the doorway. But the problems of economic theory—such as the incidence of taxation, the effects of devaluation—are by their nature quantitative questions whose answer depends upon a superposition of many different pieces of quantitative and qualitative information. When we tackle them by words, we are solving the same equations as when we write out those equations.

Now I hold no brief for economic theory. I think the pendulum will always swing between interest in concrete description and attempts to construct abstract summaries of experience, with one decade and tradition giving more emphasis to the one process and another time and place giving emphasis to the other. But I do think that when the pendulum is swinging in favor of theory, there will be kind of a Gresham's law operating whereby the more convenient deductive method will displace the less convenient.

Convenience of Symbols for Deduction. And make no mistake about it. To get to some destinations it matters a great deal whether you go afoot or ride by a train. No wise man studying the motion of a top would voluntarily confine himself to words, forswearing all symbols. Similarly, no sensible person who had at his command both the techniques of literary argumentation and mathematical manipulation would tackle by words alone a problem like the following: Given that you must confine all taxes to excises on goods or factors, what pattern of excises is optimal for a Robinson Crusoe or for a community subject to prescribed norms?

I could go on and enumerate other problems. But that is not necessary. All you have to do is pick up a copy of any economic journal and turn to the articles on literary economic theory, and you will prove the point a hundred times over.

The convenience of mathematical symbolism for handling certain deductive inferences is, I think, indisputable. It is going too far to say that mathematicians never make mistakes. Like everybody else, they can pull some awful boners. But it is surprising how rare pure mistakes in logic are. Where the really big mistakes are made is in the formulation of premises. Logic is no protection against false hypotheses; or against misinterpretation of reality; or against the formulation of irrelevant hypotheses. I think it is one of the advantages of the mathematical medium—or, strictly speaking, of the mathematician's customary canons of exposition of proof, whether in words or symbols—that we are forced to lay our cards on the table so that all can see our premises. But I must confess that I have heard of card games—in fact I have participated in them myself—where knowingly or unknowingly, we have dealt cards from the bottom of the deck. So there are no absolute checks against human error.

The Human Dilemma. In conclusion, ask yourself what advice you would have to give to a young man who steps into your office with the following surprisingly common story: "I am interested in economic theory. I know little mathematics. And when I look at the journals, I am greatly troubled. Must I give up hopes of being a theorist? Must I learn mathematics? If so, how much? I am already past twenty-one; am I past redemption?"

Now you could answer him the way Marshall more or less advised Schumpeter: forget economic theory. Diminishing returns have set in there. The world is waiting for a thousand important applications.

This of course is no answer at all. Either the young man disregards your advice, as Schumpeter did. Or he accepts it, and psychologically you have dealt him the cruelest blow of all.

I think a better answer might go somewhat as follows: Some of the most distinguished economic theorists, past and present, have been innocent of mathematics. Some of the most distinguished theorists have known some degree of mathematics. Obviously, you can become a great theorist without knowing mathematics. Yet it is fair to say that you will have to be that much more clever and brilliant.

It happens to be empirically true that if you examine the training and background of all the past great economic theorists, a surprisingly high percentage had, or acquired, at least an intermediate mathematical training. Marshall, Wicksell, Wicksteed, Cassel, and even such literary economists as Nicholson or Malthus provide examples. This is omitting economists like Edgeworth, Cournot, Walras, Pareto, and others who were avowedly mathematical economists.

Moreover, without mathematics you run grave psychological risks. As you grow older, you are sure to resent the method increasingly. Either you will get an inferiority complex and retire from the field of theory or you will get an inferiority complex and become aggressive about your dislike of it. Of course, those are the betting odds and not perfect certainties. The danger is almost greater that you will overrate the method's power for good or evil. You may even become the prey of charlatans who say to you what Euler said to Diderot to get him to leave Catherine the Great's court: "Sir, $(a + b^n)/n = x$, hence God exists; reply!" And, like Diderot, you may slink away in shame. Or reacting against the episode, you may disbelieve the next mathematician who later comes along and gives you a true proof of the existence of the Deity.

In short—your advice will continue—mathematics is neither a necessary nor a sufficient condition for a fruitful career in economic theory. It can be a help. It can certainly be a hindrance, since it is only too easy to convert a good literary economist into a mediocre mathematical economist.

Despite the above advice, it is doubtful that when you check back five years later on that young man he will be very different. Indeed, as I look back over recent years, I am struck by the fact that the species of mathematical economist pure and simple seems to be dying out and becoming extinct. Instead, as one of my older friends complained to me: "These days you can hardly tell a mathematical economist from an ordinary economist." I know the sense in which he meant the remark, but let me reverse its emphasis by concluding with the question: Is that bad?

IMPLICATIONS FOR GENERAL ECONOMICS OF MORE REALISTIC THEORIES OF THE FIRM

K. E. Boulding

In the last few years a good deal of dissatisfaction has been expressed with the theory of the firm as it has come down to us from Cournot by way of Marshall, Chamberlin, and Joan Robinson. It is hardly necessary to say that the basic principle of this theory is the principle of profit maximization, and that the marginal analysis is merely an elaborate spelling out of this basic principle. There have been two main lines of criticism. The first is that the theory is unrealistic because it does not have enough variables in it, or because the variables of the theory do not in fact correspond to the significant variables of the firm. The second is more fundamental; it attacks the principle of maximization itself, on the grounds that it does not correspond to the actual principles which motivate and direct behavior.

The first criticism is one that is fairly easily remedied within the general framework of the marginal analysis by the simple process of adding new variables. Thus in the Chamberlin-Robinson versions of the theory, I myself have argued in several places, there is a serious deficiency in that the asset variables of the firm are not included except in a highly indirect way in the total cost. The Chamberlin-Robinson firm seems to have no balance sheet, no liquidity problems, no financial problems, no cash budget, and no investment program; it maximizes a curious income variable called net revenue, of which no accountant ever heard, and presumably lives happily ever after. It is not too difficult, however, to incorporate other variables into a more generalized marginal analysis, and I have made some steps in this direction in my *Reconstruction of Economics.*[1] The balance-sheet variables, in the accounting sense, are not the only ones which can be included in a generalized marginal analysis of this type. The psychological and sociological variables of the firm, insofar as they are subject to measurement, can also be included. Thus we can count "morale" as a psychological asset, and discuss morale-building expenditures as also subject to the marginal analysis, being carried on like any other to the point where marginal gain is just equal to marginal loss.

The second criticism of the marginal analysis is more fundamental. It is directed, not at the details, but at the basic assumption of profit maximization itself. The criticism takes two forms: the first is that profit maximization is simply not what firms in fact do; the second is that even if firms wanted to maximize profits, there is no way of doing it. The criticisms of Hall and Hitch[2] and of R. A. Lester[3] are of the first kind; that of Stephen Enke[4] is of the second. Insofar as these criticisms have theoretical content, however, they come to much the same thing: that the maximization of profits is unrealistic because firms cannot possibly know when profits are at a maximum. Hence firms must adopt rule-of-thumb methods of behavior (like

---

[1]K. E. Boulding, *A Reconstruction of Economics* (New York, 1950).

[2]R. L. Hall and C. J. Hitch, "Price Theory and Business Behavior," *Oxford Economic Papers,* May, 1939, pp. 12-49.

[3]R. A. Lester, "Shortcomings of the Marginal Analysis for Wage-Employment Problems," *American Economic Review,* March, 1946, pp. 63-82.

[4]Stephen Enke, "On Maximizing Profits," *American Economic Review,* September, 1951, pp. 566-578.

full-cost pricing) which do not necessarily maximize profits but which fit into their information systems. Profit maximization is ruled out because there is nothing in the information system of the firm which reveals the marginal inequalities which would be indicative of a failure to maximize profits. The information system reveals average costs; it reveals sales, production, inventory, debt, and other figures in the balance sheet and income statements. It does not, however, generally reveal marginal costs and still less does it reveal marginal revenues. If the firm cannot know when it is not maximizing profits, therefore, there is no reason to suppose that it maximizes them.

Much of this criticism seems to be destructive, in the sense that it seems to knock down an existing theory without setting up any other in its place. The criticism is grounded, however, in the beginnings of a general theory of organization and behavior which is emerging in many fields, notably in the work of Cannon the physiologist,[5] Barnard the theorist of organization,[6] and Wiener the founder and namer of cybernetics.[7] This general theory of organization begins with the concept of homeostasis; that is, of a mechanism for stabilizing a variable or a group of variables within certain limits of toleration. Every organism or organization is characterized by a group of such variables, and the organization consists mainly in more or less elaborate apparatus to maintain these variables between an upper and lower limit. Should any of the essential variables rise above the upper limit, machinery must be brought into play to reduce it; should it fall below the lower limit, machinery must be brought into play to raise it. An organization in this view consists of an aggregate of such governing mechanisms, sometimes called control or "feedback" mechanisms. The simplest example is perhaps the thermostat, or a governor on an engine. The body contains dozens of such mechanisms, maintaining a great many physical, chemical, and even psychological variables within a limited range of toleration: temperature, blood pressure, water content, calcium content, and so on down a long list. Any organization likewise may

---

[5]Cannon, *The Wisdom of the Body*.

[6]Barnard, *The Functions of the Executive*.

[7]N. Wiener, *Cybernetics* (New York, 1948).

be characterized by a long list of variables which have upper and lower limits demanding appropriate action.

A control mechanism always involves a number of parts. There must be first a receptor of information (i) which picks up information regarding the variable to be controlled and, in particular, picks up information regarding divergence between the actual value of the variable and the limits of toleration. In the simplest mechanism, all that is necessary is qualitative information about the sign of this divergence: the minimum information is that the variable is above the upper limit or below the lower limit of toleration. This information must be transmitted by a communications system (ii) to an executive, or decision-maker (iii). The function of the executive is to transform the information received into instructions; it (or he) can be thought of as a kind of production function, receiving information by one communications system and sending out instructions over another (iv). The instructions go to effectors (v) which carry out the instructions, and can produce an effect which is carried by another communications system (vi) to the controlled variable. Thus in the thermostatically controlled furnace, we have the thermostat (i) which registers divergence of the temperature from the tolerated limits (the upper and lower limits may in this case be contiguous). This information is transmitted by a wire (ii) to the furnace control (iii), which transforms the information into instructions sent by another wire (iv) to the furnace (v), which is capable of transmitting the effect (heat) by a system of pipes and radiators (vi) to the environment of the thermostat.

The theory of the control mechanism has been developed in some detail by Wiener, and we need only mention some conclusions here. One is that a control mechanism always involves a cyclical movement of the controlled variable, the amplitude of the cycle being a function of the sensitivity of the mechanism. If the mechanism has pronounced lags, the corrective effect may only be brought into play after an extensive divergence of the controlled variable from the norm, and the correction may go too far before the countercorrection comes into play. The famous contrast between the hand-fired furnace, where the house has two temperatures, too hot and too cold, and the automatic thermostat, where the cycle is practically imperceptible, illustrates the point.

The thermostat is a very simple control mechanism because the controlled variable (temperature) in the absence of control contantly tends to diminish, assuming that the tolerated temperature of the house is above that of the outside. Action, therefore, is only needed in one direction—that of supplying heat; the only action necessary when the temperature becomes too warm is to turn the furnace off. Where the movement of the controlled variable in the absence of control is random and may be in either direction, the problem of the "effector" becomes more difficult, and it is generally necessary to have two kinds of effectors: one to operate when the uncontrolled movement of the variable is downward (e.g., a furnace) and another to operate when the uncontrolled movement is upward (e.g., a refrigerator). This also requires greater complexity in the information system, which must be capable of detecting in what direction the uncontrolled movement of the variable would be going. Otherwise we will have the mechanism switching on the refrigeration unit in winter and the furnace in summer. In the case of physical variables, this task is not too difficult. In the case of social variables, however, the information system may have considerable difficulty in delivering information which will enable the executive to choose the appropriate effector. Thus suppose a firm is faced with inventories rising above what it considers to be the limit of toleration. A control mechanism of some sort will come into play. There is, however, a choice of mechanisms. The firm may reduce prices and institute a selling campaign in order to increase sales. Or it may cut back production and allow the existing rate of sales to lower the inventory. If the piling up of inventory is a result of a faulty price and sales policy relative to the general state of the market, the first technique may be effective. If the piling up of inventory is due to a general depression and decline in income, the second technique (from the point of view of the firm) may be more effective. Information about the mere quantity of inventory is not sufficient to distinguish between these two policies.

There is yet another complication of the control mechanism which is of great importance for social organizations. In organizations of any degree of complexity there is not a single variable to be controlled but a large number of variables, and the effectors which affect one may also affect others. If each variable to be controlled has an isolated effector which is capable of controlling it, the multiplicity of variables presents no problem. We do not in general find this to be the case, however. Action which is taken to influence one variable will almost always have some effect on the others. A great deal of human frustration arises from this confusion of effectors. It is a commonplace that when we solve one problem we generally create three others. If the effectors are sufficiently confused, the problem of control will become insoluble: in endeavoring to stabilize one variable we inevitably unstabilize others; acute cycles may be set up and the organization may even disintegrate.

So far we have simply assumed the existence of certain controlled variables and of machinery to control them. Clearly, however, the theory cannot stop there. Two further questions must be raised. The first is what determines the limits of tolerance of the controlled variables and under what circumstances do these limits change. The second is under what circumstances is the organization itself changed, in one regard or another. In the simple theory of control, a divergence between the actual and the ideal value of the controlled variable sets in motion a control mechanism to bring the actual value nearer to the ideal. Suppose now that the mechanism is persistently unsuccessful and that the actual value of the variable seldom if ever falls within the ideal limits of toleration. Information of this type constitutes a different kind of challenge to the executive than simple information regarding divergence of actual from ideal values. The question facing the executive, then, is whether to adjust the ideal values in response to this situation or to reorganize the machinery itself. The answer to this question is likely to depend on the relation of the ideal values to the survival of the organization. In the case of the firm, for instance, a persistent failure to keep inventory within certain prescribed limits may result in a revision of the limits rather than a change in the organization, as action to keep inventory within specified limits is only incidental to the survival of the firm. If, however, the firm persistently makes losses (i.e., if there is a failure to keep profits above the lower limit of toleration), the executive will be seriously disturbed and will not revise the limits of toleration in the direction of being satisfied with taking losses, but will look around to see what steps, drastic if need be, must be taken in order to correct the situation.

A problem related to the above is that of growth and the life cycle. It is evident from the study of organizations of all kinds that they exhibit periods of growth, of relative stability, and of decay. This is perhaps the least understood field in the whole theory of organization. The existence of growth indicates that the controlled variables are certain rates of change through time. A firm, for instance, frequently regards some rate of growth as normal, and if its growth is not equal to this normal rate, serious concern will be aroused and steps will be taken. There are, however, important limits on growth. It is not merely that there may be certain rates of growth which are inherently unstable, as Harrod suggests for the economy as a whole and as the study of hormones indicates may be true for biological organisms. Growth at any rate, however, cannot take place without the organism eventually becoming "large," and diseconomies of scale may set in. The ideal rate of growth, therefore, may properly be regarded as a diminishing function of the size of the organization and will eventually diminish to zero. The problem of decay and death is even more mysterious, and the question as to whether death is inherent in the structure of organization itself or whether it is an accident is one that must remain unanswered, especially in regard to the social organization.

The kind of theory which I have outlined very briefly above is general and can be applied to the firm as well as to any other organization. Thus the first-approximation theory of the firm is a theory of "homeostasis of the balance sheet," treating the behavior of the firm as a reaction to changes in its balance-sheet structure, designed to restore the balance-sheet composition to its "ideal" value. On this theory, for instance, sales of product result in a distortion of the balance sheet, increasing cash (or accounts receivable) at the expense of inventory. In order to restore the previous values there must be production of product to replace the inventory lost by sale. This production will diminish cash and other items, which must also be replaced, and so on.

The next step is the theory of the selection of ideal balance sheets;

i.e., what distribution of its assets and liabilities among the various items does the firm regard as best. It is at this level, if anywhere, that the theory of profit maximization becomes relevant. At this level, also, we cannot regard the firm as simply passive in regard to its income variables, and the problem of the selection of possible rates of turnover of balance-sheet items must also be considered. Profit is evidently a crucial variable in the case of the firm, as it represents probably the most important single variable which determines the firm's ultimate survival. We shall expect, therefore, that there will be some lower limit of profits below which a control mechanism will operate. There may also be an upper limit, above which the firm will take life easy and will not bother about profit-increasing activity. Somewhere around this range presumably profits are at a maximum. The theory of profit maximization assumes in effect that the upper and lower limits of toleration coincide at the point of maximum profits. This is an assumption which is not likely to be realized. However, it is a special case of the more general theory.

A word should be added on the subject of expectations and uncertainty, especially as this subject has received so much attention in recent years.[8] There have been a great many attempts to construct a theory of "rational" behavior in the presence of uncertainty—attempts which have not as yet produced agreement even on the problem of the measurement of uncertainty itself. The only conclusion which seems to emerge solidly from all the discussion is that uncertainty creates a preference for liquidity and flexibility in the asset structure. Liquidity is a measure of the degree of perfection of the market for an asset; i.e., the extent to which it can be exchanged for any other asset in indefinite quantities without loss due to worsening terms of trade. Flexibility is the extent to which an asset can be transformed into a variety of other assets in the course of the process of production. There may also be another property of the asset and income structure which increases in value with increased uncertainty; this might be called the property of security. It is measured by the "peakedness" of the

---

[8]Kenneth J. Arrow, "Alternative Approaches to the Theory of Choice in Risk-Taking," *Econometrica,* October, 1951, pp. 404-437.

profits function. If this function has a sharp peak, so that profits are high if exactly the right decisions are made but low or negative if slight deviations from the right decisions occur, the burden of uncertainty will be great. If on the other hand the profits function is a broad plateau, so that deviations from the "best" decisions do not involve disaster, uncertainty will not create acute discomfort. It is evident that there is a problem of the relief of uncertainty-discomfort in the process of decision making, through retreat towards more liquid, flexible, and secure positions as well as through the more conventional methods of insurance. I wonder, however, whether this process cannot be described in terms of the asset-preference structure for all purposes of the economist, and whether a detailed attempt to break up the problem into a "returns" aspect and an "uncertainty" measure is particularly useful.

It can hardly be denied, I think, that the type of theory which I have outlined so sketchily above is more "realistic" than the elementary marginal analysis, if only because it offers more hope of meaningful empirical studies of the firm. Economists have had enough of asking businessmen whether they equate marginal this to marginal that and being met with utterly blank stares of incomprehension. It is quite evident that the marginal analysis, useful as it is as a tool of general static equilibrium economics, is not particularly useful as an instrument of analysis of actual business behavior. The economist, however, who asks businessmen what information comes to their desks, how they classify it, how they react to it, what kind of instructions follow from what kinds of information, what are the variables which they watch, what sort of weight do they give to various kinds of "trouble indicators," and so on, meets with an immediate response, and it seems not unreasonable to hope that armed with the kind of theory I have outlined above economists might even be of some use to businessmen, and their modest triumphs at the level of national accounting might be matched, in the next generation, in the realm of business practice. The question of this paper, however, is a different one. It is concerned with the impact of these newer theories of organization on the structure and conclusions of economics itself. Because the marginal analysis had been shown to be a rather highly special case, unlikely to be realized in practice, should we thereupon banish it from our textbooks, in spite of the admirable examination fodder which it makes, or at least relegate it to appendices which only specialists will ever read?

At the level of elementary teaching the proposal to ban the marginal analysis can perhaps be defended on the grounds that economics can get along so well without it. It is well to remember that for all practical purposes there was no theory of the firm in economics before Marshall and no theory of the individual consumer before Jevons and the Austrians. Even in Marshall the theory of the firm is practically confined to a sort of appendix on monopoly, and the theory of the firm does not become central in economics until the development of the economics of imperfect competition in the thirties. The whole of the classical economics, especially, was constructed with only the barest rudiments of a theory of the economic individual. The essential conceptual framework behind the classical economics is that of supply and demand analysis—the assumption of definite functional relationships between prices and quantities produced or consumed, and the further assumption that an improper relationship between production and consumption would have an impact on prices. The theory of maximizing behavior and the marginal analysis comes into economics at a second level of analysis—that of explaining the character of the supply and demand functions. As such it is not essential to economic analysis. It is a sort of porch to the main edifice, which may be remodeled without much affecting the central structure. No matter how much we revise the theory of the firm (or general economic organism), it would be surprising to find a conclusion that high prices generally discouraged production and encouraged consumption. We should even be surprised to find a theory that told us that under price discrimination the higher price would be charged in the more elastic market, or that a change in relative prices will cause substitution of the dearer for the cheaper factor or commodity. These conclusions which emerge from the marginal analysis will almost certainly survive a considerable failure on the part of the firm in maximizing its profits. We shall not be far wrong in concluding, therefore, that the impact of more realistic theories of the firm on static price analysis is likely to be small.

This conclusion is reinforced if we observe that many of the objections to profit maximization do not apply to the maximization of utility or preference. The substitution of a subjective for an objective maximand removes some of the difficulty in regard to the information needed for maximization. If utility is defined in terms of preference, presumably we always know at the moment whether one set of alternatives is preferred to another. Much of the marginal analysis can be rescued by substituting the maximization of utility for the maximization of profits, even in the theory of the firm. If the preference functions are reasonably stable, this theory has meaning and predictive power, for the preference functions can be investigated empirically. If the preference functions are not stable, of course, the theory amounts to little more than saying that people do what they do. Unfortunately there are many indications that the preference functions are not particularly stable, especially in regard to asset preferences. If this is the case, the only hope of rescuing the theory from sterility is the discovery of a genuine dynamics of preference; that is, stable difference equations relating present preferences to past variables. We are still a long way from this goal.

When we turn to economic dynamics in general, the impact of the theory of organization is likely to be larger, if only because the great weakness of the theory of maximizing behavior is that it has practically no dynamics in it. The general theory of organization as applied to the firm is likely, first, to draw attention to certain sensitive variables which the economist has previously neglected, such as the various asset ratios. Thus a shift in cash balances between firms and households may create considerable reactions in firm behavior, not because profit positions are affected so much as because asset ratios are disturbed. This is one of the points at which the theory of the bank, which has generally been discussed in terms of balance-sheet ratios such as the reserve ratio, could well be integrated with the general theory of the firm. In the second place, the possibility that the controlled variables exhibit a range of toleration introduces a "threshold" and time-lag phenomenon into the over-all movements of the economy. Profits, asset ratios, and other controlled variables will rise or fall for some distance without producing action until they pass the range of toleration. This fact is of great importance in the development of an economic dynamics, for it explains why the adjustments of the system are not instantaneous, and it determines the rate of adjustment. Generally speaking, the wider the range of tolerance, the slower will be the transmission of changes through the system. Even if the ranges of tolerance of the various controlled variables were stable, we would expect to find a certain asymmetry between "upward" and "downward" movements of the economy. Firms and households are more likely to be at one of the limits of toleration in one case and at the other in the other.

There is some possibility also that the general theory of organization may throw light on the theory of interactions among the few—one of the least satisfactory parts of almost any science, as the unsatisfactory state of the theory of oligopoly testifies in economics, and as the practical nonexistence of a theory of international relations testifies in political science. These interactions must clearly be confined to those variables which are in the information systems of the organisms concerned. Variables which are in the control of one organization may well be controlling variables for another organization. Consequently any change in the policy of one organization, insofar as it gets into the information structure of a second organization, may produce immediate reactions in the policy of the second, which in turn may react on the first, and so on in a kind of circular chain reaction. The nature of the information system may easily determine whether or not such a system is capable of equilibrium. There may be cases where ignorance is bliss! The phenomena of the price or advertising war and its counterpart in the arms race are good examples which need further study in the light of organizational theory.

One may conclude, then, that there is great need to integrate the general theory of organization into the body of economic analysis, and that such integration will immensely improve economics as a technique for analyzing the actual behavior of firms. Economists may even become useful to business! This extension of theory will not, however, overthrow the existing structure of analysis, which emerges clearly as an important special case. It is not likely to make any spectacular changes in a static theory; it may reasonably be expected to throw new light on economic dynamics.

Index

Section V is not indexed.